Certain Women Amazed Us

Certain Women Amazed Us

The Women's Missionary Society Their Story 1864-2002

Lois Klempa
and
Rosemary Doran

Women's Missionary Society (WD)

Women's Missionary Society (WD)
The Presbyterian Church in Canada
50 Wynford Drive
Toronto, Ontario M3C 1J7

Copyright © 2002 by Women's Missionary Society (WD)

All rights reserved. No part of this publication may be reproduced, stored in a retrieval system, or transmitted, in any form or by any means, electronic, mechanical, photocopying, recording, or otherwise, without the prior permission of the publisher.

National Library of Canada Cataloguing in Publication

Klempa, Lois, 1932-
Certain women amazed us : the Women's Missionary Society, their story, 1864-2002 / Lois Klempa and Rosemary Doran.

Includes bibliographical references and index.
ISBN 0-9731753-0-3

1. Presbyterian Church in Canada. Women's Missionary Society. W.D.—History. 2. Women in missionary work—Canada—History. I. Doran, Rosemary, 1935- II. Presbyterian Church in Canada. Women's Missionary Society. W.D. III. Title.

BX9001.K54 2002 266'.5271'06 C2002-905375-7

Design and production by Tim Faller Design, Inc.
Printed in Canada by Reliable Printing
Photos courtesy of The Presbyterian Church in Canada Archives

Contents

PART II
Women's Missionary Society, Western Division, 1914-1972

Foreword

Certain Women Amazed Us! They did it 2000 years ago. They are still doing it. From the faithful reporting of good news on the first Easter morning to the present, there are those who continue to leave us with a sense of awe and amazement. The women whose lives provide the inspiration for this book, together with the authors, editors and publishers who produced it, belong in that renowned lineage.

In 1994, at its annual Council meeting, the Women's Missionary Society, Western Division, decided to celebrate its 130th anniversary by developing a five year plan. One objective of the plan was to prepare a history of the WMS. Yes, another history. But this one would have some differences. The book would be carefully documented so that students of church, society and women's movements as reflected in The Presbyterian Church in Canada, would find in it a valuable resource and be directed to the original sources for their research. It would tell the story from the perspective of women who look back with respect and awe to those who lived out their Christian commitment to Christ and the church from the days when they had no right to speak, vote or hold office in the courts of the decision makers to the time of emerging equality, changing roles, increasing responsibilities and new uncertainties. Whenever possible, first names would be traced and restored to scores of women who had been identified only by the surname of husband or father. And, according to the plan, all this would be accomplished within five years — by 1999.

Lois Klempa

Lois Stewart Klempa, graduate of the Presbyterian Missionary and Deaconess School, was the first to rise to the challenge. With great enthusiasm she agreed to be the author of the book. She uncovered and deciphered documents written by hand in the beautiful but often obscure script of the Victorian era. She explored the Presbyterian Archives where she was confronted with more than one hundred years of annual reports, monthly magazines and minutes of weekly meetings — stack after stack. Wisely, she called for help in the person of Druse Bryan, a member of the Council Executive, who became a research assistant and valued consultant. Deadlines were adjusted from 1999 to 2000 to 2001 to 2002. Late in the process, Rosemary Doran, recently retired minister and former president of the WMS, was recruited to research and write the final section of the book. True to the tradition they were describing, these volunteers pursued their tasks with remarkable focus and energy even while maintaining active involvement in affairs of family and church. Throughout the project, the work was encouraged and facilitated by Margaret Robertson, program secretary on the staff of the WMS. By January, 2002, the manuscripts were placed in her hands for final editing and publication.

Druse Bryan

Like artists using a wide canvas, the authors described their subjects in colourful diversity. The figures appear first in small clusters with only an occasional individual in sharp relief. Many details are omitted, a person or an event being depicted with a single vibrant stroke. But the figures merge to produce the impression of a mighty procession of extraordinary movement and power. There are sombre areas, dominated by deep shadows — the tragedies of war and depression,

Rosemary Doran

the limitations imposed by patriarchal hierarchies maintaining control. But there are brilliant colours where the procession emerges into the sunlit areas of bold dreams and surprising achievements as it moves forward with unfailing commitment to the greater causes of Christianity both within and beyond The Presbyterian Church in Canada.

Margaret Robertson

To read the book is to be engaged as a participant in a long and adventurous procession with our grandmothers, mothers, sisters and daughters. The endnotes can guide us to explore the places and people of special interest which will enrich the stories of our becoming. Unanswered questions are posed to urge us into the future. But for now, let us read the book and celebrate these women who continue to amaze us.

E Margaret MacNaughton

Introduction

Women were there at the beginning of the Christian story, engaging fully in its unfolding. Women were there at the beginning of the story as disciples, apostles and missionaries, and have played a formative role throughout history in the development of its narrative. Unfortunately, like the disciples in Luke's gospel we continue to be amazed when time and again we are presented with the richness of that activity.

When the women first spread the good news of an empty tomb, Luke tells us that they were not believed. To the disciples it appeared "an idle tale" until Peter went to the tomb and saw for himself. In so many periods in the history of the Christian church, women's experience and revelation have been judged in a similar way.

One task of the modern feminist movement has been to ensure that women's story is told. It is difficult work, in that it means bringing a discerning and critical eye to the "stuff of history." But it is important work. As Barbel von Wartenburg-Potter claims, "women hold up half the sky."[1]

Elisabeth Schussler Fiorenza, a biblical scholar, has been helpful in identifying a meaningful way into such activity, and her insights are useful whether we are looking at the biblical women or women within the history of The Presbyterian Church in Canada. The first step for her is a reconstruction of women's role in the biblical story. She identifies the kind of questions that need to be asked in order to ferret out clues from a story that is not only told through the eyes of the male leadership, but whose interpretation has been almost completely in the hands of male clerics. Once this detective work is completed the clues and their interpretation need to be integrated into the Christian story and celebrated as an important part of the whole.

Fiorenza emphasizes the importance of the activity of asking questions in a poem called The Song of Questions:

Mother, asks the clever daughter,
who are our mothers?
Who are our ancestors?
What is our history?
Give us our name. Name our genealogy.

Mother, asks the wicked daughter,
if I learn my history
will I not be angry?
Will I not be bitter as Miriam
who was deprived of her prophecy?

Mother, asks the simple daughter,
if Miriam lies buried in sand,
why must we dig up those bones?
Why must we remove her from sun and stone
where she belongs?

The one who knows not how to question
she has no past,
she has no present,
she can have no future
without knowing her mothers
without knowing her angers
without knowing her questions.[2]

With this background in mind, it is clear that the present history [her-story] of the Women's Missionary Society (WMS) is vital to the history of The Presbyterian Church in Canada. In it we see how much the work of these women continues that of the women at the tomb in its commitment to spreading the good news of the gospel. We hear the names of faithful women. We come to understand their commitment to mission work, to education and diaconal ministry, and understand better how that commitment served to enhance the life of Canadians and people throughout the world. We learn of the ability of these women to raise money, and how that in no small way has time and again increased the ability of the whole of the Presbyterian Church to respond to the commandment to love of neighbour.

If the story of The Presbyterian Church in Canada is to be told in its fullness, all of those whose activity was central to the story must be proclaimed and celebrated. The names and details about the commitment of the countless women who worked and gave leadership within the WMS provide for all of us, both women and men, a piece of this story.

J. Dorcas Gordon

Acknowledgments

I began to research and write this history of the Women's Missionary Society in 1996. There were two things, as time went on, of which I became more and more aware. First, that this project was going to take much more time and much more work than I had ever anticipated. Second, although I thought I already knew something of the history of the Women's Missionary Society before I began, I became more and more amazed at the accomplishments of these feisty members of the WMS beginning with the women in 1864 and up to and including the year 2002, proving that the title I had chosen from Luke 24:22, *Certain Women Amazed Us*, seemed particularly appropriate. Although it was a great deal of work, it was a fascinating and rewarding experience for me.

First and foremost, I am grateful to the editorial committee, Druse Bryan, Rosemary Doran, Margaret MacNaughton, Margaret Robertson and Joan Sampson, who read and re-read the manuscript, giving their valuable comments for changes and corrections. Margaret Robertson, Programme Secretary for the WMS, was convener of the committee, keeping us on track, collating the manuscript and checking sources, in consultation with June Stevenson, editor of *Glad Tidings*. Margaret's computer skills were invaluable to the production of the book. Druse Bryan needs special mention. She spent much time with me doing research, reading through the chapters, checking quotations and, with her eye for detail, saving me from many an error. Thanks also goes to Druse's husband, Charles, an author himself, who offered encouragement and much helpful advice.

To Rosemary Doran, who shares authorship in this book, I owe a real debt of gratitude. When I realized, in a panic, that if I did not get help, I might never finish the book, Rosemary came to the rescue, agreeing to write the important last section (Part III) covering the period of the integration of the work of the WMS with the Board of World Mission.

I am grateful also to Keith Knight for copy-editing the manuscript and to the staff of the archives of The Presbyterian Church in Canada for providing ready and willing assistance.

Finally, and most important of all, I want to thank my family. Thanks to my husband, Bill, who, with his knowledge of the Church and its mission work, offered many helpful suggestions and much support. Thanks also to our two daughters, Catherine and Mary-Margaret, who, along with their husbands George and Jim, managed to produce four grandchildren in the interim but were still not too critical when I seemed always to be reading old WMS records or writing the history of the Society when I could have been enjoying the grandchildren. And thanks to our son Michael and his wife Melanie, who, though further afield, must also have been tired of hearing about 'THE BOOK'.

Lois Klempa

The writing of the last section of the book was — sometimes by turns, sometimes simultaneously — exciting, challenging and frustrating. Building on the good foundation and development of the theme provided by Lois, my task was to record the ongoing evolution of the WMS over roughly the last quarter of the twentieth century. This required much reading and research, writing and rewriting, none of which could have been accomplished without the help of many people. Among them I should like to mention Margaret Robertson, who patiently unearthed documents and checked details, and also past and current staff of the WMS, who willingly shared personal experiences and opinions. In this regard, special thanks go to Giollo Kelly, Helen Tetley, May Nutt and Margaret MacNaughton and to the many others I consulted who are the "living history" of the Society. Valuable assessment of the section on "Residential Schools" came from June Stevenson and Stephen Kendall, Principal Clerk of the General Assembly. Thanks must also go to Tim and Sophie Faller for their splendid work on design and layout.

It would also have been impossible for me to complete my part of the project without the help, support — and computer skills! — of my husband, Gerald, and of the many friends all across the Society, whose kind and encouraging words persuaded me to keep going.

It has been a pilgrimage through history. I am grateful to have had the privilege of being a part of it.

Rosemary Doran

PART I

Three Missionary Societies Become One

1864-1914

Chapter

1

How Did It All Begin?

Where to start? A good question! Women's ministry is as old as the Church itself. We could begin with the words of the Emmaus disciples who, in relating the story of the resurrection to the stranger, who happened to be Jesus, exclaimed, *Some women of our company amazed us!*[1]

The women in question were, of course, those women who had been with Jesus from the beginning of his ministry, who followed him from Galilee to Jerusalem, who were there at the cross and at the grave. These were the women Jesus commissioned to go and tell the other disciples that he had risen from the dead. Certain women amazed us! There have been a multitude of amazing women throughout the history of the Church — not least in the Women's Missionary Society.

The Presbyterian Women's Missionary Society had its beginning, along with many other women's organizations, in the mid to late 1800s. So, to set the stage, we have to think back to a time when Canada was young. In fact, the Dominion of Canada had not yet come into being. What was Canada like then? Louise Reith describes it in a historical skit prepared for the 100th anniversary of the Society in 1964. In those early days, she says,

> *...had we been able to fly over Canada what would we have seen? On the Atlantic Coast, settlements of people in the Maritime provinces. In the sparsely settled areas known as Upper and Lower Canada would be found a faint hum of mills and factories. Railway lines might be seen creeping East and West; indeed, imaginative people were even dreaming that* some day *a railway might link the Atlantic and Pacific Oceans. Farther west — bush-lands along the shores of the Great Lakes extending west until we see the expanse broken by the cluster of farms known as the Red River Settlement. Then 2,000 miles of endless plains, of bush country and mountains to the Pacific Coast, where we find two outposts — Vancouver Island and British Columbia — linked only by sea to the outside world.*[2]

And what was it like for women? Briefly, they could not vote. If married, employment outside the home was frowned upon and, in many cases, forbidden; if single, they were barred from a large range of male-only occupations. Women were just beginning to be allowed to attend university, and those who did faced hostility and persecution. In the church, ordination to the ministry of word and sacraments and to the eldership was denied to women and thus women had no vote in any courts of the church.

It was not all gloom and doom, for it was in this atmosphere of limited opportunity that women began to organize themselves into social and political groups, suffrage societies, charity organizations and missionary societies. These women's organizations

> *...did, however, accept for the most part the predominant view that women's primary role was played out in the home. Indeed most of the...activities were designed to ensure that the home remained the fundamental unit of Canadian society.*[3]

We see this same view expressed by Lady Aberdeen at the first annual meeting of the National Council of Women in 1894,

> *...how can we best describe this woman's mission in a word? Can we not best describe it as 'mothering' in one sense or another? We are not all called upon to be mothers of little children, but every woman is called upon to 'mother' in some way or another...*[4]

This view

> *...ensured that...women would extol the virtues of domesticity even when their participation in these organizations revealed that women were gradually discovering new roles for themselves outside the home.*[5]

It was what Ruth Compton Brouwer calls "redemptive social housekeeping on a worldwide scale." It has also been called the Dorcas tradition.[6] At the same time these organizations proved to be a training ground for women who were not allowed leadership roles in society or in the church.

Although, in the beginning, it seems the clergy kept a fairly strict guard over the missionary societies, the women themselves gradually took over the leadership and were soon conducting their own business meetings, planning their own worship services and studies, raising their own money and supporting their own missionaries.

Marjory MacMurchy, a well-known Toronto journalist, in an article written in 1916, gives us an insight into how these early women's groups operated.

> *The national missionary societies, broadly speaking, are wholly devoted to missionary work, and have consistently refused to express an opinion on public or social questions... We have then two great groups of women's associations in Canada, both highly and efficiently organized, the one with a more or less definite purpose to be heard in public affairs and to represent Canadian women; the other, with a single purpose for missionary work and an extraordinary business development, publishing magazines, books and leaflets, supporting and managing hospitals, employing, educating and supporting missionaries and deaconesses, collecting and designating an income of somewhat under half a million. This business is carried on almost altogether by voluntary effort. The only charge for management is less than three percent.*

MacMurchy continues,

> *The typical member of these associations in both groups is married, not single. She is middle-aged. She is a woman with household occupations and yet with some leisure. Her children are wholly or half-way grown and she is able to undertake some work outside.*[7]

It is almost 100 years since MacMurchy penned these words. Looking back from our own vantage point at the accomplishments of the women in those early missionary societies, it is our turn to be amazed.

Some modern writers of women's history have recognized what a fascinating story these women have to tell. Ruth Tucker, in her book *Guardians of the Great Commission*, says,

> *The role of women in the modern missionary movement has been phenomenal. No other public ministry in the church has so captured the interest and commitment of women in the past two hundred years.*

She adds,

Despite their active involvement in missions, however, women have been largely forgotten by the missions historians…women rarely had leadership roles and, as is true in any field of history, the leaders are the ones who draw the attention of researchers.[8]

In *Women and Religion in America*, Rosemary Skinner Keller writes,

The ability of females to build grassroots organizations, and to consolidate those groups into regional and national societies, created a new basis of community among women in the churches. The surprising power of women to raise thousands of dollars from the gleanings of 'mite boxes' was a major factor in making missions an identifying mark of late nineteenth century Protestantism.[9]

Today, members of the Women's Missionary Society of The Presbyterian Church in Canada, at the beginning of the 21st century, wonder, as the title of their Five Year Plan suggests, if they are indeed "threatened with resurrection."[10] In any case, whatever the future holds for the women of the WMS, as they look to the future and learn from the past, they may surely find new hope and inspiration from the multitude of amazing women whose wisdom and courage, enthusiasm and dedication have brought them to this point.

Since we are surrounded by so great a cloud of witnesses, let us also lay aside every weight and the sin that easily distracts, and let us run with perseverance the race that is set before us, looking to Jesus the pioneer and perfector of our faith. (Hebrews 12:1)

The Presbyterian Women's Missionary Society as we know it today is an amalgamation of three groups: the Woman's Missionary Society, Montreal; the Woman's Foreign Missionary Society and the Women's Home Missionary Society. The amalgamation took place on March 15, 1914. Each of these societies has a unique story to tell.

The Atlantic Mission Society, formerly the Woman's Missionary Society, Eastern Division, has its own fascinating history. Although it is not our purpose to tell their story here, the close association between the eastern and western divisions of the societies makes it important to tell something of their beginnings and to touch briefly on what was happening in their society from time to time.

Chapter 2

In Search of Our Roots

Woman's Missionary Society, Montreal, 1864-1914

The Groundwork

John Thomas McNeill in his book *The Presbyterian Church in Canada 1875-1925*, devotes an entire chapter to the contribution of women. He tells us that, as early as 1841, Montreal had an interdenominational ladies' society that co-operated with the French Canadian Missionary Society. He also says that in 1864 a Ladies' Auxiliary Association was formed to assist the Presbyterian Church in Canada in connection with The Church of Scotland in its work among the French population. It is to this Ladies' Auxiliary Association that the Presbyterian Women's Missionary Society traces its origins.[1]

The early days of French occupation in Canada were turbulent times. A little book with the big title *Historic Sketches of the Pioneer Work and the Missionary, Educational and Benevolent Agencies of the Presbyterian Church in Canada* has a chapter on "French Evangelism" taken from notes by Rev. Professor John Campbell of Presbyterian College. It begins,

Among the adventurers who came to our shores in the early days of French occupation, there was a considerable and influential Huguenot element, essentially Presbyterian.[2]

The Story of Our Missions, published in 1915 by the newly-formed Women's Missionary Society, Western Division, has a chapter on French Missions in Quebec Province. The section "Early History of French Protestantism" begins,

For nearly a hundred years after the discovery of the St. Lawrence, Canada was a country free to all who wished to seek its richness.... Among these were many Protestants...[3]

The author of *The Story of our Missions* quotes at some length from *The Tragedy of Quebec*, a book written by Robert Sellar of Huntingdon, Quebec. Sellar says that in 1615, when Champlain sailed with four Recollet priests, an edict forbidding Protestants to live in Canada was promulgated. In his book, Sellar tells of the persecution of Protestants who attempted to emigrate to Canada.[4]

A more recent account of these events comes from Rev. André Poulain, minister of Église St. Luc, Montreal from 1950-1977. In his article "French Protestants and the Foundation of Canada," he says that it was the plan of Admiral Gaspard de Coligny, leader of the Huguenots, to build a

...great French Empire in America in order to allow the subjects of the Reformed religion, persecuted in France, to freely practise [sic] *their religion*[5]

The most distinguished officers of New France were Protestant. Champlain, himself, was born a Protestant and did not become a Catholic until 1596. Henry IV was a Protestant until his conversion to Catholicism in order to become the King of France. Henry IV was an admirer of Coligny and encouraged the colonization of Canada by Protestants. His assassination in 1610, says Poulain, was a turning point in the history of New France and

...little by little the French Protestants or Huguenots were to be eliminated. The policy of Richelieu favoured the Jesuits and closed the entrance (to) Canada to the Huguenots by the Act of the Company of the 100 Associates which was entirely Roman Catholic.[6]

By 1774, except for the army, there were not more than 400 Protestants in the province of Quebec. But these hardy Protestants were not to be dismissed so easily,

We shall shed the light of the pure Gospel into every hamlet and, as far as possible, into every heart, has been the watchword of French Evangelization[7]

Both the author of *The Story of Our Missions* and Professor Campbell in *Historic Sketches* give a brief history of how French evangelization began. The first missionary was sent out by the British Wesleyan Conference in 1815. As early as 1836, the Montreal auxiliary of the Bible Society had a travelling evangelist, called a "colporteur," in Montreal and by 1838 it had another working in the country. It was Rev. James Thomson, agent of the Bible Society, who was instrumental in forming the French Canadian Missionary Society in 1839 which, although non-denominational, was largely supported by Presbyterians and Congregationalists. It was the hope that this society might be the means of uniting all the agencies and missionaries in one French Canadian Reformed Church. A synod was formed in 1858. The movement was not too successful and disbanded in 1878. In the meantime separate denominations flourished and the Presbyterian Church in connection with the Church of Scotland opened St. John's Church in Montreal.

In 1859, a movement began which had an immense influence in furthering French Canadian missions. Professor Campbell tells the colourful story of Father Charles Chiniquy, the converted priest, who left the Catholic Church, taking with him hundreds of his parishioners. Presbyterian College, Montreal, after its formation in 1865, was encouraged to become involved in the French mission work. During their vacation, the students became colporteurs and soon many new missions were established.

The situation in Montreal became volatile in 1875 and Dr. Donald MacVicar, principal of Presbyterian College, called on Father Chiniquy for help. Father Chiniquy was in Ontario at the time. He returned to Montreal and crowds of eager listeners, attracted by the eloquent preacher, attended evangelistic services which were held nightly for two months. They had to contend with angry mobs who smashed windows and stoned the preacher and his hearers, making it necessary to post guards so the meetings could continue.

Those who hearken back to "the good old days" in the church need to be reminded that the hostility between Catholics and Protestants in the not too distant past was bitter and sometimes violent. Professor Campbell speaks about colporteurs often having hairbreadth escapes, their books seized and burned, their efforts hindered and denounced.

Although, in his article, Professor Campbell never mentions the Ladies' Auxiliary Association, he speaks about the Pointe-aux-Trembles school,[8] which was supported by the women, and praises the work done by several people including Rev. J. E. and Mrs. Tanner and Miss Vernier — names also mentioned in the records of the Ladies' Auxiliary Association.

How did these Montreal women become involved in this work of French evangelism in Quebec? The minutes of that early society tell the story.

Seed-Planting Time

In the spring of 1864, a group of sabbath school teachers belonging to St. Andrew's and St. Paul's congregations,

> *...feeling anxious to enlarge their sphere of usefulness without intrenching on the ground already occupied by others...expressed their willingness to assist by any efforts in their power the French congregation under the auspices of the Church of Scotland.*[9]

With the encouragement of their ministers, this group held a meeting in the manse and, before separating, had decided to hold a soirée and sale of work to raise funds to help the synod's French Mission Committee in its work.

The first meeting of the group took place on March 4, 1864, to consider the advisability of forming a Ladies' Auxiliary Association to aid the synod's French Mission Committee. Rev. William Snodgrass, principal of Queen's University, Kingston, committee chairman, opened with prayer and gave an explanation of the history and current state of the French mission, urging the women to consider the necessity of forming a ladies' auxiliary society. Mr. Tanner, missionary for French work, also made some explanatory remarks and approved the formation of such a society.

Following a motion stating *that considering the great importance of the French mission work....and also considering that there are many ways in which an association of ladies might materially assist in the prosecution of the scheme,*[10] a resolution was passed that a Ladies' Auxiliary Association be formed. A draft constitution was submitted and accepted, stating that the association would be called the Montreal Ladies' French Mission Association in connection with the Church of Scotland with the object of rendering assistance to the French Mission Committee of the synod. Mrs. Andrew Paton[11], the wife of the assistant minister of St. Andrew's Presbyterian Church, Montreal, was the first president.

At the next meeting, collectors were appointed and the group decided they would take on the task of defraying the expense for one year of an assistant to the now ailing Rev. Tanner. Mr. Tanner suggested the name of Monsieur Geoffrey.

M. Geoffrey regularly attended the meetings of the women's association and read reports of his work. His job was not an easy one. His reports indicate that he visited both French Roman Catholic families and French Protestant families. In his first report he informed the women that he was only insulted once when a stone was thrown at him. However, by the end of the first year, the annual report says that he had been reviled and insulted on many occasions but was cheered and encouraged by those who appreciated his visits.

The association also supported a day school which had been started in connection with the mission. It was held in St. John's Church. On the resignation of the first teacher, the committee secured the services of Miss Vernier, who was interested in the work of the mission. Unfortunately, Miss Vernier had to work under horrendous conditions. For six weeks, due to some defect in the drainage of the church, the floor of the basement was covered with water to the depth of several inches and Miss Vernier had to teach the children on the stairs and landing.

The first annual meeting of the new auxiliary was held on December 29, 1864, in St. Paul's Church, with a large number in attendance. Principal Snodgrass chaired the meeting. Mr. J.L. Morris read the annual report on behalf of the secretary, Miss A.M. McIntosh. The report told how the group began and how the money, raised through collections, soirées and sales of work, was apportioned in the work of the mission. There were reports on M. Geoffrey's and Miss Vernier's work and a plea for subscriptions and donations in aid of the work. The report also included a list of 136 annual subscribers, all women except for one male. Addresses were delivered at the meeting by Principal Snodgrass, Mr. Morris and Mr. Tanner.

Although there is no indication that the women objected, it is clear from the minutes that the clergy intended to keep control of the women's association. The clergy attended most meetings, opening and closing with prayer and speaking freely on matters pertaining to ways the women could help the synod in their endeavours. The clergy chaired the annual meeting and even read the annual report on behalf of the secretary. It would seem the women's job was to raise money through soirées, sales of work and collections. As we have already seen, at the second meeting collectors were appointed and the people from whom they collected, with one exception, were women.

According to the annual report, there were evidently some who believed the church should not involve itself in French evangelism. The response to this criticism was that,

> *...since ignorance of God's word is the source of the Roman Catholic Church's errors, it is the duty of Christians to see that the people among whom their lot is cast have this infallible guide placed within their reach.*[12]

The women did not always agree to the synod's requests. In 1865, when Dr. John Jenkins, minister of St. Paul's Church, suggested that the committee might provide an annual sum for the support of a young man, Mr. Doudiet, to be educated for the ministry at Queen's University, Kingston, Ontario, the women turned him down.

The second annual meeting, at the end of 1865, found the women rather discouraged. M. Geoffrey's work, *although productive of good, had not attended with all the benefits expected.*[13] The report of the day school was more encouraging and Miss Vernier is described as discharging her duties faithfully and efficiently. The women felt that the school was perhaps one of the most important branches of the mission. The conclusion was that, although they did not have a large amount to report, they had not laboured in vain, nor without encouragement.

It would appear from the minutes that the association did not intend to continue beyond their existing mandate even though their constitution included a fee for life membership. They stopped their meetings and collections at the end of 1866. However, they were called together again by the synod in the fall of 1869 and it was impressed upon them that, since Mr. Doudiet had completed his studies at Queen's, and was ordained and inducted into the French Mission Church, there would be increased expense incurred in sustaining the mission. The women unanimously agreed to assume the work in aid of the synod's scheme. At the January meeting in 1870 the women were told of the hope of a new day school being built, since the school continued to grow. As the group was without a president, Mrs. Colin Russel agreed to fill the position.

At the annual meeting in November, 1870, Mr. Doudiet informed the women that, although the congregation was doing well, the manse was sadly in need of repair. The women agreed to hold a sale of work, the proceeds to be used for the repair of the manse and for the building of a schoolroom in connection with the church to house the sabbath school and the day school. The cost would be $500.

After the successful outcome of the sale, it was decided to hold no more meetings for the time being. However, once again the synod was in difficulty and in June of 1871 the women were called together for a special meeting where it was decided to give the money left over from the sale to help pay the minister's stipend.

New Growth

Those first minutes end with that meeting in June 1871. The auxiliary did not meet again until 1875, when the Presbyterian churches scattered throughout Canada joined to form the Presbyterian Church in Canada. The auxiliary was reconstituted under the leadership of Mrs. Jane Redpath. It had the distinction of being the first and only women's society of the newly formed Presbyterian Church. It was given a new name — The Ladies' French Evangelization Society — in co-operation with the General Assembly's Board of French Evangelization. Auxiliary groups and mission bands were formed

Jane Redpath

in congregations in the Montreal area. The mission bands were mainly children's groups but there were some for young adults.

In the spring of 1875, a house was leased on Lagauchetiere Street. Furniture was purchased and a matron hired. The house became the centre for mothers' meetings, religious instruction, Bible study, and sewing classes. It was a busy place with many people taking advantage of the classes offered.

In 1881, the society, which had devoted its efforts almost entirely to French work, was approached by the Woman's Foreign Missionary Society (formed in 1876 in Toronto) with the proposal that the Montreal society become an auxiliary of that society and help with the work in the foreign field. Worried that such a decision would cause the French evangelization work to suffer — this work having been successful and dear to the heart of the Society — the offer was declined. Still, it was clear that involvement in home and foreign mission work would certainly be of interest to their members. The decision was made to continue the work in the French field with increased vigour but to take responsibility for some work in the home and foreign fields. This called for some changes. So in April of 1882 a new constitution was adopted, and home, French and foreign work were included under one board of management. The new name? The Montreal Woman's Missionary Society of the Presbyterian Church in Canada. The motto chosen was "Thy Kingdom Come."

At the 20th anniversary of the society, in 1884, the president commented,

> *Now thirty-two auxiliaries, meaning perhaps 800 women, meeting in little companies from month to month ought to mean something to the Church of God, and surely it will if we pray as we should and allow Him, as He would, did we not restrain and limit Him, to work in us to will and do of His good pleasure*[14]

Branching Out

Mr. Lockert, who had been appointed to do city mission work in French evangelization, left in 1883 and was replaced by Madame Coté.

> *For 30 years she pursued her daily task of visiting the French poor of Montreal, Roman Catholic as well as Protestant, relieving the temporal needs of those in distress, rendering assistance in the home, ministering to the sick, endeavoring to enlighten the ignorant, to guide and strengthen the weak by reading the Scriptures and, ever and anon, repeating the 'old, old story of Jesus and his love.'*[15]

In 1887, the society raised $5,000 to remodel the girls' school at Pointe-aux-Trembles and for many years provided scholarships for the support of students. The society also contributed regularly to the Board of French Evangelism.

The society, as far back as 1888, had been anxious to produce a missionary leaflet, but it was not until 1904 that the first issue of *The Woman's Missionary Outlook* appeared. The name of the society was also changed to reflect the inclusion of auxiliaries outside Montreal. It became The Woman's Missionary Society, Montreal.

As the society increased in strength and numbers, it took on more work, appointing M. George André in 1904 to do mission work throughout the Province of Quebec and employing a student to assist during the summer months. A trained nurse, Miss McIntyre, was employed to do for the English what Mme Coté did for the French — distributing literature, linen, clothing and comforts.

As for the home mission department of the society, the claims of the northwest were pressing. In 1887, contributions, along with two boxes of clothing were sent for distribution among the needy. Contributions were also made toward work with immigrants. In 1900, responsibility was taken for partial support of a mission station in the northwest. Another was added in 1901 so that, by 1905, the society was supporting five mission stations and, by 1914, ten. The auxiliaries found this branch of the work most appealing.

Work in the foreign field was, in the beginning, mainly confined to correspondence with missionaries. The society worked hard to interest and educate the auxiliaries about foreign missions. By 1887, with membership and funds increasing, the committee responsible for foreign work was anxious to have a missionary 'to call their own'. Their chosen field was India. To their dismay, they discovered that no women missionaries could be sent to India except through the Woman's Foreign Missionary Society. They were allowed, however, to pay the salary of a missionary in China who was already on the field. The church had several women missionaries in China so, in 1892, the society decided to take responsibility to support Dr. Lucinda Graham in Honan, China. They did this with some trepidation since, at the time, auxiliaries could decide for themselves how to spend their money and it was not a certainty that the response from the groups would be generous. They need not have worried. Having a missionary of their very own, with letters going back and forth, along with reports of her work, created much interest.

Dr. Lucinda Graham, according to Alvyn Austin, author of *Saving China*, was a merry individual cutting quite a figure in the mission by striding out for walks around the town. This apparently caused the men some consternation since, as she confided to her brother, they very seldom went outside the compound themselves unless they had some special reason to go.[16]

Unfortunately, Dr. Graham's term was very brief. Just two years after her arrival, she and another worker, Mrs. Malcolm, died at their posts. Reports show that Dr. Graham was called to attend Mrs. Malcolm who was dying of cholera. Within a week, both women were dead. Funding for this branch of the work was given to the Foreign Mission Board until a replacement for Dr. Graham could be found.

Dr. Jean Dow was appointed by the Foreign Mission Board in 1895 to take the place of Dr. Graham and was assigned to the Montreal Society. Dr. Dow was a young woman from Fergus, Ontario. For twenty years she was the only woman physician in the Canadian Presbyterian Mission in Honan. She became well known in China for her work as a surgeon and was given a medal by the Chinese for her fine work during the terrible famine of 1920-1921.

Dr. Dow was one of the missionaries who had to flee for their lives during the Boxer Rebellion in 1900. At that time there was a temporary withdrawal of missionaries from Honan because of an outbreak of anti-foreign feeling in China which had paralyzed missionary efforts. Many missionaries with their wives and children were brutally murdered along with many indigenous Christians. Rosalind Goforth, in her book *Goforth of China*, relates the harrowing experiences the missionaries had to face in trying to leave. Dr. Jean Dow was there, she said, to attend to the many wounds which desperately needed cleansing and dressing. Dr. Dow returned to China after the Boxer Rebellion and laboured there until her death in 1927. She was buried at Changte and Rosalind Goforth speaks of her again as *our beloved co-worker of many years, thought of by us and others as 'our beloved, beautiful doctor.'*[17]

The society had never lost its desire to have a missionary in India. This desire was granted when, in 1900, Dr. Susan McCalla was appointed to serve in Central India. After two years, however, Dr. McCalla married and went with her husband to Honan.

Agnes Dickson

China seems to have been the society's destiny for, in 1901, the Presbyterian Church opened up work in Macao, South China and assigned to the society the work among women and children in that field. In 1904, in Erskine Presbyterian Church in Montreal, Miss Agnes I. Dickson and Dr. Isabella Little were designated for work in Macao. Within a year Dr. Little was married.

Miss Agnes Dickson was a graduate of the University of Toronto and the first educational missionary under the Woman's Foreign Missionary Society. She had charge of the girls' boarding school in Kong Moon, and was engaged in student evangelistic campaigns in Canton and in the Union Bible Women's Conferences. She served first in China and then with the Chinese in Montreal. She wrote the chapter on China in *The Story of our Missions*.

Dr. Jessie MacBean succeeded Dr. Little in Macao and was designated as missionary in St. Paul's Church, Montreal, in December 1905. In 1906, land was purchased and buildings erected in Kong Moon, three miles from Macao. As soon as property was secured plans were made to build a hospital. But how was it to be financed?

The Foreign Mission Board devised a scheme whereby it would give to whoever donated the cost of either of two hospitals in Kong Moon the privilege of naming the hospital. Mrs. Elliot Busteed, president of the St. Paul's Women's Auxiliary in Montreal, who merits a whole page in Alvyn Austin's book Saving China,

> *...immediately set on foot a scheme to raise $2,000 among the members of St. Paul's Church...to build a hospital as a memorial to Mrs. Marion Barclay, 'our esteemed pastor's wife'... The Marion Barclay Hospital was opened with great fanfare in 1912, with 33 ward beds and 23 in emergency, it had its own generating plant, one of the first in the city, and a modern operating room and it was run for many years by the diminutive Dr. MacBean.*[18]

Towards Amalgamation

The society felt it was hampered in its work due to auxiliaries' right to dispense their funds as they saw fit. It decided it was time for a change. After much consultation with auxiliaries, it was decided that all money raised should be disbursed as directed by the executive committee.

By 1914, the year of amalgamation, the Woman's Missionary Society, Montreal, had 49 auxiliaries and 10 mission bands with some 800 women supporting l0 missionaries concerned for home, French and foreign work.

It was the intention of the church to amalgamate all the women's missionary societies in the Presbyterian Church. Although the Montreal Society does not seem to have been included in the negotiations, the hope was expressed at the General Assembly in 1913 that the Woman's Missionary Society, Montreal would decide to become one of the amalgamating societies. After its annual meeting in February 1914, the Montreal Society sent official word of its decision to amalgamate with the other societies in May 1914. The motto of the Montreal Society, whose work included home, French and foreign, was "A three-fold cord is not quickly broken." The editor of *The Foreign Missionary Tidings*, in reporting the decision to amalgamate, said that the women of the WFMS trusted that this union of the three women's societies would also represent the union of a three-fold cord which would not be broken.

Not everyone in the Montreal society was happy about the amalgamation. Mrs. Elliot Busteed, the feisty president of the St. Paul's Missionary Auxiliary, Montreal, along with her entire executive, resigned in protest. The new president, in her annual report for 1914, had this to say,

> *The year 1914 will stand out as perhaps the most eventful in the life of the St. Paul's Missionary Auxiliary — certainly as the most unsettled. At the beginning of the year, the question of amalgamation of the Women's Missionary Societies began to be discussed... For the voting on the question in May our members were well informed on the subject — but conservatism was in the majority and the amalgamation was voted down. However, in the whole society the feeling was different so that the St. Paul's Auxiliary, though having voted against, was compelled to come in with the new amalgamation.*[19]

Mrs. Busteed later returned to St. Paul's Auxiliary. She took an active part in the work of the auxiliary and often spoke on her favourite subject — the mission in China. She was president of the auxiliary again in the late 1920s and until her death in 1930.

Chapter 3

Women's Work for Women

Woman's Foreign Missionary Society (WFMS), 1876-1914

Women — A Potent Force

"Helping 'Heathen' Sisters: Women's Work for Women" is the title of one of the chapters in Ruth Tucker's book *Guardians of the Great Commission, The Story of Women in Modern Missions*. This, Tucker says,

> *... was the major justification for the women's missionary movement ... It was widely believed ... that women were the most potent force available to carry out the Great Commission ... that women reaching women was the most effective means of evangelism.*[1]

A nation rises no higher than its women, says the writer of the chapter on China in *The Story of Our Missions*.[2]

Many mission-minded women heard the clarion call to do the work for women that only women could do. The male leaders in the church, although somewhat fearful that women might be a little difficult to control, were aware that local customs and taboos overseas made women's work inaccessible to male missionaries. It was to their advantage, therefore, to encourage the organization of women's groups that would finance and publicize this work. The challenge for the men was keeping the women happy without losing control of the work.

Opportunities for women were limited at home. On the mission field the opposite was true.

> *Practically every area of ministry imaginable was wide open to them. There was criticism when they overstepped the bounds of what was considered to be the 'women's sphere', but the criticism was muffled by the overwhelming needs....as well as by the fact that women on the mission field quickly proved to be more than equal to the task before them.*[3]

Women doctors, who had difficulty being accepted in their own countries, were welcomed with open arms in India and China. Male doctors were not allowed to treat women. Husbands in many cases would rather have their wives die than permit them to be seen by a male doctor. Many women went to medical school with the specific purpose of pursuing careers as medical missionaries.

Ida Scudder's story is a testimony to the need for women doctors and to the burden laid upon women to respond to this need. Ida's grandfather, Dr. John Scudder, was the first American missionary doctor. He served under the Reformed Church of America. He had seven sons. All became missionaries to India. One was Ida's father. Ida, born in 1870, from her youth was determined not to follow the tradition set by her father and uncles, who had all become missionaries. She tells the story of how, while visiting her parents in India after her graduation from Northfield Seminary in Massachusetts, three Indian men came to the door pleading for medical help for their wives who were having difficulties in childbirth. Her father would have gone but custom would not permit a male doctor to treat a woman. In the morning she heard the beating of the tom-tom. All three women had died in the night. She went to her mother and father and told them she must go home to study medicine and come back to India to help such women. After her graduation, she raised $10,000 and returned to India to set up a program of medical work for women, the beginning of the Vellore Medical Complex, offering Indian women the medical services they so desperately needed.[4]

Presbyterian Women Respond to the Call

Many women in the Presbyterian Church in Canada were well aware of the missionary groups that already existed in the "Old World" and in the United States. For some time, isolated groups in Canada had begun to draw together. Some of these groups were formed as early as 1838 in Ontario, and earlier in eastern Canada. In 1868, Mrs. Marjory MacLaren in Belleville and

Mrs. Smellie in Fergus were working to interest women in missions. In 1875, the Foreign Mission Committee, meeting for the first time as a committee of the newly formed Presbyterian Church in Canada, authorized their convener, Dr. William MacLaren, Marjory's husband,

> *...to investigate the possibility of establishing a woman's foreign missionary society such as already existed in several branches of American Presbyterianism.*[5]

A committee was appointed to draft a constitution and bylaws. It consisted of Dr. Topp and Dr. MacLaren, Mrs. Marjory MacLaren, Mrs. Catherine Ewart, and twelve other women.

The Woman's Foreign Missionary Society was organized on March 21, 1876. The constitution and bylaws were adopted and the board and officers appointed. Mrs. MacLaren was the first president with Mrs. Ewart as secretary. Its object was

> *...to aid the Foreign Mission Committee in the support of its work among the heathen women and children, to interest the women and children of the Church in this work and to call forth in a systematic way their prayers and free-will offerings in its behalf.*[6]

Catherine Ewart

Fifty women enrolled as members at the first monthly meeting held at Knox Church, Toronto on April 4, 1876. The constitution was approved by the General Assembly in June.

From the beginning *...the direction and management of the organization was entirely in its own hands with the executive board to conduct business*[7], or so they thought. Their first concern was to receive direct missionary information from the foreign field. Letters were received from Mrs. Stothert of the Scottish Free Church, Bombay, along with letters from Canadian missionaries, Margaret Rodger and Marion Fairweather. One other letter, from Mrs. Fraser of Formosa, contained all of the direct missionary intelligence available for circulation during the first year.[8]

Both Margaret Rodger and Marion Fairweather were teachers. They were the Presbyterian Church in Canada's first women missionaries and its India pioneers. Margaret Rodger was from East Settlement, near Lachute, Quebec, and Marion Fairweather was from Bowmanville, Ontario. They were paid by the Presbyterian Church in Canada but worked for an American Presbyterian agency in North India.[9] They also received financial assistance from the Woman's Foreign Missionary Society.

The aim of the Woman's Foreign Missionary Society was to form an auxiliary and a mission band in every congregation. In summing up, at the end of the first year, Mrs. Ewart, the first secretary, states,

> *Now as we are assured that no scheme of our church has suffered in consequence of this additional call upon our givings, we think we may take courage and urge the claims of the society.*[10]

Mrs. Ewart's comment would suggest that there were those who had considerable fear that money given for the work of the WFMS would mean less money for the general work of the church, a fear that has persisted throughout the history of the society. At the end of the first year there were only eighteen auxiliaries and three mission bands. The society grew slowly in the first five years, and not without opposition.

> *The end of our fifth year found us weak and struggling. The entire scheme was new, and good people looked on with amused interest or apparent indifference... Since the fifth year, the evident success has been a little more pronounced, prejudice has given away to cordiality, and in some places where there has been indifference and opposition, there is now harmonious accord.*[11]

The harmonious accord, unfortunately, was not easy to maintain. On the one hand there were powerful women who were excited about the possibilities for service that were opening up to them. On the other hand, the male leaders of the church had the power and were determined to keep the women in their place. However, the women knew, with a concern that was genuine but also, to be sure, political, that they must be careful not to step out of their proper sphere. To put it bluntly, the men said, in effect, "You raise the money, we'll make the decisions."

The WFMS apparently got the message. They were aware of the danger of over-stepping their mandate. In a seeming attempt to placate the powers that be, the fifth annual report attempted to make clear that the society knew its place in relation to the Foreign Mission Committee,

> *The position of this society, as an auxiliary to the Foreign Mission*

> *Committee of our church, affords us an excellent opportunity for doing work of a congenial kind. We are happily free from much responsibility which would be unavoidable in an independent organization. There is nothing to do which ought to bring us before the public, or which will interfere with the priceless possession 'of a meek and quiet spirit', no selection or superintending of missionaries; no puzzling questions to settle; but the simple duty of raising money sufficient to meet certain expenses for which we have become responsible.*[12]

One might be forgiven for suspecting that the above statement was made "tongue-in-cheek," particularly since, in the years after 1881, the actions of the WFMS seem to belie the pious words of the report as the society goes from strength to strength.

In 1883 the society adopted the motto, The World for Christ, and for the first time issued life members' certificates. In 1884, mission band presidents became entitled to a seat on the WFMS Board. We can probably assume that it was the adult leaders who attended.

Top priority was given to providing information about the work of missionaries to the auxiliaries. At first, letters were copied by hand and sent to the groups. In 1884, *The Monthly Letter Leaflet* was produced and circulated at a cost of 12 cents a year. The title was changed in 1897 to *The Foreign Missionary Tidings*. Other leaflets and pamphlets were produced by the publications department, as well as study material for mission bands.

Presbyterials were formed as soon as there were enough auxiliaries to make that viable.[13] The work of the society was done entirely by volunteers until 1905. Ministers were not always favourable to the society, and, in those congregations, the organization of an auxiliary was postponed.

At the close of the first decade the membership of the WFMS was 6,191 and the financial position was assured. The society's confidence grew as its knowledge of the work increased. Consequently, the women felt it was important to have more input into decisions that were made about the work they supported. This was balanced by an increasing effort on the part of the Foreign Mission Committee to share information and to consult the WFMS on matters pertaining to women's work.

It seemed the right time, therefore, to put forward an idea that had been the dream of Mrs. Ewart, one of the founding members of the society, along with a few other women closely connected with the work. That dream was to provide for young women applying for foreign service an opportunity to *receive a special training in biblical and practical subjects.*[14] The dream became a reality with the opening of a school in September, 1897. It was named the

Ewart Missionary Training Home in loving memory of Mrs. Ewart who had died shortly before it opened. Mrs. Ewart was president of the society at the time of her death.

> *...the home symbolized the persistence with which the organization pursued its goals as well as its increasing part in the church's foreign missionary enterprise.*[15]

At the time of the 20th anniversary in 1896, the membership of the WFMS stood at 19,000. The society was supporting sixteen women missionaries in Central India, five of whom were medical missionaries, along with a woman's hospital, a girls' boarding school and other buildings. At Tamsui, in North Formosa, the society was responsible for the girls' boarding school and the salaries of a number of indigenous Bible women. In Honan, China, with the opening up of women's work, the society was responsible for one woman missionary and assisted in sending several others. In western Canada and British Columbia, considered foreign fields at the time,

> *...numerous buildings have been erected for Indian educational work, and the society contributes the salaries of all who are engaged in the training of the young on the reserves.*[16]

India — A Most Important Field

India was the first and most important field for the Woman's Foreign Missionary Society. Marion Fairweather, along with Margaret Rodger, had been working in North India since 1873 under the American Presbyterian Church until our own church could establish a foothold in the country. Marion Fairweather was responsible for doing much of the groundwork in finding appropriate, unclaimed territory where the Presbyterian Church in Canada might establish its mission.

The Canadian Presbyterian Church established a mission at Indore in Central India in 1877. Rev. James M. Douglas was sent to Central India as the official founder of the mission. From the beginning of the mission, single women alone outnumbered the men. The result was that 'women's work for women' was more important in Central India than in any of the church's other fields.

Although Indian officials were adamantly opposed to attempts by the missionaries to proselytize, they were anxious to take advantage of the educational and medical skills of the women missionaries. Many high caste women lived in seclusion, shut up year after year in zenanas, as the women's part of the house was called. Wealthy Muslim women, and many high-caste Hindu women were never seen on the streets except to attend family feasts when they went in closed carriages. They embroidered, worked on lace, and a few of them would read their religious books. Women's quarters were completely inaccessible to the male missionaries. Since Indian men wanted their wives to learn English and other skills that the women missionaries could teach, the women missionaries were warmly welcomed and quickly took advantage of their privileged status.

Five girls' schools were opened for the instruction of approximately 200 children. This was not an easy task. Parents of girls from Hindu or non-Christian families were not anxious to send their children to school. This meant that "calling women" had to go from house to house each morning to try to collect the children.

Parents who did want their children to be educated were often opposed to the Christian teaching at the schools. A report in *The Foreign Missionary Tidings* from Miss Jessie Weir of the Mhow field tells of the school at Manpur which had done fruitful work. Prakashu, the small daughter of the highest official in the village, was one of the brightest little girls. One day a friend of her father who was visiting in the home asked what she had learned in school.

> *Reading, writing...and we are taught from another book about Jesus...* she said with a great deal of pleasure. *Do you see what is happening? the friend asked her father. You send your daughter to the mission school and while she is young she is taught the Christian religion...She will become a Christian.*

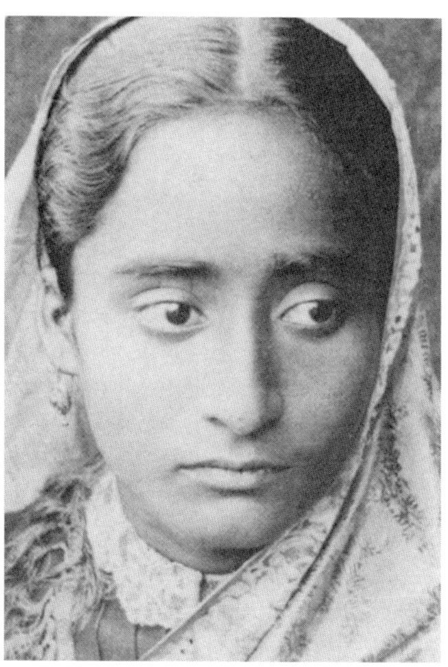

Mrs. Johorty, the superintendent for many years of the widows' industrial home in Indore, was one of the few Indian women workers whose name was well known to missions supporters in Canada.

Prakashu, Miss Weir reported, did not return to school and neither did some of her little companions.[17]

The Women's Industrial Home began in 1893 with several young women from Indore who had turned to Christianity and sought the protection of the mission from cruel relatives. They were sheltered and educated in a small bungalow with Mrs. Johory, wife of one of the Indian professors at the Christian College.

> *Words fail to describe the famine year of 1900. The cries of the hungry, the emaciated forms, the hopeless faces, the empty villages, the untilled*

> *fields — all these sights and sounds tore the heart-strings of our missionaries.*[18]

The missionaries threw themselves wholeheartedly into the rescue work. The famine brought to the Indore Women's Industrial Home many young widows and girls who could not be admitted to the boarding school or the orphanages. Later the widows' homes at Ujjain and Neemuch were amalgamated with the Indore Home and a worker was appointed to take charge of the institution with the assistance of Mrs. Johory. Miss Janet White, who began work at the Women's Industrial Home in 1903, reported that many poor widows and discarded wives found their way to the home. They all had to engage in industrial work — needlework, button making, crocheting and knitting, but Bible teaching took precedence.

Tours to Indian villages could only take place when the weather was cold. It was too wet in the rainy season and not safe in the extreme heat. The missionaries would take their 'magic lantern', an early edition of the slide projector, to show Bible pictures and tell stories. The boys would stand at the front with the men nearby. On the outskirts, or across the narrow road, there might be two or three women, drawn by curiosity but not allowed to come nearer. Women in the villages could not mix with the crowd of men who gathered to hear the preaching. Some of the women missionaries would then go to speak to women who had gathered in one of their homes.

In the late 1800s, doctors were sprouting like wildflowers, says Carlotta Hacker, author of *The Indomitable Lady Doctors*. Women doctors, whose names and work should not be forgotten, laboured tirelessly and were in many cases honoured by their universities in Canada and by the Indian government.

Dr. Elizabeth Beatty, the Presbyterian Church in Canada's first woman missionary doctor, started medical work at Indore in 1884. On her arrival, she rented a mud hut, using the lower floor as a dispensary and the upper as a four-bed hospital. She learned Hindi as quickly as she could, ministered to the sick, and trained Indian women as nurses. She was consulted by both rich and poor. Four years later, the dowager maharani, impressed by her work, provided land to build a hospital for women. This was the first women's hospital in Central India. Unfortunately, because of ill health, Dr. Beatty had to return to Canada before the hospital was completed.

> *Only six years, yet during those years Dr. Beatty had laid the foundations of what was to become one of Canada's greatest medical missions. Many women doctors were to follow her to Indore...but it was dry-humoured Dr. Beatty in her mud-hut dispensary who led the way.*[19]

Dr. Beatty's friend and colleague, Dr. Marion Oliver, joined Dr. Beatty at Indore in 1887 and spent her life there building up the mission. She presided over the opening of the new hospital and it remained under her able supervision until she returned to Canada in 1912. She died on May 22, 1913.

> *Dr. Oliver loved the people of India and gave 27 years of her life towards their uplift.*[20]

Dr. Margaret McKellar came first to Indore and then went on to become pioneer medical missionary in Neemuch, opening a dispensary in 1892. The terrible famine that began in 1900 was followed by plague. Two hundred and forty orphans were collected and a hospital was necessary. The first hospital was built in 1912. Dr. McKellar, a medical missionary for 40 years, received the Kaiser-i-Hind medal from the government for her years of service in India, and in 1929 was awarded an honourary doctorate degree by Queen's University, Kingston, Ontario.

Dr. Margaret O'Hara was the first medical missionary in Dhar, beginning work there in 1895. A hospital was built in 1898 with the maharaja donating the land for both the hospital and a bungalow. For 35 years, her many responsibilities included not only work at the hospital and dispensary but also at the Dhar Leper Asylum. She started a training school for Indians at the hospital. She was a doctor, teacher, missionary, writer, and one of Queen's most distinguished graduates. Queen's honoured her with a doctorate for her long and valued service in India and she was also awarded the Kaiser-i-Hind medal.

Margaret O'Hara in Dhar, India

Dr. Agnes Turnbull was born in Montreal. She left for India immediately after her graduation from Queen's University. She served as medical missionary at Indore and received the Kaiser-i-Hind medal for her work during a terrible outbreak of plague. When plague broke out in 1900, all doctors and nurses were taxed to the limit as they aided in inoculation of hundreds of patients a day, or visited the plague hospitals erected by the government. Temporary sheds were erected at Indore hospital for the treatment of women and children, victims of famine. Fifty to 300 meals were given out each day. It was during one of the most alarming periods of plague, with the strain of night and day duty, that Dr. Turnbull's health became so undermined that she took ill. She died at her post in 1906.

Dr. Belle Chone Oliver served at the women's hospitals in Indore, Dhar and Neemuch. During the plague, Dr. Oliver worked with Dr. McKellar in Neemuch. In 1915, she was appointed the first medical missionary to Banswara. She was actively involved in the medical education of Indians, and was appointed secretary of the Christian Medical Association of India in 1933.

Dr. Mary Mackay arrived in India in 1888, serving just one year before being married. Dr. Elizabeth McMaster arrived in India in 1904 and served for 37 years. Miss Harriet Thomson was the first trained nurse. She took up her duties at Indore in 1896, and served on the mission field for 33 years. Catherine Campbell, a teacher, arrived in India in 1894 and served for 41 years. She received the Kaiser-i-Hind award for distinguished service. These doctors, along with many nurses, teachers and other women missionaries made up the majority of workers, outnumbering, by far, the male missionaries in the Central India field.

With intensive research into letters, reports and publications, Ruth Compton Brouwer, in her book *New Women for God, Canadian Presbyterian Women and India Missions, 1876-1914*, gives a picture of the struggles and disappointments, along with the blessings and encouragements, that were part of the experience of women on the mission field. Apart from the dangers and difficulties of being in a foreign country, Brouwer points out the obstacles faced by those early women missionaries that were largely due to sexist attitudes carried over from Canada to the mission field in India by the male missionaries. These attitudes were, to a large degree, responsible for conflict on the field.

In April 1879, the Foreign Mission Committee in Toronto had formulated regulations for the Central India field that denied women any formal authority even over their own work. A mission council, all male, was to be responsible for all decision-making, and would meet quarterly or more often. The women were to be consulted on all matters pertaining to their work but the council was not obliged to follow their advice. This was accepted practice on other mission fields but the Central India field was not like other fields.

This was a field, as already noted, where women missionaries were in the majority, several of whom were doctors. Having faced hostility and discrimination at medical college, they were *seasoned veterans of gender politics.*[21] The women missionaries, who ran schools and hospitals, were not prepared to just sit quietly at council meetings while decisions were taken about their work. Marion Fairweather had a long experience of missionary work in India and was instrumental in paving the way for the opening of the central India field. She surely could rightly assume that she would continue to be considered an important voice in what happened on the field.

Even before the regulations were put in place, trouble was brewing on the mission field. Resentment toward Marion Fairweather by her co-workers, and gossip about her and James Douglas, official founder of the mission, led to her recall by the Foreign Mission Committee in October 1879. John Wilkie, the newest member on the mission station, wrote a letter attacking Fairweather's work. In spite of strong testimonials from many clergy and lay people who knew her work, the Foreign Mission Committee notified her that, as of October 1880, she would no longer be a member of its staff.

Although Margaret Rodger accepted the new regulations, Mary McGregor, a teacher from Brockville, Ontario, did not. The same John Wilkie, who had "done in" Marion Fairweather, wrote to the FMC suggesting they should send out no more single women at present, adding,

> *Some few have done excellent work but the greater number have led to trouble...we have all had not a little trouble with their financial affairs... When you realize how even in Canada some excellent lady workers can hardly be kept in their place by Cmts (committees) you can perhaps understand our position here — especially as it is all much increased through the effects of an eastern climate.*[22]

Mary McGregor was the next woman missionary to be sacrificed in order to maintain the principle that the all-male council should have authority over women's work. Her employment as a missionary of the Presbyterian Church in Canada was terminated in May, 1888. Mary McGregor, like Marion Fairweather, was one of the church's most high-profile WFMS missionaries. Knowing questions might be asked, the FMC blamed the "influence of the climate on her temperament" as the cause of the trouble and urged the Woman's Foreign Missionary Society to keep her dismissal as quiet as possible.

The Indore Presbytery was established in 1886. It was responsible for theological matters; the mission council for financial affairs. They met at the same time and the same men were members of both. Since women could not be ordained, they knew that, as far as the presbytery was concerned, they could have no voice and no vote. They also knew a simple change in regulations could allow them a vote on council. With the growth in women's work, the Foreign Mission Committee in Toronto decided that, to avoid discord, change was necessary.

Wilkie, who had been instrumental in the dismissal of both Marion Fairweather and Mary McGregor, now seemed to recognize that it would be in his own best interests to cultivate the support of the growing number of women on the field. He wrote to the Foreign Mission Committee saying that, in his opinion, the ladies should be allowed to have control over their own work. He suggested a separate women's council, reporting to the Foreign Mission Committee through presbytery and including wives of missionaries as well as the women missionaries.

Most of the male missionaries in the Central India field were absolutely opposed to "women's rights." John Campbell, chief spokesperson for the conservatives, wrote saying that,

> *Much as he valued their help and co-operation, he would rather do without women workers in his station than share authority with them.*[23]

The women themselves said that women should either have their own council or else (preferably) the right to vote in a mixed council on matters affecting their work. They thought missionary wives should be excluded since they would just be "mouthpieces" for their husbands.

The women were gaining confidence and, as their confidence grew, so did their indignation. The usually mild-mannered Margaret Rodger wrote to the Foreign Mission Committee to say that, if women missionaries were not considered capable of taking charge of their own work, they should not have been sent from Canada in the first place. Dr. Oliver added her opinion.

> *...to speak of oversight of women's work among women in India even by such an august body as a presbytery sounds very like sending a man to the kitchen to oversee his wife's cooking... Nor can I imagine any gentleman save from a love of showing authority being willing to assume the oversight of work of which he can have no thorough knowledge...*[24]

They were certainly not subordinates, or employees, the women said, and Dr. Beatty added that perhaps women should have a say in the choosing of an ordained missionary sent to their station, just as women and men in Canada do when calling a minister. She went on to deplore the fact that young men fresh from Canada immediately had a voice in the affairs of the station simply because they were men, and suggested both sexes should have to meet a minimum residency and language requirement before being allowed to vote. The women's final act of rebellion in this round was to send their views directly to the Foreign Mission Committee in Toronto rather than through the mission council.

In 1891, new regulations were adopted by the Foreign Mission Committee. Women missionaries could participate in all council deliberations and could vote on all matters affecting their own work. New mission workers, both male and female, had to spend one year on the field before they could vote and they must have passed their first language examination. This was certainly no solution as far as the men were concerned. Everything the council did, they said, seemed to have some relation to women's work, which would mean the women could speak and vote on everything. Being in the majority, they would control the council.

This called for drastic measures. In March of 1894, council was dissolved by some of the ordained ministers due to lack of a male quorum. A presbytery meeting was called to outline problems and to propose new arrangements. The men said it was not in the interest of the mission that the ladies should be on an equal footing with the men and recommended two new structures: a presbytery, and a separate women's council to oversee women's work, or the women's council could include the Canadian Finance Committee and have missionaries' wives as corresponding members. This was rejected by John Wilkie and by the women. The men admitted their intention was to exclude the women from their business. The idea that women might control the work of ordained men was highly offensive to them.

Later in 1894, new interim regulations were sent by the Foreign Mission Committee (FMC) to re-establish the council. These new regulations improved the situation of the women missionaries only slightly. The FMC warned the missionaries that there were members of their committee who were in favour of a mission council where women would have full equality.

The women grew more militant. Dr. Marion Oliver told the FMC that if these issues were not resolved and women given an equal voice, she would not return to Central India. Five other women threatened to resign as well. Dr. Margaret McKellar, throwing all caution to the winds, wrote:

> *You, perhaps, and other ministers of the church will lay great stress upon the fact that most of our brother missionaries are ordained and that therefore it is not right and proper for us to have the same footing according to Presbyterian teaching. Away with such a reason, for Christ taught differently and we have been 'foreordained' by God Himself to engage in this grand and glorious work of winning souls for Him.*[25]

Four of the women missionaries dissociated themselves from the call for equal rights. The right of women to deliberate in council and to vote on their own work was one thing, but equal rights? That was going too far!

Most ordained missionaries on the field opposed the new regulations citing familiar objections and adding a few new ones — the affairs of Indian Christians would effectively be controlled by women; women could conceivably be in control of ecclesiastical affairs; other missions would be reluctant to work with the mission on new ventures. This last objection was backed up by quoting from a letter they had received from John McInnes of the Scottish mission in Rajputana.

> *We are so disgusted with your board's wild action in regard to the ladies that we won't even speak of union till it comes back to reason and Scriptural position... So far as I know, not a soul of us sides with Wilkie and his band of Graces, rather ecclesiastical Amazons.*[26]

In May 1897, the FMC advised that they were recommending at the next General Assembly the abandonment of the equal rights council and the creation of separate councils for women and men. The women's council was to be limited by the fact that their estimates would be forwarded to the FMC through the presbytery for comment. An amendment in 1898, however, allowed the women to send their estimates directly to the Foreign Mission Committee.

The dreadful famine that devastated India in 1900, and the plague that followed, overshadowed all past difficulties as all mission workers were united in the task of administering famine relief. It was the work on behalf of orphans that had begun near the end of the century, even more than the educational and medical work, that brought the greatest success in terms of Christian converts in India. Children and widows who were left homeless were raised or trained as Christians and became the core of the church in Central India.

Dr. Belle Chone Oliver, in her annual report to the WFMS, says,

> *As we see our clean, bright, intelligent, happy helpers going about their work, making up subscriptions, putting on bandages, nursing the sick, singing, reading and giving the Gospel message, we often rejoice and thank God, for the harvest we have reaped from the famine. Nearly all our workers are girls who were gathered in at that time. This year six of our helpers took the St. John's Ambulance Association course in first aid and all passed. I suppose they are the first women in India who have taken the course in Hindu.*[27]

The views of the male missionaries did not change and the women, for the most part, resigned themselves to separate councils. Dr. Belle Chone Oliver who, after attending a mixed missionary conference in 1913 in Calcutta, told of what a wonderful experience it was to sit with men and women together and she thought how good it would be to have a united council for the mission in Central India.

> *We c'd do better work together, provided we came together in the right spirit, and I hope to be in C.I. when this comes to pass, as I believe it will. Both the men and women have suffered for lack of it.*[28]

Formosa — The Beautiful Island

Dr. George Leslie Mackay was appointed by the General Assembly of the Presbyterian Church in Canada to serve in China. He left on October 19, 1871, but felt compelled to go to Formosa instead. He learned that, although there was a flourishing mission established in south Formosa, nothing had been done in the north. He made Tamsui his headquarters and, consequently, it is the oldest mission station of the Canadian Presbyterian Church.

Some of the strongest converts were women who served as Bible women. Their salaries were paid by the Woman's Foreign Missionary Society. A college for boys and men was opened. Later, in 1833, a school for girls was built by the WFMS. The most important work of the WFMS began in 1905 when the first two women missionaries arrived in Formosa — Miss Jane M. Kinney and Miss Hannah Connell. Work was difficult in the beginning. In spite of the offer of free board, tuition, travelling expenses and free clothing, parents could hardly be persuaded to send their girls to school even for a few months. The girls' school, which had from its beginning been open to

"Bible woman" with a patient from Mackay Memorial Hospital, Tamsui, Formosa

women and to wives and families of students, was reorganized in 1907 as a school for girls only. A school for women opened in 1910.

The Woman's Foreign Missionary Society had no practical part in the medical work of the mission until 1913. The old hospital in Tamsui, the Mackay Memorial Hospital, had no WFMS representatives on its staff. The opening of the new hospital in Taihoku (Taipei) in 1913 added another department to the work of the WFMS. Miss Isabel Elliott, a Canadian nurse, organized a nursing department with a number of Chinese girls as nurses in training.

Missionary Wives or Missionaries' Wives?

The words of Ruth Tucker, quoted earlier, bear repeating,

> *The role of women in the modern missionary movement has been phenomenal...despite their active involvement in missions, however, women have been largely forgotten by the missions historians...*[29]

Of all women missionaries, missionary wives have been the most neglected. Ruth Tucker, at the end of her introduction, does not forget the wives of missionaries.

> *...the accomplishments of married women in ministry should not be overlooked or minimized. Despite their heavy domestic responsibilities they made significant contributions to the missionary enterprise.*[30]

Tucker quotes from Helen Barrett Montgomery's classic *Western Women in Eastern Lands.*

> *You might almost think there were no women, to read the ordinary school history. So also in missionary history, there is a tendency to pass over lightly the contribution of missionaries' wives and mothers.*[31]

Montgomery's claim is supported, says Tucker, by another writer, a man, who says,

> *American historians usually write with a male bias and ignore the role of women in our culture, but no one can ignore the role of the missionaries' wives and daughters without distorting the history of the missionary movement.*[32]

In the beginning of the missionary era, the only women who went overseas were missionary wives. Some who married missionaries went reluctantly, others happily, but there were also those who believed they were called to the foreign field themselves. Marrying a missionary was the only way to get there.

Although the missionary wife's first obligation was to look after the welfare of her husband and their children, there is no question the expectation of the male church officials was that these women should participate fully in the work on the mission field, particularly since their husbands needed them to teach the women on the field. This was, in fact, spelled out in a farewell sermon preached in 1812 to two missionary wives before they left for India.

> *It will be your business, my dear children, to teach these women, to whom your husbands can have but little, or no access....*[33]

Of course, there was no question of remuneration for wives of missionaries. In fact, the names of the wives were not even included on the missionary charts published by the church, although one can safely assume that most of the men who went as missionaries to the foreign field were married.

Charlotte and John Geddie were the first missionaries sent by Canadian Presbyterians. In 1848, they went to Aneityum in the New Hebrides and served for 24 years. A memorial in the New Hebrides says, "When he landed in 1848, there were no Christians here, and when he left, in 1872, there were no heathen." The fact that Mrs. Geddie's name was not included on the memorial underscores Ruth Tucker's and Helen Barrett Montgomery's statements regarding women in mission work.

The Geddies moved to Australia in 1870 to complete the translation of the Aneityumese Bible. John Geddie died there in 1872. Charlotte spent her "retirement" serving the Presbyterian Church in Victoria, Australia. For 30 years she was a member of the Ladies' Benevolent Society in Melbourne. In 1890, Charlotte, along with another woman, founded the Presbyterian Women's Missionary Union. By the end of the first year there were 28 branches and 1,500 members, and four young women had offered themselves for missionary service in Korea. Charlotte died on New Year's day, 1916, at her home in Victoria, Australia.[34]

The chapter on the New Hebrides in *The Story of our Missions* pays tribute to the wives of

> *...these noble missionaries of our church, women of great devotion to the work... Through long years they, too, labored amid unnumbered trials and difficulties...*[35]

The missionary wives worked with the women workers on the field and had close links with the Woman's Foreign Missionary Society. The early WFMS annual reports list all the "lady missionaries" and also the "wives of missionaries." Many of the missionary wives had stories and reports of their work printed in *The Foreign Missionary Tidings*, giving evidence that they were certainly "missionaries" in their own right.

It was a hard life and a heartbreaking one for there were few families where at least some of the children did not succumb to disease and death. Rosalind and Jonathan Goforth lost five of their eleven children. Rosalind

Goforth was a frequent contributor to *The Foreign Missionary Tidings*. In the June 1911 issue she tells of her time among the women of Hsien Hsien.

> *March 6th, Chi Hsien. At the close of the Hsun Hsien Fair I came on with my two women helpers to this place... I have been here now almost a week and have had just a grand time preaching morning, afternoon and evening. Women have filled our place... We have kept up the preaching nine and ten hours a day, but it has been such a strain I am quite worn out... The two women I have helping me are good earnest Christians, but do not know how to hold a crowd so I have been obliged to do most of the preaching myself...*[36]

An added bonus for the church were wives who had nursing or teacher training. *The Foreign Missionary Tidings* of January, 1912, reports that Mrs. Mitchell's school work at Wei Hwei was unexpectedly broken into by the illness of her little girl with severe typhoid. The WFMS had no trained nurse on the field who could meet the extremity. Fortunately, Mrs. Auld, the wife of one of the missionaries, had taken a partial course in nursing before her marriage and arrival in Honan. She was happy to help. It was then suggested by members of the board that Mrs. Auld's example in taking hospital training might be commended to other wives of missionaries before leaving for the foreign field.

Children were a real asset in helping to reach out to women with the gospel message. Mrs. Bruce, reporting from China, says that evangelistic work among the women had been quite encouraging and adds that baby Agnes had assisted very much by her bright smile and clean face and clothing. More women came out when they heard the baby was with the missionaries.

Many of the wives initiated work themselves. Mrs. Barker in Korea reported that she had rented a building and was doing what she could teaching the women and girls. She said that they hoped to have a girls' school built before long.

At the annual meeting of the WFMS in 1912, Mrs. Emily Steele, in her president's address, refers to the great need for more workers, and adds,

> *...let us not forget those who, though not on the salaried list, are nevertheless being of great service in all the fields — I mean the wives of our missionaries, of whom there are seventy-one.*[37]

The WFMS recognized the work done by missionary wives as well as by local workers. A report from Formosa in the June, 1912, issue of *The Foreign Missionary Tidings* says that, as in all the fields, much assistance was given by the wives of the missionaries and trained local helpers. A report from Formosa in the annual report of the WFMS of 1913-14 tells that Mrs. Jack and Mrs. McLeod had led a Sunday afternoon Bible class with the women and adds that the married women gave their help in many different branches of the work.

Rosalind Goforth

Rosalind Goforth wrote a book in 1935 entitled *Goforth of China* which gives a glimpse of what life was like for her as a missionary wife. Rosalind was one of those women who felt called to the foreign field herself, but recognized, that, as the wife of a missionary, she had no status. She does not even put her own name on the cover of the book but simply says "by his wife."

In writing about Goforth, she tends to apologize whenever she includes something about her own life. However, like many other missionary wives, she believed that God had called her as well as her husband and her work was important. She taught the women during the day and played the baby grand organ for the meetings at night. She certainly did not feel inadequate for the task. She tells of an instance when her husband was setting off on a revival tour. On hearing that he was to go, some of the leading Christians at Changte

> *...came to me in a body, begging that I take charge of my husband's field in his absence. Knowing I could not decide this myself and that it was most unlikely that presbytery would agree to it, I endeavoured to put them off. But when the men sank down on their knees, begging with tears streaming down their cheeks, for me not to leave them, but to take my husband's place, I agreed that a deputation should go immediately and lay the matter before the presbytery which was still in session. Presbytery, however, decided "there was no Presbyterian precedent for such a course."*
>
> *Preparations at once began for the break-up of our home, for it had been decided by presbytery that I should return to Canada with the children.*[38]

The Story of Our Missions mentions an incident that occurred when Dr. Goforth wanted Mrs. Goforth to go off with him on an extended evangelical tour. The author says that for six years in succession, Mrs. Goforth took her family and, at the risk of health, joined her husband in touring in the newer parts north of Changte, living in Chinese rented rooms and setting before the people the example of Christian family life.

Rosalind Goforth relates the story differently,

> *As I listened, my heart went like lead! The vision of those women with their smallpox children at Hotsun, crowding about me and the baby, the constant danger to the children from all kinds of infectious diseases that this life would mean…and the thought of our four little graves, all combined to make me set my face as adamant against the plan…*
>
> *Oh how my husband pleaded!.. he assured me that the Lord would keep my children from harm…. He was sure God was calling me to take this step of faith….he went further. He said: "Rose, I am so sure this plan is of God, that I fear for the children if you refuse to obey His call. The safest place for you and the children is the path of duty. You think you can keep your children safe in your comfortable home at Changte, but God may have to show you cannot. But He can and will keep the children if you trust Him and step out in faith!"*[39]

Rosalind went. Since none of the children died during that time, Rosalind concluded that her husband was right. She deemed her reluctance to be a lack of faith, vision and courage.

Missionary wives worked very hard. It was only when the work they were expected to do, along with family duties, became too much for them, that church officials reluctantly decided that single women could apply for overseas work.

It was through a concern for the families of missionaries and single women missionaries that a suggestion came before the board and general meeting of the Woman's Foreign Missionary Society that, with the co-operation of the Foreign Mission Committee, a house be provided in Toronto where missionaries returned on furlough might find accommodation. It was received with favour and the women's board was given a free hand to manage this matter as they considered best.

On May 12, 1914, at the last annual meeting of the WFMS, three days before the amalgamation of the three societies on May 15, the question of a missionary residence was brought up again in the president's address. It was reported that the Foreign Mission Board had secured a lot in the north-east end of the city. Only a small payment had as yet been made on it, and because it was not in the budget scheme, private donations would have to be found. Mrs. Emily Steele, the president, said that they were recommending that $10,000 be donated for the building as there would certainly be missionaries on their staff who would benefit from such a residence. One of the last decisions to be made by the Woman's Foreign Missionary Society before amalgamation was to grant this sum of $10,000 toward the building of a residence for missionaries on furlough.[40]

Working with Aboriginal People

Western Canada, in those early years, was considered a foreign field and came under the purview of the Foreign Mission Committee. The Woman's Foreign Missionary Society was involved in the work with Aboriginal people right from the society's beginning in 1876. As the years went by, the financial burden of the work was placed more and more on the shoulders of the WFMS.

The annual reports of the Woman's Foreign Missionary Society, along with *The Foreign Missionary Tidings*, give a picture of the heavy involvement, both financial and otherwise, of the Woman's Foreign Missionary Society with the Aboriginal people. The February, 1911 issue reports that of the whole estimate, four-fifths, for Aboriginal work undertaken by the Presbyterian Church, was met by the Woman's Foreign Missionary Society. This did not include the bales of clothing, quilts and other items which were always an important part of the work.

To be sure, the writers of these reports reveal some of the prejudices and paternalistic attitudes that were held by the majority of the people in Canada at the time. However, from these reports, we also learn of the genuine care and Christian concern that most of the missionaries showed for the Aboriginal children under their care at the schools and for the older folk on the reserves. Although study books and reports are often inclined to present a favourable picture, we certainly hear as well about the frustrations caused by lack of funds, poor accommodation and long working hours for the staff.

The story of our church's work with Aboriginal people began ten years before the formation of the Woman's Foreign Missionary Society. For some time, a little colony of Red River settlers had begged the church to send out a missionary for the "red men." Finally, the General Assembly gave its consent and on June 6, 1866, Rev. James Nisbet of Kildonan, Manitoba, along with his wife and little child and several helpers, set out in an ox cart looking for a suitable place to begin the first Presbyterian mission to the Aboriginal people in the northwest. After travelling 200 miles in 66 days, they arrived at a spot near the banks of the Saskatchewan River. They secured a tract of land for the Presbyterian Church located near a band of Cree. The site was later to be known as Prince Albert. The winter of 1868-69 was particularly severe and starving families came to the mission for help. Mr. Nisbet offered supper to everyone who would come to night school for a lesson in English and a Bible story. He established a mission among the Aboriginal people in that area and later opened a school for their children.

Mr. Nisbet asked the church to send a female teacher so Aboriginal children could be kept at the mission while their parents were away hunting and fishing. Lucy Baker, a teacher from Lancaster, Ontario, responded to the call. Miss Baker travelled west with Rev. and Mrs. Donald Ross, who had been appointed as missionaries to Prince Albert. They travelled under difficult conditions as far as Winnipeg. The Rosses, both being very ill, were unable to go further. Lucy Baker continued on the journey. She describes her trip by Red River carts

> *...which were made entirely of wood, and as they journeyed on, kept up a continual screeching... On coming to a stream which could not be forded, they were taken apart and formed into rafts... We were six weeks making the journey...arriving at Prince Albert on October 28th, 1879, with the thermometer standing at 28 degrees below zero.*[41]

Miss Baker bought land, built a home and taught at the Nisbet Academy.

Not many years later, ill health forced the Nisbets to retire. By this time, treaties had been made by the government with the Aboriginal people. The little band of Cree had been settled on a reserve about 60 miles from Prince Albert with their Chief Mistawasis, Mr. Nisbet's first convert.[42] Rev. John McKay, who had worked with Mr. Nisbet as his interpreter, along with his wife, responded to a request from Chief Mistawasis for a missionary for their reserve, and a second mission station was opened up. Mr. McKay's daughter opened a school for the children at her own expense. It was later taken over by the church.

Lucy M. Baker

According to *The Story of our Missions*, in 1890 Miss McKay married Mr. MacVicar, B.A., an Aboriginal and a teacher in several mission schools under the church. Oddly enough, *The Royal Road* has Miss Christina McKay, who was in charge of the school at Mistawasis, marrying a Mr. Mills of Prince Albert and becoming one of the honorary presidents of the Saskatchewan Provincial WMS. *The Royal Road* also tells the story of a Mr. MacVicar who was the son of Chief Mistawasis. This Mr. MacVicar was educated at Manitoba College and was given the English name Donald MacVicar after the principal of the Presbyterian College, Montreal. After graduation, according to *The Royal Road*, Mr. MacVicar assisted with mission work on the Crowstand Reserve where he married a daughter of Old Fiddler, a Christian baptized by Rev. John Flett. Mr. Flett was an Aboriginal who had been with the Nisbet party. Mr. MacVicar worked among his people until he died in 1896, leaving his wife and one daughter, Victoria. At the time of his death, he was translating the New Testament into Cree.

Rev. D.H. MacVicar, is mentioned in several of the letters from the Mistawasis reserve. In *The Monthly Letter Leaflet* of 1891, Mr. Nicol writes,

> *Since last I wrote you, Miss C. B. McKay, who has so long discharged the duties of teacher resigned her position. She is succeeded by Rev. D. H. MacVicar, B.A., who also acts as my interpreter, and assists in the general work of the mission.*[43]

These first missions,

> *...were rich in converts to the Christian faith as the Indians had not yet had much opportunity of coming in contact with white men, except the Hudson's Bay Company's men; and while these Highlanders may have had Indian wives, they were, as a rule, very religious men who had brought their Bibles with them from the Old Land.*[44]

During the Riel rebellion in 1885, Lucy Baker gave up her house in Prince Albert for use as a hospital. She devoted her time to caring and cooking for the sick and wounded. After the capture of Riel, the orders of the day found on him were translated from the French by Lucy Baker, who was fluent in the language. She went back east for a rest, returning to teach at the Nisbet Academy until a government high school was established.

Lucy Baker's colourful career did not end there. Some Sioux from the United States had settled near Prince Albert.

> *With the return of peace and the loss of Nisbet Academy, Miss Baker was left without occupation. Then, at her own expense and personal risk, she learned to paddle her canoe across the swift flowing Saskatchewan* (River) *and commenced mission work among these pagan Indians.*[45]

Later the Presbyterian Church became responsible for the work. A log schoolhouse was built with the Woman's Foreign Missionary Society providing for a mission house.

> *There Miss Baker worked among the Indians…raising calves for them, chickens and even kittens; going to town with them to sell their loads of wood… She showed them how to plow, to bluestone their seed wheat. She taught the women to knit and sew… The sick she nursed; the hungry she fed. She also wrote their letters and read to them the replies…* (She) *supplied paper and stamps. This brought the Indians to the mission house often and gave the opportunity of telling them the Old, Old Story, to which they were willing to listen for hours. Lucy Baker had studied the Sioux language and spoke it like a native. On Sundays she preached in three languages, in Sioux for the benefit of the old Indians; in English for the school children; and in French for the neighboring Metis, whose children attended day school and therefore came as well to the Sunday services.*[46]

Lucy Baker maintained the school by herself until 1893 when her health broke down and an assistant was appointed. She stayed on in Prince Albert, though ill health caused her to retire from teaching.

> *The Indians loved her as a mother, and many, young and old, first learned the name of Christ from her lips.*[47]

She died in Montreal in 1905, after thirty-one years of service. She was the Woman's Foreign Missionary Society's first missionary.

The early WFMS documents indicate that the missionaries did not see the work in the residential schools separate from the mission work on the reserves. Many of the Aboriginal people were Christian and many of the reserves had churches, some with active WFMS groups. The close connection between the work on the reserves and the schools is seen in the stories of how some of the schools got started.

The boarding school at Portage la Prairie began with the women of the town wanting to do something for the children of a band of Sioux who were camping nearby. They started a school with Miss Sebastian as the first teacher. These women carried over the meals for the children until 1888 when they wrote to the Woman's Foreign Missionary Society asking the society to take over the work. This was done and a boarding department was added with Miss Fraser as the first principal. The school increased in numbers until, with a new building and Rev. W.A. Hendry as principal, the numbers rose to seventy-eight.

In 1884, Rev. Dr. Hugh McKay began work at the Round Lake Reserve. He began in a small way by taking a few starving and half-naked Aboriginal children into the little log house where he lived. He fed, clothed and taught them. The school began in a primitive log building. Later a stone and frame building was provided as a residence for the children. Mr. McKay was principal of the school for many years and missionary to the four reserves under his care. Mrs. McKay was matron of the children's residence for many years until ill-health forced her into retirement. The chief was a frequent visitor at the mission. *He cannot forget the kindness of the missionary and his wife in times of trouble and illness.*[48]

Work was begun at File Hills Reserve in 1886 or 1887. In the early days there was so much opposition from the Aboriginal people to the 'Jesus Message', that many of the missionaries gave up in despair. One of the missionaries, Kate Gillespie, later Mrs. Motherwell, was the first to win their confidence, after which the school and reserve work steadily advanced. She often visited them in their tepees, caring for their sick, although she was forbidden by them to mention the name of Christ.

Miss Kate Gillespie was appointed principal of the boarding school, a position usually given to a man. Miss Gillespie was no shrinking violet. She announced that she would like any man coming to File Hills ...*to understand that my authority in the school is just the same as is invested in any male principal.*" [49]

In a letter to Toronto, she also commented about the difference in salary because of her gender.

> *I must confess to being a little piqued that the committee should ask me because I am a woman to fill a position for a salary less than they had ever paid to any man. I suppose that is the misfortune of being a woman but I care not for the salary itself further than it would enable me to do perhaps a broader work.*[50]

Mission work began at Hurricane Hills Reserve in 1885. A day school was opened but the Aboriginal people did not co-operate so the school was closed and the children sent to school in Regina. Mission work still continued. In 1911, the Indian Department opened a day school. The first teacher was Miss Lawrence. The missionary, Rev. Ewan Mackenzie, ministered at this reserve for seventeen years. He was much loved by the Aboriginal people. When he died after a lengthy illness, Aboriginal men acted as pall bearers. After his death, the Aboriginal people requested that Mrs. Mary Mackenzie take full charge of the mission, which she did, serving for many years. The congregation at this reserve, like several others, had its own women's missionary auxiliary.

Some of the reserves had churches built by the Aboriginal people themselves. The church at Bird Tail Reserve, built by a Sioux tribe, refugees from the United States after the Minnesota massacre of 1862,

> *...is the pride of the congregation, and a heartier, more devoted people to the church and their missionary would be hard to find. There you will see every Sunday a typical Indian congregation, the women seated on one side of the church with their children, the papooses in the oldtime moss-bags, and the men seated on the other side... At the service the Indian elders read the scriptures and take the prayers, the missionary gives the sermon, which is interpreted for the older Indians... And the singing, how they love it! Morning service over, the missionary returns to the boarding school, leaving the Indians to conduct the Sunday school, evening praise service or YMCA. During the week come the prayer meeting and the WMS auxiliary.*[51]

The government had agreed that they would look after the physical welfare of the Aboriginal people, and that the church, with its missions, would be better able to help them morally and in the education of their families.

According to *The Story of our Missions*, the boarding schools operated in the following way: The Aboriginal boys and girls studied the regular public school course and, when they reached the higher classes, the girls took their turn in the sewing room, cleaning the dormitories or working in the kitchen and laundry room. The boys were given training in mixed farming, gardening and the care and use of farm machinery. A proper proportion of their time was given to healthful outdoor sports. In holiday time, the month of July, the children went to their parents' homes, or, if it was a busy time on the farm, the older boys would be allowed off duty early to help their parents.

Day schools were semi-boarding schools, for the children had to come long distances and stayed from Monday to Friday during the winter. The government supplied part of the food, but the Aboriginal people helped, and mission boxes provided comforts in the way of bedding and clothing. In spring and fall two large wagons were provided and every morning the children on the reserve were collected and taken home at night.

The Indian Department paid the salary of the teacher in the day school. The Indian Department gave boarding schools a per capita grant for each pupil up to a certain number. If the WFMS owned the school building an extra grant was given to cover the cost of repairs.

> *The Women's Missionary Society in all these schools meets the salaries of the staff, except that of the nurse and the farmer. The former was paid by the government; the latter by the farm.*[52]

By 1911, supply work for the northwest was well established. In each issue of *The Foreign Missionary Tidings*, there was a section called "Acknowledgments." These were letters from the mission workers at the reserves thanking the women's groups for the bales of clothing and other supplies. A letter from Miss Bruce of Swan Lake says,

> *Although the winter has been beyond Manitoba's worst experiences, the school has not been closed one day for non-attendance nor for any other cause and that is saying a good deal as most of the children live almost two miles away. The boys and girls are in good health and high spirits and are doing well in their studies... What they would have done if the comfortable warm clothing and quilts had not been sent them is impossible to imagine....*[53]

Bale work was efficiently organized. Each year the magazine published a list of the reserves and the particular presbyterial that was responsible for the bale going to that reserve. A list was sent to each presbyterial giving the number of children and their measurements. Presbyterials were earnestly requested that, at their annual meetings, committees be appointed to receive and repack the supplies for the northwest and to see that only clothing of good quality was forwarded. Furthermore, clothing for reserves should include quilts and clothing suitable for old men and women and for children under five years of age.

In 1911, *The Foreign Missionary Tidings*[54] records that Stratford Presbyterial sent a plentiful supply of clothing to the west, 13 bales, weighing 840 pounds, and valued at $520.51. Although the government reimbursed the WFMS for the cost of freight on the bales sent to the schools, they did not reimburse it for bales for the reserves. When the children were signed into the school as wards of the church, the school received a certain grant for their maintenance. Although this grant went a good way towards the expense of running the school, it was barely enough to feed the children. Clothing, fuel and other expenses were met by the church.

At the Conference of Presbyterian Workers Among the Indians in July, 1911, Rev. Dr. Hugh McKay made a special plea for the Muscowpetungs, Pasquah and Piapots reserves. He told of a recent visit to these reserves at their own request. He said the burden of their cry was the education of their children. After the men from the reserves had spoken, Mr. McKay said, a woman asked to speak. She said the men did not speak strongly enough about their need for schooling and urged that at least a day school be provided. A young man also spoke, saying that they loved the Presbyterian

Church and were baptized in that church. He asked Mr. McKay to speak for them so they could have their children educated under their own church and not another. He said they would help to support the school. Mr. McKay said that a list of thirteen children had been brought to him and when he was asked if these children could be taken into his school, he had to tell them there was no room. Later at the conference a decision was made to ask the Foreign Mission Board to start a day school on these reserves and that it be supported by the church if the department would not do so.

The issue of discipline is rarely mentioned in these reports. At the conference mentioned above, at which papers were given on different subjects, Mr. Donaghy of the Okanase Reserve dealt with the issue of discipline in the schools. He said that these children could not be dealt with in the same way that white children were and that it was important to try to get the co-operation of parents.

In December, 1911, the Woman's Foreign Missionary Society reviewed the situation in regard to Aboriginal schools. They clearly recognized that the government's funding was inadequate.

The position of the schools in relation to the Canadian government and the church, says their report, was given serious consideration by the board of the Woman's Foreign Missionary Society. Tactfully, the women state that it was the government's wish to support the schools more adequately, but what they allowed for the cost of maintaining the schools was inadequate and was becoming an increasing drain on the mission funds of the church.

It is also clear from this report and later ones that the WFMS and the staff working at the schools realized that cleanliness, good care of the children and proper ventilation in the buildings were crucial in order to maintain good health and to avoid disease. The government was becoming concerned, they said, about tuberculosis among the Aboriginal people and the menace this presented for the schools and the community if things did not change. Experiments show, they add, that in schools where special care and medical attention was possible, where proper ventilation in school room and dormitory was carried out and where isolation wards or cottage hospitals existed, it was possible to resist the disease or wipe it out altogether.

Their report explains that the government had decided to grade the schools, A, B and C, and per capita grants would be granted depending on the class of the building and its equipment. Birtle was the only school that could claim a class A standing with the understanding that there were improvements that needed to be made. None of the other schools came up to even the lowest grade according to the regulations for air space and sanitary arrangements. The WFMS was directly concerned since the support necessary for these schools over and above the government grant came wholly from them.

There were two alternatives. The church could own the buildings, appointing the staff and having care of the children, with a grant from the government of $125 per child per year, or the government could own the buildings with the church still appointing the staff and having the care of the children with a per capita grant of $100.

The WFMS board sent on a resolution to the Foreign Mission Board saying that they were prepared to take preliminary steps to go forward with buildings at Birtle and Round Lake, but would leave the responsibility of further action until after the annual meeting of the society in 1912.

Some reports speak of the terrible housing conditions and of the sickness and disease prevalent in the schools. In March 1912, Mr. Hendry of Portage la Prairie reported that they had passed through an anxious time. A virulent type of measles had broken out in the school with twenty-two children contracting the disease. This was followed by an epidemic of pneumonia.

The April, 1912 issue of *The Foreign Missionary Tidings* printed a letter from Mrs. Ledingham of the Round Lake school who apparently did not believe in mincing words. She vents her frustration regarding the terrible conditions at the school, the problems of staffing, and the financial difficulties they were having.

> *...the building is in a wretched state — creaky worn-out floors, with neither paint nor oil, a broken cook-stove the only means of cooking and baking, crowded dormitories and store-rooms and you have some idea of the work to be done.*
>
> *You will think this a very pessimistic letter. Well, sometimes I do get discouraged, when at night I am so tired that I cannot sleep. But then there is a pleasant side to the work. I really enjoy it, especially when I see the wonderful change to appearance and dress of some of the children in a few weeks' time. The pupils, too, are both bright and affectionate, and soon learn and take a pride in doing housework. So far I have managed to keep the mending done, but I was almost in despair this week for the clothes were so worn and old that almost every article in the wash required a few stitches. But your welcome parcel has relieved me. If you could only send a few good women to help with the work...*
>
> *The things you sent us are just what are needed... The financial problem here is a very hard one. We find that the amount given by*

> *the government is barely enough to provide food alone for the children. This means that all equipment, clothing, fuel, and other expenses must be met by the church. There are many, many things still needed... But we are hoping to have new buildings and new furnishings very soon.*[55]

Some of the reports speak about improvements that had taken place in school attendance and in the health of the children.

In 1911, Miss Craig, the secretary for the northwest, reported encouraging results during the year — decrease in the death rate, better school attendance, a growing stability and appreciation of education by the Aboriginal people, and an increase in things both material and spiritual on the part of the older Aboriginal people. There were two Aboriginal girls on the staff, said Miss Craig, one was second assistant matron at File Hills and one assistant nurse at Birtle Indian Hospital.

Rev. W. McWhinney of Crowstand admits that mistakes were made.

> *It is forty-five years since this work began at Prince Albert under James Nisbet. Both the government and the church at that time were experimenting, but since that time we have learned many things. Since then the schools have changed their policy in many regards. We know that in early years the death rate was high... Our people did not understand him, the effect of the school life in many cases was to undermine his health...the children in our schools...demanding, and rightly, better food and better treatment in every way than we were able to give them in those first years... We all feel that more should be done....*[56]

The new school at File Hills, built by the Indian Department, was finished in 1912. The Indian Department had urged the improvement of all the schools and had promised to add to the grants when this was done. With this in view, the WFMS board was considering the matter. The Foreign Mission Committee and the provincial society of Winnipeg gave their opinion that the WFMS board should go forward in equipping and enlarging all the schools requiring improvement.

A report from Miss Grant, a teacher at Alberni, said that the work had been growing steadily from the time it was first started in 1895, although there was some concern about tuberculosis among the Aboriginal people. Miss Grant said that they were being careful about hygiene. The children were being taught that tuberculosis was preventable and could be cured. They drilled every day in the open air, and the children were taught deep breathing. Consequently, there had been little sickness in the school in the past year.

Susette Blackbird of Birtle was the first Aboriginal woman to attend the Presbyterian Missionary and Deaconess Training Home. Arriving there in the fall of 1910, she completed her courses in the spring of 1911 and returned to Birtle School to become assistant nurse and matron. She later married the principal of the school, Rev. W.W. McLaren. It seems this marriage was not acceptable to those in authority in Toronto and Mr. McLaren was transferred to the school at Round Lake.

After months of delay and disappointment, a new church was opened at the Okanase Reserve on November 17, 1912, "with a choir second to none." The Aboriginal people devoted time and labour as well as the material for the building. The Women's Auxiliary at Okanase, organized by Miss McGregor, the field worker, had been doing great things to clear off the debt.

Mrs. G.H. Pattison, president of the Minnedosa Presbyterial, attended the opening of the new church.

> *Leaving home at 6:45 on the evening of November 18th, we journeyed over twenty miles of good road to attend the concert given at the opening of Thomas Hart Presbyterian Church at Okanase Reserve... The church was nearly full... I was delighted to meet a number from the Bird-tail Reserve who had come to visit and enjoy the festivity of this church opening. Okanase also has a Woman's Foreign Missionary Auxiliary who are doing good work*

The Okanase Reserve WFMS Auxiliary

and labouring just now for their new church... Mr. Donaghy also showed a number of lantern slides, many of them taken on the reserve. I only wish a number of the 'board ladies' had been present to see the mirth and enjoyment of those people... The evening proceeds amounted to $107, this with the collections of the Sunday services will help their building fund.[57]

All the reserves, with the exception of Alberni, were represented at the Pre-Assembly Congress in May, 1913. The executive of the board of the Woman's Foreign Missionary Society met with the workers to hear about their difficulties. Among other things

> *...they pleaded for closer co-operation with the older Indians. Our system has robbed them of their ability to care for their own families. We...sympathize with the Indian's viewpoint. Some of the workers think the policy of separation in the colony system is not for the best. Others think the boys and girls, after graduating, should be followed up more sympathetically when they go back to their homes... We can learn something from the Indian.*[58]

Mr. Donaghy, the missionary at Okanase Mission, who had attended the General Assembly Pre-Assembly Congress, reported on a different gathering that had come hard-on-the-heels of the congress. This time the gathering was made up almost entirely of Aboriginal people. It was their YMCA's annual convention, June 26-29, 1913. Addresses were given by leading Sioux from the United States. A communion service was held on Sunday morning when a memorial tablet was donated by Mrs. Hart in memory of her husband, an early pioneer who had worked with Aboriginal people. Many of the non-Aboriginal people residing in the district were present to hear the Aboriginal speakers and, Mr. Donaghy said, it was probably a revelation to them to hear such splendid addresses from men who were wearing the blanket.

The September 1913 issue of the magazine reported that the Portage la Prairie school was soon to be relieved of its crowded conditions by a new site and buildings. Birtle School was remodelled in 1913 to meet government regulations. About forty new pupils were promised which would increase the government maintenance and ease the financing which had been one of the acute problems of the school.

The March 1914 issue of *The Foreign Missionary Tidings* had a description of the Christmas party at Round Lake Reserve.

> *We invited the parents of our scholars to come down and spend an evening with their children. The day was cold, but they came in*

comfort; with their tents pitched on their sleighs a little stove kept the tent comfortable... One hundred and fifty invited guests sat down at a well-filled table, so there were over 200 who were provided for, and they did all eat... The room was beautifully decorated for the occasion, the Christmas tree occupied a corner. The five men who occupied the platform looked dignified and beautiful, each one gave an address in the Cree language, and then a fine address from the teacher in the same language... Chief Walter is chairman and the teacher, secretary...

The next hour and a half was given to the scholars...then the distribution of presents... On the following morning most of our scholars went to their homes for a week.

It was always our custom to go out on the reserves, and taking provisions along...and have dinner with the old people and those who could not come to Round Lake, but this winter the Indians invited us...the following day we drove to church and met with the Indians of Kewistahaws band.[59]

Poverty on the reserves was widespread. As one missionary, addressing his band, so quaintly put it, as long as you are healthy, God expects you to support yourself, but if you are sick and in need, the friends of Jesus will not be slow to help you.

Rev. Sweet of File Hills School tells of a visit he made to the Qu'Appelle Reserve, and makes a plea for help.

In the chief's house I found a bright but pinched boy, a grandson of the old chief. I persuaded Muscowpetung and his wife to sign him into the school. I hated to take the boy, but, oh, the little fellow is not having a thing put into his life; he needs clothing, education, shelter, cleanliness, fresh air, love — but, most of all, the Saviour's love. I promised to help the old people. They need clothing, a suit of underwear, socks, clothing, shirts, etc., for the old man. These things need not be new. And clothing for the old woman — a quilt or two. I thought perhaps you knew of some good man or woman of means who would like to take these two decrepit, blind, old people and provide something for them periodically.[60]

Another report speaks about the gratitude of the Aboriginal people to the government and to our missionaries in making the transition step in their life easier but adds that there are many of the older people who dream of bygone days of freedom and plenty and who find life today one long struggle. The report makes a plea for sympathy and help for the Canadian Aboriginal people.

A letter from Rev. W. Heron, speaks about the poverty of the older people at the Pasqua's Reserve and says how happy the poor old people were to get the clothing when the bales came. The younger people were doing fairly well and their condition was generally improving, but the old people seemed to get more hopeless and helpless and hungry as they grew older.

Mr. Heron, in his acknowledgment to the Toronto Presbyterial for their help for the Qu'Appelle Reserves, enclosed photographs of two elderly Aboriginal people who were helped by the bale they had sent.

> *One of the enclosed snapshots is Chief Muscowpetung — standing beside his castle, a little mud plastered, sod roof, log hut...he is a feeble old man, tottering on the brink of the grave. He and his blind wife were very grateful for the quilts we gave them.*
>
> *The other photo is of an old woman we overtook in the valley. She has a small sleigh loaded with wood. She had evidently had a slight accident while chopping the load in the bush as she had a great smear of blood on one of her cheeks. Just before we came up to her the harness had broken... She had on a man's ragged coat, a cotton dress in much worse condition than the coat, her head-dress a rag. She looked worn out with her day's work... We gave her a quilt and a heavy coat... I mended her harness... Another old woman we gave a quilt to lives in a mud plastered hut, about 8 x 10, no floor but the earth. She had just finished plastering it for the winter, her hands had served for trowel but she wiped them on her ragged dress before shaking hands with us... Three others, an old man (Strong Eagle) and two old women, I can see them yet standing in a row of the door of their mud hut, with their WFMS quilts, each trying to outdo the others in expressing their thanks. These are a few of the many we might mention. I wish more could be done...*[61]

Included in the reports are items that give an insight into the staff and what it was like for them. We discovered that many of the staff spent long years at the schools, often leaving because of a breakdown in health.

Dr. Gilbart, in a talk on the health of the workers given at the Conference of Indian Workers in July 1911, said that health usually broke down from two causes; overwork and monotony. It would be wise to have two or three extra workers, he said, who could relieve the schools in times of illness or furlough. He added that there should be a retiring allowance for women workers who have toiled all their days in the service of the church and for whom no provision was made as there was for the men.

Mr. McWhinney of Crowstand at the end of his report in June 1911 speaks about the very menial work members of the staff had to engage in. Miss McLeod of Birtle Indian boarding school served for almost twenty years. Mrs. Ross, the matron at the Ahousaht boarding school, was connected with the school for sixteen years. She was a diligent, faithful mother to the children of the school. Under medical advice, she had to take a leave of absence as her health was shattered. A report in April 1913, announced the resignation of Mr. and Mrs. Ross due to her ill health. Mr. Ross, formerly missionary at Ucluelet, took charge of Ahousaht boarding school in 1910. In their letter of resignation, Mr. Ross adds,

> *Before leaving Ahousaht we wish to tender our thanks to the WFMS for the many kindnesses we have received from the society during all the years. On every occasion the WFMS has cared for our many wants and we always felt that there was no lack of interest shown by the society in our needs for the work at Ahousaht…*[62]

Ahousaht was the most distant and isolated of all the missions. In 1913-14, Mr. Ross reported that the land was so barren it hardly paid to cultivate it.

A report from Birtle School in December, 1913 said that Miss McLaren, who had been matron of the school, was retiring after 25 years of service. Her affection for the Aboriginal people had grown with the years, and the work had become part of her life. Her retirement would bring relief from the long strain, yet would carry the pain of separation.

A later report told that Miss McLaren had received from the session of the church a handsome club bag, the gift of the members of the congregation in which she had faithfully laboured. In addition, the women of the congregation presented to the children of the school an enlarged photo, to be hung in their classroom, of this lady, Miss McLaren, who was known throughout the whole province by the inscription on the photograph "The Red Man's Friend — Birtle, January 1914."

Miss McLeod, who was for eighteen years assistant matron at Birtle, had shared long years of devoted labour with Miss McLaren. The welfare and development of the Aboriginal children, both in and out of school, was largely due to the real "heart interest" shown by these two women. The board granted to both an honorarium of a quarter's salary.

In 1914, the Indian Department at Ottawa agreed to place trained nurses in the boarding schools and signified its willingness to meet the salary of two of these as a first trial; one to be placed at the Cecilia Jeffrey School, the other at File Hills. The appointment would rest with the church.

In her final report, the WFMS secretary for Indian work in the northwest, Miss Craig, listed all the schools under the care of the Presbyterian Church, and reported that at Crowstand and at Round Lake the need for more accommodation was great. She said that Rev. Dr. Hugh McKay had written to say that there were fifty children in a school that only had room for forty and that twenty more were asking for entrance. Of course, there was no way to accept them. Miss Craig 'warned of the danger' that these children might drift into the Roman Catholic schools where there was always room.

Miss Craig also reported the closing of the mission at Prince Albert where Lucy Baker had laboured for over 25 years. Mr. Hendry, principal at Portage la Prairie Boarding School, reported that the past year had been one of the most successful they had ever enjoyed. The discipline had never been better and the children had co-operated with their teachers and performed their duties faithfully and cheerfully. He added that they had been free from sickness throughout the entire year. The Misses Bruce, missionary and teacher at Swan Lake, reported that during the year no deaths had occurred among the pupils and those who attended regularly made as marked progress in their studies as did the average white children.

Mr. MacWhinney, principal at Crowstand, did not have such good news to report. The buildings were in a most unsatisfactory condition, and it was hoped there would be no more delays in the erection of new ones. The health of the reserve continued to be fairly good. At the close of the year whooping cough had made its appearance and he was afraid there would be some deaths among the small children. However, he said, in recent years there was a marked improvement in the care of the sick, and especially of the little children. Pneumonia, with its frequent accompaniment of tubercular conditions, continued to be the most frequent cause of death among the Aboriginal people.

In 1914, when the Woman's Foreign Missionary Society amalgamated with the Women's Home Missionary Society and the Woman's Missionary Society, Montreal, the work with residential schools then came under the care of the new united Society, the Women's Missionary Society, Western Division.

Steps Leading to Amalgamation

For thirty years, the Woman's Foreign Missionary Society had *...pursued its way without any special indication that it might not continue on its original basis for an indefinite period of time.*[63]

In actual fact, mission officials had been trying to persuade the WFMS since the early years of its existence to include home mission work in its mandate, but the society was riding on a wave of success and it was not anxious to change. Perhaps the women felt they had earned the right to decide their own future. After all, they had laboured hard and successfully over the years in work that could only be done by women. They had co-operated with the Foreign Mission Board and had contributed generously to the mission work of the church. They believed their work was unique, 'special work', and they were not about to jeopardize it by giving in to male pressure to pass on to women even more of the church's responsibilities — at least not if they could help it.

On October 8, 1889, a conference took place at Knox College between the executive of the Woman's Foreign Missionary Society and the Assembly's Home and Foreign Mission committees. The conference was held to deal with a resolution of the June, 1889 General Assembly asking the society and the Home and Foreign Mission committees to consider a proposal to widen the constitution of the WFMS to include home missions.

Dr. Cochrane spoke first, urging the desirability of the proposed change. Then Rev. D. J. Macdonnell spoke against the multiplying of organizations within the church and stating that there should be only one women's society in a congregation and adding that *people were beginning to think they would be better to spend more time at home for the good of their own spiritual life and that of their children.* Dr. Warden, chair of the committee, spoke against the women focusing only in one direction. He had no sympathy, he said, with the argument of 'women's work for women' contending that home missions were no less for the benefit of women and children than foreign missions. Dr. Robertson spoke next, setting out the home mission scheme, speaking of a current deficit and the imperative need for increased funds.

The women of the WFMS executive were then invited to speak about the proposed change. Mrs. Harvie introduced the recording secretary who read the paper prepared by Mrs. Catherine Ewart, who was unable to attend. Mrs. Harvie pointed out that the proposal had been discussed at length by the board and that the secretary would read the minute respecting it.

Among other points, Mrs. Ewart's paper spoke of the expressed declaration of the society against any attempt to depart from their original purpose and the danger of introducing an element of confusion and possibly discord into a hitherto harmonious organization. The paper pointed out that the WFMS had neither salaried officers nor any provision for travelling expenses and incurred no outlay except for postage, printing and incidental expenses of meetings.

After reading the minutes, Mrs. Harvie reiterated that the WFMS had been organized for a specific purpose, namely, evangelizing of women and children in foreign lands. She said that the members of the executive understood the importance of work in Canada and individual members of the

Presbyterian Church were contributing towards it. In response to the argument of too many meetings, she said that often the auxiliary was the only meeting that brought the women together. These meetings were of great good spiritually. If there were no auxiliaries there would be no representative body or woman's board of any kind. Mrs. MacLaren added that the women of the WFMS were already overworked and it was not reasonable to ask them to do more. If the Home Mission Committee needed help, why not ask boys and young men in the church. Mrs. Campbell pointed out that the WFMS work was small, self-denying efforts, over and above their individual church work. She suggested that if the Home Mission Committee would furnish information that would reach all the members of the church as Foreign Mission news does, the means would soon be forthcoming.

Principal Grant, Dr. MacLaren and other members of the Foreign Mission Committee made appropriate addresses in support of what the women's executive had said. Mr. Mcdonnell asked permission to say a word more. He said that he thought that the sentiment that only women could raise the money for work among women was absurd and maintained that men, no less than women, could pity the condition of the sisters shut up in zenanas. He protested that the proposal had not been discussed on its own merits, and said that the ladies had come with their minds made up. Dr. Laing said that he thought too much was made of our foreign missions and too little of those labouring in the home field.

After the Home Mission executive withdrew, the Foreign Mission Committee framed a resolution to be transmitted to the woman's board saying that, although they sympathized with the Home Mission Committee, they were convinced that it would be highly inexpedient to change, in the manner suggested, the constitution of the WFMS, or to interfere with the work of an association which God had so signally blessed, and that the committee was the more confirmed in this judgment by the strong and unanimous opinion expressed by the executive of the WFMS in opposition to the proposed change.[64]

The pressure continued. Immigrants were pouring into Canada and the northwest was opening up. The formation of the Women's Home Missionary Society in 1903 did not resolve the situation. The question of amalgamation was constantly being brought forward and meetings were held between the women's boards with representatives from the home and foreign boards in attendance. Some churches were unhappy with two separate mission societies in the congregation, one anxious to gain support for foreign mission work and the other for home missions. The Women's Home Missionary Society was in favour of amalgamation but the Woman's Foreign Missionary Society feared that their emphasis on women's work would suffer with such a union and that a united society *could become a mere fund-raising arm for the general work of the church.*[65]

The only indication in *Our Jubilee Story* of the increasing pressure on the Woman's Foreign Missionary Society to amalgamate, and the recognition that the gentle persuasion was really an offer they could not refuse, comes in one sentence. *At length, in 1910, the FMC 'definitely requested' the WFMS to consider sympathetically some plan of amalgamation with the W.H.M.S.*[66]

The Foreign Missionary Tidings, 1911 to 1914, gives a detailed account of the events leading up to the amalgamation of the women's groups. The March 1911 issue reports,

> *The matter was first considered in conference by the two boards in June last... It will be apparent from a reading of these documents that the boards are merely reporting progress made and that a further conference will follow.*[67]

A document prepared by the WHMS containing suggestions for a basis of union was presented to the WFMS. The WFMS took issue with some of the suggestions.

Regarding the name of the amalgamated society, the Women's Home Missionary Society suggested the name the Woman's Missionary Society. The Woman's Foreign Missionary Society preferred the Woman's Home and Foreign Missionary Society

> *...thus indicating the lines of work hitherto carried on by both societies. Such a name would, in our opinion arouse more interest, and, what is the more important point, would limit and define the objects of the organization.*[68]

The name suggested by the WHMS, the WFMS said, would stand for a plan of work unlimited and undefined in its scope.

The WFMS also expressed a divergence of views regarding the estimates. The WHMS constitution, they said,

> *...indicates work, which in our opinion, encroaches upon the general work of the church... This clause indicates a scope in general home mission work which would be practically unlimited... While the work of the WFMS has been distinctively a woman's work, ...we differ somewhat from them.*[69]

The reply came back swiftly from the WHMS in April of that same year stating clearly that they desired to adhere to the name the Women's Missionary Society of the Presbyterian Church in Canada. In regard to estimates, they would be willing to make some concessions but they did not feel it necessary to eliminate any part of the work of either society and they added,

> *The phenomenal growth of the Women's Home Missionary Society indicates very clearly that the women of our church realize as never before the gravity of the home mission problem facing Canada today… At no time in the history of Canada has there ever been such need for aggressive home mission work, especially is this true of the present year, when nearly half a million immigrants are expected to enter our borders.*[70]

Two documents for a basis of union, one prepared by the WHMS board and the other by the WFMS board, were published in their respective magazines and brought before the delegates at the annual meetings held in May 1911. The main differences were singled out.

The WFMS said that if the fundamentals of the work of a united society could first be agreed upon, the matter of the name might rest for later decision. However, they felt strongly that if the work undertaken by the women of the church was to be placed under one society, it should be defined.

> *We should recognize it as the first duty of every woman member of the church to support the general work of the church through its schemes; the justification of woman's work being separated and made a special department is not to secure increased means for the maintenance of general church work, but because there are parts of the work of our church in which the closer touch of woman's influence, sympathy and aid in administration are necessary to better progress. This has been the main principle for the existence of the WFMS and should hold good in any larger sphere of work which a united woman's missionary department of our church may be asked to assume.*[71]

The WFMS added that they recognized the great need in Canada to press on in home mission work. However, they expressed the view that the elimination of the support of home mission fields did not prevent women of a congregation from sharing in any special work in their individual church.

At the annual meeting of the WFMS in 1912, it was reported that the WFMS, at the request of the Foreign Mission Committee, had considered the question of amalgamation with the WHMS and had been in conference during the year with that Society. This resulted in some points being cleared, but some difficulties still remained unsolved. The WFMS had asked the Foreign Mission Committee what steps they would now wish them to take. A reply came in early May with a suggested basis of union, which was sent to each of the women's boards.

The General Assembly met in Edmonton in June 1912. Mrs. Emily Steele, president of the Woman's Foreign Missionary Society, and Dr. Margaret McKellar of India, represented the society on foreign mission night. Mrs. Steele reported they were well received and adds,

> *The women of our Canadian Presbyterian Church have never sought publicity at Assembly time. They have been content to be enthusiasts in the background. Gradually, however, they are accepting the changes due to modern times and are prepared to take the rightful place which the Assembly stands ready to offer in publicly acknowledging the power which the women's missionary societies are in the work of the church.*

Mrs. Steele could not resist a little jibe,

> *It was a pleasure, therefore, to see the recognition which was proffered to the representative women who were in attendance — the first time in thirty-five years' history of the work of the society. Hitherto we were satisfied to receive a passing comment embodied in the general Foreign Mission report, nor did we seek more, though for some years the WFMS treasury, eastern and western divisions, has represented one-third of all the money given for the foreign mission work of the church.*[72]

The Foreign Missionary Tidings of May, 1913 announced that the boards of the WFMS and the WHMS were arranging for a mass meeting of women to be held in Cooke's Church, Toronto, on June 4, at the time of the Pre-Assembly Conference. It would be followed by the 37th annual meeting of the WFMS. The Pre-Assembly Conference, the women's mass meeting at Cooke's Church and the 37th annual meeting of the WFMS were written up with a flourish in the July-August 1913 issue of *The Foreign Missionary Tidings*.

> *No meeting in the history of the 37 years of the society has been ushered in with such a prelude; no meeting in our history ever closed with such momentous happenings as this one. The prelude was the great Presbyterian Congress in Massey Hall, followed on the Wednesday with the mass meeting of representative Presbyterian women...in Cooke's Church. The closing event was the decision of our WFMS to pass from a distinctive organization into a larger sphere by its union with the other women's societies — a momentous happening; the larger vision had been caught of woman's work wherever her hand is needed in all missionary departments of our church banded together under one women's missionary society — a few who could not see wisdom in the step held back, but as with the larger union question at the General Assembly, the atmosphere was*

> *charged with the spirit of the times, unite and advance, and so the WFMS joined in the forward step, but not without many tender thoughts for the years that have passed...*

The report continued,

> *To look at the vast audiences in Massey Hall was a sight never to be forgotten... Long before the hour on Wednesday afternoon, the auditorium of Cooke's Church was crowded to its limit...*[73]

The meeting of the WFMS board took place on Wednesday morning before the mass meeting of women on Wednesday afternoon. Dr. Alfred Gandier, convener of the Foreign Mission Board, along with Dr. R.P. Mackay and Dr. A.S. Grant, had been instrumental in drawing up the basis for union. Dr. Gandier was asked to present the question to the general board of the WFMS. He began by saying that, for some time past there had been a growing feeling that there should be one WMS for the whole church and that the union of the two great missionary societies of the church, the WHMS and the WFMS, was desirable for the well-being of congregational life. He reviewed the union question up to the time when the boards approached the Assembly's Home and Foreign Mission Committees asking them to prepare some simple basis on which they might unite. The committees knew, he said, that there were members of the WFMS board who would prefer further changes, but they saw these changes could not be considered without delaying the way to union.

Dr. Gandier then read the basis of union to the board, clause by clause, commenting when necessary. He noted that, for clause three, it had been the desire of the WFMS that the work both at home and abroad should continue to be distinctly women's work, that it should not simply duplicate the general missionary work of the church which is provided for in the congregational budget. Now, said Dr. Gandier, the principle for which this society has all along contended is specifically stated in this basis of union. Our work in the foreign field, he said, is changing in character *...it is not necessarily work among women and children, but it is woman's work nevertheless...*[74]

This may sound like double-talk to some but, nevertheless, the women's board was at one with Dr. Gandier and agreed that the work had long since passed the stage of work among women and children in the foreign fields, but that the principle of woman's work which the WFMS had all along stood for and the granting of this principle as stated by Dr. Gandier was satisfactory.

Dr. Gandier further stated that the class of work to be undertaken after the union would be decided by the Home and Foreign Mission Committees after consulting with the women's board. There were bound to be new phases of work within this new country and in the foreign fields, he said, which the Assembly's committees might feel was a work that would appeal to the women of the church and work that they best could do. Hence the basis must be left open for such conditions and with this the women were again in accord. Dr. Gandier also commented on clause eight.

> *To take away any misunderstanding that might be in the minds of any, let me say that this does not suggest in any way that the money raised by The Women's Missionary Society will be a part of the general budget. There is no thought of that here whatever. The women's work and the women's budget will be something quite apart from the general budget of the church...*[75]

Mrs. Steele then asked if the board was ready to make a recommendation to the general society. After a standing vote of thanks for Dr. Gandier, the vote was taken and *heartily carried in favour of the adoption of the basis.*[76]

On the following day, the 37th annual meeting of the Woman's Foreign Missionary Society convened in St. James' Square Church. It was from this church that many missionaries had gone to the foreign field. Two presidents of the WFMS also came from its membership, Mrs. Catherine Ewart and her daughter Mrs. Emily Steele.

The president, Mrs. Steele, in her presidential address, said,

> *It is with peculiar feelings that I stand before you today in St. James' Square Church, to which as a young woman I belonged, in whose sabbath school I taught, and with whose mission band I was connected in the first year of this society's existence... On May 5, the Rev. Dr. Gandier, convener of the Foreign Mission Board, brought the amended basis to our board meeting and put before us very connectedly and clearly the reasons for amalgamation and the good results to be expected therefrom. These were all in harmony with facts that had come to our secretaries in letters from individuals and societies from time to time, during the last two or three years...the great difficulty of finding officers for two auxiliaries in very many of the smaller congregations and sometimes, even in the larger ones; the uncomfortable and very undesirable overtone of rivalry that often develops when there are two auxiliaries working alongside of each other for two branches of one great work, and with the same object in view... When amalgamation was first suggested a few years ago, the board, as a whole, did not enter heartily into the idea, but circumstances have so changed, that now we believe the hand of God is leading us forward to union...*[77]

The question regarding amalgamation was put to the delegates on the Friday of the annual general meeting. After brief discussion, the representatives gathered there accepted the basis and agreed to go forward with the union of the women's societies of the church.

The 38th and last general meeting of the Woman's Foreign Missionary Society was held on May 12, 1914, just three days before the amalgamation. In her president's address, Mrs. Steele left no doubt that there were many who had not been in favour of amalgamation.

She announced that the current membership of the society was 19,000, with 1,084 auxiliaries. There were 553 mission bands with a membership of 6,367. The income for the year was $104,000. It was not until 1906, she added, that board members even received travelling expenses. She spoke frankly to the society and it is clear where her sympathies lay. She had fought long and hard to keep the WFMS a separate society with a concern that their work should be work for women and children, separate from the general work of the church at large. It was with a real sense of sadness that she gave her report. After assuring the women that no part of the work would be changed, she spoke frankly.

> *Let me now speak directly on that subject which is as an undercurrent in all our minds today — the union of three societies... We do not pretend to say that the constitution...is perfect...but we do say that to us it seems to be a workable constitution....*
>
> *But let me add a word of warning and counsel to these same friends in the various auxiliaries, east and west. A great deal of responsibility now rests on you to make this united society a successful one. You who have told the boards for years of your difficulties where there were two auxiliaries in the one church, you have had a great deal to do with bringing it about and you must be patient with those who have not agreed with you...*
>
> *I do not need to tell you to consider what there is to do in Canada, you are hearing of it constantly from the pulpit, the platform and the press. But we do need to make ourselves acquainted with what God is doing in foreign lands...*
>
> *Some of us are facing this future with a vague feeling that 'all is not well'...but this is not as it should be. Certainly our society is losing its identity as a separate body, but it is a case of evolution or merging of other lines of usefulness with what we are doing now. The amalgamated society is to be responsible for carrying on two of the main lines of mission work in our church, work in Canada and work in foreign fields... No mean task is this...a task quite impossible for mere human wisdom and ability but quite possible for those who yield themselves to the guidance of Him who has called us to be co-workers... We must work as if everything depended on us; we must pray as if everything depended upon God.*[78]

Chapter
4

Winning the West

Women's Home Missionary Society (WHMS), 1903-1914

A Treasure More Precious Than Gold

Strange as it may seem, the formation of the Women's Home Missionary Society is linked to the discovery of gold in the Klondike. Dr. James Robertson, superintendent of missions for the Northwest Territories, realizing that someone should go who could tell them of a treasure more precious than gold, raised the call for pioneer missionaries to follow the gold-seekers with the gospel. Rev. R. M. Dickey, Dr. A. S. Grant and Dr. John Pringle responded to the call. Mr. Pringle describes his visit to the hospital in Atlin,

> *Lying on a low cot was the man whom I had come to see, and on pole bunks around were five others, injured and diseased. At the door was a rough box with a dead body in it, and outside was another... The only nurse was a so-called abandoned woman, who nursed, cooked, and washed for the hospital without reward. God bless her for her work. That scene decided me to ask the church for two nurses.*[1]

An appeal for help came from Mr. Dickey,

> *There will, I fear, be a great deal of sickness and a great many accidents. What is to become of the sick*

and wounded if we do not do something for them? If trained nurses, with the love of Christ in their hearts, could be sent there would be a great work for them to do. The people are mostly too eager after gold to care for the sick. I am in great hopes something will be done by the ladies soon. A man cannot do much in such work.[2]

A meeting of representative Presbyterian women was held on March 15, 1898, in St. Andrew's Church, King Street, Toronto, to consider the appeal of Mr. Dickey. Mrs. James Maclennan presided at this meeting. A small committee, with Mrs. Maclennan as convener, was appointed to confer with the Home Mission Committee.

An urgent plea came from Mr. Pringle in October, 1898, who was ministering to 1,200 miners in Atlin, British Columbia, to say that men were dying for lack of care and asking for an immediate response to their request. In the spring of 1899, the committee that had been appointed was enlarged to include representatives from nearly every congregation in Toronto. Mrs. J. K. Macdonald was named president. Circulars were sent out to inform congregations of the need. Soon $1,500 was in hand, allowing the committee to go ahead and appoint and equip two nurses. On June 28, 1899, Miss Elizabeth Mitchell and Miss Helen Bone were designated in Westminster Church, Toronto, for service as missionary nurses to the Klondike. They left on July 22. A month later, Miss Mitchell wrote describing the hospital:

The government agent gave us a cabin for a hospital. It had a roof of mud, a floor of sawdust, and only two small panes of glass for a window. It held four cots; the pillows were made of packing that came around our cots and filled with the hay in which our dishes were packed. When the cabin became crowded a tent was put up beside it.[3]

Dr. Pringle, writing home that fall, said,

The work of the nurses for one month has done more to make the people believe we have the spirit of Christ than a year's preaching could.

He reported on a visit he made to the hospital on a cold winter's night,

...I visited the tent and cabin used as a hospital. There I found Miss Mitchell caring for the three sick men. The tent was 12x14 and had a stove in the middle of the floor, around which, as near as safety would permit, were the three canvas cots. The nurse sat almost against the stove, her fur coat buttoned round her. I could not sleep that night. The picture of that tent, the three patients, and the nurse were before me all night. In the morning I called at the nurses' home, then a shack 12x18, and said: "I am going to build a hospital"...[4]

In 1900, St. Andrew's Hospital, Atlin, British Columbia, was erected. It was the first Presbyterian hospital to be built in Canada. Mrs. H. M. Kipp says,

> *Little did Dr. Pringle think that his appeal would be the beginning of a chain of Home Mission hospitals dotting the frontiers of our great Western prairies or nestling in the mountain fastnesses of our magnificent Western sea coast province.*[5]

News travelled fast, even in the early 1900s. Hearing reports of how money had been raised to send nurses to the Klondike, frontier missionaries and others began writing to the Home Mission Committee to ask for similar assistance. This brought before the Atlin Nurse Committee the possibility of enlarging their scope in the area of home missions.

In the meantime, Dr. James Robertson brought before the 1901 General Assembly his concern for the conditions of the ever-increasing numbers of new settlers in the northwest. He proposed legislation which would put into the capable and experienced hands of the Woman's Foreign Missionary Society the responsibility of this work, under the direction of the Home Mission Committee. When his motion was lost, his response was that nothing now remained but to organize a Women's Home Missionary Society. Individual organizations did their best to respond to Mr. Robertson's appeal for help but it seemed that the Atlin Nurse Committee which was already in existence would be the most logical way of dealing with the situation.

On May 18, 1903, the Atlin Nurse Committee and other interested women, along with other members of the Home Mission Committee, met in Knox Church, Toronto. Dr. Warden presided and the following motion was carried unanimously: That in the judgment of this meeting it is desirable that a Women's Home Missionary Society should be formed in connection with our church.

On June 9, 1903, the Atlin Nurse Committee disbanded to form the new Society which took as their motto "Canada for Christ." The object of the new society was

> *...to aid the Assembly's Home Mission Committee by undertaking nursing and hospital work at such points in the newer districts of the country as the committee may select; by engaging in any other work of a kindred nature that the committee may deem it advisable to have taken up; and by co-operating with the committee in raising funds for the general home mission work of the church.*[6]

One of the first duties of the organization committee was to change their constitution to include men in its membership. There seems to be no record of just how successful this decision was, particularly in view of the name of the new society. The 29 auxiliaries already in existence formed the nucleus of the new Women's Home Missionary Society and the first report showed 33 auxiliaries with a membership of 442.

Requests for help began to pour in from all over the country. A travelling secretary, Matilda Robinson, was appointed and was successful at organizing new auxiliaries. The society's publication, *The Home Mission Pioneer* monthly magazine, was launched in 1903. Ten thousand copies were printed and sent free to every minister and missionary in active work in the church. Within five years the magazine was self-supporting and by 1914 it had a circulation of 22,403.

In 1904, the Home Mission Committee requested assistance from the newly-formed Women's Home Missionary Society in maintaining mission fields on the lonely frontiers of British Columbia, Alberta and Ontario. The women became enthusiastic supporters of the work on the home field. Medical work became so urgent that the Home Mission Committee, which had no funding for this purpose, called upon the Women's Home Missionary Society to develop this phase of the work.

Home Mission Hospitals

Thousands of immigrants from Europe were pouring into western Canada, dotting the Prairies with foreign colonies. The next call from the Home Mission Committee to the Women's Home Missionary Society was a request to meet the need and the exceptional opportunity for medical service at Teulon, Manitoba, a foreign colony 40 miles north of Winnipeg, made up of Ruthenians. These were Ukrainian immigrants — the largest group of foreign-born people to come to Canada.

With the barrier of language, the best line of approach was through medical assistance. Rev. A. J. Hunter was appointed missionary. He boarded close to the settlement, practising medicine among the people and becoming acquainted with them, even picking up a smattering of their language. The building of a hospital was at the suggestion of Dr. George Bryce of Winnipeg and work was begun in the fall of 1903. The building was ready for use at the beginning of the new year with patients coming in almost before the building was finished. The Teulon hospital opened in 1904 with Rev. A. J. Hunter as medical missionary. Miss Elizabeth J. Bell was the first female superintendent and first nurse to be sent out by the society to work among foreigners. Miss Isobel Beveridge, also a nurse, arrived in 1910.

The building was erected largely on faith and assistance from the Church and Manse Building Fund, the Woman's Missionary Society, Montreal, Dr. Bryce, Dr. Hunter and the people of the district. The newly formed Women's Home Missionary Society took over the hospital, becoming responsible for the debt.

In 1905, Rev. J. C. Herdman made an appeal for a hospital to minister to the needs of a foreign colony of 45,000 immigrants near Vegreville, Alberta. The erection of a hospital here was made possible by a generous gift from Mrs. Boswell of Elora, in memory of her late husband. The Rolland M. Boswell Hospital was opened on October 29, 1906.

Looking for a new homeland, people from France, Quebec, Germany and the western United States, along with some Hungarians and Ruthenians settled in a district south of Prince Albert, Saskatechewan. They were mainly Roman Catholics. In the heart of this district lay Wakaw.

In 1903, Rev. George Arthur, missionary at Rosthern, was asked to establish the Wakaw Mission. Barriers of language and culture presented difficulties.

> *With splendid initiative he built and operated a store, and had a post office opened. He erected also a stone mill...and became the miller of the district. He was appointed a justice of the peace, and...had the opportunity of adjusting the differences of the most contentious of the district.*[7]

They were a people who had no experience in western farming and were sinking into debt. They lived in crowded, poorly ventilated houses and were consequently subject to sickness. In 1906, the Anna Turnbull Hospital was built. Hospitals were usually named after people who gave generous donations, often in memory of a husband or wife.

In 1907, Dr. and Mrs. Arthur were appointed to Vegreville and Dr. R. G. Scott was appointed medical missionary to Wakaw. Even though the majority of the people were Roman Catholics, Dr. Scott was able to gather the people around him, holding religious services, organizing a sabbath school and even a choir. A new hospital was built, opening on October 31, 1912.

In 1910, Rev. Alexander Forbes was appointed missionary in Grande Prairie, Alberta. He and his wife, Agnes Sorrell Forbes, travelled hundreds of miles into an almost unknown section of northern Alberta. Settlers soon found the Forbes' home

> *...a haven of rest and mercy in time of sickness and trouble, and the work of caring for them became so heavy that Mrs. Forbes, who did everything for them herself, as well as the entire domestic work of the household, sent an appeal to the WHMS for the services of a nurse, who was sent that same autumn. Distances are so great that, in order to visit some of her patients, the nurse had to purchase a horse and sometimes ride fifty miles on horseback.*[8]

Work increased rapidly. In 1912, Mr. Forbes asked that a hospital be built. Mr. R. W. Prittie of Toronto had given a donation of $5,000 to the WHMS, to be used for the building of the hospital to be known as the Katherine H.

Hospital, Canora, Saskatchewan

Prittie Hospital. The major portion of the money came from the WHMS. The hospital opened in June 1914.

Mission work in Canora, Saskatchewan, was made possible by a generous donation, $25,000, from Mrs. Waddell of Peterborough, Ontario, to build a hospital in memory of her husband, Mr. Hugh Waddell. Ten acres was donated by Mr. Graham of Canora. An annual grant for maintenance was given from the Canora town council which was supplemented by the WHMS. Local doctors gave their services gratuitously. A female superintendent and three nurses staffed the hospital which opened in June 1914.

Medical mission work was carried on at Ethelbert and Sifton, Manitoba, at two missionary dispensaries. Work began at Sifton in 1900 by Dr. J. T. Reid and three years later was taken over by Dr. R. G. Scott. The first nurse arrived in 1906 with others following later.

> *No night was ever too cold, or drive too lonely, or trail too rough for them to respond to the call from suffering humanity. They faced all kinds of perils, have relieved suffering thousands and saved many from death.*[9]

Medical mission work would be incomplete, says the author in *The Story of Our Missions*, without reference to the Pacific Coast mission ship. When the Women's Home Missionary Society took over this mission, medical work was added. The medical missionary's work was carried out by a walking church and a floating hospital. The work was also known as the Loggers' Mission.

The Story of Our Missions gives us some idea of just how these early women missionaries carried out their work,

> *Our missionaries have taken with them a portable organ, perhaps packing it on their backs for some miles, and with its help have made large use of song and hymn. A bunkhouse service may open with a song like "Annie Laurie" or "Home, Sweet Home," after which the loggers will be asked to join in one of the hymns familiar to their childhood; the word of God will be read, and the love of God to sinners proclaimed. It is not easy to give Christian testimony in these surroundings and at times it has been found prudent not to preach but to substitute lantern pictures or selections on the gramophone. Good literature, too, has always been distributed…*[10]

The closing down of lumbering activities at the outbreak of the First World War brought an end to the work.

Dr. and Mrs. Fred Inglis were faithful and efficient missionaries for several years at Telegraph Creek, British Columbia. The work was aided when the government built a hospital in 1909. In 1910, two trained nurses were sent there by the WHMS. Apparently, Telegraph Creek was notorious for its immorality. As a French factor[11] exclaimed, "Telegraph is hell." Due to consideration of their growing family, Dr. and Mrs. Inglis left in 1913. The nurses left as well. Dr. Inglis thought highly of the nurses and said that their influence and splendid service in Telegraph Creek could never be over-estimated.

School Homes

Shortly after the medical work was established, the need for education, especially among the non-English speaking children, became apparent. Many of the children lived great distances from schools and attempts were made to find accommodation for the pupils.

Educational work had its origins through the missionaries and nurses in the hospitals who took non-English-speaking children into their homes. They taught them English and supervised their studies and tried their best to make them Christian Canadians. School homes were built in many places and as near to foreign colonies as possible.

> *The School homes stand in the same relation to these children as do our own homes to our own children — a place of shelter, loving care and Christian influence, where nothing is neglected that tends to develop body, mind, and spirit, and instill Christian principles in the boys and girls.*[12]

When Dr. and Mrs. Arthur were appointed to Wakaw, Saskatchewan in 1903, unfamiliarity with the language made it impossible to conduct religious services, so a school was opened. At first, many parents were reluctant to send their children, but interest increased and the following winter educational work was undertaken on a larger scale. Because of distance for some of the children, the Arthurs boarded them in their home at a cost of $1.00 a week. Even this was too much for some of the families. The Arthurs' home was dubbed the "Polyglot Manse." Five different languages were spoken in that little home. As numbers of children needing accommodation grew, conditions became intolerable. The WHMS came to the rescue by sending the money to assist in completing a house which Dr. Arthur had already begun to build.

The hospital at Teulon, Manitoba, almost from the date of its opening, had been a home for Ruthenian children. It allowed them to attend the village school. Both Dr. Hunter, missionary at Teulon, and Dr. Arthur missionary at Wakaw, strongly believed that,

> *...in education lay the only sure highway to evangelization, and that all evangelistic endeavor must fall far short of its aims unless some means of communication were established between the races. Kindness, and sympathy, and love, epitomized in the hospital and its healing, were doing their part to break down the barriers; but this was not enough.*[13]

Dr. Hunter wrote,

> *The work which seems to me now to be of the greatest importance is educational... The provincial government has established at Teulon a rural model school, intended to train teachers specially for work in the country schools of this district... What is required now is a residence where the most promising children of the district can receive good Canadian home training while attending this model school. In this way we can do for the Ruthenians at comparatively little expense what is being done for the Indian by the industrial and boarding schools.*[14]

In January 1912, a residence was opened. Applications were so numerous that it was necessary to complete the attic of the building to allow for extra accommodation. Miss Isobel Beveridge was the first and only matron. Much of the success of the school was due to her wise oversight.

Dr. Hunter wrote,

> *If only we had the means, we could extend the educational work very advantageously... Medical work is valuable as a means of missionary approach, and it is good to feel that one is relieving the sufferings and lengthening the lives of individuals; but if we can prepare some of the brightest youths to be leaders and helpers of the*

people, we shall do a work, the influence of which will continue far into the future.[15]

Dr. and Mrs. Arthur had been transferred from Wakaw to Vegreville to take charge of the Rolland M. Boswell Hospital. Mr. Arthur's vision of an educated young manhood and young womanhood, made possible by the efforts of the Presbyterian Church was not dimmed. Mr. Arthur strongly believed that the children must be taken away from the old home influences while they were young and taught Canadian manners and customs. A boys' residence was opened with Mrs. Arthur as matron. The next year a girls' residence was opened and, a year later, two more residences.

Vegreville became an important educational centre. The government erected a seminary there to train non-English-speaking Canadians as teachers. It was the hope and expectation that boys from the Vegreville homes would enter Albert College, becoming ministers and teachers to their own people. No school homes were built at Ethelbert or Sifton. The mission houses were used to accommodate the children. This put a tremendous burden on Dr. Gilbart and the nurses but they were deeply conscious of the importance of the work.

Although it was not possible to carry out the active educational programs at Wakaw as had been done at Teulon and Vegreville, Dr. Scott, missionary at Wakaw, was also convinced of the importance of these programs,

Boys' School Home, Vegreville, Alberta, one of the first to be established by the Women's Missionary Society

> *Just as the great reformers of Scotland saw that schools were an essential part of the Protestant movement, so it is being learned again that a rational education is essential to sound religious progress.*

He continues,

> *Illiteracy, relative and absolute, hangs over the people like a dark cloud… When a person who has been blind…has his sight restored, he must, like a child, learn from the beginning, and much painful experience is necessary before sight becomes normal.*[16]

These missionary doctors, nurses and teachers, rightly or wrongly, strongly believed that by taking the boys and girls aside while their prejudices were still unformed, their thoughts and ideas unhampered by old-time customs, it would be possible so to educate and train them that there might not be this "slow and painful transition from darkness unto light."

The government is doing its part, the writer in *The Story of our Missions* says, by establishing schools,

> *…but it has been left for the church to make the connection between the school and the child; to foster the desire for learning…to remove the barriers set up by poverty, by uninterested and unintelligent parents, or by distance from school centres; in short, to help these newcomers and one-time strangers in our land to gain such an education as shall really be a "leading out" from the trappings and darkness and superstition of the old life, into the glorious light and fullness of one where life means service for God, and king, and humanity.*[17]

Other Areas of Concern

A new phase of work opened up for the WHMS when a letter from the chairman of the Missionary and Deaconess Training School, endorsed by the Home Mission Committee, indicated the need for employing deaconesses in aggressive Christian work.

The first deaconess employed by the Women's Home Missionary Society was Miss Adelaide Sutherland. She was appointed in September 1910 and sent to Prince Rupert, British Columbia, where she was employed in home and hospital visitation and work with young girls. The following January, a second deaconess, Miss Margaret Cameron, was appointed to work with immigrants in the city of Winnipeg. Later that same year, Miss Agnes Cowan was appointed to work in the city of Edmonton. Soon other deaconesses were serving as congregational deaconesses in Toronto, with Aboriginal children in Deseronto and among Ruthenians in Toronto.

The work opened up and deaconesses were employed in frontier towns and at ports of entry. Their services were given in a multitude of ways: mothers' meetings, sewing classes, Bible classes, organizing women's auxiliaries, visiting in hospitals and homes, meeting and caring for young girls who travel alone, visiting the sick and the lonely, dispensing food and medicine and clothing to those in need, finding work for the unemployed or befriending strangers.

In 1908, the Presbyterian Church, through the Foreign Mission Committee, began its first mission to the Jews. The WFMS assisted by employing a woman missionary, followed later by another and two voluntary workers, one of whom was a nurse. In 1912 Jewish work was transferred to the Home Mission Committee and became part of the responsibility of the Women's Home Missionary Society. The society assumed support for five women missionaries, one in Winnipeg and four in Toronto. The first Christian Jewish synagogue in connection with the Presbyterian Church was built in Toronto in 1913. The minister was assisted by a staff of five, three of whom were supported by the WHMS. In 1910, the work had been extended to Winnipeg and, in 1914, to Montreal. Christian Jews were often persecuted by their families and friends and looked upon as outcasts, says a report in *The Story of Our Missions*. The work was not easy and, the writer admits,

> *A strange apathy still holds back many of our Christian Gentile people from sharing in this branch of the work...*[18]

The supply department was also an important part of the WHMS work. This was natural, said the writer in *The Story of our Missions*, when there were so many hospitals to be equipped and stocked with bedding and linen and so many school-homes to be furnished and foreign children helped. This gave a practical side to the work for members in auxiliaries and many "willing hands" were glad to help. As *The Royal Road* delightfully puts it,

> *The imprints of their needles have traced many a path of the loving heart, whether across the wide expanse of quilts or circling the borders of little flannel petticoats.*[19]

Library work was another department that brought literature into lumber and construction camps in northern Ontario and British Columbia and furnished libraries for camps and needy Sunday schools.

The increasing demands soon brought financial problems for the WHMS. In 1908 the treasurer, Miss Helen Macdonald, requested the assistance and co-operation of a finance committee to prepare estimates and frame policy. Special efforts were put forth and financial creativity came to the fore.

The sale of calendars illustrating different phases of the work brought in sufficient funds to allow for the extension of educational work in western

Canada. The children were not forgotten and were invited to participate in the solution to the financial bind by providing five miles of pennies, each yard representing 36 pennies. The money raised was to be used to furnish and name wards and cots in the home mission hospitals. A considerable sum was also raised by the children through a share scheme. A large sum was raised through the sale of a deaconess story called *The Gold Coin*. Part of the proceeds from the story were used to open home schools in Quebec. All this, on top of the usual schemes for raising revenue saved the day; the usual schemes being mite-boxes, life membership fees, autumn and Easter thank offerings, Home Helpers, Ladies' Aids, boys' clubs, young people's guilds, Bible classes, Sunday schools, legacies and individual gifts — plus freewill offerings.

In 1910, the Home Mission Committee (HMC) put the responsibility of their department of the stranger, which was included under the Department of Immigration and Migration, into the hands of the Women's Home Missionary Society. Strangers' secretaries visited the sick in hospitals and often provided newcomers to Canada with necessities. Presbyteries were instructed by the HMC to work with the WHMS in this area. Miss Mary C. Murray was the first hospital visitor appointed by the society.

Up to the time of amalgamation, the society's financial obligations included the support of seven hospitals, eleven mission fields, seven school homes, eight deaconesses, three workers in the stranger department and three in the Jewish department. And that is not all! Grants were given to the loggers' mission on the Pacific Coast, to Galician (Ukrainian) students in Winnipeg, to the Galician Church and the Robertson Memorial Institute in Winnipeg and to students studying medicine preparing themselves to be medical missionaries. Grants were also given to the Missionary and Deaconess Training Home in Toronto, and loans made for mission work in northern Ontario. When supplies were needed for hospitals, school homes, and needy mission fields, the women were always prepared to meet, sew and give generously. In 11 years, 1903-1914, 27 fields were assigned to the WHMS. Sixteen became self-supporting.

Recognition at Pre-Assembly Congress

General Assembly held a congress in Massey Hall in Toronto in 1913. Many missionaries and their families came from remote outposts on the frontiers to attend the congress as guests of the Church. The year also marked the 10th anniversary of the Women's Home Missionary Society and their 10th annual meeting was the largest in the history of the society. The Assembly committee asked the corresponding secretary of the society to present to the congress the story of the ten years work. This was well received and appreciated.

Moving Towards Amalgamation

Still there were problems. Local churches found it increasingly difficult to support two separate groups — one for foreign and one for home missions. The question was being constantly raised, "Could some plan be devised whereby both branches of the work might come under one society?" Several meetings were held and step by step the two women's societies dealt with the differences separating their societies.

The Last Annual Meeting

At the last annual meeting of the Women's Home Missionary Society there was an undertone of sorrow and a note of sadness. At the opening of each session the women responsible for the devotions prepared the women for the larger vision which Mrs. Marjorie Herridge brought to them in her opening words,

> *Although this is the last meeting of the Women's Home Missionary Society as a separate organization, we hope that by the blessing of God the union of the societies will yield marvelously greater power and that each branch of mission work will be strengthened and stimulated by contact with the others... We are being led more and more to see that the words "Home" and "Foreign" are not important words, and that the outstanding word is "missions." The true missionary zeal knows no dividing line. It begins at home, but it cannot stop there...*[20]

The editor of the magazine described the solemnity of the moment when the audience gave their approval of the constitution by a standing vote which "had to be experienced to be appreciated." The program announced the meeting for the amalgamation of the Women's Home and Foreign Missionary Societies, but to the hearts of a multitude of women it was the 'consummation meeting,' the fulfillment of a 'prayer-born hope', the realization of a vital need.

The president's address was printed in full in *The Home Mission Pioneer* of June 1914. The president, Mrs. J. Somerville, begins,

> *Long before 1903 when the WHMS was organized, there was a longing in the hearts of many women in our church to come to the aid of the Home Mission Committee... The grand old hero, Dr. James Robertson, had a clear vision of the wonder that would ere long be throughout the boundless West and never doubted for a moment its future. The tide of immigration had scarcely begun to rise in those days, but he saw it coming when other eyes were blind. Yet, with all his optimism, we wonder if he would have hazarded a*

prediction, that in 1913 there would crowd into our country from other lands, 418,870 people... Several attempts to have the women enlisted in this service for the home-land failed. The cry from the West for aid waxed louder till at last the cry became such an appeal that the women in Zion could no longer sit still.

Mrs. Somerville goes on to give a brief summary of the work of the WHMS over the years, ending,

We now reach the last station on our road, when the WFM line and the WHM line which for eleven years have run parallel to each other, are to converge and meet and form one line...

In this brief review of the history of our society we are filled with amazement at its marvellous growth...at the end of eleven years we have 46 presbyterials, 1,119 auxiliaries, an active membership of 25,077, and have raised during the year just closed the goodly sum of $89,979.20...

It is with feelings of pride and profound thankfulness that I recall the noble way in which the auxiliaries, almost without exception, came to the help of the board. The cost of buildings this last year was way beyond anything we anticipated, and the thought of being in debt was a great burden to us...time was passing, amalgamation was drawing near and still there was that debt to face... Personal letters went to every auxiliary.

The response was wonderful... I am sure every member of the board heard the gentle rebuke of our Lord — "Wherefore didst thou doubt, O thou of little faith." Shall we not claim the fulfillment of His promise and ask...that the windows of heaven be opened, and that He pour out such a blessing that there will not be room to receive it — the blessing of regenerated lives, transformed homes and uplifted communities, among the people who are coming to our land and may the time soon come when His dominion shall be from sea to sea, and from the river even to the ends of the earth....[21]

Chapter 5

Eastern Sunrise

Woman's Foreign and Home Missionary Society, 1876-1914

The WMS Rises in the East

The first women's missionary organization in Canada took shape over a century ago in Prince Edward Island. The Princetown Female Society for Propagating the Gospel and Other Religious Purposes was formed at Princetown, or Malpeque, in 1825. This society predated by nine years the Society for Promoting Female Education in the east formed in England. Other mission groups were organized in the Maritime provinces and were a great help in the promotion of missions.[1]

The Halifax Woman's Foreign Missionary Society of the Presbyterian Church in Canada, Eastern Section,[2] was formed on October 13, 1876 in St. Matthew's Church, Halifax. Mrs. Burns was the first president. The first Mission Band of the society was organized in 1878.[3] Two presbyterials, Halifax and Pictou, were formed in 1885, and at that time the name was changed to the Woman's Foreign Missionary Society of the Presbyterian Church in Canada, Eastern Division. The publication of their magazine, *The Message*, began in 1893 with a subscription price of 12 cents per year.

Over the years other auxiliaries and presbyterials throughout the Maritime provinces were added to the society. The society was auxiliary to the mission boards of the church and did not initiate work on its own. It chose from lists recommended by the church boards and offered help where needed.

The women in the Maritimes were largely responsible for the opening of the Korean Mission in 1898. Their initiative in this exciting work, and their contribution to the work in the New Hebrides and Trinidad must not be forgotten.

New Hebrides

John Williams was the first missionary to the New Hebrides. He was sent by the London Missionary Society in 1839 and met a martyr's death on the Island of Erromanga. The Presbyterian churches of the Secession Synod of Nova Scotia[4] sent the first missionaries, John and Charlotte Geddie. They landed on Aneityum in 1848 and worked there for 24 years.

Erromanga was called "The Martyre Isle." In 1857, this field was opened again and George and Ellen Gordon, missionaries from Prince Edward Island, arrived at Erromanga. The people blamed the missionaries for an outbreak of measles that had been introduced by traders, and they murdered the Gordons in 1861. Gordon's brother, James, came to take his place and ten years later he also was murdered. Other missionaries from Canada followed and the situation improved. Later, the charge and oversight of the mission, with the consent and help of Scottish and Canadian churches, was assumed by the large Australasian Presbyterian Church there.

Rev. T. Watt Leggatt has a lengthy article in the November 1911 issue of the *Foreign Missionary Tidings*. The article, "The Position of Heathen Women in the New Hebrides," gives a shocking account of the treatment of women, including a description of their inferior position in society.

> *In some places she cannot pass in front of a man. She may be bowed to the earth with a heavy load, but if a man comes along the path she must crush herself into the bush at the wayside to allow him a clear road. When he is seated she must make her way behind him, and if he is of high rank crawl out of his sight on her hands and knees.*[5]

Rev. John Geddie, in a letter written in May 1850, explained that things were different for Christian women. They had, he said, gathered a little society about them who had totally abandoned heathenism. Christian women were treated as equals and had "laid aside the cord." (Every married woman in Aneityum used to wear a cord around her neck by which she was strangled on the death of her husband.)[6]

Trinidad

Annie Blackadder

Rev. John Morton, a young Nova Scotia minister, visiting Trinidad for his health, came home with a concern for the 25,000 East Indians who had come to Trinidad as indentured immigrants. Little had been done for their moral or spiritual welfare. Their need had touched his heart.

He asked the Maritime Synod to send him back as a missionary. In November 1867, John Morton, his wife Sarah and their small daughter sailed from Halifax. After a tempestuous voyage they landed in Trinidad the following year. The success of the work in Trinidad was attributed in part to the splendid educational system and the place given to children. To help with the teaching, twelve women in succession went from Canada. Miss Annie Blackadder was the first teacher to go overseas from Canada and the first foreign missionary sent by the Woman's Foreign Missionary Society, Eastern Division. She went to Trinidad in 1876 and served for 38 years.

Korea

The Story of Our Missions gives a glowing report of the work in Korea. Wonderful stories were coming from the missionaries. No other non-Christian land had heard the gospel so quickly or so gladly. The Presbyterian Church in Canada was given the north east corner of Korea, which was under Japanese control. William McKenzie of Korea was the name first associated with the mission. It was an appeal McKenzie sent home from the little band of converts that led the Canadian Presbyterian Church to say, in 1898, through its women in the Maritimes, "We will take up the work." The women in the Presbyterian churches had been touched by the need of the Korean women. God used their cry to stir the Maritime church, and the mission in Korea was begun. The work grew so quickly that the missionaries' plea to the church in Canada was that enough workers be sent until the indigenous church could stand alone. WMS auxiliaries were established in each of the Korean station congregations and there were plans to establish branches in the out-districts as well. The

Society supported a Bible woman, Kim Miriam, an elderly woman of fine character, who spent a month in each county of the field as evangelist.

Two sisters, Louise and Elizabeth McCully, made an outstanding contribution to the mission work in Korea. Louise, who had been serving in China, came to join the small band of pioneer missionaries in Korea. Her sister, Elizabeth, remained at home in Truro, Nova Scotia, to look after their mother. However, she did not remain idle at home. She, along with another sister, established the Berachol Mission in Truro. Elizabeth also wrote a book on the life of William J. McKenzie, pioneer missionary to Korea. It was not until the death of her mother, when she was well past middle age, that Elizabeth was free to go to Korea. Her heart had always been there and, although she was well past the age of acceptance by the board, her outstanding qualifications in education and music made her a worthy candidate and, with her salary guaranteed by friends in Nova Scotia, she went off to Korea.

The work in Korea advanced quickly. Soon there were schools for both boys and girls. This was a wonderful change, says the writer in *The Story of Our Missions*, especially for the little girls, for they were not supposed to need an education. There were still many mothers who needed to be coaxed to send their girls to school. Parents believed it was a waste since the girls could attend only until 13 or 14 years of age at which time they were sent to the home of their mother-in-law to learn housekeeping. The young girls often went to school with their little baby sister or brother strapped on their back while their mothers worked.

Christians were building their own churches and supporting what day schools they could afford. Since most of the schools were for boys, the women had to continue work with girls until Koreans better appreciated the need for the enlightenment of their women. The first school for girls was opened at Wonsan, the oldest of the mission stations. Soon another was opened at Song Chin and then at Ham Heung. A few years later Koreans suddenly began to realize the benefit to these girls, and schools for both Christian and "heathen" were opened all over the country.

Louise and Elizabeth McCully established the Martha Wilson Memorial Institute, in memory of their mother. This Institute supplied Bible women for the church, greatly adding to the church's strength. Elizabeth was a most articulate and interesting writer. It was she who wrote the chapter on Korea in *The Planting of the Faith*. Early in her story, Miss McCully speaks about the change taking place in the women of Korea with the coming of Christianity.

> *....news was whispered about of old women going to school. There was no doubt about it for there they sat, old grandmothers, widows, mothers-in-law, too many to count, studying hard at the new Book*

for weeks together. They dispersed only to scatter every-where, working fresh mischief by teaching hundreds of other women the new worship. For they listened by the way-side, at the markets, in their kitchens; while they washed at the brooks or trod the heavy rice-mill; when they tarried for a little gossip at the well-sides, perhaps even as they made an offering to the spirits under the sacred trees or at the hillside shrines; whenever the strange word was spoken there were some to believe and turn from the age-old ways.[7]

Miss McCully gives us a sorry picture of the plight of the Korean women. No wonder they listened so eagerly to the good news of the gospel.

...physical health, enduring muscles and ordinary good nature, but most of all maternity give a woman a bear-able existence...should her mother-in-law be not too violent. She expects nothing, claims nothing, knowing herself to be a mere machine, nothing to the man she serves, save his cook, his laundress and the mother of his children. Never a word of sweet courtship before marriage, never a word of love after. His life is lived far apart from hers. She cooks for guests but never meets them...she has no name unless she become mother of somebody. He is clad in snowy linen and silk...while she...must be dirty, unkempt, uncombed, unattractive. Her joys are all in mother-hood and the baby on her back is a precious burden. Let her boy grow up and he will be as far removed from her in the world of letters as is his father... Only a low dancing girl may be clean and well-dressed...Only among women of shame will he find any able to read or converse... His wife dares not pronounce his name, may not even know it. His daughter is but a disappointment for she might have been a boy.[8]

And so, writes Miss McCully,

...the kindling of the light went on until a dozen places saw its steady gleam...as the Spirit of God moved upon the new believers over all Korea in a mighty tide of power...The Church in Eastern Canada had now a work to do beyond all she had planned. No tiny New Hebrides was this she had touched, no Trinidad, child of her love, but a great appealing nation that now looked to her to complete the task she had begun...

A contagion of evangelism had seized upon the Korean Christians... The desire to win another soul seemed to fire every heart, sending every believer to teach his neighbor. Even children caught the contagion... The multiplying came so fast that the missionary could never overtake his whole task.[9]

Women were the "heaviest care," says McCully, for they were, for the most part, ignorant mothers of bright happy scholars, unlettered wives of clever men, toiling, unlovely, neglected brides — all of them to be lifted into the Light that transforms, or Korea could never be truly Christian. Yet for this, says McCully, God had provided help and a way to train the women who already loved His Word, that for one solitary teacher there should be an 'army of women' to publish it. In honour of a mother who had loved Korea there was founded the Martha Wilson Memorial Bible Institute.

For the students in the schools, there was no need for rules, for they were so eager that rules were superfluous. These were students who could hardly be persuaded to stop studying. From this Institute came

> *...a score of Oriental deaconesses in a uniform of clean white cotton, heads crowned with a white turban of neatly folded cloth, feet shod "with the white straw sandals of their land and with the preparation of the Gospel of Peace."*[10]

Miss McCully names each of them and gives a brief description of who they were and what they did, but best known of them all, she says, was Hannah who made her own decision to leave an unlawful husband to obey the Word, and who travelled on foot hundreds of miles, year after year, by the side of her missionary friend.

Among all the fine teachers, there was one, well known in Canada, who particularly stood out. Her name was Grace Lee. Devoted to the pioneer missionary, W.J. McKenzie, she was brought by him to offer her service. A teacher of many gifts, parents hastened to send their children to sit at her feet. The students loved her. Her influence grew as she spent some winters in the Women's Bible Institute teaching, studying, taking her diploma with the rest.

Medical work grew slowly. The first medical missionary, Dr. Grierson, arrived in 1898. In 1901, Dr. Kate McMillan was sent out by the Woman's Foreign Missionary Society, Eastern Division. Koreans, says the writer in *The Story of Our Missions*, were ignorant of the laws of health and terrible epidemics occurred. They never imagined that diseases of the skin or the eyes could be caused by living in smoky rooms and by lack of bathing. The writer quotes Dr. McMillan who tells of a little sick boy brought to the dispensary by his father,

> *The doctor ordered a bath. The father looked surprised and said the women of the house would not allow it, as they feared a bath would bring on convulsions, for their little girl had died from that after the first bath. She asked how old the little girl was when she died. "Two years," was the reply.*[11]

The Japanese who were then in control of Korea were interested in medical work and were establishing hospitals throughout Korea. The hospitals were government-owned and free for those too poor to pay.

The nursing profession was slow to attract young Korean women who were fearful of entering such a field of work because of public opinion. Mary Tak was the first indigenous nurse.

> *Mary knew all the lazy excuses against bathing the babies and washing the sick; she knew the unsanitary, dirty habits that foster disease; she could devise ways to obey laws of health in spite of small, unventilated houses, and poverty that could not afford to be clean "like the foreigner."*[12]

Such nurses were multiplying in all the stations. Unfortunately, they could not be spared from hospitals to take part in community service where child-welfare, preventive measures, duties of motherhood, laws of hygiene could be taught to women to whom such themes were unknown and mysterious.

The Home Field

In 1905, with some hesitation, the Woman's Foreign Missionary Society, Eastern Division, had undertaken to assist in home mission work and in 1910 they added the words "and Home" after "Foreign" in their name. Work in Canada grew steadily. The northwest held a special place in the affections of the women but increasing needs in eastern Canada, due to the influx of immigrants, demanded the larger share of their givings.

When the church, through the Maritime Synod, took up work in the different industrial centres, the women gave what help they could. In Sydney, they built a small church, St. Stephen's, and a school. They provided a kindergarten and a teacher, Miss McIvor. A church and a school were opened in Scotchtown in 1915, where a number of immigrants had settled and the WMS(ED) women paid for the ground, the equipment of the school and the salary of the teacher. Miss Grant was the first teacher. The society helped maintain these and other missions to immigrants in the Maritimes.

The Decision Not to Amalgamate

The 1914 annual meeting of the Woman's Foreign and Home Missionary Society in the east was held on September 15-16 in Amherst, Nova Scotia. It was reported to be one of the best in their history. The three aims of the society had all been reached — increase in membership, in liberality and in labourers for the fields both at home and abroad. The attendance was the largest in its history, the reports the most encouraging, the offerings the greatest, and the obligations for the next year the heaviest.

The General Assembly, at its meeting in June 1914, had suggested the union of the foreign mission boards, east and west. The Woman's Foreign and Home Missionary Society in the east, while expressing sympathy for the apparent wisdom of uniting the Assembly's foreign mission boards, decided that their society would not amalgamate with the societies in the western division but would remain auxiliary to the Maritime Mission Board since their society's method of work differed from the Women's Missionary Society of the west. The aim of the WMS(ED) had always been to assist the general missionary funds of the Maritime Foreign Mission Board and to assist in home mission work, while, they said, the WMS(WD), carried on specific work termed woman's work, with all the breadth that such a term involved.

In 1914, the same year as the three western societies amalgamated to form the Women's Missionary Society, Western Division, the Woman's Foreign and Home Missionary Society, Eastern Division, added a social service department to their mandate and changed their name to the Woman's Missionary Society, Eastern Division.

Chapter

6

The Three Become One

Women's Missionary Society, Western Division — WMS(WD)

General Assembly, June 1913

Dr. A. Gandier presented the following recommendations to the General Assembly in June 1913:

- that the Assembly express its cordial approval of the unions of the Woman's Foreign Missionary Society and the Women's Home Missionary Society to form the Women's Missionary Society of the Presbyterian Church in Canada and also expresses the hope that the Woman's Missionary Society of Montreal will at its next meeting decide to become one of the provincial societies which are to constitute the Women's Missionary Society of the Presbyterian Church in Canada.
- that the boards of the three societies concerned be requested to appoint a joint committee.
- that a joint meeting of the societies uniting be called for May, 1914 in the city of Toronto to adopt a constitution, choose a general council for the first year and as far as possible complete the organization of the new society.

Dr. A.S. Grant then moved the adoption of the proposal and the Clerk of Assembly, Dr. Campbell, seconded it. Dr. R. P. Mackay supported the motion. The Assembly then sang a verse of a hymn and a prayer was offered.

The Montreal Society Decides

After their annual meeting in February 1914, official word was received from the Montreal society of their decision to be one of the amalgamating societies in May 1914.

Amalgamation — May 15, 1914

O greatly blessed the people are
The joyful sound that know;
In brightness of Thy face, O Lord,
They ever on shall go.

As the congregation of women blended their voices in the singing of Psalm 89, the three societies — the Woman's Missionary Society, Montreal, the Woman's Foreign Missionary Society and the Women's Home Missionary Society — became one.

The union, or nuptials as the General Assembly's Foreign Mission Board called it, was formally consummated in Knox Church, Toronto, on May 15, 1914. On the platform were the three presidents of the uniting societies, Mrs. I. C. Sharp, Mrs. J. J. Steele, and Mrs. J. Somerville. With them sat five prestigious representatives of the General Assembly — the Moderator of the General Assembly, Dr. Murdoch MacKenzie; the representative of the Foreign Mission Board, Dr. R. P. Mackay; the representative of the Home Mission Board, Dr. A. S. Grant; Dr. A. Gandier and Dr. J. Somerville.

After the singing of the Psalm, Dr. Somerville led in prayer, Dr. Gandier reviewed the history of the three uniting organizations and the General Assembly minutes regarding the union. The agreed upon constitution was then read and adopted, "the whole audience rising in token of acceptance." The names of those nominated for the General Council were read and accepted. Dr. MacKenzie led in a prayer of dedication and the representatives of the *Foreign Mission Board* and *Home Mission Board* expressed their satisfaction about the union. Dr. Gandier then pronounced the benediction.[1]

Getting Down to Business

The general council of the new Women's Missionary Society, Western Division, met that same afternoon, May 15, 1914, for the election of officers. Mrs. J. J. Steele was unanimously elected president with Mrs. I. C. Sharp, Mrs. J. Somerville and Mrs. G. H. Robinson as vice-presidents. The delegates from the several provinces met in the evening to draft the list of officers for the provincial boards.

WHMS Board and Associate Members at Amalgamation

The basis of union provided:

- that all the present obligations of the uniting societies be assumed by the united society until such time as they are fully discharged
- that the work of the Women's Missionary Society be distinctly women's work
- that its budget be entirely separate from the budget of the church
- that the WMS budget be submitted to the Assembly's Home and Foreign Mission Boards for their approval
- that the general council at its annual meeting allocate to each provincial society its share of the whole budget

The new society took the motto of the Woman's Foreign Missionary Society, "The World for Christ."[2]

PART II

Women's Missionary Society, Western Division

1914-1972

Chapter 7

The War Years

1914-1918

An Overwhelming Task

With the impressive union service of May 15, 1914, still fresh in their minds, the united society faced, with fear and trembling, the great responsibility of the combined work of the three societies and the complete reconstruction called for in the new constitution. The General Assembly, at its June 1914 meeting, adopted, by a standing vote, a resolution expressing gratitude to God that the women of the Western Division had united all their missionary work under one society but the task at hand was overwhelming. Nevertheless, no time was lost and the July/August issue of the new magazine *The Missionary Messenger* was circulated to the auxiliaries. *The Missionary Messenger* replaced the magazines of the three uniting societies, *The Missionary Outlook, The Foreign Missionary Tidings* and *The Home Mission Pioneer.*

The July-August 1914 issue lists the society's work under the newly formed Women's Missionary Society.
Canada:

- nine pioneer hospitals for foreigners.
- seven educational homes for immigrant children, with a staff of about thirty-four in all.

- eight boarding schools and six day schools for Canadian Aboriginal work with a staff of about forty-five.
- nine deaconesses for city mission work, four for Jewish work, two for educational and evangelistic work among French Canadians, which work was to be largely extended.

Foreign Fields:

Departments of work came under three general divisions: evangelistic, educational and medical. Single women missionaries numbered about sixty, among whom were seven medical women, five of whom were in Central India, one in Honan, one in South China. The other missionaries were distributed among the many avenues of work in the boarding, day, and high schools, the industrial institutions, and the hospitals. Others were set apart for village and zenana work, or for assisting in translation work.

The report adds,

> *Nor must we omit the valuable work done by the wives of the missionaries; this also is supported by the W.M.S. In fact all woman's work under the missions of the Western Division will now be estimated for under this Society. Our responsibilities are therefore of no mean proportion, and will require for the coming year an estimate of about $200,000.*[1] (See Appendix C)

Three short months after the union of the three societies, war broke out. Already dealing with the difficulties of amalgamation, the new society now had to face the unexpected difficulties brought on by the conditions of the war. Among those who felt the call of duty to King and country were two members who were prominent in the work of the WMS. Miss McHarrie, a nurse in India, home on furlough, asked permission to stop off in France and enter one of the Allies' hospitals where Indian soldiers were being cared for. Miss McHarrie felt that, equipped as she was with the language, she could be of special service. The other member was Miss Bessie MacMurchy, corresponding secretary of the WMS general council. Miss MacMurchy was a graduate of the New York General Hospital and, though she had since remained at home, when duty called she joined a band of sister graduates in a hospital for the allies outside Paris. Later, other medical missionaries would answer the call to serve their country, leaving a shortage of workers in the field.[2]

Official notice was sent to all missionaries in Canada and overseas advising them to keep down expenses and to stop extension work until further notice. In September the following message appeared,

> *It has been thought advisable to let the whole Society know that the treasury is almost empty, so that all may do promptly whatever is in*

Bessie MacMurchy

their power. The amount required every month for salaries and other expenses is very large...[3]

In spite of it all, the work went on but "retrenchment" was the watchword.

The response from missionaries on the Prairies to the financial crisis in which the new society found itself was heartwarming. Extracts from missionaries' letters to the board from western Canada indicate their willingness to do everything in their power to help until better days dawned.

I do not think the Board would be justified in doing any building whatever during the great scarcity of money. We will make out with our present hospital accommodation for another year.

If the grant is still forthcoming I will undertake to run the institution on it, and will be personally responsible for any deficit, for a few months at least.

Until things improve, I will do without the $50 a quarter for hospital drugs, and $50 a quarter of my salary. The workers each agree to offer $10 a month off their salaries...

Kindly convey to Dr. Grant and to the women our cordial sympathy in this difficult crisis, but say that we will try a good many schemes sooner than agree to quit the work.[4]

Pointe-aux-Trembles School, Quebec

The first annual meeting of the newly-formed society took place in May 1915 in Montreal. The delegates were treated to a visit to the Pointe-aux-Trembles School.

A motion from the Manitoba Provincial came before the council expressing concern about the urgent need for female medical missionaries on the foreign field, and asking for permission to set up a special fund to aid young women willing to qualify as medical missionaries. The matter was sent to the executive board for consideration.

Another motion came from the British Columbia Provincial recommending that WMS estimates be included in the budget of the General Assembly's Committees on Home and Foreign Missions, and that the WMS be granted a representative on these committees. Prompting this motion was the criticism, often expressed, that WMS money bypassed the local church's budget when, if included, it could help the local church meet its allocation. After discussion, the motion was defeated for several reasons, the main reason being that the WMS would lose control of its own budget.

A further motion, made with a view to easing the financial crisis facing the society, asked a year's notice be given for a change in the constitution that would allow for triennial meetings of the council instead of annual meetings, with the executive board having the right in any year to call a meeting of the general council.

The Moderator of the General Assembly, Rev. W. T. Herridge, in an address on missions, possibly given to the women at council and printed in the July/August issue of *The Missionary Messenger*, includes a few disparaging words about women. Although he was probably just voicing common sentiments of the men of his day, his words would strike women today as rather insulting, as they probably struck women in 1915.

> *The men go forth and fight, the women stay at home and wait and work — work mightily. Even the most frivolous women in Canada, the women whose lives have hitherto been unproductive, are justifying their existence now and doing some good in the world...*[5]

The editor of *The Missionary Messenger* ends the year with this sentiment,

> *Christmas comes to us this year with veiled face and gentle footfall ...for heartache is universal and the hurt of sorrow widespread. The world's great conflict still rages, and the angel-song of peace and good-will seems strangely silent.*[6]

The New Year's message from the president in the January 1916 issue of *The Missionary Messenger* voiced a new problem. The temptation of auxiliaries and Mission Bands to divert their givings from the treasury of the WMS to the Red Cross, Belgian Relief and Social Reform was causing real concern.

> *Each and all of these and similar channels of helpfulness claim our generous attention but not at the expense of our society's fund.*[7]

The April issue of the magazine speaks even more strongly. Reports from auxiliaries made clear that over and over again money given directly by the auxiliaries and Mission Bands for the estimates of the WMS was being divided by them and half given to other schemes of the church, already provided for in the Assembly's budget and to other emergency needs. These were all urgent and worthy needs. However, the editor pointed out, such efforts to aid the Red Cross or other patriotic work was at the expense of WMS work already pledged and would mean that work must be closed down if the money was not there. This manner of giving, the editor said, did not mean sacrifice for the giver, but called for sacrifice on the part of our schools and hospitals.

This practice was widespread in women's missionary societies all over the world. A report of the international secretary for Women's Missionary Societies was quoted in *The Missionary Messenger* as saying that many of the societies were giving time and service to the Red Cross and other patriotic work, which before the war, had been devoted exclusively to missionary interests and undertakings.

The second annual council meeting of the society was held in Winnipeg in May 1916 at the same time as General Assembly. The council delegates attended the opening meeting of the General Assembly and also the sessions of the Home and Foreign Mission Boards. Arrangements were made for the WMS delegates to council to go by special train to visit Teulon. Dr. Hunter, as their host, gave them a tour of the school, the hospital, the school home and the church.

Mrs. Steele's presidential address to council delegates brought home the seriousness of the society's financial situation.

> *When the members of Council separated last year in Montreal at the close of their first Annual Meeting, little did we think that we, as a nation, would be called upon to pass through such a year of anxiety and sorrow and loss as this last has been... To your Executive Board...it has been a year of mingled encouragement and anxiety.... The volume of work undertaken was large, and anxiety was felt because not at any one time since last Council meeting was there sufficient money in the treasury to place the balance on the right side of the ledger... When the last installment of money from Provincial Treasurers was received at the end of January and it was found that not only was there nothing to meet the expenses of doctors, nurses, teachers and others for the current month but that there was a large deficit... A few at once wished to retrench but the large majority thought and believed that to dismiss members of staff and close a Home here, a Hospital there either in Home or Foreign field would not be approved of by the society, so the appeal was made...and the response has been very hearty.*[8]

In reference to the recommendation sent down from the 1915 annual meeting with regard to the fund for the education of women medical missionaries, the motion was amended to say that the WMS place this need among the estimates. This council also dealt with the notice of motion from the 1915 annual meeting asking that meetings be held every three years. It was moved in amendment that the meetings be held annually.

The corresponding secretary, writing at the close of 1916, commented that prayer and study were the bulwarks of the Women's Missionary Society and reminded the delegates of the importance of the Day of Prayer that was held annually in January. She also announced the publication of the new study book *The Story of Our Missions*, edited by Mrs. Janet MacGillivray, editor of *The Missionary Messenger.*

At the third annual meeting of the general council in May 1917, a resolution came before the delegates from the Board of Home Missions and Social Service respectfully suggesting that the WMS authorize presbyterials, where requested by presbyteries, to co-operate in social service work, provided no expense to the WMS was involved. This request was refused on the grounds that the branches of work already undertaken by the WMS would require expansion which they were as yet unable to meet. The fact of the deficit weighed heavily on the minds of the delegates and it was their hope that the president's appeal to the auxiliaries to wipe it out would prompt a good response.

Included in the 1917 resolutions was one protesting the desecration of the Lord's Day, registering the society's disapproval of permitting work for the greater production of food on the Lord's Day. Another resolution deplored the fact that no definite action had been taken by the government to restrict the gambling and other evils of the racetrack.

The 1918 general council meeting planned for Calgary in June was cancelled. The feeling was that members would see this as an unjustifiable expense when the Empire was facing such a crisis and bending every effort to win the war. Besides, the Passenger Association of the Canadian Railways had decided to give no special rates to any convention in Canada during 1918.

Mrs. Steele, in her president's message in October 1918, reported that there had been progress in 1917. Not only was the society able to carry on all the existing work, but was able to do more than had been planned for at the beginning of the year. She adds,

> *Because you did not disappoint us, we were able to close the year with a balance in hand of several thousands of dollars. But do not think for a moment that we could not have spent all this, and more, too, for as an Executive we will never be satisfied till we have enough money left over on December 31st to carry us through till the first quarter's money comes, in the end of March.*[9]

The Forward Movement

In 1918 the General Assembly, in response to an overture and looking forward to the coming of peace, inaugurated the Forward Movement and invited the WMS to co-operate with them in bringing before the people of the church the need for united prayer and for the re-consecration of life to the service of the Lord. A five-year program was adopted. Arrangements were made by the Forward Committee of the WMS in conjunction with the men's committee for a representative of the society to present the needs of WMS work to each presbytery.

In the first year of the Forward Movement an educational campaign was carried on and the needs of the church's work were placed before every synod, presbytery, provincial and presbyterial society, auxiliary and Mission Band in Canada. The WMS prepared a set of ten charts with accompanying literature and sent one set to each auxiliary and two additional charts for each Mission Band.

For some years the WMS board had felt the need for a closer link with the committees of the church for whose work they were partially responsible through large financial support.

> *The women of our Presbyterian Church have not blazed the trail by seeking recognition from the highest council of the Church on the different Mission Boards,*[10]

However, the time had come to take action. A memorial[11] went to the General Assembly in 1918, on the matter which they hoped would be given "rightful consideration."

> *That in view of the larger problems before the Church, and in order that we work with a better understanding and more in uniformity with the policy of the Presbyterian Church, that in addition to the present membership on the Presbyterian Missionary and Deaconess Training Home, and the Board of Pointe-aux-Trembles Schools, the WMS ask the privilege of representation on the following Standing Committees of the Church, viz.: The Foreign Mission Board; The Home Mission Board; Committee on Sunday School and Young People's Work, and in view of extension work among women in connection with our theological colleges, representation where this work is being developed.*[12]

The General Assembly in June 1918 remitted the resolution to a committee to report to the next General Assembly. The WMS(ED), at its September 1918 annual meeting, passed a resolution referring to the petition of the WMS(WD), requesting a similar representation.

The need for co-operation with other missionary societies also had long been felt by the WMS. More than 30 years before, the WFMS had become a member of the World Union of Women's Foreign Missionary Societies. In 1918, the WMS joined the Federation of the Women's Foreign Mission Boards of North America and became a constituent member of the Council of Women for Home Missions in the United States. Steps were also being taken for the formation of a Federation of the Canadian Women's Mission Boards. In this new atmosphere of inter-denominational co-operation, the

Forward Movement became an inter-church movement and its second year featured the great National Peace Thankoffering.

In the December 1918 issue of *The Missionary Messenger*, the editor writes,

> *The coming of a world peace is drawing very near. We can almost hear the rustle of its wings. Its calming spirit is already in our hearts... The challenge now is to the Church to get into the hearts of the people of all nations the spirit of the Prince of Peace... We must go forward and, please God, we shall. And the church shall lead us. She cannot do otherwise for to her has come a vision of service and sacrifice on a vaster scale than was ever imagined and a vision of unparalleled opportunity which she has summed up in two words vibrant with life and action: FORWARD MOVEMENT...we, as a WMS have been asked to take part.*[13]

Indeed, the church had invited the WMS to co-operate in the Forward Movement, and even to enter the intimidating courts of the presbyteries where, says the editor,

> *...the ministers and elders of our Church have always had entrance, and it is surely indicative of a new day when this privilege was graciously extended to include representatives of the WMS, who sought to lay before the ministers the work of our society and its objective in the great Forward Movement.*[14]

The representatives from the WMS were kindly received at most presbytery meetings. One exception was the misunderstanding on the part of a moderator who, instead of arranging for the WMS representatives to address the presbytery, called a public meeting of women only. However, on another occasion the WMS representative was asked to sit as a corresponding member which was considered to be a gracious act of courtesy on the part of the gentlemen. Another presbytery took a still further step by appointing four women with the six men on the presbytery's committee of the Forward Movement.

Change certainly seemed to be in the air. Helen Smith, the student secretary, in an article written in the January 1919 issue of *The Missionary Messenger*, had this to say,

> *In this day and generation the choosing of one's career is not the simple matter it once was. Where twenty-five years ago, a woman was expected to marry or teach, now she is not only free to do but is expected to do the work of a man even in the sacred precincts of Parliament and the pulpit. In their wildest dreams our mothers hardly thought to live to see the day when women would sit in the*

British Parliament, much less occupy Presbyterian pulpits as did our eight women missionaries in the West last summer.[15]

The women in the WMS were discovering their voices and realizing that they had an exciting and impressive story to tell which the rest of the church did not seem to know much about.

Our committees of women of the Presbyterials are going fearlessly forward in seeking to make the needs of the WMS known. Not so many years ago it was with hesitancy that women of the WMS ventured to speak in public especially before a mixed audience, and though there still is a natural preference to speak only before their own constituency they are willing to forget themselves in the greatness of the message they have to present.[16]

The Forward Movement was, for the church and the WMS, the outstanding feature of the decade. It was at the forefront of all the WMS plans. Their estimates for 1919 were high, an advance of more than 33 per cent over those of 1918.

Our hopes are high and our faith strong that the women of our Church are seized as never before with the world situation, and are ready to rally to their place and part in the great new battle front that righteousness and peace may become the law of all nations and Christ be recognized as King.[17]

The WMS closed the books for 1918 with the largest increase in expenditure in the whole history of its work. In spite of financial successes, the society's emphasis throughout the Forward Movement campaign was on the importance of prayer. It ran like a golden thread through all they did as they put their hopes and dreams for the mission work of the church into an imaginative set of charts, lantern slides and talks.

I believe implicitly in the power of prayer, said Mrs. McKerroll to the WMS board before setting out on a seven-week itinerary in the west on behalf of the Forward Movement. Before returning, she had travelled 4,000 miles and delivered 30 addresses, with the outdoor temperature at a constant 60 degrees below zero. At the close of the last meeting with the Manitoba Provincial she asked, *What is the most vital thing we can do for the Forward Movement?* The answer, said Mrs. McKerroll, was God-inspired. *Devote one hour a day to prayer for the Forward Movement.* To test the feeling of the meeting the chairwoman asked: *How many women will pledge themselves to one hour or to a definite time every day for prayer for the Forward Movement?* and every WMS member in that packed church rose to her feet.[18]

The articulate and poetic editor of *The Missionary Messenger*, Mrs. MacGillivray, began 1919 with these words,

> *The darkness, the storm and the conflict have passed and over the war-worn world the Unseen Hand has cast the rainbow of peace. The night is over, the dawn has come, a new day calls.*[19]

The fourth annual meeting of the general council of the WMS in May 1919 was the longest in the history of the society due to the fact that council had not met during the war years. It began with the Moderator of the General Assembly, Dr. Colin Fletcher, leading in a service of thanksgiving for victory and approaching peace. Dr. Somerville led the society in the prayer of adoration and thanksgiving, a prayer that would become for them a hallowed memory as Dr. Somerville died shortly after the May meeting.

> *We think of him,* says the editor of *The Missionary Messenger, and of his gracious and kindly service to us as a society and individually, and of the last words that we heard fall from his lips, 'I am glad to do this for you for I have been in love with the WMS for a great many years, and I believe its organization to have been the greatest blessing that has come to The Presbyterian Church'.*[20]

A request at this annual meeting, that the second Sunday in September be set apart as WMS Sunday, met with the approval of the whole council. A similar request had already been granted the Saskatchewan Provincial by their synod. The Saskatchewan Synod had gone the second mile by sending a letter, under the names of the moderator and the clerk of the synod, to each minister within the bounds asking them to comply with the decision of synod.

One of the important decisions of this council was the adoption of a resolution which would lead to the Federation of the Women's Mission Boards of Canada. This caution was added,

> *...it being clearly understood that we are not binding our Societies in any way, and that no interference is intended with the constitution by which they are governed.*[21]

The WMS had not yet received a response to their resolution to the 1918 General Assembly, asking for representation on the several committees of the church. The committee appointed reported to the 1919 General Assembly that, after careful consideration, they found themselves in so much doubt as to the precise meaning of the action of the last Assembly that they

> *...resolved to ask this General Assembly for an interpretation of the resolution, and for more definite instructions, any action, in the meantime, being delayed.*[22]

The committee was instructed by the Assembly to meet with the various boards interested and with the boards of the Women's Missionary Societies, and to report to the next General Assembly on the whole question of the representation of the Women's Missionary Societies on the boards of the church.

In November 1919, Mrs. Janet MacGillivray resigned as editor on account of illness in her family. Her work was taken over by Miss Fraser, the editorial secretary. Mrs. Emily Steele, the first president of the united society, was forced, due to failing health, to retire from office in 1919. She had led the society through the difficult days of amalgamation and the trying years of the war. She was succeeded by Mrs. MacGillivray.

The year 1919 ended on a rather sad note. Apparently the WMS board had held its weekly board meetings at the Deaconess Training Home. An announcement in *The Missionary Messenger* reports,

> *The Executive Board felt suddenly homeless when the announcement was made that the Deaconess Training Home management required the room, used as our weekly meeting place since amalgamation and before, for lecture and study purposes. The problem of where to meet was solved by the action of the Session of Knox Church who kindly placed their large Social Room at our disposal for Board meetings, and a smaller room for the use of Committees.*[23]

The WMS board expressed its appreciation of the gracious attitude of the various principals of the home, their pleasure in meetings with students and the thoughtfulness of the staff as they passed out of a building *dear to us through the association of years.*[24] It seems a rather ungracious action on the part of the managers of the home. Perhaps they had forgotten that the Ewart Missionary Training Home had been the dream of WMS members, particularly Mrs. Ewart,

> *...whose desire it was to arrange a plan whereby young women applying for foreign service could receive a special training in Biblical and practical subjects.*[25]

The Women's Missionary Society had not forgotten. In June 1921 Miss Jean Macdonald wrote "The Presbyterian Missionary and Deaconess Training Home: A Child of the WMS," in which she says,

> *To know the past years of the Home is to pay tribute to the vision and persistent efforts of those of the Deaconess Committee and Board, who have developed it. And those who know the past know,*

too, 'the mothering care' of the Women's Missionary Societies of the Church over this child of theirs. Their contribution in the earlier days made the work possible; the child has grown but it records its gratitude for this nurturing care.[26]

Canada

Reports from the missionaries in western Canada during the war years speak of the difficulties faced by both missionaries and the immigrants who were trying to begin a new life in Canada. Over and over we hear of the poverty, the extreme cold during the winter months, the lack of water, the distances people had to travel to get to the mission hospital and the frequent accidents that brought them there. Dr. Hunter, medical superintendent at Teulon, Manitoba, reports,

...this year the great majority have had hard work to get bread and many families are close to starvation. Nine-tenths of the settlers in the North have not sufficient land cleared to make a living and depend chiefly on working in the summer.[27]

The report from the Rolland M. Boswell Hospital in Vegreville, Alberta, says that the winter season was particularly trying, especially in the nurses' quarters and the office *...during the severe weather blankets had to be placed on the radiators in the office to keep them from freezing.*[28]

Mrs. H.M. Kipp, hospital secretary for the society, on a visit to the home mission hospitals, commented on the lack of water, and called it the west's great trouble. Nearly every hospital had stories about the lack of water. Several speak about having to cut and melt ice. The Hugh Waddell Memorial Hospital at Canora, Saskatchewan, reported that their entire water supply had to be hauled in barrels and tanks to the hospital. A picture of just what this meant for the staff comes in a report from Canora informing that the WMS board had approved a grant for the installation of a laundry machine which was very much needed and which would solve the difficult problem of doing enormous washings by hand.

The reports are full of accidents of all kinds. Shooting accidents were common, especially during the winter months, and distance was a real problem. A report from Grande Prairie tells of a prospector who had an infected hand. He walked over eighty miles to get to the hospital, arriving in bad shape. He told them of the terrible pain he suffered and of having to plunge his arm and hand into the creeks to try to ease the fearful burning and throbbing.

Probably the women in the foreign colonies felt the hardships of the new life worst of all. Alone all day, usually with several children, they were often far from relatives and friends and without enough money to feed and clothe their families. Added to that were their frequent pregnancies, sometimes with complications and far from medical help.

When the war began in 1914, the WMS was responsible for hospital work in nine areas. The hospital at Telegraph Creek had been closed for several years for lack of a medical missionary, and the Pacific Coast Mission was also closed during the war years. A fire in the autumn of 1914 had swept over Atlin, British Columbia, burning down a large area of the town. The hospital, fortunately, escaped damage. It was the hope of the WMS that these hospitals would eventually become self-sustaining. They were pleased to report that, by 1919, three of the hospitals had reached the point where they no longer needed assistance from the WMS.

Due to financial worries, new work was being planned only for exceptional cases. The new hospital at Ethelbert, Manitoba, was finally opened on December 29, 1915. Two years later, the hospital escaped destruction by a fire that destroyed part of that town. It was not the first fire on the hospital property and the staff was well prepared. They had three good wells and a large supply of quilts. They also had plenty of help. The men and boys worked on the roofs, the women carried water and wet quilts to cover the roofs and windows, and the children ran around putting out small fires in the stable and yard. There was practically no damage to the hospital.

Another new hospital was added in 1917 in Bonnyville, a small, remote settlement on the Alberta-Saskatchewan border. Rev. William Simons had appealed to the WMS for assistance in evangelizing the French-Canadian settlers at Bonnyville. Despite strong opposition to the mission from the Roman Catholic Church, the work was encouraging. Miss MacDougall, a nurse at Bonnyville, wrote saying that she loved the work and that her whole heart was in it. She rode the mission pony to visit her patients.

In the 1918 *The Missionary Messenger*, Dr. Hunter of Teulon was pleased to announce that Miss Annie Korzak had been appointed head nurse. Miss Korzak came to the hospital as a sick little child when she was eight years old. After professional training she returned to Teulon, and was probably the first Ruthenian nurse in Canada. The hospital at Teulon was re-named the Hunter Hospital by the WMS board in honour of Dr. Hunter, veteran medical missionary who had been at the hospital in Teulon since its inception in 1904.

By the end of the war, Spanish influenza, a world-wide scourge, was sweeping westward. Hospital reports told of the heaviest year's work on record. "Canora Hospital Filled To Overflowing With 'Flu' Patients" was the headline of a report in the *The Missionary Messenger* in 1918. Many of the

Bonnyville Hospital, on the Alberta-Saskatchewan border

staff were also victims. The R. M. Boswell Hospital at Vegreville was constantly full. The high school had opened again but the public school would not open until the New Year. In fact, in the latter part of 1918, every hospital was filled far beyond its normal capacity, necessitating, in some cases, turning the nurses' sitting rooms, operating rooms and corridors into emergency wards in order to meet the demands of the community. Miss Jean Stewart, who had retired from Bonnyville in May 1918, offered her services during the influenza epidemic, and was sent to Tofield where, after nursing several severe cases, she was stricken with the disease and died.

In a report to the Home Mission Board, the WMS said that since the church had declared itself again and again in sympathy with the establishment of the public school system, the women were watching with eagerness its growth in the western provinces where "the foreign element" was strong. The WMS was prepared, the report said, to gather in the children from the less favourable districts into Christian homes and give them the privilege of attending a good public school and in the school home, by means of a clean wholesome environment, teach them "a love of truthfulness, justice and true Christian gentleness."

Eager for education, more children were applying for admission to schools and school homes than could possibly be accommodated. The parents were so anxious to have their children educated that they were increasingly willing to give what they could afford toward the support of their children in the homes.

Two new homes were opened in 1917, one at Vermilion, Alberta, the other a larger building for the girls at Vegreville. Vegreville was the centre of a large Ruthenian colony, so large it was said the Ruthenians outnumbered the English-speaking people two to one.

After a long wait, the girls' school home at Teulon had its formal opening on November l, 1918. Even before it opened four girls had moved in — two Ruthenians, one Icelander and one Canadian. Mrs. Freeland, the matron, tells of one little girl whose father had been burned out and had lost everything.

> *I have had my first experience of cleaning up one of the neglected little ones who has been deprived of her mother. She is only 8 years old and has been playing mother to two brothers and a sister and a baby one and a half years old…she came yesterday — a wee old woman, her coat down to her boots which were 3 sizes too large for her and a dirty toque on a mass of coal black hair, with a pair of the most beautiful brown eyes looking out from under long lashes, as if they would read your very heart, and such a plaintive little smile, such as would say to you, "I have suffered; are you going to be good to me?"*[29]

The Canora Home for Girls was opened in October 1919, thanks to the generosity of Mrs. Waddell, who had also financed the Hugh Waddell Hospital in memory of her husband.

Every school home was full to overflowing and only the question of financing prevented the opening up of many more. If accommodation was lacking, children often lived at the mission or at the hospitals and even in the homes of the missionaries in order to be able to attend the public schools. The teachers and matrons of the home schools reported that the children of the immigrants not only held their own with the Canadian pupils but often surpassed them. Children in the mission homes also had better knowledge of the scriptures due to the religious atmosphere in the homes. Toward the end of the war, at least one hundred children were under the care of the WMS, attending public schools and receiving religious and domestic instruction in the homes.

The Missionary Messenger reports that several new homes would be opening in the near future: Rossburn, Manitoba; Edmonton, Alberta; Cochrane,

Ontario — the latter two to include children of French parentage. A further school for missionaries' children was expected to open in the west.

For some time, Rev. J. U. Tanner, the district superintendent of Home Missions in Quebec, had pleaded for the establishing of homes near schools in certain places in Quebec so that families living too far from the schools could leave their children there during the week. Mr. Tanner asked the WMS to take charge of this phase of the work. A school home was opened in Namur, Quebec. A grant of $600 was given toward rent, matron's salary and furnishings. The auxiliaries in Quebec provided blankets, sheets, towels, and other necessities. The children attended the Protestant school in Namur. The school was kept up by the taxes of the community supplemented by the Home Mission Board.

A second school home was opened, at the request of Miss Davidson, secretary for French work, at St. Philippe de Chester. The property already belonged to the Presbyterian Church but was badly in need of repair. The WMS paid for the repairs, for the matron's salary and some maintenance. There was no church or school at St. Philippe de Chester. The missionary taught the scholars at the manse. The matron had charge of the girls, living with them at a house nearby. The boys stayed at the manse.

The WMS offered two scholarships to girls at the Pointe-aux-Trembles School to enable them to attend Macdonald College in Ste. Anne de Bellevue, Quebec. In 1916, Principal Brandt informed the WMS that both girls had successfully passed their examinations at Macdonald College and that one would be employed as a teacher in one of the city mission schools while the other had already found a place in a country school, awaiting an opening in one of the mission schools.

It was reported in November 1918 that, due to a quarantine that had been rigidly enforced, the Pointe-aux-Trembles School had been relatively free of influenza. New school homes were opened at several other places including Tourville where the people were anxious to have a school and were doing as much as possible themselves. School work in Quebec suffered severely with the influenza epidemic in the fall of 1918. Many of the schools had to be closed.

There were changes in the work with Aboriginal people. The General Assembly's boards of Home Missions and Social Services amalgamated in

1915. The new board stated in its report to the General Assembly in 1916 that, since the contract with the government under which the church had conducted the work with Aboriginal people had expired in April 1915, the board had decided that,

> *Inasmuch as the Indians are the wards of the government, and the main concern of the Church is the moral and spiritual welfare of these people, it is the opinion of this board that the Church should assume in future no responsibility for buildings or farms or equipment, but confine its support to the salaries of workers as hereinafter set forth.*[30]

The terms outlined were: that the church would provide the salaries for principals, matrons, teachers and farm instructors in boarding schools, the government for teachers in day schools, farm instructors and all employees not otherwise provided for.

The WMS, in its estimates for 1915, reduced the amount for residential schools by $4,000. This was not, they said, that there would be any lessening of the work but because of the new policy as stated by the Board of Home Missions and Social Services. The WMS had been contributing about $20,000 annually to "Indian work," exclusive of the government grant and the supplies of clothing for the aged and needy on the reserves and for the children in the schools.

According to WMS records, the years from 1914 to 1918 saw many improvements in both the quality of the residential schools and in the health of the students. A report from Portage la Prairie speaks about the magnificent new buildings the government was erecting that would have accommodation for over 70 children. It seems attendance at the schools was no longer a problem. Most of the reports speak of overflowing classrooms with many students having to be turned away. It was quite different, said one report, to a few years before when, if they wanted students, the teacher had to go around and pull them out of bed and bring them to school. A report from the Cecilia Jeffrey School said that they no longer had to ask the parents to send their children to school because more children wanted to come than they could accept. There was also a great improvement in the health of the children in the schools. Mr. McWhinney of Crowstand attributed this to good nourishing food and plenty of fresh air.

The churches on the reserves were growing, many of them with active WMS groups. An encouraging factor in the reports during these war years was the increasing involvement of the Aboriginal people, not just in the building of their own churches but in the leadership they took in their church services and in evangelism.

A new church opened on Ahousaht reserve in British Columbia in 1915. Due to the enthusiastic help of the Aboriginal people it was all paid for and no help was needed from the WMS. Rev. John Ross said that he would require more seating because the Aboriginal people were good church attenders. Ever since Joseph Samuel, one of their graduates, had begun to take the morning services, attendance of both young and old was very regular. The WMS field secretary reported that many Sunday schools were carried on by the Aboriginal people themselves because the missionary did not have time to be present after his sermon in the morning. Many of the WMS auxiliaries on the reserves functioned on their own.

Thomas Shewish, the son of an Aboriginal chief and graduate of Alberni school, had been the missionary to his own people at Dodger's Cove, British Columbia since 1913. He conducted services on Sunday, ministered whenever possible and taught day school during the winter months where the Aboriginal people located for the cold season.

Many of the missionaries felt the disadvantage of not being able to speak to the Aboriginal people in their own tongue. Rev. Matthews at the Rolling River Reserve found the work encouraging, feeling that almost every barrier had been overcome, except the barrier of language. He was thankful for the progress of the work but felt it was small compared with what it might have been if he could only preach the gospel to them in their Aboriginal tongue. This, he believed, was the really weak link in the whole chain. Several reports mentioned that Mr. Dodd, principal of the Cecilia Jeffrey School, preached to the students in their native tongue.

Rev. Dr. Hugh McKay of Round Lake Reserve told of his travels with Jacob Bear to the people along the valley,

> *The people here are Ojibway and we tried to speak to them through an interpreter, reading the story of the great supper. Jacob then addressed them and I felt the contrast between speaking through an interpreter and the direct appeal. Then the closing prayer by Jacob, full of earnestness and pathos... We spent the night in an Indian house... I was glad Mrs. Mackay persuaded me to take a pillow, but my hip bones were sore and the night was cold...*[31]

Sometimes it was not just the language. Rev. Fernie of Moose Mountain Reserve and Day School in Saskatchewan commented on the Sunday service. He said,

> *At the Indian Service we avail ourselves of the services of any present who can read the Indian Bible for the Scripture Lesson...*

He added that, at this service, Mrs. Fernie, who was a teacher on the reserve, would give the address.

I do not succeed in giving satisfaction, either to those present, or to myself. Whereas, Mrs. Fernie seems to have no difficulty in reaching their understandings... She gives a good Gospel address in a way which appears to go home to their minds.[32]

From The Rolling River Reserve the missionary laments,

We cannot give the Gospel to them in their own tongue and our long experience has proved that the best spiritual results cannot be obtained in any other way. No matter who the interpreter is, the message does not go direct from the heart of the speaker. For two weeks we had an Indian evangelist, Jacob Bear, holding services and there was no doubt about the power of the Gospel when rightly applied.[33]

The name of Jacob Bear appears several times in the reports. He is mentioned as one of four or five Aboriginal people who worked among their own people at Telegraph Creek. Notable among the workers, says the report, was Jacob Bear of Round Lake who had laboured over 30 years and had the love and respect of all. He is mentioned again in Mr. and Mrs. Fernie's report. Mr. Fernie says that they had tried to secure the special service of Jacob Bear from Mr. McKay of Round Lake for whom the Aboriginal people had great respect. Unfortunately, the winter began early and his coming had to be postponed until spring or early summer. A report from Round Lake Boarding School from Mr. McKay makes it clear just what an asset this Aboriginal man was in the mission work in the west.

We regret that our aged missionary, Jacob Bear has been seriously ill... He has been doing good work, not only among the Indians of Prince Albert, but visiting Mistawasis, File Hills, Pia-pots and the reserves north and east. His last trip was to Rolling River Reserve, where he held two weeks' evangelistic meetings. He is 77 years of age...and has been a helper for over 30 years to the missionary at Round Lake.[34]

There is a strong emphasis in all the reports on the necessity for an educated Aboriginal missionary who could tell the old, old story directly to the Aboriginal people in their own language.

Something else that came out in the WMS reports was the patriotism of the Aboriginal people during the war years. One band contributed over $500 to the Patriotic Fund while File Hills contributed $1,600. Aboriginal women on many of the reserves knitted and sewed for the soldiers. Many Aboriginal youth from almost every reserve enlisted.

Their voluntary service to the Empire will ever stand to their credit. One regiment of Indian lads found themselves in the city of

Edinburgh and as they marched down the streets they were cheered and shown great honor by the citizens of that historic city...[35]

At the end of 1915, a report from Rev. W. A. Hendry, principal at Portage la Prairie, offers a word indicating the change that had taken place in the thinking of many of the missionaries over the years.

...a word about the trend of our efforts with the children. We must win them by sympathetic interest and guide them along in an unobtrusive manner. Many good people with bad judgment have thought by cutting the ties of affection and looking down upon the aged and non-progressive members of the family, a shorter way to civilization is gained for the child. It does not work out in practice. The better plan and the more humane one, is to develop love for the father, mother and home. This love is a wholesome instinct planted in the children for a wise end.[36]

On October 20, 1918, a report in *The Missionary Messenger* from the Cecilia Jeffrey School in Kenora brought the bad news. Two of the boys had taken ill. Miss Folliott said she put them to bed and treated them for what she thought was Spanish flu. More of the children took ill and soon every boy and girl in the school was in bed. Not long after Dr. Matthews, principal of the school arrived, he confirmed that it was the Spanish flu. They worked day and night, reported Miss Folliott. She and the nurse took turns at night and there were some serious cases. One little girl died from pneumonia. Dr. Matthews had been ill himself on his arrival at the school and, in spite of all that could be done, he became worse. Miss Folliott ends her letter,

I am too tired to write more. I hope the morning brings better news. But no matter what happens we shall all do our very best for the good of the school. The little girl who died was a grandchild of Chief Redsky. I had sent for him and he came just before Martha passed away... The children have all been so good and patient...[37]

Dr. Matthews did not recover. He developed pneumonia and died. Anxiety for the welfare of the pupils, forgetfulness of self, overwork and exposure, the report said, contributed to his death. Influenza was rampant on the reserves and the percentage of fatalities was large. The schools fared better with fewer deaths among the children owing to good care, proper sanitary arrangements, and dedicated staff.

The WMS, in its report for 1918, said that it was doubtful if the work with Aboriginal people had ever been in a more encouraging position. With the assistance of the extra per capita grant the government had given as a war bonus, all the boarding schools had closed the year with a satisfactory credit balance.

During the year 1914/15, the WMS was responsible for nine deaconesses: two each in Toronto and Winnipeg, one each in Hamilton, Edmonton, Fernie, Nanaimo (summer of 1914) and Montreal.

In 1916, the Ontario Provincial reported that the growth of Mission Bands was phenomenal. An average of over one per week was being organized. The problem, as always, was leadership. The report berates the auxiliaries for not living up to their responsibilities and states that auxiliaries need to realize their moral indebtedness to the Mission Bands. Auxiliary officers should be visiting and assuming responsibility for organizing new groups.

The Mission Bands certainly did their share. As well as contributing to the bales, their givings went directly into the treasury of the WMS for mission work. In 1916, the Mission Bands contributed $24,000 to the WMS. Each issue of *The Missionary Messenger* contained a program for Mission Bands. Study material on mission work was also published for the bands. Although the financial contributions of the Mission Bands to the WMS were laudable, the women were anxious that Mission Bands should be looked upon as missionary educational centres and not simply money-making organizations. In *The Missionary Messenger* of September 1918, the Mission Band secretary of the general council had praise for the little folks who held such a big place in her heart. She commended the children for the way in which they had 'measured up' and for the example they set to older members.

The July/August issue of *The Missionary Messenger* reports that CGIT (Canadian Girls in Training), an institution of the Presbyterian Church, was sweeping the country. The WMS already had a place for CGIT in its program of studies.

Two field secretaries were employed by the WMS and travelled far and wide across Canada. Miss Eliza MacGregor reported in 1916 that throughout the year she had visited 197 congregations, delivered 264 addresses, organized 41 auxiliaries and five Mission Bands, besides being present at and taking part in two provincial and several presbyterial meetings.

As the war progressed, the deaconesses assumed a new role. In May 1918, *The Missionary Messenger* reported that for two years the deaconesses had been asking to be sent to the west to home mission fields to "carry on" where men were not available. Their primary aim was not the filling of vacant pulpits, but "to keep the home fires burning." At their March annual meeting, the Board of Home Missions and Social Service decided to appoint a number of women missionaries to undertake work on mission fields, under the same conditions and at the same salaries as men. Many men were enlisting and there was a scarcity of male missionaries. Each mission field, says *The Missionary Messenger*, had three congregations and the drives for the Sunday services ranged from twenty-two to thirty-two miles for the round trip. The women were each furnished with a horse and buggy. Rev. Peter Strang, in assessing their work, said,

> *I am satisfied that women such as these can do, during the summer, satisfactory work on any ordinary rural western mission field and that our church can with profit continue their services.*[38]

The aim of the WMS was to have a strangers' secretary in every provincial, presbyterial and auxiliary. Salaried chaplains at the ports, and women workers in Montreal, Toronto and Edmonton helped to secure necessary information from the immigrants which was then passed on to the Home Mission Board and to ministers in the local churches. The WMS gave particular attention to young women who were seeking employment as domestics. The WMS also made hospital visiting a priority. These were all concerns of this department.

During the war years the women were involved in patriotic service as well as responding to pleas for help from the poor and needy across Canada. Bedding, linens, garments and equipment were required for the comfort of patients in the various hospitals under the care of the WMS. Approximately 100 foreign children in the school homes were clothed, and equipment provided for the homes. In the Aboriginal boarding and day schools about 500 children were provided with clothing. Bedding and linens were provided for the schools. A supply of clothing was also sent for the old people and young children on the reserves.

Bales were sent to missionaries in the new and poorer parts of the provinces. They were especially appreciated by the Ruthenian minister who ministered to a large foreign population where a great deal of poverty existed. The wife of one of the missionaries wrote that the bales had brought great joy to the people in their district. She said that she was able to make up fifty-four parcels for the Christmas tree. Another missionary wrote to say that the women who sent the bales would be amply repaid for their labour of love if they could see the tears of gratitude running down the cheeks of those who went away with a bundle under their arms. All this was made possible by the combined efforts of auxiliaries, Mission Bands, and with the cooperation of Bible classes, infant classes, grandmothers and friends who knitted mittens, stockings and made a large number of quilts.

Bales sent from Mission Bands often included marbles, mouth organs and horns for the boys, with dolls, scrap books, picture books and hair ribbons for the girls. The writer comments that there need be no fear for the future of the society when we know that the children have caught the spirit of giving.

The home helper's department was organized for women who were unable to attend auxiliary meetings but who wanted to keep in touch with, and contribute to, the work of the society. It also attempted to arouse interest among women not yet interested in mission work, and secure their cooperation and support.

Providing Christian literature became a priority as women and children in China learned to read. The first Christian paper for boys and girls of China was issued March 1, 1915. It was made possible through the Federation of Women's Mission Boards of North America. Mrs. Elizabeth MacGillivray, the wife of Dr. Donald MacGillivray, missionary in Shanghai, was the author of the publication *Happy Childhood*. About 2,800 copies were printed with 2,500 paid up subscriptions. Mrs. MacGillivray accepted the position of editor of the magazine. She wrote *The Christian Ideal of Marriage and Home* in Chinese. It was illustrated by a Chinese artist. She met all expenses herself. The first edition of 1,000 copies sold out.

India

In a report from Dhar on December 16, 1915, Dr. Margaret O'Hara, veteran missionary, reminisces. It is the cold season and Dr. O'Hara is 'in camp' at Digthau. She snatches a few moments from the busy day to write of precious memories, and adds a glimpse at present crowded hours,

> *It is twenty-three years today since I was designated to medical work in India. There is no comparison between the joy then and now. At that time it was all untried, but now the joy of service is beyond expression…seventy-six patients at first camp…next camping spot had scarcely settled when people began to call…visited eight homes in the afternoon and in some of them found the whole family down with malarial fever… Never did I realize more deeply the privilege of being a medical woman than in days such as these…*[39]

The missionaries often spoke of itinerant work in the villages as something they truly enjoyed. Sometimes, however, it was not so easy. Reports from Ujjain and Mhow speak about the work being more difficult and discouraging in these areas than in past years. Miss Jessie Grier reported that the women were hard to reach and did not want to listen to the missionaries. Often they told the missionaries to go away as they had been told by their Brahmins not to listen to their religion.

Miss Bella Goodfellow, on the other hand, reporting from Kharua, says that touring among the villages had yielded greater results than ever before. The sad part was that wherever the missionaries went

> *...there was ever the sight of misery and suffering of the women and children due to ignorance; broken and disjointed limbs hanging useless; faces almost unrecognizable from aches and sores; bodies badly burned to relieve suffering; children's backs, chest, abdomen burned so deeply that medical aid was almost too late. Again there were the little children made stupid through opium to relieve the overworked mother; or the sad child-widows and wives; a little child just able to walk, screaming for its mother and being forced through a marriage ceremony, not knowing in any sense what it meant.*[40]

Many of the children had sore eyes, and there were many adult cases of blindness resulting from neglect. Infant mortality was appalling.

During the war years plague and cholera were constantly breaking out at different stations adding to the regular medical work. The surest way to escape the plague was to leave the infected towns. Families would move into temporary huts or tents in the jungle just outside the city. In the rainy and the cold season the huts were uncomfortable and the children often contracted pneumonia and many died. In Rajputana in the north, there was severe famine and many of the village people wandered through Central India with their herds of cattle, and their children and household goods in ox carts. From six in the morning until six at night a steady stream of these poor people with all their belongings passed the front of the Mission House.

Doctors on the field were always under a heavy strain. "Please send us more doctors!" was the constant refrain. The British government in India had appealed for the services of medical women for war work. Several of the doctors had been called to help at hospitals at the front. Dr. McKellar was stationed at Simla and was on a committee with three other medical women whose duty it was to select medical women to form units for service in military hospitals in India. At the request of the government, Miss Emmeline Smillie of Indore also went to care for wounded soldiers on a hospital ship. Nurse McHarrie went to Scotland and Dr. Laura Moodie to Bombay for similar duties. Dr. Margaret O'Hara and Miss Janet White postponed their furloughs indefinitely due to the dearth of workers.

The training of qualified hospital assistants and nurses became more and more important. Mrs. Kipp, secretary of Home Missions, in an article on medical missions, says that without the faithful band of Indian Christian women only a fraction of the work could be done. She adds that one of the most encouraging features in connection with the development of the medical work was the training of indigenous girls as nurses and medical assistants.

> *These native workers, in times of famine and plague do not spare themselves. Such service is like a broken box of alabaster whose perfume fills all the house of God with its fragrance.*[41]

Besides the indigenous nurses and hospital assistants, the work of the Bible women was invaluable to the missionaries. Bible women were required to take a five year course. We hear more and more about these women and they are often named in the reports. Thanribai, says Miss Coltart at Dhar, is a treasure and is the one on whom everyone depends. Miriambai has been a faithful helper and Bible woman, says a report from Mhow.

In 1915, three new fields were opened up at the request of the people themselves. At Bagli and Banswara, a grant of land was offered by the indigenous officials for the erection of hospitals and schools for women and girls. The third field was among the Balais.

Dr. Belle Chone Oliver was appointed to Banswara where Dr. McKellar had previously done itinerant work. Miss Catherine Campbell was appointed to do the evangelistic work. They were particularly hoping to reach the Bhils, the indigenous people. A government bungalow was put at their disposal and local people were employed at a fair wage to do the work on the new buildings. In the evening all the Bhils would gather at the bungalow where a short service was held.

Even the children helped. A report in *The Missionary Messenger*, "The School That is Different," tells us that the children were asked to gather stones for the building and, as they passed material up the ladder, assembly-line style, they were taught to count and to work in time to music whereby they learned lines of hymns.

The Women's Hospital in Hatpiplia in Bagli State was completed in October 1916. The land was a gift of the local officials at whose request the mission entered this field. Miss Ethel Glendinning opened a school for girls after the families who had moved away during the plague returned. The parents seemed quite pleased but became alarmed when they heard the missionaries were teaching the children Christian hymns and some of the parents stopped sending their children. Persuasion was to no avail. "No, you will make Christians of them," said the parents.

The Women's Christian College in Madras was opened in the summer of 1915. Anglican, Presbyterian, Methodist and Baptist churches in Britain, the United States and Canada had united in this new interdenominational effort. The WMS, at the council meeting in 1916, was asked to support the work. The hope was to open another college at Bombay in the future. If that happened the WMS would transfer its support since Bombay was the natural centre to which they would hope to send their students who wished to take up advanced work.

"Shall India Be Christ's?" was the question asked in an article in the August 1916 issue of *The Presbyterian Messenger* that told of the remarkable turning towards Christianity through an 1915 evangelistic campaign in South India. Plans were made for a similar campaign in North India in which the Central India Mission would share. Preliminary training brought amazing results. Christians were rising in a united evangelistic campaign for the winning of their country for Christ.

In 1918, the new year brought an unexpected gift. The Raj Bahadur Seth Sarupchand Huken Chand, recognizing the value of the teachings of Christianity and inspired by the work of the missionaries, gave $8,000 for the completion of the new Indore High School for girls including the erection of an assembly hall. It was decided to name the hall the Huken Chand Hall. The tablet sent out by Old St. Andrew's Church, Toronto, in memory of Miss Amelia Harris, first principal, was placed in the hallway of the new building as a reminder of the way "the Lord led the school from its small beginning in Neemuch to its new home in Indore." The school was opened on August 17, 1918.

By 1918, Miss Florence Clearihue in Kharua was asking permission for the mission to go ahead with plans to build a girls' school. She was pleased to report that the political agent who had visited Kharua felt that they did not have enough land so an additional three acres was given to them at a low lease.

The terrible influenza epidemic which had been world wide in its sweep did not miss India. Every mission station was visited taking a terrible toll on many of the local Christian helpers. With startling suddenness it took from the mission Miss Emmeline Smillie who had waited untiringly on the sick until two days before she died. There was also great fear of famine. Dr. Laura Moodie wrote that, on top of the scourge of influenza, the rains had failed for 12 months and there was no food for people or cattle. *The Times* of India said that the poor had eaten up all their food and were wandering from place to place in the hope of securing assistance. A report from Central India says,

> *The year's outlook over our field is touched with pathos, for sorrow and sadness have reigned; first plague, then influenza, now famine is at the door…we wonder how our young medical worker, Dr. Oliver, came through, for at one time with the dread epidemic of influenza raging around the whole district she stood alone. The city government dispensary was closed, only the mission hospital left, and that with only a hut for a dispensary and a ward off the missionary's house, and verandah for a hospital…*[42]

China

Miss Margaret McIntosh, senior missionary of the WMS in China, celebrated twenty-five years of service at the Honan mission station in December 1914. She was one of the first women missionaries to enter Honan while the people were still hostile and the danger from mobs very real. She was also among those missionaries who suffered terribly while escaping to the coast during the Boxer Rebellion of 1900.

What changes are seen in Honan today!, exclaims a 1915 report: Cities and towns were open to the gospel; an indigenous ministry had its own presbytery with kindergartens, schools, colleges and hospitals in several of the larger cities; Christians were ministered to in many other towns and villages. The WMS was represented at six centres by fifteen missionaries, not forgetting the equally important work of the missionary wives.

A class for the training of Bible women, the first of its kind, was held in January at Changte. Whereas, in the early years, the education of girls was unthinkable, in 1915 the Chinese government was beginning to recognize the value of education for women as well as for men.

By the fall of 1914, the new buildings for women's work in the city of Wei Hwei were ready for occupation. Celebrations were planned for October 15-17. As a prelude, the regular Sunday afternoon service was to be held on the 11th in one of the classrooms. The chapel was not to be used until the formal opening. However, the large numbers who attended the Sunday service made that plan impossible. Miss Margaret McIntosh, senior missionary, was the speaker at the service. While she spoke in the chapel, Miss Isabel McIntosh took the women who were more advanced in Bible study to her own room. Here, as they sat in a group,

> *…learning of the first Lord's Supper, by a beautiful coincidence they numbered just twelve, all believers. The thought of what they as witnesses for Christ may do in their Jerusalem touched their hearts.*[43]

Rosalind Goforth was guest speaker. In her address at the formal opening she spoke of the new building as one of the most ideal she had yet seen in China. Throughout the three days, visitors were numerous and the whole yard was alive with women of all classes and their children. The chapel was crowded at every service.

Evangelistic campaigns under the united auspices of the Anglican, Methodist, Baptist and Presbyterian missions, had been held in China in 1913 and 1914. The campaign workers in 1914 had been overwhelmed by the number of women signing up for Bible classes. They were determined to be better prepared this time. Intensive preparations were made before the campaign in the fall of 1915.

Miss Margaret McIntosh reported that the campaign was a huge success. Miss Gregg of the China Inland Mission, who had just finished an evangelistic campaign for women in different parts of the province, agreed to help with the campaign in Changte city. It was held in December, rather late in the season, but it turned out that the days were warm and the women came faithfully day after day. About 1,300 in all heard the gospel message. Miss Gregg attracted the women with her speaking.

In South China, Dr. Jessie MacBean reported from the Marion Barclay Hospital in Kong Moon to say that she was glad to hear about the appointment of a nurse for the hospital. A nurse, she said, was badly needed to look after the hospital and to train the indigenous nurses. She added that she hoped the society would be able to build a nurses' home because the present three nurses had to sleep in a little room without a window. They had to sleep, eat and sit in this room which staff frequently had to pass through to get to the operating room. Good news came in March 1915, giving permission to go ahead and build the nurses' home. A member of the WMS in Montreal had contributed $500 for the home. Dr. MacBean said they were delighted and felt grateful as she knew that because of the war, money was scarce at home and there were many pressing needs. But, she added, we really needed this building.

The 1916 annual report says that, with the present staff in Honan and Shanghai, it was impossible to maintain even the already established work, much less keep up with its continual growth. This would be even more impossible, the report said, if it were not for the assistance which the married women gave.

Dr. Jean Dow worked under impossible conditions at Changte. The new hospital was still in the future. Even much-needed equipment was lacking.

A report in *The Missionary Messenger* said Dr. Dow was carrying on her work without even a sterilizer. For twenty years, Dr. Dow was the sole woman physician at Changte. She devoted herself, without even a break for vacation, to her hospital and dispensary patients. Dr. Dow had informed the WMS that her beloved assistant, Dr. Ui, had died after a lengthy illness, leaving her bereft of a helper and a friend. She added that she really missed Dr. Ui very, very much, but was grateful for the years of fellowship they had had together. Dr. Chan, a schoolmate of Dr. Ui, had come to work at the hospital, Dr. Dow said, and was proving to be a good helper.

During the summer of 1916, a conference of missionaries from the various missions in North and South Honan was held at which plans for the "Five Years" Forward Movement were adopted. However, in 1917, China was devastated by floods. With 90,000 square miles of North China under water, it was one of the greatest deluges known in China since the beginning of the mission work there. The rain began to fall in June and continued in torrents throughout July. Some villages were completely destroyed and people saved themselves by climbing into trees or fleeing to higher ground. Much sickness and poverty were brought on due to the devastating floods. A special appeal was launched and the WMS opened a flood fund.

Dr. Jessie MacBean wrote in 1919 that they had had a terrible visitation of Spanish influenza. She also told of the urgent need for a maternity hospital and asked if the board could help. She said China had suffered so much from flood and famine that it was impossible to raise much money there.

Formosa

1914 marked the close of an old and the promise of a new era in the history of the girls' school in Tamsui, says a report from Formosa. The old school, built in 1907, had become unsafe and too small for the number of girls wishing to enter. New buildings had been promised but the war had delayed the plans. With great rejoicing the new school was formally opened on June l, 1916. Many important guests were in attendance, including the Civil Governor of Formosa and the acting Minister of Education. The Tamsui students proudly wore their new uniforms for the first time — light blue cotton waists and navy-blue cloth skirts. Also in attendance was Rev. William Campbell of the English Presbyterian Mission of South Formosa who had recently been granted a Doctor of Divinity by Knox College, Toronto and had been decorated the year before with The Fifth Order of the Rising Sun by his Imperial Majesty, the Emperor of Japan. His address was of particular interest since, having been a missionary on the island for over 40 years, he could compare the old and the new in girls' and women's education in Formosa.

He said he saw Formosa when girls' education was unknown, when girls were often named "Not Wanted" or merely "Girl," when they were cast out and uncared for. Later, girls were tolerated but were not yet considered able to learn anything. Gradually, he said, it was discovered that the girls could be taught and, what is more, were more useful if somewhat educated. Young men wanted wives who had some education. Now, he said, the time had even come when in many homes some sacrifice was made in order that daughters as well as sons might receive some education.

Reports in regard to evangelistic work in 1915 indicated that more direct personal work had been done among the women and children than in any previous year. Extreme parts of the field were visited and hundreds of women and girls gathered about the missionaries to listen and be taught for the first time. It wasn't only the bright young boys and girls who were interested in the gospel.

> *Often they are weary, middle-aged women, who never studied in their lives, who are in need of teaching... But such a task as it sometimes is!... One dear old woman in Tamsui, having only one eye and it rather dim at that, came trotting into Church one day...she told jubilantly how she had learned to read. She said, "I just learned one letter at a time and went around at my work saying, 'Lord, don't let me forget.'"* [44]

There were some disappointments in the work. Mission workers spent three weeks in the spring and fall of 1915 in the large city of Gilan. In this city of about 20,000, only two or three of the women attended the church services and they were too old to learn to read. They memorized a few hymns. There was a reason for the poor attendance. Almost all the women in the city had bound feet and seldom left their homes.

It was only after 1913 when the new hospital in Taihoku (Taipei) was opened that the WMS had a representative in the medical work of the mis-

Isabel Elliott's graduating class, Missionary Training Home

sion. Miss Isabel Elliott, a nurse from Canada, had organized the nursing department. By 1918, she had a staff of 10 girls, including two graduates of her first year's class.

Mrs. Bella Koa, daughter of George Leslie Mackay, trained a splendid staff of Bible women. The Bible women and the wives of the missionaries were given high praise in the reports. One worker says that the Canadian church should thank God every day for such Bible women as Peng-a-chim who was an inspiration to everyone. A missionary, in speaking about the work of the wives of missionaries, commented that the story of the work they do could fill a book and the wonder was how they could do such splendid work and manage their homes and families as well.

The Missionary Messenger in May 1916 reported that the Governor-General of Formosa had given friendly approval of the work of Christian missionaries. The previous spring Chinese evangelists had gone from place to place holding three-day meetings. The chapels were packed and everyone had nothing but praise for the "Jesus doctrine."

In addition to the regular work, two things stand out prominently, said Miss Mabel Clazie in the 1917 annual report. One is a series of special meetings for women held in the largest city church and the other is a special evangelistic campaign during the Government Industrial Exhibition. Since the exhibition was for the whole island, the English Presbyterian Mission of South Formosa united in this special evangelistic effort. The exhibition lasted five weeks and never before in the history of the mission had there been such an opportunity to spread the gospel. The people were formerly opposed to Christianity but now they were beginning to show interest and come out to services.

By 1919 the influence of the Japanese government was being felt and the opening up of mission day schools was becoming more difficult. The system of public school education was being promoted and it was up to the Christian church to adapt. The missionaries counted on the young girls who had gone to their schools to give leadership.

Korea

The Missionary Messenger of October 1915 reports that Miss Elizabeth McCully of the WMS (ED) had graciously given a large part of her furlough time to making known the Korean mission to the members of the western division. The editor of *The Missionary Messenger* says,

> *We will follow Miss McCully as she travels back to another term of service and to her beloved work at the Martha Wilson Memorial Institute, Song Chin, which she and her sister have mothered from its infancy...*[45]

The WMS executive was fortunate to have Dr. Kate McMillan from Korea visit on her way home to the Maritimes. She had, by this time, 14 years of experience in pioneer medical work. The hospital building in Song Chin, she reported, was being enlarged and was soon to be ready. When she began, she said, she had no building. Later she had a small local hut that was often so crowded work was difficult. The floor had to be used for an operating table and medicines used for dispensing were kept wrapped in paper. She had the assistance of two Korean doctors and a Canadian nurse, with four young girls in training.

The Severance Union Medical College Hospital and Nurses Training School in Seoul was an interdenominational college. The WMS(WD) had been asked to provide a nurse and $500 for maintenance. Miss Hughes was appointed, thus linking the WMS(WD) with other churches seeking to make Christianity a working force in Korea.

The Korean people, especially in the north, were beginning to show themselves particularly susceptible to the gospel message. In the northern district of Kanto, they were free from the restrictions that the Japanese government placed on the medical and educational work of the missionaries in Korea proper. The urgency of medical work in the north resulted in several donations that made it possible to proceed with a building at Yong Jung. The new building opened in 1918.

Miss Maud Rogers, writing from Song Chin, tells of one group of women that had organized a women's missionary society. The young pastor could not go among the women so the new Christians asked for a Bible woman. These women were poor but their collections, together with help from the central auxiliary at Song Chin, enabled them to keep a Bible woman. The Korean authorities, as well as many Koreans, were now opposed to the church, so there was considerable persecution.

A report from Miss McLellan at Hot Ryung tells that she and her Bible woman spend their days doing house to house preaching. It was difficult work. Miss McLellan was grateful for her Bible woman, Onhai, who was so enthusiastic that she needed no assistance in preaching. She marvelled at Onhai's zeal and knowledge and the boldness of her preaching.

Mrs. Barker sent a letter to the home society from a missionary society in Yong Jung. The letter said that their little society had been in existence for only about eight months and that there was another society about three miles from them. The two societies had united their contributions and chosen a Bible woman to work for the two groups. They were happy to inform their sisters in the Canadian missionary society that they now felt ready to take up the work in earnest.

In a letter published in *The Missionary Messenger* in 1918, written from Wonsan, we hear again about Grace Lee. Elizabeth McCulley writes that Grace Lee and her Bible woman, Tabitha Chong, are both with her organizing women's missionary societies. She says she is fond of Tabitha, and can depend upon her judgment. She adds that Grace has done a great deal of work translating the consitution and bylaws and helping plan mission studies.

In another letter from Miss Elizabeth McCully in the October issue written from Chong Chin, she described a trip where she, along with Grace Lee, had gone to teach classes in the north. The distance was only 34 miles but they travelled by cart at two miles an hour over terrible roads. It took two days to arrive at their destination.

By 1919 changes were taking place. Korea was passing through critical times to which, says a report in *The Missionary Messenger*, no reference could be made in the individual reports. The report goes on to say that they must wait until the more moderate party was able to put down the militarists who were ruling with an iron hand.

Eastern Division

The 40th annual meeting of the Woman's Missionary Society, Eastern Division was held in the fall of 1916. Even with the strain of the war, the society had, when their books closed, met all the responsibilities called for in their estimates. In response to the call of the Foreign Mission Committee to place women's work in Trinidad on a more equal basis with that of men's work, the society had decided to take a step in that direction as a tribute to Mrs. Sarah Morton's work among girls in Trinidad. Mrs. Morton had gathered girls in her home and taught them side by side with her own little daughter. From this had grown the girls' high school and dormitory, established first in Princestown and then in San Fernando. The new home built by the WMS(ED) was called the Sarah Morton Dormitory. In 1916, Mrs. Morton wrote, *John Morton of Trinidad*, telling the story of their work in Trinidad.

Mrs. W.G. Wilson of Moose Jaw attended the 43rd annual meeting of the WMS(ED). She gave her impressions in *The Missionary Messenger* of December 1919. She said,

> *Unlike our Division, their work is not confined to work for women and children, nor do they disburse their own money; but they work entirely under the Boards of the Church.*[46]

Mrs. Wilson further reported that attendance at the meeting was the largest in the history of the WMS(ED) and their offerings the greatest. They unanimously decided to raise as a peace offering the sum of $50,000, one tenth of the total asked by their synod for the Forward Movement.

Chapter

8

After the War

Changing Times for Women

The Changing Status of Women in the Foreign Fields

Janet T. MacGillivray, who became president of the society in 1919, was editor of the new study book *The Planting of the Faith*, written in 1921. In her foreword she says that, although it was only seven years since the publication of *The Story of our Missions*,

> *...momentous events have occurred in world history which have hastened the need of a second volume of our story... Missionaries reaching these lands today find themselves in the heart of a great renaissance, and in the forefront of the new movements is the problem of the place of its womanhood.*[1]

The object of this book, MacGillivray says, is to show the results of our missionaries' intensive work and its relation to these new movements and changes.

Dr. Margaret McKellar, who served as a missionary doctor in India from 1890 to 1931, wrote the chapter on Central India. In "Present Position of Indian Women," she says,

> *Much has been written about the new status of women in non-Christian lands, and for every indication of improvement we give God thanks.*

> *In India there are small communities who encourage their women to enter higher education... It is from among such women that a few, from time to time, have appeared in mixed public audiences...and have attended Women's Conferences in Europe.*

She adds,

> *In a remarkably efficient manner they have voiced sentiments similar to those of the best aggressive, modern women of Western Nations, in favour of equal rights, opportunities and privileges with men, in home and state affairs.*[2]

In spite of these changes, Dr. McKellar said, women in the villages still did most of the hard work in the fields, and there were millions of women who were still shut up in women's quarters. If some of them did go out, they had to wear shroudlike burquas with small slits in the cloth for the eyes. India would not advance, said Dr. McKellar, until women were emancipated. The key to India's advance, she said, *hangs at the zenana door.*

Dr. McKellar quotes an "enlightened Indian gentleman" in his address "Importance of Women's Education."

> *Education is essentially a question of social reform...and in education I would give first place to education of girls. The education of a single girl means the uplifting of a whole family in a larger sense than the education of a single man.*[3]

Women's suffrage had not yet come to India. In a rather astute application of scripture to women's plight, Dr. McKellar comments that

> *...it is given to us 'to preach deliverance to the captives and the opening of prisons to them that are bound'.*[4]

These early missionaries were not the only ones to realize that women's lives were being changed in India, China and other countries.

Ruth Compton Brouwer tells us in *New Women for God* that women missionaries were much praised by contemporary social reformers in India and the west. Some historians have argued, she said, that the training and example the missionaries provided were the most important factors behind the revolutionary changes in Indian women's lives in the late nineteenth and early twentieth centuries. She quotes L.S.S. O'Malley, from his *Modern India and the West*, published in 1941,

> *It would...be difficult to exaggerate the part played by Christian missions in the emancipation of Indian women... Christian missionaries, in the face of apathy and open hostility, steadily and patiently pursued their self-appointed task of emancipation and equipped Indian women for the responsibilities which they to-day are undertaking.*[5]

Ruth Compton Brouwer cautions against giving all the credit to the work of the women missionaries. There were, she says, other forces at work, but adds,

> *...it is probably true that women missionaries were the most accessible and directly helpful mentors for many of the thousands of Indian girls and women who forsook centuries of tradition during the late nineteenth and early twentieth centuries to obtain a formal education and enter professional life....mission medical schools laid the foundation for medical education for women, and for many years Christians were significantly over represented in the population of Indian women doctors.*[6]

William Ernest Hocking, in his book entitled *Re-Thinking Missions* published in 1932, in a chapter entitled "Women's Interests and Activities," says,

> *In this forward movement of eastern women, Christian missions have played a significant role, a fact admitted without reserve by leaders of the Orient like Dr. Muthulakshmi Reddi, who repeatedly voices the feeling that "the women of Asia have been placed under a deep debt of gratitude to the missionary agencies for their valuable contribution to the educational uplift of Indian women."*[7]

Women of the east were gaining in a single decade what it took western society over a thousand years to accord its women, says an article in *The Missionary Messenger* in January 1916. In China and Japan, as in India, women were being released from the suffocating seclusion that had been forced on them and entering public life. Japanese wives had stopped blacking their teeth, formerly a witness that they no longer wished to appear beautiful to other men. The Anti-Mother-In-Law Society was formed in an attempt to suppress the power of the mother-in-law in the home. The Anti-Footbinding Society, led the way to the organization of Chinese women who walked for miles to get to women's conferences. Christians were unbinding or refusing to bind their little girls' feet and were targets for criticism and sneers. The Japanese authorities, after trying for years to persuade parents to stop this abuse, finally gave orders that feet should not be bound and those already bound should be unbound.

The Japanese Presbyterian Church, at their 1920 General Assembly, decided that men and women were equally eligible for both the eldership and the ministry. Caroline Macdonald, known as the White Angel of Tokyo for her work among prisoners and their families, was among the first women to be ordained as elders in the Japanese Church. Seven women were ordained — all Japanese except for Caroline.

The Changing Status of Women in Canada

In 1917, British Columbia, Alberta, Saskatchewan, Manitoba and Ontario extended the provincial and municipal franchise to women on the same terms as to men. In the four western provinces the women were given the right to be elected as well as to vote.

In an article in *The Missionary Messenger* of July 1920 on "Canadian Christian Citizenship," Mrs. Ella Mutchmor Thorburn of Ottawa, a faithful member in the WMS and active in many fields, had this to say,

> *Political parties, and we have four to reckon with now, are on the look-out for leaders to organize women, politically. Their eyes naturally turn to women who are leaders in church work, whose experience will be helpful and whose church connection might not be considered a drawback. Women are no longer merely an influence — women voters are now a power.*[8]

At the annual general meeting of the WMS held in 1919 one of the resolutions asked that, as a body of enfranchised Christian women, every delegate urge women to have their names placed on the voters' list at the earliest possible date to be ready for the approaching referendum. Mrs. I. C. Sharp, president of the Quebec Provincial Society, at their 1922 annual meeting said that the denial of voting privileges for women in Quebec was an insult, especially when women in the other provinces had already be given the vote. She said that the denial of voting privileges for women in Quebec was an insult, especially when women in other provinces had already been given the vote.

The women in the WMS, along with many other women, believed that the war had changed everything. *The world will never be the same again for women*, states an article in *The Missionary Messenger* of January 1919. The editorial in the January 1920 issue begins,

> *With all the force of a new idea there has suddenly come to us the realization that we are not only entering a New Year, but that we are living in a new world.*[9]

The Missionary Messenger, in the years after the war, had several articles with titles like "The Challenge of the New World Order to Christian Women," and "The New Woman in the Orient and Woman's Place in the World."

The 1919 study book, *Women Workers of the Orient*, by Margaret Burton, was considered most timely. It appeared when the women of the world were being drawn together as never before in a great fellowship of toil and suffering. An article by this same Margaret Burton, "Women and the New World Order," appeared in *The Missionary Messenger* of November 1919.

The interdenominational links, particularly with the United States, certainly gave the women in the Women's Missionary Society food for thought. In 1920, the magazine printed extracts from an address given by Mrs. E. C. Cronk of Richmond, Virginia to the Conference of Foreign Mission Boards. In her address, "The Challenge of the New World Order to Christian Women," Mrs. Cronk frankly states that

> *...the attitude of some of the Boards of the Church to the women's work has been one of suspicious watchfulness because of an ever-present fearful uncertainty as to the next move of the feminine contingent, mingled with judicious courtesy because of the ever-present need for the funds which have steadily poured in from the Women's Societies, no matter how other agencies have flared and faded.*[10]

One section of a report on the world conference and the North America conference printed in the March 1920 issue of *The Missionary Messenger* ended on this interesting note,

> *Much more we could tell but we close this section with a reference to the devotional exercises and to the reading, in one case, of Romans 12, substituting the word woman for that of man. It was most impressive and put a new meaning into it for all.*[11]

Later, the same report noted that the question had come up whether the women's board and the general board of a denomination should be amalgamated. A Dr. Corey had opened the discussion by saying that he was never able to see any valid reason why women should not be represented on all the boards of the church since they numbered 63 per cent of the membership, and were naturally as intelligent as the 37 per cent, and just as self-sacrificing. Mrs. Lucy Peabody, a Northern Baptist, spoke of women's previous condition of servitude, and affirmed that women had to develop their voices, men had to rest theirs. She suggested that this begin with the church and that there be both men and women pastors, both men and women on boards of deacons, and so on. Miss Hodge, of the Presbyterian board, thought the ideal would be one board with men and women working together as individuals, chosen because of special qualities.

The question of what happened to the resolution that went to the 1918 General Assembly of the Presbyterian Church in Canada from the WMS asking for representation on the different boards of the church had still gone unanswered. The committee appointed by the 1918 General Assembly had come back in 1919, asking for clarification and were told by that General Assembly to meet with the appropriate boards and with the WMS. The

General Assembly in 1920 received the next report from the committee, which began with this comment,

Not being seized with the greatness of the task assigned your Committee and the infrequency of some of the Board Meetings, the duties were not commenced early enough in the year to enable us to have sufficient communication with the various Boards to admit of reaching conclusions that would be satisfactory to all concerned...[12]

The committee ended by craving the Assembly's indulgence and asking for more time. After two years they had done nothing.

An address by Mrs. Lucy Peabody before the National Laymen's Conference of the Inter-Church World Movement in Pittsburg, Pennsylvania, was reprinted in the April 1920 issue of *The Missionary Messenger*. Mrs. Peabody begins,

Our Lord Jesus Christ lifted up women as no other great religious teacher and founder has done. But for a long time the Church overlooked the powers of women... I am very glad that the Inter-Church Movement has recognized women's activities, and back of that, women's part in the Church... We have listened to the very many discussions of woman's place in the world. I think if we could lay them all aside and...point out what God meant when He created woman...it would settle a great many discussions... They were given the first message of the resurrection of the Lord Jesus Christ. They were there to receive it, and when He said, 'Go, tell my disciples,' it didn't take a theological education for them to go and tell that Jesus had risen from the dead.

Mrs. Peabody also mentions Priscilla,

...who served on the faculty of the first theological seminary.[13]

It was not just in the United States that women were speaking out. On January 26-27, 1921, Toronto's first Interdenominational Conference on Foreign Missions was held at Convocation Hall of Wycliffe College. A Miss Cartwright spoke on "The New Place of Women in the World." She stressed, as did Mrs. Peabody at the conference in Pittsburg, the equality of women and men in creation and named women in the Old Testament who wielded great influence. She pointed out that Jesus *dealt exactly alike with both man and woman.*[14]

In the Presbyterian Church in Canada the question of the place of women in the church had been frequently discussed. It had come up as early as the second General Assembly in 1876. The *British American Presbyterian* at the time advocated their admission to *such subordinate offices as they can fill with advantage.*[15] Theological education for women had been advocated by Principal D. H. MacVicar of Presbyterian College, Montreal, and by others for many years. In the early 1900s, St. Andrew's College, Saskatoon and Knox College, Toronto were graduating women students with distinction. During the war years, deaconesses were employed by the Home Mission Board to minister on mission fields in the west.Women missionaries overseas were certainly ministers of the word, if not of the sacraments.

The concrete issue of the representation of deaconesses and other trained workers in the church courts came before the Assembly in 1922 in an overture from the Presbytery of Regina. The General Assembly appointed a committee to report to the next General Assembly issuing, at the same time, this paternalistic statement,

> *There is no evidence of a widespread demand for the ordination of women throughout the membership of our church... In view of the variety, the intimacy, the gravity and the burdensome nature of the work of ministry on the one side, and in view of limitations, necessarily involved in the fact of sex on the other, the Assembly is not prepared to direct that women be ordained to the office of ministry.*[16]

In 1923, a new overture on the question of the ordination of women to the ministry came from the Presbytery of Saskatoon. Both overtures, along with recommendations from the committee struck to deal with the 1922 overture, were sent down to presbyteries by the 1923 General Assembly instructing them to explore the whole question of how best to bring to bear on church work "the viewpoint of women."

Thirty-three presbyteries responded to the questionnaire sent down by the General Assembly. Seven approved the ordination of women; six approved in special circumstances and six disapproved. The majority favoured postponement of the question *owing to the transition through which the Church is passing.*[17] When the question was raised again at the 1924 General Assembly the issue was again deferred "in view of the present situation in church life."

John T. McNeill, Professor in Church History at Knox College at the time, comments in his book *The Presbyterian Church in Canada, 1875-1925*, that,

> *Trained women are seeking, in the Church, opportunity not rank. Many of them are strongly of* (the) *opinion that they could do better service if admitted to committees of presbytery and to meetings of sessions... The demand for the admission of women to the ministry seems to have come largely from men... The question of their admission to the courts as constituent members is distinct from that*

of their admission to the order of the ministry; though it may be looked upon by many as a step in that direction.

To back up his words, Dr. McNeill quotes from an address given by the president of the WMS, Mrs. Janet MacGillivray, which, he claims, represents the views of many women on the subject.

Does it not seem a paradox that it should be the Church (we speak of our own) into which she (woman) has put her best work and thought, where the seeds of training for service were first sown, which should be the last to let down the bars? Is there a danger of so separating the other spheres of life from the Church that the best of our young womanhood, brought up in the atmosphere of the Church, now prepared and fitted for service in other walks of life, will grow away from active interest in the Church? We do not refer to the missionary as such, but to the woman in the pew. We are not pleading for women to enter the pulpit (though the public press headlines would understand it so). Our women are conservative on that point, but where the need arises and she is academically prepared, and is actually doing the Church's work under the appointment of the Assembly's boards, why should recognition be withheld in the courts of the Church? Has the day not come also when the relationship of the Women's Board of the WMS to the Assembly's Mission boards should be cooperative rather than auxiliary.[18]

After Mrs. MacGillivray's words about the society's conservatism in the above quote there follows a big "but":

...but where the need arises and she is academically prepared, and is actually doing the Church's work under the appointment of the Assembly's boards, why should recognition be withheld in the courts of the Church?

This does not sound like a woman opposed to the ordination of women. We certainly cannot conclude that Mrs. MacGillivray, and probably many other women in the WMS, even at this early date, believed that most women were simply seeking "opportunity, not rank." We have seen how, in the early 1920s, women in the WMS were fired up with the challenge of the New World Order for Women. However, they had other priorities within their society that had been ignored for years. The women in the WMS had seen how their resolution to General Assembly requesting representation on the boards of the Church had not been taken seriously or considered important enough to merit time or effort. This did not go unnoticed. In an earlier presidential address to council in 1922, Mrs. MacGillivray had this to say,

The request that went to the Assembly four years ago for the

Janet MacGillivray

> *representation on those Assembly Boards, where our work was affected, has not yet been answered... It is from no spirit of aggressiveness as individual women that we have sought such favors, but that the WMS of our Church may more intelligently relate the work the Assembly Boards have entrusted to us, to the work as a whole.*[19]

The quotation Professor McNeill used in his book is taken from a long address given by Janet MacGillivray on "The Women of the Church, 1864-1924," at the Jubilee Celebrations of the WMS in 1924. Mrs. MacGillivray uses some strong language in this address. She chastises the church for lagging behind the rest of society. As noted, she says,

> *Does it not seem a paradox that it should be the Church (we speak of our own) into which she (woman) has put her best work and thought, where the seeds of training for service were first sown, which should be the last to let down the bars?*[20]

This leader and representative of the Women's Missionary Society, Janet MacGillivray, who, after all, did have her master's degree, says, in the same address, in another part not quoted by Dr. McNeill, that it had taken many years,

> *...for woman to gain even the privilege of education. Given an education what might not she attain! "By stealth," we are told, "a few*

> *with some friendly help had managed to climb over and eat the fruit of the Tree of Knowledge, but the wall still held."*

She adds,

> *What a debt we owe to those pioneer women who struggled for equal rights… It took the courage of extremists to break down the prejudice of man-thought, but it broke, and woman, frail and tender, considered solely a hot-house plant, came at last out into God's open sunshine of life to be given a common chance with man.*[21]

Mrs. MacGillivray, in her address, had probably quite rightly judged the temperature of the society to be conservative on the question of the ordination of women. But in her address, she gets back to the issue that really concerns the WMS.

> *Has the day not come also when the relationship of the Women's Board of the WMS to the Assembly's Mission Boards should be co-operative rather than auxiliary?*[22]

Later she comments on the change and growth of the society.

> *In the beginning our gifts of money were administered wholly by the Board to whom we were auxiliary.*

Then, hearkening back to a particularly meek and humiliating statement made in the fifth annual report of the WFMS, she adds,

> *I doubt if the Society would be willing to-day to subscribe to the following which occurs in the Annual Report of 1881*

She quotes from that report:

> *We are happily free from much responsibility which would be unavoidable in an independent organization. There is nothing to do which ought to bring us before the public, or which will interfere with the priceless possession of a meek and quiet spirit; no selecting or superintending of missionaries; no puzzling questions to settle; but the simple duty of raising money sufficient to meet certain expenses for which we have become responsible.*[23]

In her research for her article, Mrs. MacGillivray must have found it shocking to read the above quotation from 1881 and frustrating to know that forty-three years later the society, with a membership of close to 100,000 and a budget of $414,000, was still auxiliary to the mission boards of the church.

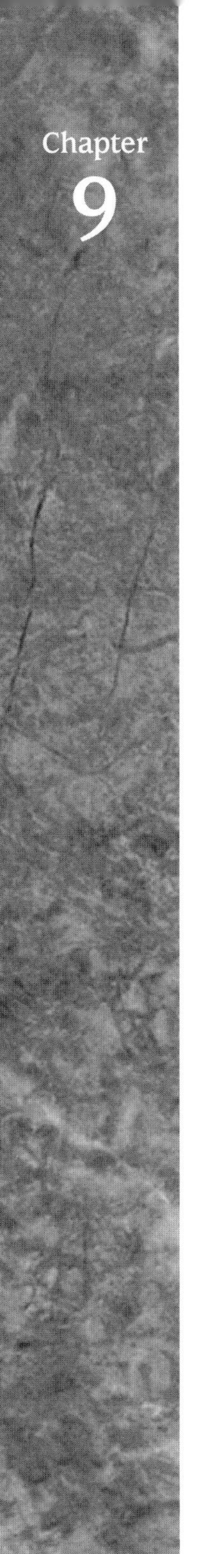

The Flourishing

1918-1925

The Great Inter-Church Movement

The editorial in the September 1919 issue of *The Missionary Messenger* begins with these words,

> *The great Inter-Church Movement which is gradually taking on more definite and complete form will be one of the greatest movements in the history of Church-life and work on the continent of North America.*[1]

The November issue of the magazine picks up the same theme,

> *The Forward Movement has caught the imagination of our women, so also has the great Inter-Church Movements into which the Forward Movements of the various churches have been coordinated, and to-day in Canada myriads of women of all the leading Protestant Communions are thinking — Forward.*[2]

On Sunday, October 5, 1919, the Inter-Church Movement was inaugurated by the reading of a manifesto in every Protestant church in Canada. The appeal and the challenge was for each and every member of the churches to take part in the unparalleled opportunity of service that had come to the Christian churches.

In this post-war period, the Forward Movement which had merged into the great Inter-Church Movement, had gripped the imaginations of the women of the Women's Missionary Society. The new age of inter-church co-operation had dawned and the WMS was anxious to be part of it. The Inter-Church Movement was welcomed by the society.

A national Inter-Church Forward Movement convention took place at Massey Hall, Toronto, November 24-25, 1919. Anglicans, Methodists, Baptists, Congregationalists and Presbyterians appeared together officially to unite in a campaign which covered every phase of ecclesiastical and evangelical activity in Canada and in lands beyond the seas. It was the first in a series of Inter-Church Forward Movement conventions which were to be held from the Atlantic to the Pacific. Long before the opening, Massey Hall was filled and every inch of standing room was taken. Many had to be turned away. Representatives of the five Protestant churches were on the platform, along with members of the boards of their Women's Missionary Societies that had been linked with the movement since its inception. Behind them was the mass choir and above them a banner with the words, "Speak Unto the People That They Go Forward."

Dr. Alfred Gandier of The Presbyterian Church in Canada briefly outlined the purpose of the movement, which, he said,

> *...was not a movement for church union — not a merger as the name implied. It was an Inter-Church Movement, which meant that each church loyal to its own traditions, true to its own teaching, following its own forms of worship and methods of work, unites with other churches to arouse the nation by united effort to fulfil the mission of Jesus Christ on earth. To each communion the same call had come, a call to penitence, to prayer, to personal consecration, to a new sense of stewardship and to a share in the great peace Thank-offering of twelve million dollars. What an end to have in view. What a purpose on which to unite!*[3]

Events were moving quickly. The committee that was working out plans for the Federation of the Women's Mission Boards of Canada was arranging to have a united prayer service under the auspices of the Women's Missionary Societies throughout the Dominion. This service would take the place of the annual prayer service which the Presbyterian WMS had held during the first week of each new year. Friday, January 9, 1920, was to see the inauguration of the first Dominion-wide interdenominational Women's Day of Prayer.

Wider, still wider was the circle to grow. In January 1921 an invitation came from the Women's Federated Boards of North America to unite with them in a national interdenominational Day of Prayer on March 3. This so commended itself to the WMS executive that they decided to accept.

After the war years, with the impetus of the Forward Movement, the WMS flourished. Their work had grown to such proportions that it was decided to secure the services of another paid worker with the recommendation that there be a salaried treasurer and a bookkeeper. The low cost of administration was due to the fact that the work of all secretaries of the executive board was voluntary. In five years, 1916 to 1921, membership had risen from 59,018 to 80,302, and the society's income from $179,843 to $451,484 for the western division alone. A surprise "even to ourselves," they said. *The Missionary Messenger* had a circulation of 40,900.

New things were happening in the WMS. The idea of having a WMS Sunday had been passed at council in 1919. It was decided it was time to make it an annual event for the whole church. A recommendation went to General Assembly asking that one Sunday in the year be appointed for the presentation of the society's work. The third Sunday in September was selected.

With the inception of the general board of the church in 1920, the WMS was given representation on that board. Their request for representation on other boards, specifically the Home and Foreign Mission Boards, had not yet been granted.

In 1921, an addition was made to the WMS constitution that any groups that took up regular mission study and contributed to the WMS funds would be recognized as a branch of the society. This meant that CGIT groups and Sunday school classes could have a connection with the mission work of the church which the Mission Bands already had. Something new! In 1921, a young people's page was added to each issue of *The Missionary Messenger*.

In 1921, a Canadian School of Missions was established. It was the first of its kind in Canada. The inaugural meeting was held in Convocation Hall of Wycliffe College in Toronto on November 8th.

It was also in 1921 that the Board of Home Missions and Social Service approached the WMS for the second time on the subject of social service. The matter was considered sympathetically by the executive board, and the general council in 1922 made the decision to organize a Social Service Department.

The membership of the WMS now stood at 92,058. This number included WMS auxiliaries, Young Women's Auxiliaries, affiliated CGIT groups and Home Helpers. The society had two objectives in view for the diamond jubilee celebration in 1924: 100,000 members and 45,000 subscribers to *The Missionary Messenger*.

Mrs. Emily Steele died on February 24, 1923. She had been president of the Woman's Foreign Missionary Society from 1911 to 1914 and of the Women's Missionary Society, Western Division, from the time of amalgamation in 1914 to 1920. A service in her memory was held on March 1, 1923 in Old St. Andrew's Church, Toronto. She was deeply loved and the April issue of the magazine was full of memorials to her.

At the annual meeting in 1923, the president, Mrs. Janet MacGillivray, addressed the council. She announced that the executive board would be inaugurating the new plan that had been agreed upon at the general council meeting in 1922 that, thereafter, a meeting of the full board would be held only every second year. She said,

> *With a conservatism true to our history, the Society hesitated long before making the change...but force of circumstances, largely financial, caused us to try out such a plan.*

Mrs. MacGillivray may have had the church union debate in mind when she ended her address,

> *The women of our church stand banded together from ocean to ocean. May our earnest prayer be that this unity be preserved unbroken and this coming year be one of preparation to worthily offer our songs and prayers of thanksgiving at the approaching Jubilee of our WMS...*[4]

At the annual meeting the deficits of the home and foreign mission boards were reported and the WMS decided to assist in the support of three home mission fields and the partial payment of the salary of Dr. Pringle of the Pacific Coast Mission to the amount of $1,500. It was at this same meeting that a motion of the finance committee was adopted that the expenses of delegates attending the WMS board meetings be met by the society, including tickets, berths, and meals, en route. Previously, members had paid their own way.

In June 1923, *The Missionary Messenger* announced that the WMS was sending out twelve missionaries to the foreign field, the largest number in the history of the society. Eight would be going to fill vacancies and four to prevent further vacancies through a breakdown in health by overwork.

Among those leaving for foreign fields was Dr. Victoria Chung, the first Chinese woman from Canada whose training was made possible by the WMS. Dr. Chung's outstanding scholarship and pleasing personality had won for her the coveted position of intern in one of the largest hospitals in Canada. She was appointed to South China. In her presidential address to members of the board Mrs. MacGillivray says,

> *What a joy to Dr. MacBean will be the coming of Dr. Chung, our first Chinese young woman carrying her Canadian degree, splendidly fitted as a missionary doctor to join our Council in South China, an example of China's hope fulfilled of leadership from among her own people, in line too with Dr. Cheng's illuminating message as President of the National Christian Church that the church of China must be left free, gradually to become an independent, self-supporting, self-propagating church free to develop according to those physiological and psychological characteristics of her people.*[5]

The WMS had received, from Mr. J. K. Macdonald, a memorial gift and Victory Bonds of $12,000 plus accrued interest to build and equip a girls school in Gwalior, India, in memory of his daughter, Miss Helen Macdonald who, for so many years and up to her death, was the beloved treasurer of the WMS. This gift was held, with Mr. Macdonald's consent, until such time as the development of the work justified the erection of the school.

Ringing in the Jubilee

The approach of the diamond jubilee of the society in 1924 brought forth a significant proposal which was eagerly endorsed by the board. The proposal was that this great event be commemorated by publishing a short history of the three societies up to and including the time of amalgamation. *Our Jubilee Story* was published in 1924. It was edited by Miss Elizabeth Laing, the society's historian. Miss Laing said in her foreword that the intention had been to write the history of the three societies after the amalgamation in 1914 but the war had interfered with that plan. It was entirely appropriate that the story be told at the time of the 60th anniversary, the diamond jubilee; hence *Our Jubilee Story!*

The diamond jubilee of the Women's Missionary Society, Western Division was celebrated at the biennial meeting of the general council held in Erskine Church, Montreal, May 27-30, 1924, with the president, Mrs. MacGillivray, presiding. There were 400 women in attendance from east to west in Canada with representatives from India, Africa, China and Korea. A communion service was held on Tuesday morning, conducted by Rev. George Hanson, minister of the host church.

Tuesday afternoon was devoted to jubilee celebrations. Mrs. MacGillivray gave an address on "The Women of the Church 1864 to 1924." "Recollections of Pioneer Days" were given by pioneer women who were then presented with a copy of *Our Jubilee Story* and an old-fashioned bouquet of flowers by their granddaughters.

Gold long-service medals were presented by the president to missionaries who had served twenty-five years or more, a bar being added for each additional five years. Silver jubilee medals were presented by the vice-president, Mrs. Mary C. McKerroll, to workers who had given longest service in other departments. Honourable mention was made of the missionary wives who had served for twenty-five years or more. During the ceremony the audience stood while the president read out their names. At the request of the council, Mrs. MacGillivray, who had been editor for twenty-one years and president for five, was presented with a gold long-service medal.

At this annual meeting the council ratified a recommendation of the finance committee that the property which had been purchased at the time of amalgamation for the purpose of building a home for missionaries be sold, and the proceeds invested, allowing interest to accumulate until the society might be in a position to secure and maintain a home that would be of real service to missionaries.

The council delegates were asked to endorse a resolution that had come from the general board of the church and been passed by the executive of the WMS asking the WMS to send representatives to meet with the treasury board to discuss plans for

> *...a campaign in the autumn to raise the givings of the Church to the Budget, and that such representatives be authorised to state, that all Auxiliaries and Affiliated groups of the WMS will be notified that they have the support of the Council in responding to invitations to meet with others in the congregation in preparing and carrying out local campaigns.*

Everyone was not in agreement and, after much discussion an amendment was moved and seconded:

> *That whereas, the position of the WMS as an organization within the Church carries with it certain responsibilities for different work under certain specified Boards of our Church, and whereas, the request comes from a Board to which as a WMS we are not auxiliary — asking that as an organization the WMS assist in a work outside that for which it is organized.*
>
> *Therefore, we cannot, as an organization, accede to this request from the General Board of the Church. As members of the Church, we are aware of the necessity of an increased Church Budget, and would assure the General Board of our sympathy with them in the present difficult financial position. We have confidence in assuring the General Board of the Church that any appeal they may make to the membership of the Church on behalf of her general work, will*

> *find the WMS women ready to discharge their primary obligations as Church members, co-operating loyally in both service and gifts as their individual ability and judgment may make possible.*[6]

In spite of this lengthy, clear explanation of the WMS position within the church and with a conservatism true to their history, as Mrs. MacGillivray might say, the amendment was lost and the original motion carried. However, in granting the request of the general board, the women wanted it clearly understood that this campaign was solely to raise the budget of the church. It was not to be confused with the WMS estimates. The responsibility for the campaign lay with the congregations.

It was clear that there was some uneasiness about this decision and in reporting the estimates for 1925 it was reiterated that,

> *...in the administration of this budget, the Board has agreed that the income for 1925 must be applied only to the definite work for which the WMS is responsible.*[7]

This decision was not the only thing causing uneasiness. Church union was imminent and the members of the WMS were certainly not united in their loyalty to the cause. Henrietta Bundy, secretary of finance, in presenting the provincial budget allocations for 1925 says,

> *Conditions are not normal we know, but in spite of this, such confidence have we in the spirit that has characterized our women in the past, so assured are we of their loyalty to the budget they accepted, and to the work at home and abroad which it carries, that we have every reason to believe, when it comes to the final closing of the year all will be well.*[8]

Other resolutions made at this jubilee council meeting in 1924 included the following:

- that Miss MacMurchy, who has served for 32 years, be decorated with one of the jubilee gold medals.
- that we protest with all the strength of our mind and spirit against any backward step being taken in the cause of temperance.
- that the women of this council now in session do strongly protest against war as a solution of any of the world's problems...do hereby register ourselves as opposed to war in any form, and further, are resolved to do all in our power to promote peace and universal brotherhood.
- whereas the need of teaching Scripture in the mother tongue to the non-Anglo-Saxon pupils in our school homes would be in the best interest of the parental homes and of the cause of Jesus Christ, be it therefore resolved that this council authorize the board of the Women's Missionary Society to secure competent matrons, instructors or deaconesses to teach

the Bible in their mother tongue to Ukrainian and French pupils in our school homes.

- that we recommend to our auxiliaries that definite time be devoted to the study of social service problems; also that, as individual members, we hold ourselves ready to co-operate with our own social service workers in the community.
- that a more strict observance of the sabbath be practised by all members of the WMS and that they pledge themselves to attend church, and to bring their visitors with them. That we encourage every endeavor to get every child enrolled in Sunday school, and to promote Sunday services at summer resorts.
- that we, the Women's Missionary Society of the Presbyterian Church in Canada, feeling the Lord's Day Act as a safeguard of the Lord's Day Alliance, will, to the utmost of our ability, with prayer, influence and money, support this act.

The May 1924 issue of the magazine announced the single honour conferred upon Mrs. Ella Mutchmor Thorburn of Ottawa, in her appointment by the Dominion government as representative of the Canadian women at the British Empire Exposition.

Canada

The latest development in medical work in Canada was the hospital unit, one of the schemes of the Forward Movement. It was "just a comfortable little home" where a nurse and deaconess or two nurses could live and work together and, when necessary, take in and care for two or three patients.

The hospital unit at Francois Lake in the Cariboo district in British Columbia was opened in December 1919. Since there was no doctor available to minister to the patients at the hospital, the WMS was compelled to make a temporary appointment, and Dr. Maysil M. Williams was sent out for a year. This was the first time that the WMS had appointed a woman doctor to serve in a frontier post in Canada. Dr. Williams was a native of Beeton, Ontario, a 1921graduate of the University of Toronto. She had been an intern at the Women's College Hospital, Toronto, for a year and arrived at Francois Lake in 1922. She later reported how much she enjoyed the work.

Other hospital units were soon to be erected at Hearst, northern Ontario, at Cold Lake, Alberta and at Pine River, Manitoba. The hospital unit had gripped the imaginations of the people and many more requests were coming to the WMS. These units were a God-send to the mothers in particular, who could not otherwise have had any medical help at the birth of their children.

By 1919, the WMS had work at 23 centres, including eight hospitals, one hospital unit, one dispensary, one nurse at St. Columba House, Montreal, and work in connection with the Pacific Coast mission in British Columbia.

After the war, the auxiliary of Rosedale Presbyterian Church in Toronto decided to organize a Young People's Circle as a branch of their auxiliary. The circle planned to raise $1,000 for a nurse's salary as a gift to the Peace Thank-Offering Fund and as a war memorial to those on the honour roll of their church and to relatives of members of the circle who had laid down their lives during the Great War. They decided to change their objective to $5,000 for the establishment of a cottage hospital. They raised the money through musicales, bake sales, rummage sales and special offerings and also held sewing meetings to make layettes for the hospital. The board of the WMS recommended Matheson in northern Ontario as the site for the hospital. The dedication and formal opening of the Rosedale War Memorial Hospital in Matheson took place on September 14, 1922.

In August 1922, work was begun on a hospital building at Hearst in Northern Ontario. St. Paul's Hospital in Hearst was dedicated on June 1, 1923. It was a gift of St. Paul's Presbyterian Church, Ottawa and was a memorial to their fallen heroes. Through the generosity of a Hamilton woman, a nurses' home was built at Hearst. It was much needed and greatly appreciated.

From their share of the Forward Movement Memorial Fund, the WMS had fourteen centres of medical services in Canada by 1923.

This section cannot end without emphasizing the important part the nurses played in the story of hospital work in Canada. We recall the story of the first nurses sent by the Atlin Nurse Committee to the Yukon. Over the years their dedication and courage was repeated over and over again at hospitals and hospital units throughout the west and into northern Ontario.

> *When the history of this country comes to be written, historians will find woven into the lives of Canada's early pioneers the impress of other lives, and foremost among them will be that of the Christian nurse whose courage and faithfulness, tender, efficient skill and great sacrifice, were blended into one magnificent, heroic and patriotic service for God and country and humanity. All honor to such women, co-workers with the Great Physician...thousands of men, women and children have been helped, relieved, rescued from death and restored to their loved ones.*[9]

Of these nurses, we can only mention a few here: Elizabeth J. Bell of Teulon, Manitoba, a daughter of the manse who held the longest record in the home mission hospitals; Kate E. McTavish, of St. Andrew's Hospital, Atlin, British Columbia, who served over 14 years; Agnes Sorrell Forbes who

Annie B. Korzak

initiated the hospital work in Grande Prairie, Alberta; Agnes Baird, the first graduate nurse to enter the medical work in Grande Prairie; Jean Kellock, another daughter of the manse, who gave distinguished service in Atlin and Ethelbert, Manitoba; and Annie B. Korzak, the first Ukrainian nurse to serve under the WMS.

A tribute is paid to the nurses by Rev. John Jackson of Manitonas in an article on the "New Canadians in Northern Manitoba" in *The Missionary Messenger*, 1923.

> *And one cannot refrain from mentioning the fine work done by the nurses themselves, particularly by those in charge of the hospital units. In cases where the doctor cannot get up on account of bad roads, the nurse has to take the initiative and fill the place of both.*[10]

A new hospital was opened in Cold Lake, Alberta, in the winter of 1924. Forty-five miles from the nearest doctor, the responsibility fell on Miss Schmidt.

> *Because of the long distance from any doctor, Miss Schmidt, the matron nurse, does work that would otherwise be done by doctors. She is successfully treating minor cases of surgery, and a number of wounded in the saw mills and in the fish industry, and trappers from the North as well as settlers throughout the whole pioneer district come for treatment to the Hospital. But the Hospital is particularly a blessing to the women and children and a God-send to the whole community.*[11]

School homes were for the benefit of children living in small towns and rural districts where there was no high school and few students in the higher grades in the public school. Boys and girls from such places had to leave home and go into towns and cities to board in order to secure a secondary education.

A summary of work in *The Missionary Messenger*, May 1921, reports that the WMS now had work at eight centres with fourteen homes, six for girls, six for boys, and two for both. During 1920, four new homes had been opened: the Lucy M. Baker Home for girls in Prince Albert; a home for boys and one for girls in Battleford; a home for boys in Edmonton. The home at Prince Albert was purchased and equipped out of the WMS share of the Peace Thank-Offering. It was named after the "first lady missionary to the Northwest Indians," Lucy M. Baker. The Battleford Home was also purchased, renovated and equipped from the Peace Thank-Offering. The boys' home in Edmonton was a rented building and was equipped by the WMS.

Because of financial restraints, no new work was undertaken in 1922 except for work funded by the Forward Movement Memorial Fund or the Peace Thank-Offering. Eleven appeals from presbyteries for school homes were still unanswered.

In 1922, the outstanding event of the year was the opening of a new home for boys in Vegreville, Alberta, on the same block as the home for girls, the cost of which was met from the Peace Thank-Offering.

File Hills, Manitoba and Round Lake, Saskatchewan, represented two types of residential school buildings. One was government-owned and the other church-owned. The government was realizing, says a report, its responsibility in this matter and the hope was expressed that within a few years all buildings would be government owned and equipped, and the church, through the WMS, would only be responsible for the education and care of the Aboriginal children.[12]

The May 1923 issue of *The Missionary Messenger* announced that the residential schools were crowded almost beyond their capacity with many awaiting admission. The WMS now had 700 pupils under its care.

Rev. Dr. Hugh McKay, the beloved principal of Round Lake Boarding School, gives a glimpse of the life of Mrs. Jacob Bear in the January 1924 issue of the magazine.

> *For forty years she belonged to that large class of missionaries — the ministers' wives — who are missionaries without a salary. Her generosity was known far and wide, and, during the hard years when many of our Indians were suffering from lack of food, she would cut her last loaf in two lest her neighbors leave her door hungry.*[13]

Mrs. Bear was brought up in the home of a missionary. She married Jacob Bear from Cumberland House on the Saskatchewan River. She worked with her husband for the Hudson's Bay Company, and then for forty years for the Presbyterian Church. She died on October 22, 1923.

The Missionary Messenger, in reporting on Rev. Dr. Hugh McKay's retirement, takes the opportunity to tell of his long, faithful ministry. Mr. McKay graduated from Knox College, Toronto in 1877 and became a pioneer missionary on Manitoulin Island. Seven years later he offered himself to the Foreign Mission Committee for work among the northwest Indians. He went west in 1884 with Rev. George Flett, the veteran Aboriginal missionary. He travelled through Manitoba and into the very heart of Saskatchewan, finally reaching the Round Lake Reserve in the beautiful valley of the Qu'Appelle River where he started what has since come to be known as the Round Lake Mission.

Mr. McKay, in his farewell address, tells what it was like when he began his ministry. The condition of the Aboriginal people at that time was pitiable, he said. The building of the CPR had driven the buffalo and moose north, and game was scarce and food expensive. Added to this were long, severe winters which caused much sickness and suffering. Mr. McKay said he began by visiting the Aboriginal people in their tepees offering help and counselling. He gathered the children about him in the little three-roomed mission house which he had built and thus started Round Lake School. The people were suffering from lack of clothing so he appealed to the WMS and their response marked the beginning of their supply work. Mr. McKay taught the Aboriginal people farming and how to care for their cattle. Later the mission house was replaced by a log school and in 1887 a larger building was put up by Mr. McKay and Jacob Bear, his faithful assistant. In 1900 a church was built and paid for by the Aboriginal people. In 1920 a large modern well-equipped school building was erected.

After 40 years of ministry to the Aboriginal people, Mr. McKay retired. At his farewell service, Jacob Bear read John 14 in Cree and gave an address on "Avoiding Discouragements," proclaiming that, although they were losing Mr. McKay, they still had the church and the minister and the Bible; that heaven was awaiting them, and they would all meet again. The people at Round Lake did not forget to pay tribute to Mrs. McKay who had been a strong helper and wise counsellor throughout all the years.

The largest centres for Chinese mission work were in Victoria and Vancouver. The Chinese church with its Chinese minister in charge was the centre of activities in Victoria. Here Miss Cronkhite, assisted by Mrs. McQueen and Mrs. Louie, a young Chinese woman from South China, carried on the kindergarten work and classes during the week. The Chinese women of the mission in Victoria had formed themselves into the first Chinese WMS in Canada. The October issue of the magazine tells of a farewell party given to Dr. Victoria Chung by the Chinese WMS of Victoria before she left for South China.

It was at the request of the Women's Federated Boards of North America, in 1914, that Mrs. Elizabeth MacGillivray of Shanghai, China, was asked to begin a magazine for the children of China. It was called *Happy Childhood* and by 1924 had a circulation of 12,000. Mrs. MacGillivray's work as editor was entirely voluntary. This was the only paper of its kind for the Christian children of China, and was very popular in the Sunday schools of all Protestant denominations. Mrs. MacGillivray, however, was breaking down under the strain and needed a qualified assistant. She said that she could not put in another winter like the winter before since her eyes were failing her. In response to this appeal, the literature committee of the women's boards asked that Miss Edith MacGillivray, who was a recent graduate of the University of Toronto, be sent to Shanghai as assistant to her mother.

What Mrs. MacGillivray was doing in China, Mrs. Jean Mackay was doing in Central India. Mrs. Mackay had been in India since the late 1800s. She was an educator and founder of the girls' high school in Indore. She was also a writer and, says the editor of *The Missionary Messenger*,

> *...stands in the same relation to the little Indian children as does Mrs. Donald MacGillivray to the children of China, being the first to provide them with a S.S. paper. Six years ago there did not exist in all India a paper for children similar to our "Jewels," and Mrs. Mackay was appointed to supply this need among the children in the Hindu-speaking area, and "Jyoti Kiran" was the result. No charge can be made for it as the people are too poor... In this our Society has a share, giving $500 yearly.*[14]

India

Motor cars changed the lives of missionaries on the foreign field. The gift of a motor car to Dr. Elizabeth McMaster in India was much appreciated, saving much time in travel as well as conserving the strength of the missionaries. Dr. Margaret McKellar made an appeal for a sterilizer and a car.

> *Now that Hat Piplia Hospital has a medical woman from Canada and an A1 Nursing Superintendent, what is needed is an up-to-*

> *date sterilizer and a Ford! Fancy the waste of time and energy of such qualified women driving in 1923 in an ox-cart! Ox-carts go sometimes at the rate of 2 miles an hour, whereas a good Ford would cover the distance in a few minutes.*[15]

The Missionary Messenger had a special "birthday greetings" article on Dr. Margaret O'Hara who was 70 on April 11, 1925. A letter of congratulation from the president, Mrs. Janet MacGillivray, to Dr. Margaret O'Hara followed the article.

The article begins with her appointment and designation in 1891, followed by some excerpts from her diary telling of her arrival in India and the important events of those early years. In 1896, she speaks of the bitter opposition they had to face in their work. The owner of the house they were renting asked them to vacate his house by the evening at the latest. He did not want it to be used as a place where Christianity was to be taught. She also spoke of the problems with the caste system.

> *One evening a woman had a very sick child in her arms; my sympathies were all with the poor child, and I took her in my arms. At once a number of people fled from the dispensary, crying out: "The Miss Sahib has become a sweeper; she has touched a sweeper and is unclean!" There is no sadder sight than to see a number of sweeper children on Sabbath standing outside listening to our hymns. I often ask them to come in, and they shake their heads and say: "We are sweepers; we must not go where other people are." We have three Sunday Schools, to which 150 children come — wild, dirty and almost naked. I was very sorry I had nothing but nuts to give them for Christmas.*[16]

Dr. O'Hara tells of how she adopted a baby, the daughter of a Hindu woman. The mother had been doing coolie's work in the bungalow. Dr. O'Hara said she had pitied the little mite because the mother used to nurse it, then give it a large dose of opium and go on with her work. One day the mother asked her to take the baby. *I told her*, said Dr. O'Hara, *that if she came with a government statement I would take her.*

In 1924, the 13th and last General Assembly of the Presbyterian Church in India met at Wilson College in Bombay during Christmas week. It was not an ordinary Assembly. The great question to be discussed was church union. A year earlier, the Presbyterian Church had adopted a new constitution which was framed with the definite purpose of facilitating union with other evangelical churches. The Congregational churches in Western India had already agreed unanimously that they were ready to unite with the Presbyterian Church on the basis of the new constitution, and, for substance of doctrine, on its existing Confession of Faith which had been drawn up about twenty years before when the Presbyterian Church in India was formed.

The debate on union in the Assembly lasted about two days. The debate was vigorous but free from bitterness. When the final vote was taken, forty-seven members supported the committee's proposals and only seven opposed them. Later, when the Resolution of Union was being passed by a standing vote, all members stood, and thus made the action unanimous.

On Tuesday, December 30, the Presbyterian Church in India and the Union of Congregational Churches in Western India passed out of existence, and the United Church in India (North) came into being. A letter of congratulations was read from the South India United Church which was the first Church in India to "overcome the barriers of western sectarianism." *The Central Indian Torch*, from which this article in *The Missionary Messenger* is taken, records that,

> *This Union is a very significant event. Denominational differences which have been imported from the West mean little or nothing to the Christians of India. There has been in recent years among Indian Christians a growing impatience of such differences, and the Union is merely one visible sign that that impatience will certainly translate itself into action. May the United Church which has been formed be richly blessed of God, and do its part to fulfil the prayer of our Divine Master, "That they all may be one..."*[17]

China

The Chinese script had always been regarded as one of the most beautiful but most difficult ways of communicating thought. Missionaries, although mastering the old written forms themselves, devised various systems of simplified writing, but only the converts would consent to use it, and they often unwillingly, so great was their reverence for their ancient symbols. The government, stimulated by the example of the new missionary methods, devised a new script. One immediate result was an open Bible for Christians and masses alike. Newspapers adopted the easy writing and the possibility of an education was opened to millions to whom the venerated ideographs were a hopeless puzzle.

On December 16, 1919, one hundred and twenty Christian leaders, Chinese and foreigners, gathered in Shanghai at the invitation of the China

Continuation Committee, which acted in China as the agency of the Inter-Church World Movement. They launched the China for Christ movement. This was the Forward Movement of the Chinese Church. The conference decided the Forward Movement in China should be a Chinese movement. Its watchword was, "Christianity, the Hope of China."

Agnes Dickson writes about Crisis Days in China in *The Missionary Messenger*, July 1920. It was almost impossible, she said, to keep abreast of the political situation. There were two governments, one in the north and one in the south. Those in the south, claim that the north is trying to rule the country, wanting to place the government in the hands of the military clique, which would be departing from the constitution as laid down by the Republican Government. She also says that, before she went on furlough, they had witnessed some revolutions in their part of the country. Many of the Chinese had come to the missionaries bringing their children and valuables and asking the missionaries to care for them. Some even lived in the mission compound for protection. Where the fighting was severe, she said, many officials sent their wives and children to the mission compounds. Some men came too.

> *God placed a great opportunity at our very door for these women and children would not have come otherwise. As a result of the revolution in one part of the field many of the official class have come into Bible classes and some into the Church.*[18]

In the pages of the November 1920 issue of *The Missionary Messenger* an appeal came to all auxiliaries and Mission Bands urging them, through the channels of their own church, to do their part to aid in relieving the terrible famine conditions that existed in North China. The famine was severe, said a cable from the Presbytery of Honan. Millions of people were destitute and dying. Relief funding was urgently needed. The Canadian churches were asked to respond liberally "out of the abundance with which they were blessed."

Several reports of the famine appeared in the magazine over the next few months. The February *Honan Messenger* reported that on New Year's Eve

> *...snowflakes fell thick and fast. In one respect they were welcome for they have not a little to do with the promise of a good crop in the spring, but, at the same time, they made the workers sick at heart for they knew they would intensify the suffering. The cold weather lasted for nearly two weeks and every day people were discovered who had been frozen to death. They had parted with their wadded winter garments and bed quilts in order to procure money for food.*

At Wei Hwei missionaries even took the clothes from their own beds and sent them into poverty-stricken homes where there was great distress. Chinese helpers at Changte reported, on returning from their tours, that there was not a village where people were not found frozen to death each morning. The storm also interfered with famine relief operations by making the roads impassable and preventing the workers bringing the grain and the starving people together.[19]

During the early period of the famine, Dr. Jean Dow and Dr. Isabelle MacTavish of the Women's Hospital at Changte, planned special help for women by establishing a maternity department. Four hundred and eighty-nine women were cared for, receiving careful medical attention and nursing entirely free with a monthly grant for mother and child on their return home.

It soon became clear that many women could not come to the hospital. They lived too far away and travel was difficult. A plan was adopted to help women in their homes. The list of recipients was gradually enlarged until they were reaching about 4,000 mothers. They then decided to extend their help to widows who had no one to care for them, reaching approximately 3,800 widows. Toward the end of the famine they made a special distribution to helpless women, and even helpless men, over 55,000 people, costing $90,000. This report from the *Honan Messenger*, reprinted in *The Missionary Messenger* tells how

…at one place our Chinese inspector arrived just in time. As he approached a village he chanced to hear a faint cry in a lonely field. Some of the villagers came along at the same time and they found a little baby which had been thrown away. They guessed to whom the little thing might belong and took it to the hovel where these people lived. They found them starving and in desperate plight. When told of the relief we were granting their desperation gave place to joy and the mother wept over the babe that had been restored to her.[20]

Political conditions did not improve in South China during 1923. From all parts of the field word came of boat travel being discontinued because of the frequent attacks by pirates and the constant fear of bandits in villages and towns. All this greatly interfered with the work. Miss Isabel Leslie gives us a picture of the situation in Honan.

This year we are well guarded by soldiers who patrol the hills at night. As you will see by the papers China is at the present time in a very chaotic condition. Robber bands, or bandits as they are called,

> *loot and plunder at will. A favorite form of raising money seems to be by taking foreigners captive and holding them for ransom. There are several people here who have been in the hands of bandits. South Honan has suffered very much more than the North where we are.*[21]

The editorial in *The Missionary Messenger* in 1925 reports that the situation in South China was critical. Two missionaries resigned because of illness. Dr. Jessie MacBean and Dr. Victoria Chung were carrying on without a Canadian nurse. The hospital, meant to accommodate 22 women and an equal number of men had, during the flood an average of 60 women patients a day. From the Forward Movement money a new hospital was erected for the men, and the WMS then took over the other half of the Marian Barclay building, making it wholly a women's hospital.

Formosa

Formosa too, was celebrating its Jubilee. An audience of 1500 people, the largest gathering of Christians that had ever been held in Formosa, met together on June 5, 1923, in Tamsui where Dr. George L. Mackay had begun mission work and where, 50 years before, the first five converts had been baptized. There were addresses by two of the Formosan pastors who, as students in the early days, travelled from place to place with Dr. Mackay. The audience listened to descriptions of the days before the Japanese came, days when bandits were numerous, when there were no government schools offering education, when there were few good roads, no railroads, when foot-binding, opium smoking and gambling were carried on without restraint, where there were only a few Christians and those few suffered terrible persecution for their faith.

The meetings on the second and third days of the celebrations were held in Taihoku (Taipei). One of the highlights was the opening of a large new church in Mankah, a section of Taihoku city.

Japan

An entirely new field of work was undertaken in 1920 in Japan when the WMS board agreed to give an annual grant of $2,500 to the settlement work carried on by Miss Caroline Macdonald in Tokyo, thus linking up the work in Formosa and Korea with Japan itself.

Caroline Macdonald was featured often in the pages of *The Missionary Messenger*, either through her visits to the WMS council and board or through her articles. She was one of the missionaries at a luncheon at the semi-annual meeting of the Foreign Mission Board and members of the

WMS executive in 1920 where she expressed regret that the Canadian Presbyterian Church had no mission in Japan proper, adding that the Presbyterian Church in Canada did not know the history and struggle of the Protestant church in Japan. They only knew of Japanese militarism in Korea.

Miss Macdonald went to Japan in 1914 as national secretary of the YWCA.

> *Five years ago she was unconsciously thrust into work for men in prison resulting in a plan for the establishment of a constructive piece of settlement work in the heart of Tokyo's industrial centre where one million laborers dwell in vice and poverty with not even one missionary living among them.*

The Interchurch World Movement of the United States endorsed the project. Then Miss Macdonald said,

> *Anything that can be done by The Presbyterian Church in Canada will be appreciated by The Presbyterian Church in Japan.*[22]

In a letter from Miss Macdonald that appeared in *The Missionary Messenger* in 1921, she shared news of her election as an elder.

> *You and the ladies of the WMS will be interested to know that I was elected an elder of the Japanese Presbyterian Church two weeks ago tonight, and that last Sunday, with seven other women (all Japanese but myself) and several men, I was ordained. The Japanese Presbyterian Church decided at its last General Assembly in 1920 that henceforth, men and women were equally eligible for both the eldership and the ministry... The Japanese Presbyterian Church is a pioneer in this at least.*[23]

In 1923, when news of the terrible earthquake in Japan reached Canada, a report in *The Missionary Messenger* announced that word had come of the appalling disaster that had befallen Japan. *Our sympathy goes out in richest measure*, said the editor, to the Japanese people and to the missionaries in their great anxiety and loss. The members of the WMS were asked to join in prayer for the nation so grievously stricken, and for Caroline Macdonald in Tokyo in whose work they were particularly interested.

In Caroline Macdonald's article "The Japanese Disaster" in *The Missionary Messenger*, December 1923, she said she was homeless with temporary abode in the home of Miss Kaufman of the YWCA. She adds that she had wanted to move for some time but was moved without any volition on September 1st when the house was badly shattered by the earthquake. The stalwart young men who had been coming to Bible study moved her furniture out of her house which was menaced by fire. Practically the whole city was burning, she said, with the lower part completely wiped out.

> *Letters are coming from the prisoners I visit... I should be so grateful if the WMS would give me an added grant of $2,500 a year for two years at least... The church to which I belong is burnt; the school I taught in is burnt. I know you will do what you can. I have cabled friends in New York to see if they can help... You have done much for me the past three years... God has called me again, I believe to these added opportunities... This is a call from Macedonia...*[24]

A note appended to the article in the magazine informs the members of the WMS that $500 was sent in addition to the yearly grant of $2,500 and, although they could not double the grant as she had asked, there was a committee of gentlemen, outside the church, who had stood by her work, and had issued a public appeal through the press for funds.

A letter from Janet C. Coates, Tokyo, in the February 1924 issue of the magazine tells about the opening of the new Shin-rin-kan (Friendly-neighbour-house) which Miss Macdonald had been able to obtain from the Anglican Church. It was only the third day after Miss Macdonald had taken over the building, but already things were humming. During the day every available corner of the capacious premises had been occupied with women sewing quilts for distribution to the destitute. There were many special speakers at the ceremony, among them the busy pastor of the largest Presbyterian Church in Tokyo of which Miss Macdonald was an elder.

The Japanese government honoured Miss Macdonald by bestowing on her the Order of the Sacred Treasure, Sixth Class, for meritorious services. The editor of *The Missionary Messenger*, says,

> *Miss Macdonald is ranked among the ablest social service workers of Japan and her tireless energies directed towards the relief of unfortunate classes have won for her the sincere respect of all who know her. Immediately following the earthquake, she organized a settlement house which simultaneously provided remunerative employment for refugee women and produced large supplies of clothing and bedding for refugees whose property had been destroyed by the fire.*[25]

We would extend, says the editor, *our hearty congratulations to Miss Macdonald*. WMS assured her of their delight that she had been so signally and deservedly honoured.

Korea

In Korea, a dark background of revolution and unrest characterizes the reports of 1919. The Koreans, after many unhappy years of Japanese rule, made an attempt to gain independence. This affected the educational and evangelical work, although hospital work flourished as a direct result of the revolution.

By August 1919 conditions had intensified which led the WMS to send a resolution to the General Assembly expressing their sympathy for the Korean church in the current crisis and assuring the General Assembly of WMS support in any effort the Assembly might take towards improving the situation. The General Assembly adopted a resolution that recognized much that was commendable in the Japanese administration in Korea but protested against the methods employed by Japanese officials in dealing with unarmed and unresisting Koreans, and against the brutal treatment of prisoners and more especially against such treatment of women and children.

Leaders of the revolution were sought out and imprisoned by the hundreds. Grace Lee was teaching in the girls' school when the bloodless revolution broke out in March 1919 and, as an officer in the Women's Patriotic League, she was arrested and sent to prison. Grace was kept for seven months awaiting trial in an unheated prison. After a sentence of a year's imprisonment, appeal only brought six month's delay.[26] Two years later, in September 1921, Grace Lee was released from prison and though she still suffered from the effects of the long confinement, she was able to be at her post again as assistant teacher to Elizabeth and Louise McCully in the Martha Wilson Memorial Bible Institute, Wonsan. The work of the institute was greatly helped by the new buildings provided from Forward Movement funds.

Mary Tak, the WMS(ED)'s first indigenous nurse, was giving a demonstration on hygiene to a group of women assembled for Bible study, when she was arrested as an agitator. Suffering unspeakable indignity and physical torture in prison for long months, Elizabeth McCully said, she was *chastened, but not killed, cast down but not destroyed*. Miss McCully added that such nurses were multiplying in all the stations, but, as yet, they could not be spared from hospitals to take part in community service

> *...where child-welfare, preventive measures, duties of motherhood, laws of hygiene should be taught to women to whom such themes still appear as useless as they are mysterious.*[27]

The cry of the Korean Church was: "Become Christian; raise the standard of women; educate the children." Already in their Forward Movement plans they had prepared a chart and one of their WMS auxiliaries had promised ten per cent of a Bible woman's salary.

Women's missionary societies in Korea dated back to 1910. By the close of the decade, there were 125 societies, with about 50 more not yet fully organized. Once each year a synodical missionary meeting was held. In the collection for foreign missions in 1921 there were 31 wedding rings, three silver wedding ornaments and three new hair-ribbons (given by little girls).

The Women's Missionary Society, Western Division, contributed $500 in 1919 towards the model village which was to be built for the accommodation of medical and theological students and their wives. A grant of $3,000 was also made by them to the Martha Wilson Memorial Bible Institute at Wonsan.

Chapter 10

The Disruption

1925

The WMS and Church Union

The records of the Women's Missionary Society in the years before 1925 are strangely silent on the question of church union. Their silence does not mean that the society was unaware of what was happening in the church. Had they been told to keep quiet by those in authority over them as some have assumed? Did their auxiliary position to the mission boards of the church mean that they had no say at all in the future of their society? Their records tell a different story.

References to church union before 1925 are few and far between. A reference is made to union churches in the WMS annual report of 1915. It is a rather oblique reference and comes in the western field secretary's report.

> *Some auxiliaries we have lost through the merging of the local church with some other denominations... We find it extremely difficult to keep up our denominational WMS in the new Union Churches that have recently been organized, although a few are still in existence and doing good work.*[1]

In 1917, Mrs. J. A. Macdonald, member of the WMS board, visited mission fields in the Orient and heard something about the missionaries' thoughts on church union. In her report on a visit to Canton Christian College she says,

> *It was here I realized more than ever the necessity for Church Union in China… The missionaries are beginning to feel that much better work could be done if there was more united effort, although there are some still who hold to the motto, "Ourselves alone." There are five medical schools and any one can see that a great deal of time and labor is wasted. We should be behind our missionaries in all their efforts to foster a spirit of union. The missionaries say that they are afraid to bring up the union idea to their home churches and Boards, and that we should set them the example.*[2]

Another reference was made to church union during the time the inaugural meeting of the Canadian School of Missions was held in Convocation Hall of Wycliffe College, Toronto on November 8, 1921. Mrs. G. A. Gollock of London, England, was one of the speakers. She was the secretary of the Board of Missionary Study of Great Britain and joint editor of *The International Review of Missions*. She spoke to the executives of the Women's Missionary Society boards on the following day. She expressed her conviction that the more capable women are in administration, the more necessary it is that their boards have a vital connection with the men's boards.

> *We who are standing together in missionary work are doing more to bring about Church Union than those who are working for it. Not only is foreign missionary work linking denominations at home, but in the foreign fields denominations are linking in a most wonderful way. As women we must see that we further every means of working together, and seek to look out with a wide, living outlook on all God's work in the world.*[3]

In closing, Mrs. Gollock appealed to the women to get away from their narrowness.

When church union was mentioned in the WMS reports before 1925, it was usually in connection with churches in the west that had already become union churches. Questions had arisen regarding the WMS groups in these churches. The January 1923 magazine reports that the Presbyterian women, members of the WMS auxiliary in Vegreville, organized 14 years earlier, who, although they had clung to this link with their church in the past, had now decided to disband and concentrate their efforts on the union society.

In Manitoba's provincial report of their annual meeting in 1923, the secretary says,

Membership has increased in four Presbyterials, and decreased in three. The latter is partly due to the many churches becoming union, for we have 67 union societies, who report only half their membership to us, out of a total of 193 Auxiliaries. In spite of this, there was an increase of 282 members with 35 new Auxiliaries.[4]

The Saskatchewan provincial of the same year reported,

The remainder of the morning session was taken up with the discussion of Union Societies… While these are not of such vital importance in the East, here in the West where whole Presbyterials are composed of Union charges, there is urgent need for some guiding principles to standardize to some extent the management of such societies, both in respect of study and of finance. It was moved that all monies be divided every month; that these be divided on a fifty-fifty basis before any allocation is made; that in reporting membership the half of the total membership be registered to each denomination; but the ultimate finding of the meeting was that a committee be now appointed to meet with the Methodist Convention in May, at Regina, and confer on Union Societies.[5]

Even in 1924, there was little mention of church union in WMS reports, as the society looked forward to the celebration of its diamond jubilee.

In her address on "The Women of the Church 1864-1924" during the jubilee celebrations, the president, Mrs. MacGillivray, makes an oblique reference to church union, ending with these words,

With the close of our 60th year there appears a turn in the road and we face still larger things. To some there is a cloud in the sky. What of the future?… As a Society we have but the one great purpose. The Christ for Whom we have worked in the past, will still be the Christ for Whom we shall all work in the future — "not the Christ of a Western possession but the Christ of a Universal Trust."… May that gentle spirit of the Master quiet our hearts to-day, and keep us great and united in that one purpose, "Christ for the World," to the end.[6]

What can we conclude from the relative silence of the WMS on the issue of church union over the years? Lack of interest? Helplessness? Not at all. Even with no voice in the courts of the church, women were not about to let this hold them back.

The Presbyterian Church in Canada, including all its boards and agencies, was, in all likelihood, going into union. This included the Women's Missionary Society which, as an auxiliary of the mission boards of the Church, would have no choice in the matter. However, there were many women in the WMS who were pro-union. The president, Mrs. MacGillivray, was herself an ardent unionist. Clergy and lay people in the church who opposed union were dissidents and had to work outside the structures of the church. So, too, the women in the WMS who were opposed to union were dissidents and had to work outside the structures of the WMS.

Outside the Structures of the Church

Presbyterians who were opposed to church union had formed the Church Federation Association. A pamphlet put out by the federation entitled the Church Union Question said that,

> *...an organization of ministers, elders, laymen and women from all parts of Canada had been formed within the Presbyterian Church, to oppose this suicidal policy.*[7]

Who were these women who were involved in the opposition to church union? It is clear that a good number of them were WMS members. We just need to look at many of the men prominent in the leadership of the Church Federation Association to see that it is not too much of a leap to assume that their wives, prominent members of the WMS, were also involved in opposing union.

Priscilla Lee Reid in *Enkindled by the Word*, says,

> *During the days of the church union struggle, there were ministers' wives who spared no effort in the cause of preserving the Presbyterian Church in Canada. One of these was Mrs. Ephraim Scott of Montreal, the former editor of the Woman's Missionary Outlook, organ of the Woman's Missionary Society, Montreal. She had always been a leader among women, therefore, it is not surprising that in a time of crisis, she came forward with her husband, Dr. Ephraim Scott, the editor of the Presbyterian Record as a fiery champion of the cause, and as an inspiration to others...*[8]

Reid also says,

> *Another was Mrs. D.T.L. McKerroll, wife of the minister of Victoria Church, Toronto. Although always known as a strong leader and a forthright person, it was in 1925, following the disruption that she earned the title 'woman of the hour'. Elected the first president of the WMS (WD) reorganized in June of that year, she, by word and example, rallied the Presbyterian women...*[9]

Mrs. Mary McKerroll had been a member of the executive of the WMS since the amalgamation in 1914 and first vice-president of the society for several years up to and including 1925 when she became president.

Other women, wives of ministers prominent in the union movement were:

- Mrs. Helen Strachan, wife of Rev. Daniel Strachan, and a vice-president in the WMS.
- Mrs. Alice Inkster, wife of the minister of Knox Presbyterian Church, Toronto. Records show her involvement with the WMS and the dissident movement.
- Mrs. Campbell, wife of Robert Campbell who had been a major leader in the opposition movement from its beginning. Mrs. Campbell was actively engaged in the Woman's Missionary Society, Montreal from 1864 to 1912, holding nearly every office in the society.
- Mrs. Marjory MacLaren, wife of William MacLaren, principal of Knox College, was the first president of the Woman's Foreign Missionary Society. She was a close adviser and trusted counsellor of the WMS board.

These women were all wives of ministers who were prominent in the movement to preserve the Presbyterian Church in Canada.

Mrs. Ella Mutchmor Thorburn was another prominent woman who, after the disruption, came forward and rallied the women for the purpose of re-establishing both the church and the WMS in the Ottawa valley. Mrs. Thorburn was also a leader in civic and national affairs, who, among other things, represented the church abroad at the League of Nations in Geneva and at the World's Conference of Women held in Denmark. In 1924, she went as Canadian Women's Commissioner to the British Fair held in Wembley.

After the General Assembly in 1913, a letter was sent out announcing that a new national organization was being formed to preserve the Presbyterian Church. A list of 150 names of lay supporters was presented to the union committee in 1913 consisting mainly of professional men. The resistance movement which had formerly been in the hands of the clergy, was now controlled by lay people. The new organization was called the Presbyterian Church Association.

It was John Penman of Paris, Ontario, an active lay person in the resistance movement, who had the idea that the women should organize separately in the defense of the church.

> *Since Penman's major interest in the church was missions, he was well aware of the effective work being done by the Women's Missionary Societies. He was confident that the women would prove to be a great asset to the resistance movement.*

Not everyone agreed with him. T.B. McQuesten of Hamilton declared that this would be a terrible mistake because women organizing women would lead to all sorts of petty jealousies. He said,

> *The best results in organizing women, as all political organizers knew, would be obtained by a male organizer.*

It was pointed out to him that Mrs. Frances McCaskill had already done splendid work in Montreal and

> *...in view of the excellent leadership she and other women were displaying it might be difficult for McQuesten to sustain his objections.*[10]

The Mysterious Women's League

The federal executive of the Presbyterian Church Association met in Montreal in January 1923. At the same time,

> *...another meeting held in Montreal was the first meeting of The Ladies' Auxiliary of The Presbyterian Church Association.*[11]

At their meeting, they passed the following resolution in which they called themselves the Presbyterian Women's League.

> *We the members of the Presbyterian Women's League, meeting at Montreal on January 17th, strongly protest against the proposed action of the General Assembly regarding Church Union. We regard this action as tending to deprive the Presbyterian Church of its name and status among the great churches of the world. We affirm our determination to uphold in every way in our power the action of the Presbyterian Church Association for the preservation of their church.*[12]

Keith Clifford, in his book *The Resistance to Church Union in Canada*, assumes that many, if not most, of these women were members of the Women's Missionary Society, since he follows his comments on the league with a brief sketch of the WMS.

> *For years...Presbyterian women had been making a significant contribution to the church's missionary effort. Since 1876 when the first Women's Missionary Societies were formed in the Presbyterian Church, they had grown rapidly... In running these societies women had proven that they were capable not only of raising large sums of money to support women missionaries at home and abroad, but also of efficiently administering their property and funds...many Presbyterian women decided to put their organizational abilities to work for the resistance movement.*[13]

At this first meeting of the Presbyterian Women's League, Mrs. Frances McCaskill, who had already done splendid work in Montreal, was elected corresponding secretary. Mrs. McCaskill was the wife of Rev. J.J. McCaskill, the minister of Maisonneuve Church in Montreal. She was a member of the Women's Missionary Society and is listed among the charter members of the newly reconstituted WMS group of Maisonneuve Presbyterian Church in May 1925. Mrs. McCaskill became the organizer for the Presbyterian

Women's Leagues throughout Ontario and Quebec. When her throat gave out from so many speaking engagements she enlisted the help of Mrs. E. H. Howson of Peterborough and Miss Minnie Gordon of Kingston, daughter of principal Daniel Gordon of Queen's University, Kingston. Dr. Gordon was also an active member of the Presbyterian Church Association. Keith Clifford quotes Mrs. McCaskill as saying,

> *It is only by will power that I keep going just now. My choice would be to crawl into a dug-out and stay there for six months rest.*[14]

At a meeting on April 24, 1923, of the union committee held in Knox College, communications were received from branches of the Women's Leagues of the Presbyterian Church Association in Toronto, Ottawa, Cornwall, Montreal, New Glasgow, and the Maritime synod. These communications pointed out that,

> *...although women had no voice in the Union Committee for General Assembly, the actions of both would affect woman's work in the church, and if the present legislation went through, they would be forced into the new denomination against their will. They therefore recommended that the Union Committee seriously consider "a better way to preserve the unity and peace of the church."*[15]

These resolutions were noted in the minutes of the Presbyterian Church Association without comment and, according to Keith Clifford, appear not to have been taken very seriously.

By June 1923, Frances McCaskill announced a minor organizational miracle. In less than six months, the Presbyterian Women's League

> *...had enrolled 173 members in Eastern Canada, and she told J.W. MacNamara that "this is just the beginning." Equally startling was the fact that they had raised $4,750 and turned over $3,000 to the Presbyterian Church Association. By providing much needed financial support and paying for all their own organizational expenses the Presbyterian Women's Leagues became the most important new factor in the resistance movement and certainly the most successful element in the association's reorganization prior to the 1923 General Assembly.*[16]

Although there were Women's Leagues in many of the larger cities, the records of the group in Toronto seem to be most complete. Dr. Roberta Clare in her essay, "The Role of Women 1921 to 1928" in *The Burning Bush and a Few Acres of Snow* points out the significance of comparing the minutes of the Toronto Women's League with the Women's Auxiliary of St. Andrew's

Church. The comparison shows that many of the leaders in the Women's Auxiliary were on the executive of the Women's League. The minutes of the Toronto Women's League were discovered in St. Andrew's Church, Toronto.

The Toronto Women's League was formed in March, 1923, and held its meetings in St. Andrew's Institute, the same building where the Presbyterian Church Association met, as did the Women's Auxiliary of St. Andrew's Church. The first task of the executive of the Toronto Women's League was to outline its mandate and submit it for approval to the executive committee of the Presbyterian Church Association.

The Presbyterian Church Association (PCA) wanted the Toronto League to appoint a woman organizer. The Women's League turned down the request as, they said, this would involve full membership on the executive committee of the PCA, which would be undesirable for many reasons. They believed, they added, that a woman who was a paid official was handicapped in making an appeal which expects of others disinterestedness and sacrifice. Furthermore, they said,

> *The Committee do not recognize any difference whatever in the position of men and of women in regard to the preservation of a Church in which their obligations of membership are identical, and believe that any method of rousing the Church members to a sense of the present danger, which divides the sexes, merely causes delay and adds to the overhead expense.*
>
> *The members of the Committee approve of the place by which the Church is governed by men officials, and believe, therefore, that the work of educating and rousing the members can be done much more effectively by men who appeal to the large body of the people, irrespective of sex... This system of government enables a man, through his position in or influence on the Session and Board of Managers, to force the issue and gain an entrance to a Church where the minister is in favour of union.*

Therefore, the committee recommended that

> *...the women members of the Presbyterian Church in Canada be permitted to serve individually as may be necessary, or required under the direction and at the request of the Executive Committee of the Presbyterian Church Association, but that the official education and organization of the entire membership be undertaken by qualified men exclusively.*[17]

The women apparently believed, like McQuesten, that women needed male leadership. Their response to the request gives some credence to a comment made by Douglas Campbell in a working paper produced by the

Presbyterian Church Association that women preferred their inferior position in the Presbyterian Church to the promise of equality in the other one.

One might be surprised to see this powerful Women's League in Toronto displaying such a submissive attitude, deeming it a noble gesture to sacrifice their equality for the sake of preserving the Presbyterian Church in Canada. What happened to all those forward-looking "new women" we read about in the records of the WMS? It makes one think that perhaps most of them were going happily into church union.

The Toronto branch of the Women's League handed over its money directly to Mr. MacNamara, secretary of the Presbyterian Church Association. It contributed to three main areas of the anti-union campaign: finances, literature, and membership drives. Roberta Clare says,

> *The League bore the bulk of the financial burden of the Toronto Presbyterian Church Association.*[18]

Their minutes of March 26, 1923, just three weeks after their formation, report that Mr. C.S. McDonald, treasurer of the Men's Association, had written to the league's treasurer noting that expenses of the association had been borne by a few but that help from others would now be welcomed.

By December, the league's treasurer had reported that they were the only organization contributing to the enormous expense under which the Association was labouring. Roberta Clare reports that, in less than two years, the Women's League raised $5,293. In addition, they paid for their own expenses such as stationery and postage. More important, as the March 14, 1924 minutes note, they paid for the services of Crussel, the association's lawyer. Their drive for funds was independent of the Presbyterian Church Association. The league paid the fees of top name speakers for public rallies and meetings. They also published their own literature and pamphlets.

No wonder the women were praised to the skies after 1925. R. G. MacBeth, one of the early opponents of union, in his book, *The Burning Bush and Canada* is lavish in his praise in a chapter entitled "Faithful Women."

> *When the existence of the Presbyterian Church was threatened by the so-called Union Movement, the women of the Church sprang to its defence, and Women's Leagues, organized to canvass in congregations, had much to do with the fact that this great historic Church continues its work at home and abroad. This uprising of the women was no surprise to those of us who had worked on frontier mission fields and amongst peoples who came from other lands. The manifest determination of women to keep the Church alive and active, though the men became engrossed in other things, always asserted itself. It is the superior loyalty of womankind that the poet visualizes*

against the dark background of the arrest and the crucifixion of Jesus Christ, in the words, "Not she with traitorous kiss the Master stung, Not she betrayed Him with unholy tongue, She, when disciples fled, could danger brave, Last at the Cross and first to reach the grave."[19]

It would not be presumptuous to assume that the women of whom MacBeth spoke, for the most part, were members of the WMS since the rest of his chapter on "Faithful Women" gives a history of the Women's Missionary Society and ends with quotations from *The Glad Tidings.*

The first post-union issue of *The Presbyterian Record* is more subdued in its praise of the faithful women.

The women have had a large share in bringing their church safely through her crisis... Their church is dear to them and owes them much.[20]

Ephraim Scott, who in 1925 became the Moderator of the Continuing Presbyterian Church in Canada, is extravagant in his gratitude to the Women's Missionary Society in "A Message From the Moderator of the General Assembly to The Women's Missionary Society," which begins *Greetings! Congratulations! Benedictions! — and if there be aught else I can give, it is yours to command.*[21]

In his 1927 report to the General Assembly, Rev. S. Banks Nelson, vice-convener of the General Board of Missions said,

The WMS also has for its Foreign work provided a generous estimate as their own report will show, and, judging by the remarkable income of their Budget this year, and the grace and enthusiasm that mark all their work, we feel that it is the men in our ministry and membership who need to get up on the watch-tower, for our sisters are already there waiting for the men of God to rise up.[22]

It seems the Toronto branch did become somewhat less self-effacing as time went on and less involved with the Men's Association. In March 1924 they planned a large conference along the lines of one held by the Montreal League. One of the major projects of the Toronto branch in 1924 was to send a letter to the Members of Parliament in anticipation of the union debate.

The letter shows the extent to which the League had outgrown its original mandate and become the driving force of the dissident movement. It had assumed the responsibility of an advocacy organization representing and defending the concerns of its constituency — women in the church — in the union debate.[23]

Their letter said, in part,

> *It is estimated that the membership of the Presbyterian Church is more than sixty percent women. As our Church is constituted none of the courts have women as members. It is a well-known fact, however, that in all branches of church activity and support, the women bear no small part, the WMS alone in 1922, did (sic) work that called for expenditures of over $450,000... If the question of Church Union, involving, as it does property rights which the sixty percent membership of women had no small share in securing, can be settled in church courts, where there are no women representing women, (this means) 60 percent of the Presbyterian Church has had no voice or part in the disposal of the church property which they have through the years, helped to secure and maintain...*[24]

The Toronto branch of the Women's League disbanded on May 10, 1926, after the Union Bill became law. However, the women in the church continued to work to build up the beleaguered Presbyterian Church as it struggled to bring order out of the chaos caused by the disruption. It was the Women's Missionary Society who led the way. It is to their story that we now turn. What part did the WMS, as a society, play in the church union movement?

Inside the Structures of WMS — A Divided Society

The silence in WMS reports in the years before church union was primarily because of their determination that their work, both at home and overseas, should not be jeopardized. However, many of the women in the WMS were excited about the possibility of strengthening their witness by uniting with the other churches. Many board members, including the president, Mrs. Janet MacGillivray, were in favour of church union, but not all. The women knew that, as an auxiliary of the mission boards of the church, like the other boards and agencies, they would automatically go into union if and when the church made the decision to do so. When the time was right, those members of the executive board who had decided to remain Presbyterian, sprang into action.

At the beginning of 1925 the executive board of the Women's Missionary Society could no longer avoid the problems arising in the society over the issue of church union and the fact that almost half of their executive were not entering the union and that many, many auxiliaries were following them out.

A report on the last annual meeting of the executive council held on June 1-3, 1925 at Old St. Andrew's in Toronto, appears in the July/August 1925 issue of *The Missionary Messenger*. The writer casts the dissident members in the role of those who are backward-looking, timid, fearful of the future and lacking in vision, while those entering the union are cast in the role of those who are forward-looking, adventuresome and willing to take risks.

> *There was a delightful air of comradeship everywhere, warm greetings of old friends meeting after long absence, but there was also a strain of deep feeling underlying the deliberations as one realized the significance of it all, not only in the annals of our Women's Missionary Society, but in the history of our beloved church. The phrase "weathering the storm" has been used over and over again lately. Let us remember that those who stay in the harbour may feel the surge of the sea, and hear the roar of the wind in the riggings, but they advance not a whit! It is only they, who, visioning a greater thing to be, and putting out for the unknown land reach the first port safely, that can be said to "weather the storm."*[25]

In presenting her report, Miss Elizabeth Laing paid tribute to the services of the president, Mrs. MacGillivray, through the long and trying period of the past months. She announced that in 1924, the jubilee year, the splendid objective of 100,000 members was almost reached with a membership of 99,716.

In her presidential address, Mrs. MacGillivray had this to say,

> *Outstanding surely is the movement within our Church itself to join with two sister communions in declaring before the world a positive faith in God and in our Divine Lord and Saviour, Jesus Christ, a creed which I have no hesitancy in its acceptance. It is the greatest movement of our day and we earnestly pray will prove a steadying influence for the youth of our land and so needed in the thought of our times.*
>
> *It was this side of the whole question which steadied me in the difficulties that faced us in seeing with deep regret the division within our own denomination. In the face of the great world need of Christianity and the issues at stake in the great foreign fields and our own land, having also carefully studied the Basis of belief as set forth in the terms of The Writ issued by those representatives of the non-concurring membership which requires acceptance of the Westminster Confession in its original entirety, there was only one answer which could satisfy my conscience, that of going forward into the United Church…*
>
> *It has been our one regret that any division of opinion should have been evident among our Board membership. The severance of a connection which has been happy and unbroken for many years is always painful. We believe that each one has conscientiously done what she felt was right and though some may now go by a divided path, we pray that the Master may use each one of us for His purposes and find us loyal and obedient servants to His Will.*

She ends her address,

> *May we as women of the United Church, so soon to be, face the future with glad hearts, strong in that secret strength that faith and trust in our great Divine Leader, which has made possible the story of the Women's Missionary Societies of all the Churches down through the years!*[26]

The magazine includes a full report of the inaugural service of The United Church of Canada which took place on June 10th, 1925.

> *The vast arena held three audiences during the day, numbering in all more than 8,000 at each service...*[27]

The historian's report of the Presbyterian Women's Missionary Society of the Continuing Presbyterian Church in Canada tells the story of those members of the executive who were remaining Presbyterian.

> *When our Women's Missionary Society held its Diamond Jubilee in Montreal, May 1924, the Dominion Parliament had not yet passed the Church Union Bill. That was passed during the summer vacation, and when the Executive Board convened again in September, those of its members, who intended to remain Presbyterian, knew that it was high time to think of the future of their beloved Society.*[28]

The report goes on to tell about a meeting on September 24, 1924, when five of the executive met at the home of one of the members. The minutes of that provisional Women's Missionary Society meeting begin,

> *An informal meeting of some members of the Executive Board of the WMS who desire the continuance of The Presbyterian Church in Canada was held at 19 Laws Avenue on Wednesday, September 24th.*[29]

There were only five women present at that first meeting, Mrs. McKerroll, Mrs. Strachan, Mrs. Grant, Miss Pringle and Mrs. Taylor. So few on that first day — only five! Would there be many to follow? Much of the time at that first meeting was spent in prayer, and it was the same at all future meetings.

They rose from their knees to work. At the very first meeting they agreed:

1. That auxiliary relationships had not proved satisfactory.
2. That synodical divisions might be better than provincial.
3. That possibly independent boards, with co-operating committees might better and more easily carry on the work.[30]

They also agreed that Mrs. McKerroll, Mrs. Horne, and Mrs. Strachan form a committee to discuss these matters with the Provisional Board of

Missions, appointed by the Presbyterian Church Association and report as soon as possible to this group. At the next meeting on September 27, it was reported that Mrs. Horne and Mrs. Strachan, illness having prevented Mrs. McKerroll from attending, had met with Dr. Eakin and his committee. They reported that they

> *...had been received with much courtesy and understanding. There had been frank discussion as to the best machinery to be set up for future work, the best and wisest way of carrying on WMS work in the Continuing Presbyterian Church.*
>
> *Our suggestion had been that the WMS might be a Board of the Assembly, co-operating with Home & Foreign Mission Bds. It had been agreed by the men that the greatest contribution that the women of this committee could make would be to declare openly that there were members of the Exec. Bd. who were not going into the Union Church, and that in the Continuing Presbyterian Church there would still be a Women's Missionary Society.*[31]

The women reaffirmed their loyalty to existing obligations as members of the executive board until June 10, 1925, and declared their intention to dedicate themselves, their time and talents after that date to the work of the "continuing" Women's Missionary Society of the "continuing" Presbyterian Church. There were some "like-minded" members of the board who were away or ill but eventually there were eighteen in the group:

Mrs. I.C. Sharp, Montreal, Honorary President
Mrs. D.T.L. McKerroll, lst Vice-President
Mrs. H.R. Horne, 2nd Vice-President
Mrs. D. Strachan, 4th Vice-President
Miss B. MacMurchy, Corresponding Secretary
Mrs. Robert Ross, Secretary for Honan
Miss J.I. Inglis, Courtesies Secretary
Miss I.S. Pringle, Associate Hospital Secretary
Mrs. D. Inglis Grant, Candidate Secretary
Mrs. J.W. Dill, Mission Band Secretary
Mrs. W.J.F. Mallagh, Secretary for South China
Mrs. James Logie, Home Helpers Secretary
Miss H. McEwen, Student Secretary
Miss C.I. Davidson, Montreal
Mrs. J.G. Potter, Montreal
Mrs. T. Wardlaw Taylor, Asst. Secretary for India & the Foreign Committee
Miss Jessie Parsons, Secretary-Treasurer of Publications
Miss M.C.G. Fraser, Editor of the Missionary Messenger

One of the first undertakings of the continuing Presbyterian WMS members was to prepare a statement of the position of the group to be submitted to the executive board. The women knew that their actions would lead to misunderstandings and broken friendships, but that, *never-the-less, to stand for the right, as God enabled them to see it, was the one thing to be done.* The statement was read at a meeting of the executive board of the WMS, but under protest and no discussion was allowed. Their request to have it printed in *The Missionary Messenger* was denied.

Mrs. Alice Inkster, in her memoirs, gives us a personal insight into her experience as a "dissident."

> *By 1921 it* [Church Union] *was being seriously considered and these years were very busy ones for "Continuing Presbyterians," The Council Executive of the WMS was quite evenly divided on the question. The President, Mrs. John MacGillivray, was ardently in favor, while the "antis" had four very able and devoted women, who by their intelligent foresight and activity saved the society for Presbyterianism. These were Mrs. Henry Horne, Mrs. Daniel Strachan, and Mrs. D.T.L. McKerroll, all wives of ministers, and Miss Bessie MacMurchy, daughter of the well-known principal of Jarvis St. Collegiate Institute and sister of two famous women, Marjorie, afterwards Lady Willison, and Dr. Helen, one of the first women doctors in Canada. The Society was fortunate indeed in having four such able and devoted women to build up its shattered ranks… "The Big Four" I called them. All honour to them!*
>
> *Presbyterianism in Ontario was strongest in Toronto and Hamilton. Many meetings were held to organize these Presbyterials and help others in Ontario. The date of the consummation of union was June 10, 1925. Accordingly plans were made to preserve the continuity of Toronto Presbyterial. This was to be done by presenting a declaration at the May meeting of the Executive and I, as the wife of the minister of Knox Church, was to read it at the close of the regular business.*
>
> *That was a long, miserable day for me, with butterflies abundant and active. The President of Toronto Presbyterial was Mrs. Johnston, as strongly in favour of Union, as her sister, Mrs. W.J. Anderson was opposed to it. They were sisters of our veteran missionary in India, John Wilkie.*
>
> *When the day's business was finished, I asked for permission to speak. It was granted and I went to the front, the document in my hand. Not more than a dozen words were needed to reveal the*

purport. Up went the president's hand "Stop — not one word more." Mission accomplished, I took my seat, shaking from head to foot.

In May, a similar procedure for the Ontario Provincial Society was followed in St. Andrew's Church, London. The Presbyterians withdrew to New St. James. Here the meeting was duly constituted by Mrs. McKerroll and the officers elected.[32]

As soon as it was known that such a movement had begun in the ranks of the executive board, the group was flooded with letters from auxiliaries asking for information and advice. There were also requests from all over Ontario for speakers. Those skilled in speaking could not meet the demand and others who had never before addressed a meeting had to go and do their best.

In October, a letter was sent to each WMS missionary and home worker, who was understood to be remaining Presbyterian, carefully stating the position of the informal group but with no attempt at coercion. The purpose was to let those at a distance know that there would be a strong Presbyterian Church and Women's Missionary Society after June 10th. Later the statement that had been presented to the executive board was sent to auxiliaries.

A meeting was held in November 1924 in St. Andrew's Church, Toronto, at a time when WMS leaders from out of town were in the city. This informal group was constituted a provisional executive board with power to add to their numbers. Their action was confirmed in February 1925, at the time of a large gathering of members from all parts of Ontario of the Women's League. This Women's League had done so much for the cause of Presbyterianism.

The women were so anxious not to injure the existing WMS work in any unnecessary way that they did not appoint a treasurer for some months. No money was asked for from the auxiliaries for necessary expenses. Many who wrote saying that they had ceased giving to the WMS were told that their provisional executive board would deprecate such an action. While they belonged to the present society, the contributions of their auxiliary must go to its maintenance. In March, the appointment of a treasurer became a necessity and Mrs. R. C. Donald was appointed.

May 7, 1925:

Many of the groups wishing to remain Presbyterian were isolated and without information. The provisional board decided to send an encouraging message to them informing them about current happenings. An Easter message went out in April and along with it a pamphlet prepared by Mrs. Helen Horne and her committee entitled *Information and Instructions for a Women's Missionary Society of the Continuing Presbyterian Church* outlining the procedure necessary for groups that did not wish to go into union. They would have to disband before June 10, 1925 and form a provisional organization. The wording for disbanding was given in the pamphlet along with other information and forms for reorganization were included in the mailing.

Miss Fraser, former editor of *The Missionary Messenger*, was appointed assistant editor of the *Bulletin* in April, "the splendid temporary publication" that did so much for Presbyterian and WMS work. The WMS board undertook to pay half her salary.

The *Bulletin* was a joint effort of the provisional WMS with the provisional board of the Continuing Presbyterian Church. There were to be five issues published. The May issue was the WMS number and it was sent to all those who had sent in subscriptions for the new WMS magazine. This issue of the *Bulletin* told about the new provisional Ontario Provincial WMS that had come into being on May 7, 1925. It told why groups must disband and reorganize before June 10. It listed branches that have transferred their affiliation to the continuing Presbyterian Women's Missionary Society. It told non-concurring groups where to send their money. As many were enquiring about the powers of the recently appointed commission appointed by the Ontario Legislature, the *Bulletin* gave a brief summary of the provisions of the act. It announced the historic annual meeting of the council of the Women's Missionary Society of the Continuing Presbyterian Church in Canada to be held on June 11-12, 1925. At this council meeting the new magazine would be sponsored and named. There was much more in this issue of the *Bulletin* but what must be mentioned is a great photograph, stretching over two pages, of the non-concurring delegates who attended the meeting in New St. James Presbyterian Church, London, Ontario, on May 7,

new provisional Ontario Provincial WMS

1925, at which a Provincial Women's Missionary Society of the Continuing Presbyterian Church was organized.

On May 14, the members of the provisional executive board were told that they were no longer members of the executive board of the existing society. A protest against this — what the members of the provisional executive board called "summary and unjust action" towards the life members of the society who were faithfully discharging the duties of their various offices and who had expected so to do until June 10 — proved of no avail. These members gave their resignations on May 20 but declared their intent, as duly elected members of the board, to retain their membership until June 10.

On May 27 the members of the provisional board sent a memo to the executive board of the WMS offering to take over certain parts of the work until the report of the Dominion Commission. The reply to their communication, dated June 8, 1925, leaves no doubt as to the feelings of the WMS board toward the non-concurring members.

> *Dear Miss MacMurchy,*
>
> *Your communication of May 27th, 1925 was read before the Annual Meeting of the Executive Board of the General Council of the Women's Missionary Society W.D. of the Presbyterian Church in Canada in session in Old St. Andrew's Church, Toronto on June 1st, 1925….*
>
> *You have referred to* ***"that portion of the Board which is entering Union."*** *Lest there be any misunderstanding as to the position taken by this Board, we feel compelled on account of this reference to the Board to re-affirm the position to which we have always and still do adhere, viz:-that the Women's Missionary Society of the Presbyterian Church in Canada enters the United Church of Canada on June 10th, 1925, as Auxiliary to the Home and Foreign Mission Boards of the Presbyterian Church in Canada pursuant to the terms of the United Church of Canada Act passed by the Dominion Parliament….*
>
> *You further refer to the* ***"Society which is remaining in the Presbyterian Church."*** *From the context we assume that you here refer to those members of the Women's Missionary Society of the Presbyterian Church in Canada who do not desire to enter Union. As the United Church of Canada Act distinctly states that the Presbyterian Church in Canada including all its Boards and Societies enter the Union on June 10th 1925 we cannot allow your reference to go unchallenged and must again re-affirm our position*

that those who "remain in the Presbyterian Church" are those who enter the Union. Any other position would be inconsistent with legislation.

In view of the provisions of Sec 5 of the United Church of Canada Act, this Board is of the opinion that it cannot consider the proposals submitted as they concern work and property which after June 10, 1925 will belong to the United Church of Canada:- nor can this Board according to its Constitution do so without consulting the Home and Foreign Mission Boards of the Presbyterian Church in Canada to which it is Auxiliary and receiving their sanction....

Signed on behalf of the Executive Board of the Women's Missionary Society W.D. of the Presbyterian Church in Canada.

Janet T. MacGillivray, President
Jessie Wilson, Recording Secretary
Eliza Laing, Corresponding Secretary[33]

On the same date, another letter went out from the above members of the board, in reply to Bessie MacMurchy's letter of June l, 1925, requesting 100 Life Membership Pins and 200 unsigned Life Membership Certificates, to inform her that they could not accede to the request,

These pins and certificates are the property of the WMS of the Presbyterian Church in Canada by whom and by whom only they can properly be used. As the Society enters the United Church of Canada on June 10th, Life Membership certificates can be issued only on written request from an Auxiliary or Mission Band of the Presbyterian Church in Canada, which according to the Act enters the Union on June 10th...[34]

The above letter was written on June 8, two days before the society was to become part of the United Church of Canada at which time the certificates would be of no use to anyone except the members of the continuing Presbyterian Women's Missionary Society.

Another letter from Bessie MacMurchy, also dated June 1 had gone to Mrs. MacGillivray to say that the seventeen members of the executive board who were remaining in the Presbyterian Church...desired to extend to their *fellow workers,...with whom we have worked long and successfully*, their best wishes for the success of their work in the future.

May we all unite in earnest prayer to our Heavenly Father that He will bless us in the future in all our undertakings as He has blessed us in the past.[35]

Janet MacGillivray, in replying to the letter, makes clear her stand on

> *...those who were members of our Executive Board and who do not wish to remain with the Presbyterian Church in Canada as it enters the United Church of Canada.*

Still, she ends on a softer note,

> *Our prayer is that though our paths may at this time divide, we each may seek only to fulfil the wise purposes of Him whose we are and whom we all seek to serve.*[36]

As the hour of adjournment of the General Assembly approached on June 9, 1925, the drama of the final separation began to unfold. A protest signed by 79 commissioners was declared out of order, unconstitutional and unprecedented. Keith Clifford describes the scene,

> *As everyone rushed out after the benediction, the dissidents gathered in the northwest corner of the church to reconvene the assembly... C.W. Gordon instructed the organist to play the Hallelujah Chorus at full blast to drown out all further discussion...reporters who were present said it was impossible to hear what was being said, but they saw Dr. D.G. McQueen, a former Moderator lead the group in prayer and then everyone put up their hand to indicate their agreement with a motion to adjourn to Knox Church at 11.45 p.m. standard time. Wardlaw Taylor later explained to the press that the meeting at Knox Church was to keep the Presbyterian Church alive over the midnight hour when according to the Church Union Act the union of the three denominations became effective...*
>
> *For two hours prior to 11.45, Dr. Inkster led those who had assembled at Knox Church in devotions. Then at 12.05, Dr. McQueen declared the court open for the transaction of business.*[37]

The Glad Tidings, the new magazine of the continuing Women's Missionary Society of the Continuing Presbyterian Church in Canada describes, rather dramatically, the experience of some of the women of the WMS who attended this historic meeting in Knox Church.

> *It was midnight of June 9th — that mystic hour that divides night from day, darkness from dawn, the yesterday from the to-morrow, the past from the future, when the prayer meeting which shall ever remain engraven on the hearts of all who were present, convened in Knox Church, Toronto. The hour was unusual. For thousands, the day had been crammed with the inspiration of the great Pre-Assembly Congress; for the commissioners to the General Assembly,*

seared with the memory of the bitter parting of the ways. Few, we thought, would attend. But, impelled by some high yearning, we decided to go. Never shall we forget the strange sense of the unreal as we drove through the streets of the city lying silent and still, saw the homes of the people in darkness, then suddenly came upon the great Church, every window alight, and the streets, far as eye could see, lined with waiting motors. Threading our way through the crowd that stood pressed to the very doors, we finally gained entrance — to find the great auditorium packed with people bowed low in prayer. And when we learned that for over two hours, intercession, silent and audible, had never ceased...that night we saw our Church reborn out of strife, sorrow and heartbreak; re-baptized by the Holy Spirit; rededicated by the Interim Moderator of the reconstituted Assembly to the service of man and the glory of God.[38]

Still to come was the mass meeting of women to be held the next day, June 10, also at Knox Presbyterian Church. Edith Taylor, WMS historian, describes it thus,

And then came June tenth, and the wonderful W.M.S. meetings in Knox Church, Toronto. Who that was privileged to be present will ever forget them? With one heart and one mind the women thronged that great Church until there was not even standing room left, united in thanksgiving to God for His guiding hand through the days of the past, and in fervent prayer for His divine blessing on the days to come.[39]

Chapter

11

A Time to Build

1925-1931

After 1925

After the exhilaration of the mass meeting that took place on June 10, 1925, the women of the Women's Missionary Society who had made the decision to remain Presbyterian, settled down to business. Their annual meeting began the next day, June 11, with Mrs. Mary McKerroll, president of the provisional executive board, in the chair.

Every part of Canada from British Columbia to Quebec was represented, 959 women altogether, plus 35 women from the Maritime provinces, and some visitors.

> *As we glanced over the vast audience that filled every seat and stood at every door, we looked not with the faces of strangers, for amongst them were some eighteen officers of the former Executive Board, Presidents or Secretaries of every Provincial and Presbyterial society, and officers or members from nearly every Auxiliary or Band in Canada.*[1]

Mrs. Sharp of Montreal, honorary president of the provisional executive board, was in charge of the opening service. Miss Mortimer Clerk, representing the Women's

Gavel of Indian teak wood

League, Toronto Branch, that had done so much to preserve the Presbyterian Church, gave a resume of the work of the league in the two and a half years of its existence.

Mrs. McKerroll outlined the work undertaken by the provisional executive board during the interim and asked the members to ratify their actions and accept these provisional officers until the election of officers which would take place later in the meeting.

The meeting also endorsed the action of the provisional board which had assured the missionaries remaining with the Presbyterian Church that the WMS would undertake their support. Mrs. McKerroll then presented the meeting with a gavel of Indian teak wood, sent for the use of the President of the WMS by Dr. Buchanan of India. The box containing this gift, and one for the Moderator of the General Assembly, had been carried thirty miles through the jungle by a Bhil runner.[2]

The women of the provisional board had not forgotten their determination, from their first meeting on September 24,1924 when only five were present, to have their status changed from an auxiliary to the mission boards of the church to a board of the General Assembly. Immediately after June 10, while the General Assembly was still in session, they sent a deputation to bring greetings from the WMS to explain their request for an altered relationship and to present the strength of the WMS to date. Surely, after all the women had gone through in working for the preservation of the Presbyterian Church in Canada, they were justified in asking for this change.

Mrs. Helen Strachan presented the report of the constitution committee stating that the amendments were largely based upon the fact of changed relations.

> *The auxiliary relationship to the Mission Boards is now at an end, and henceforth, the WMS is an independent organization, administering its own funds, making its own appointments, holding its own property, and carrying on its work subject only to the policies formulated by the newly created General Board of Missions of the Church. But on this Board, and helping formulate all policies, sit ten members of the Council Executive of the WMS who are nominated by the Council and elected by the General Assembly.*[3]

Other changes were in names of departments: Foreign Missions would be called Overseas Missions; Home Missions would be called National Missions and instead of Strangers' Work, Welcome and Welfare.

It was unanimously decided that the magazine of the WMS(WD) be called *The Glad Tidings*.[4] It was also unanimously decided that the present motto The World for Christ be kept and if this were not possible to take as the motto Christ for the World.

Mrs. McKerroll was unanimously chosen president. Rev. George Ross of Montreal and Rev. William L. Clay of Victoria, representing the General Assembly, conducted the installation service, marking *the cementing of the bond between the Chief Court of the Church and the WMS.*[5]

Before 1925 was over, a new school home in New Liskeard had been dedicated and another call from the northland for a hospital in South Porcupine had resulted in the purchase of a two-storey building. A request from Fort McMurray for a hospital unit had been laid before the council in June 1925 and in July a nurse, Miss Olive Ross, was appointed.

In the work with Aboriginal people, four reserves in Manitoba had remained loyal to the Presbyterian Church. It was from these reserves that Birtle Residential School drew its scholars. The people on the reserves were anxious that the Presbyterian Church should take over Birtle School.[6]

In the meantime, deaconesses who had remained with the Presbyterian Church would continue the work they had been doing. Three new deaconesses were appointed: two for the summer months in northern Ontario and one in Montreal.

Deaconesses worked where congregations were scattered and where there was a need for visiting families, building up Sunday schools and women's groups. They also held church services and other church activities where

Laura Pelton

necessary. Two missionaries, Miss Ethel Reid and Miss Luella Crockett, formerly of South China, helped with this work.

In 1925, Agnes Dickson formerly of the China field, was sent to do deputation work in the west and to assist in the organization of societies. Returning from the west, she said that she had just returned from a lightning trip through Manitoba, Alberta and Saskatchewan, where she had addressed forty-four meetings in six weeks. She was struck, she said, by the optimism of the west — people whose churches had been "shot to pieces" were meeting anywhere and everywhere and were full of hope for the future.

Miss Laura Pelton was a "field secretary extraordinaire" in the years after 1925. She worked as a volunteer helping to reorganize WMS groups across the country from Vancouver to Quebec. She was given the name "honourary field secretary" and was formally appointed in 1926. She was a person of great ability and her name and reports of her work appear over and over again as the WMS rebuilt itself after church union. After two months of travelling in Ontario in 1925 her reports were most encouraging. She had attended meeting after meeting and found the members full of life and interest. Young women's auxiliaries were well organized and enthusiastic. She met with people in minority groups whose spirits were undaunted.

In 1926, Laura Pelton visited the four western provinces. She gave an address at the annual meeting of Victoria presbyterial where there was a good attendance, and a spirit of thankfulness and optimism prevailed. The publicity secretary for the presbyterial, in her report of the meeting, said that Miss Pelton

> *...struck the keynote of the Presbyterian Church in its declaration of the Divine Sovereignty and the preservation of belief in the authority and supremacy of God, following hand in hand with the conscious presence of God in Jesus Christ as the dynamic force of all effort. This was the heritage handed down and entrusted to the coming generations.*[7]

The WMS groups in the western provinces that remained Presbyterian set to work immediately to rebuild their societies. On July 23, 1925, a meeting was held in Old Kildonan Church to plan the rebuilding of the Manitoba Provincial Society of the Presbyterian WMS.

News from the presbyterials in British Columbia was heartening. Both presbyterials of Westminster and Victoria were fully organized and ready for work. The auxiliary in Cranbrook was reported to be stronger than ever. A mass meeting of Presbyterian women was held in St. Andrew's Hall in Victoria on September 11, 1925, where addresses were given by women who had attended the Pre-Assembly Congress, the General Assembly, and the WMS meetings in Toronto in June.

Minority groups, that is people who wished to remain Presbyterian but whose churches had voted to go into union, were urged to organize WMS auxiliaries even if they only had a few members.

In January 1926, the Presbyterian Church opened the new Presbyterian Missionary and Deaconess Training Home at 648 Huron Street, Toronto. The establishment of this home was important as many appeals were coming to the WMS for workers in national and overseas missions. Later in the year the school moved to Bedford Road and then finally, in 1927, to 156 St. George Street.

The WMS was appealing for twenty-five candidates for the foreign fields and an equal number for Canada. The society did not know what fields the Dominion Property Commission, appointed by the federal government, might apportion to them. They needed to be ready when that decision was made.

The publication of *The Glad Tidings* was authorized on June 12, 1925 and before the second issue was out 10,000 paid up subscriptions had been received. The objective for 1926 was 25,000 subscribers. The society did not reach this goal but by the year 1927 it had over 21,000 subscriptions.

In 1926, the WMS council approved the appointment of a girls' work secretary, Miss Edith Sinclair. Their concern for youth was shown in their choice of guest speakers at the council meeting. Miss Hilda Neatby, a student at Saskatoon University, spoke to the delegates about the student volunteer movement. She told how the members of this association, while still at university, discussed and sought to solve the problems which confronted those who were considering Christian missionary service. Miss Kathleen Patterson gave a presentation of the Student Christian Movement from the student's standpoint. She felt it was a valuable movement in its original purpose if it were not influenced by a type of modern philosophy.

Mrs. Grace, who had represented the WMS at the Student Christian Movement conference for western students at Saskatoon University in December 1925, gave a frank report mentioning its helpful side but sounding a warning against the ultra modernistic views expressed which might undermine the faith of the students.

The WMS appointed provincial student secretaries to follow-up on students away at university as well as young people who went off to train as teachers and nurses. Student representatives had been sent to student conferences and the plan was that, by means of an enlarged grant, a number of students would be able to attend other conferences in the future.

The WMS was anxious to promote and support the young women's auxiliaries. In March 1931, the editor of *The Glad Tidings* announced that there would be a new page in the magazine especially for them.

> *One of the most encouraging features in our membership is the increasing number of young women who are coming forward to share in the work and bringing with them their business and professional talents, interest and influence...from now on a certain space in the magazine is to be devoted to them and the page is to be entitled "Young Women."*[8]

The Dominion Property Commission Makes Its Decision

On September 22, 1926, the Dominion Property Commission approved the division of foreign mission fields agreed upon by the mission boards of the United Church and the Presbyterian Church. The national mission work was not approved until April 17, 1927. The Commission also directed that the Presbyterian Church reimburse the United Church for all money expended since June 10, 1925 on the fields that were now Presbyterian. This meant that the WMS had to pay whatever had been expended on women's work in these fields since that date.

By the terms of the commission, the Presbyterian Church was to be responsible for the following:

Overseas Missions

North Formosa [now northern Taiwan]

British Guiana

India — Gwalior, South Bhil District and West Nimar Districts, comprising Amkhut, Alirajpur, Jobat, Mendha, Sardi, Barwani

National Missions

Cecilia Jeffrey Residential School,	Lake of the Woods, Ontario
Birtle Residential School,	Birtle, Manitoba
Lucy Baker Girls' School Home,	Prince Albert, Saskatchewan
Hugh Waddell Memorial Hospital,	Canora, Saskatchewan
Girls' School Home,	Canora, Saskatchewan
Boys' and Girls' School Homes,	Vegreville, Alberta
Rolland M. Boswell Hospital,	Vegreville, Alberta
Chinese Mission,	Victoria, British Columbia

The Chinese Church in Victoria went to the Presbyterian Church, but the women workers were under the direction of and supported by the Women's Missionary Society. The WMS also had two workers in the Vancouver Chinese mission.

Previous to 1925 the church paid part of the principal's salary in the Aboriginal schools. In March 1927, the Board of Missions agreed, by vote, that all Aboriginal boarding schools should be under the care of the WMS and that the WMS should be responsible for their support over and above the government grant. All reserve work was to be under the care of the church.[9]

Canada Celebrates Its Diamond Jubilee

Bonfires and beacons lighting up hilltops, maple trees being planted, diamond jubilee concerts and parades — in 1927, everyone was celebrating Canada's sixtieth birthday. Even the WMS made its annual meeting a Confederation Council with flags and insignia and the theme of confederation sounding throughout speeches and programs. The new study book, *The Royal Road*, was published in November 1927 to mark Canada's diamond jubilee year. The author was Muriel J. Gray, a member of the WMS council executive.

A resolution came before the council in 1927 directed toward WMS members themselves.

> *That we, the General Council of the Women's Missionary Society(WD) of the Presbyterian Church in Canada...reaffirm our belief in the sovereignty of God; in the infallibility of the Bible; and in the doctrine of our Church as set forth in the Westminster Confession of Faith.*[10]

A further resolution, on the same theme, indicating the importance the WMS had always attached to the nurture of children and youth in the church, asked that the WMS

> *...earnestly solicit the co-operation of our women, on behalf of the children and youth of our Church; that these young people may be*

more thoroughly taught the word of God; that of memorizing Scripture and the Shorter Catechism be encouraged; and that the polity of our Church may be frequently brought before them — to the end that the coming generation may be truly loyal to the Faith of our Fathers.[11]

In their report to this annual meeting in 1927, the council executive stated that in 1926 their work had to do with the beginning of things again, and with the bringing of order out of the chaos into which the events of June 1925 had plunged the church. It would seem, now that the dust had settled, with these two resolutions the WMS believed that it was time to ask the question, "Why am I a Presbyterian?" or at least do some serious thinking about "Why I am a Presbyterian."

Canada

The hospital aid groups were indispensable to all the hospitals. Their hard work and generosity was remarkable. They made donations of hospital equipment, furnished the rooms, even put in a new furnace at Vegreville, and a shadowless operating room lamp at Canora. They also donated food. There were gifts from others as well; memorial gifts, such as the Mary McCulla surgical bed and the Mary E. Johnson convalescent chair. Donations from presbyterials were also generous.

This help was badly needed. The Rolland M. Boswell Hospital in Vegreville, Alberta, reported that 1930 had been a hard year financially with many of the public ward patients unable to pay due to crop failures. Wood, meat and vegetables often had to be accepted for payment of accounts.

The Hugh Waddell Memorial Hospital in Canora, Saskatchewan, reported that the first part of 1930 had been satisfactory but, as a result of the financial depression, the fall collections and number of patients admitted showed a noticeable decrease. Little did they know that this was just a foretaste of the terrible years that lay ahead.

Two hospitals were opened after 1925: South Porcupine, Ontario on February 17, 1926; and Fort McMurray, Alberta. Miss Olive Ross[12] reports in 1931 that this was her fourth winter there. It had been the longest and coldest winter in twenty years. Apart from her nursing duties, she provided some entertainment for the patients. The women in Edmonton had sent her a gramophone which was a great help. On one occasion, she said, she had a little boy deliver it on his sleigh to a woman down the river who had not heard any music for three years. She also had a large number of books which had been sent to her, along with several magazines which formed the nucleus of a library. She had started a Sunday school but found it difficult to keep the children interested. In 1932, on the advice of the Alberta Advisory Committee, the hospital unit at Fort McMurray was closed. It was felt that, in spite of Miss Ross's exemplary work, there was no longer any need for it.

The study book, *The Royal Road*, ends the chapter on the Aboriginal people, with a question, "Has this work among the Indians been appreciated?" The author quotes extracts from a letter written February 17, 1927, which she believes shows the loyalty of some Aboriginal people to their country and their church. The letter is signed by three councillors on behalf of the Sioux Indian Village at Portage la Prairie.

This is a long letter and, when read in full, it becomes obvious that what the people of the Sioux Village of Portage la Prairie were really concerned about was the decision handed down from the Dominion Commission after church union in regard to Aboriginal work in Manitoba. The letter is asking the WMS to

> *...take fully into consideration and look into this matter carefully and....settle this matter which would make things easy for us and our children.*[13]

The letter stated that ever since the Presbyterian women started mission work among the Aboriginal people five years before, they had been loyal to the name of the Presbyterian Church. Now they were told that their children would have to go to a different school. They opposed this as the new school would be too far for them to visit their children. They said that they did not know about the union vote until it was too late. They also said that the people at the Long Plain Reserve were in agreement with them and wanted them to make the appeal against the decision about the school settlement since they had been with the Presbyterian Church for such a long time. Did the letter get results? It seems it did not. The reserve was not listed among those allotted to the Presbyterian Church.

A report in *The Glad Tidings*, May 1929, says that even though the Presbyterian Church had not held services in Mistawasis for nearly ten years, the people had remained loyal to the church. *They are such staunch Presbyterians*, says the report, *really we should be very proud of them.*[14] For some time Mrs. Moore and her son, Rev. W.W. Moore, who was the missionary on the reserve, along with the WMS auxiliary and with the support of the people, had been petitioning the church and government to open an improved day school. Finally, after much negotiation, the government gave its permission in 1928. Miss Sadie McQueen was appointed teacher. Mistawasis was added to the two schools, Birtle and Cecilia Jeffrey, which had already been allotted to the Presbyterian Church by the Dominion Commission. The WMS report to General Assembly in 1929 says,

> *A small day school, is carried on at Mistawasis to help meet the wishes of the Indians that their children be educated under Presbyterian auspices.*[15]

The new Cecilia Jeffrey residential school was opened January 1929. Whereas the old school was built with the funds of the WMS, a new policy had been inaugurated and the new school was built and equipped by the Department of Indian Affairs. Mr. Byers, the principal, reported that the discipline at the school had improved since he initiated a self-government system for the boys and girls at Cecilia Jeffrey, using the tribal idea of chief and counsellors. He also reported that many of the children knew for the first time the thrill of skating and hockey. The children were attending the newly established Presbyterian congregation in Kenora and were attending the Mission Band.

The dedication and official opening of the new residential school at Birtle, Manitoba, took place on October 29, 1931, before a gathering representative of all the departments of the Church, many districts of the province, different departments of the government, co-workers and friends. The chapel was crowded beyond capacity. Halls and corridors were packed and hundreds could not gain admittance. Many of the guests had come great distances and a number of Aboriginal people from different reserves had travelled 100 miles or more with pony and buggy. Because many Aboriginal parents were disappointed at not being able to gain admittance to the opening ceremony, Mr. Currie, the principal, arranged a second service for Friday evening, with 300 present. Mrs. Robson, the matron, reports:

> *The Indians arrived a couple of days before the opening, and we counted 35 tents across the track behind the new school and 10 or 15 more down by the old school which Mr. Currie let them use as there was a stove there…*
>
> *…when the opening services were over tea was served… Then a number of the parents wanted their children "home" (home being the tent) with them and Mr. Currie was kept busy giving permission to the pupils to go with their parents…*
>
> *…Friday afternoon we drove to the Indian encampment and visited 25 tents. At the first one the squaw was making bannock at an open fire…. At one tent two Indian women, who were ex-pupils, surprised us by saying, "Are you the ladies we read about in The Glad Tidings?" At another tent two bright women talked such good English I asked them what school they had attended, and they said*

> *"Regina," and it was in Mr. Angus McLeod's time, whom I knew so well, and one of them said, "Do you ever hear anything of Mrs. McLeod?"... There were several chiefs, and on Friday night Chief Rattlesnake spoke...*[16]

The December 1930 issue of *The Glad Tidings* reports on a new WMS group organized by the Aboriginal women on the Okanase Reserve at Elphinstone, Manitoba. Mrs. Mackay Flett was appointed president; Miss Mary Flett, treasurer; and Miss Jemima Blackbird, secretary. Miss Blackbird was a former pupil at Birtle School. All the officers were Aboriginal women.

The new Chinese church in Vancouver was dedicated on September 2, 1930. The children and the CGIT girls sang. The Women's Missionary Society, which had taken an active part in furnishing the dormitories, was represented by Mrs. Muriel Ledingham, provincial president, and Mrs. R.M. Thompson, presbyterial president. Miss Sibyl Crawford and Mrs. Louie were in charge of the Chinese church's WMS. With the new church building, Chinese work was growing considerably. It was a busy place from 9:30 a.m. till 10:30 p.m. every day except Saturday and Sunday, when they had half-day classes and evening service.

Grace Lee

In Victoria, Miss Grace Lee of South China had been appointed to work among the Chinese women and children. The kindergarten was large and Mission Band, CGIT and Sunday school were flourishing. There was also a WMS. In

Regina, Saskatchewan, Mrs. Martin worked as a volunteer with the Chinese women. Toronto had opened a much-needed kindergarten in 1928. Another "first" happened that same year. During the month of June, Saturday training classes for leaders were held in Park Road Baptist Church, and, on July 3, thirty vacation Bible schools were opened with a total enrollment of about six thousand children. Among them was the first vacation Bible school for the children at the Chinese church. It was with some trepidation that the workers had entered upon this new venture, but the attendance and interest certainly justified the attempt.

Supplies were pouring in from every quarter; equipment and furnishings for the school home in New Liskeard and for the South Porcupine hospital; clothing for the All People's Mission at Selkirk, run by Mrs. Mary Mackenzie, formerly of Hurricane Hills, for new Canadians of all nationalities; supplies for Aboriginal people on the reserves; for Jewish work and for the sick and the lonely stranger; plus Christmas gifts galore for an army of little children. We can only guess at the great number of quilts that were made and clothes that were sewn, along with innumerable other things collected or made, not only by the women in the auxiliaries but also by the children in Mission Bands and the girls in CGIT.

The WMS was responsible for supplies for four hospitals, six school homes, two residential schools, and one day school, for the deaconess and Chinese departments and the ever-increasing needs of home mission fields and reserves. The society was responsible for renewing furniture and equipment in the various institutions and they also furnished the dormitories in the new Chinese church in Vancouver and supplied such things as organs, victrolas, radios and collection plates where needed.

For the new Canadians who were struggling with the language, the library department of the WMS stood ready to send suitable literature. Material was sent to ministers and missionaries in remote charges, to lumber and mining camps and to isolated individuals and new settlers in lonely places. There were many calls to this department for books, Bibles and hymnals for groups with no church building, and for Sunday school papers, picture rolls and libraries.

Deaconesses' duties were many and varied. Dorothy Jenkinson had a three-point charge twenty-five miles north of Winnipeg. Her home, she says, was a room above the church. Dorothy had three meeting places; Walkleyburg, Mayfield and East Selkirk. East Selkirk was the main point of the field.

In Walkley-burg, the furthest point, 10 miles from East Selkirk, the church service was held in a school house. She also held Sunday school here, carried on the young people's society and organized a Mission Band. However, the work at Walkley-burg was difficult and the field was closed in 1930. At Mayfield, five miles east of East Selkirk, there was no organ. When Dorothy Jenkinson told the people in her little home church at Scarborough, Ontario, that she needed an organ and a victrola, both were sent to her. The church service, Sunday school and Mission Band were combined with East Selkirk. Gradually, Miss Jenkinson was able to have separate Sunday school sessions, one at 11 a.m. and another at 1:30 p.m. with regular church service at 3 p.m.

A new church was built at Mayfield in 1932. This was just one result of Miss Jenkinson's splendid work, said the report to council executive. The land for the church was a gift and much of the material was donated. The work was voluntary and the building made possible by a legacy. The church was dedicated in August 1932. The little church was completely full. At the first communion service, tribute was paid to the work of Miss Jenkinson by Rev. J. M. Niven of Winnipeg. He said that she had been encouraged in her work with a group of girls who had given evidence of real conversion. They had each made their profession of faith at the preparatory service. These girls formed the nucleus of a communion roll.

Mrs. J. F. MacLean gave a brief account of her work in British Columbia. In 1929, she visited twenty-seven localities with a view to assist and promote the work and growth of the Presbyterian Church in Canada. She was authorized by the Synod of British Columbia to hold sabbath day services if other supply was not available. So as not to offend anyone by her presumption, Mrs. MacLean carefully explained that she was simply doing this as a Christian worker to prevent lapse of service. In each place she contacted the Presbyterian minister and explained the nature of her work and asked for the help and co-operation of the church officials. She visited homes and addressed public gatherings. During the year she visited 400 homes and addressed over 80 gatherings.

Deaconesses, it seems, did just about everything — even preaching. But they had to be careful, as did Mrs. MacLean, to make it clear that when they led Sunday worship services and preached, it was only because there was no minister or student minister available.

The WMS was anxious to preserve all the links that had bound them to other mission boards. When the WMS president, Mrs. Mary McKerroll, along with three other representatives, attended two foreign missions conferences held in Atlantic City in January 1926, she reported back that

> *...so persistent had been unionist propaganda that surprise appeared to be felt by a few that even four individuals were not in the 'Union'; and we were considered rather brave to come, until they found out about the strength of the Church we represented.*[17]

The Federation of Women's Boards of Foreign Missions and The Foreign Mission Conferences of North America met January 1930. The Federation of Women's Boards held the first session with representatives from forty boards. The federation had three areas for co-operative service: The Day of Prayer; Christian literature and women's union Christian colleges. One of the speakers at the conference was Miss Margaret Wong, Christian Literature Secretary for Africa. She gave an address on "What Shall Africa Read?" and pointed out how the size of that vast continent made it impossible for missionaries to keep in touch with all parts and to what extent the written word might assist in the enlightenment of indigenous people.

Christian literature had become an urgent issue. What could more tellingly reveal, says the WMS literature secretary in her report, the crying need for Christian literature in overseas lands than the picture of the little Indian lad demanding, "Now that you have taught me to read, what are you going to give me to read?" The children's magazine *Treasure Chest* had been edited in five Indian languages; while in China, *Happy Childhood* was filling a gap in the lives of children. But the gaps were numerous and not only among juniors.

Mrs. Elizabeth MacGillivray in Shanghai reported that, although China had been terrorized and ruled by the military and in many places mission work had suffered much, in Shanghai they were able to go on with their work of preparing Christian literature. Mrs. MacGillivray gave many years of service to the literature department in China. The department was in good shape, she said. There was a new building for Christian literature, with almost one whole floor devoted to literature for women and children. However, more funding was needed for this work. Three different women's boards provided women to help with the work.

The Federation of Women's Boards of Foreign Missions was responsible for Christian literature. Sixty different women's boards participated in its work; the Presbyterian Women's Missionary Society was one. The WMS was well aware of the great importance of this work and funding was always included in their estimates.

India

In the two Presbyterian strongholds, Gwalior and the Bhil district, the missionaries showed unswerving loyalty and devotion to the Presbyterian Church. In overseas work all the expansion in buildings was in India. Plans included:

For the Gwalior Field — a new bungalow for WMS missionaries in Jhansi and another girls' hostel; the erection of a small bungalow at Toran Mall where summer school was held and where missionaries went for rest and holidays.

For the Bhil Field — plans were for a new bungalow in Jobat; a much-needed training home for nurses in connection with the work at the Jobat Hospital; a children's nursing home at Amkhut.

Besides the compound at Jhansi, the Gwalior mission had land at Baragaon where eight Bible women worked in Jhansi City and the stations in the surrounding area. Indigenous preachers and their families lived in the outstations, each preacher having twenty-five villages under his care.

The Gwalior mission also had 1,200 acres at Bronsonpura which they called the farm. It offered refuge to any who might be driven out of their own village. Farming was also taught so people could become self-supporting.

For many years the missionaries on the Bhil Field, in Amkhut, had felt the need for a home for the motherless babies that were brought to them from time to time and the need for a hospital where the mild cases of sickness among the school children could be treated. A memorial gift of $5,000 from Mrs. M. G. Abey of Brandon, Manitoba, meant that this dream could become a reality. By October 1930, the Jobat bungalow was finished and the M. G. Abey Memorial Children's Nursing Home at Amkhut was nearly completed. Back in Canada, Miss Mildred Soutar was designated and set apart as a missionary nurse for service among the Bhils and appointed superintendent of the newly erected M. G. Abey Home.

China

The Dominion Commission had made the decision in September 1926 to put the South China field under the care of The United Church of Canada. Of the WMS staff in South China, five remained loyal to the Presbyterian Church: Miss Agnes Dickson, Miss Agnes Dulmage, Miss Ethel Reid, Miss Luella Crockett and Dr. Jessie MacBean.

Agnes Dickson and Ethel Reid were assigned to work on the WMS staff with the Chinese in Canada. Miss Reid later returned to China and worked for the Church of Christ in Kwangtung Province. She was in charge of the women's work in one of their presbyteries and was the only woman missionary in that district. The WMS grant for her work was used to pay for much needed Bible women and for Miss Reid's assistant. Miss Reid later married

Jessie MacBean

but continued to send reports of the work in South China to the WMS. Miss Dulmage died in 1926. Miss Luella Crockett returned to China, this time to Manchuria; Dr. Jessie MacBean stayed in China and worked at the Hackett Memorial Hospital.

After 1925, political conditions in China had become more and more unsettled, with communist, labour and anti-foreign agitation, and a violent anti-Christian movement. Many missionaries had to withdraw from their fields and many weaker Christians fell away from the church. Christian leaders felt it was time for an aggressive Christian movement. The missionaries understood the confusion caused with so many different Christian denominations and sects that had no historic significance for the Chinese people. Another great difficulty was that, in China, Christianity was perceived as a foreign religion. Chinese leaders and the missionaries came to the decision that, if China were be won for Christ, it must be won by a united church. The new church, therefore, must be a Chinese church, inspired by the vision of a new China. Delegates from churches in all parts of the country met at Shanghai to organize the Church of Christ in China. The first General Assembly of the new church was held in October 1927. The WMS gave a grant of $1,000 a year for evangelistic work in the new Church of Christ in China.

Formosa

The fifth annual meeting of the Formosan WMS took place in Taipei on November 22, 1927. Mrs. Helen Strachan, one of the WMS(WD) members who had travelled to the Orient with a delegation from the Presbyterian Church in Canada, attended their meeting. The meeting was opened by an old woman from Gilan, the first woman elder in the Formosan church. She was Mrs. Bella Koa, daughter of Rev. G. L. and Mrs. Mackay. She welcomed Mrs. Strachan as an officer from the mother society in Canada and presented her with a membership pin.

Mrs. Koa gave the president's address. She said they were now supporting three Bible women. The address of the morning was given by Mrs. Mitsui from the Japanese Presbyterian Church. Mrs. Mitsui had been chosen to go to Washington to present a petition to the president in the interest of peace. Mrs. Koa visited 30 churches during 1930, helping the three Bible women, holding meetings for women, distributing Christian literature and promoting the work of the Formosan WMS.

Several new missionaries had been appointed to Formosa in the late 1930s but a woman doctor and a music teacher were still needed. Some knowledge of music, said one report, was not a 'frill' among the Formosan Christians, but was one of the strong forces in building up the native church.

Mrs. Jean Mackay was in charge of the work of the Bible women and Mrs. Lillian Dickson was also interested in it. For some time they felt they would like to have these Bible women gather together for a few days of Bible study and prayer, but they lacked the necessary funds. The Bible women received such a meager salary that they could not be expected to pay. Mrs. Jean Graham, one of the missionaries, offered a gold piece that she had been given by the Huron Presbyterial. She felt that no better use could be made of it than to finance a retreat.

Most of the Bible women were over fifty. The Chinese respect old age and they were able to gain entrance to homes that were closed to young women. One of the Bible women, Chi-Oang, had facial markings of the Taroko tribe — the fiercest of the savage tribes still on the island. A broad blue band was tattooed right across each cheek and a band down the forehead. For years the mission people had been praying for some means of contact with this tribe on the east coast. This woman had married out of her own tribe and knew the Formosan language. She had been baptized into the Christian faith and was attending the Bible women's school at Tamsui. The Formosan WMS was paying her expenses at the school in the expectation that she would go

Chi-Oang

back to preach to her own people. She was probably the only woman of her tribe who was a Christian.

In 1930, Mrs. Margaret Gauld, called "the best loved woman in Formosa," celebrated 38 years of missionary work in Formosa. Her husband, former principal of the theological college in Taihoku (Taipei), had died in 1924. Mrs. Gauld continued to devote herself to the musical education of the Formosan people, which she had begun in 1901. That same year their two daughters had joined the staff of the Mackay Memorial Hospital, one a nurse and the other a doctor. When Mrs. Gauld left Formosa in 1930 she had charge of the singing in the theological college and in the girls' school, the boys' school, and the women's school. She also taught piano and organ and worked in two Sunday schools. Shortly before his death, Dr. Gauld had translated "Come, Let us Sing of a Wonderful Love" into Formosan for the closing of the girls' school. This hymn won its way into the hearts of the people and as Mrs. Gauld sailed away from Keelung on her return to Canada, far out from shore she could still hear her Formosa friends singing the refrain of this hymn.

March 31, 1930 was a happy day for Dr. Gushue-Taylor of Formosa for on that day the finance department of the government gave him a cheque as a subsidy towards the Happy Mount Leper Colony and towards the expenses of the out-patient clinic which was already in operation. The colony was to have fifty cottages, walks and roads, an open air exercise ground, a chapel and a dispensary for the blind and infirm. The government had promised land for a site. The WMS had agreed to contribute to the work and chose to build the chapel at a cost of $5,000.

The kindergarten department was the newest department and was under the direction of Miss Ada Adams, a graduate of the Kindergarten Training School at Oberlin, Ohio, USA.

> *...although only eight or nine years have passed since it was started, there are already five kindergartens in as many churches, one is self-supporting while the others receive help from the Mission.*[18]

There were nine teachers, one of whom was a graduate of a government school while all the others were from the Tamsui Girls' School.

Lillian Dickson and Dr. Gushue-Taylor at one of the cornerstones of a leprosarium

Tamsui Church was bursting at the seams. Mrs. Mackay says,

> *We have one Girls' School, one hospital, the nursing department, one school for women, and a kindergarten. We have been trying for years to put up a church large enough to accommodate the Tamsui congregation as well as the hundreds of students. It is quite a sight to see the congregation assemble for service at 9 o'clock on a Sunday morning. All the front pews are filled with Girls' School pupils in*

their blue and white uniforms. The back of the centre and one side are packed tight with Middle School students in their khaki uniforms. The Women's School students sit behind the girls in the centre. The members of the Tamsui congregation are crowded into one side, the men squeezed in at the back...or standing around the door. And the worst of it is that the roof has been pronounced unsafe. The Tamsui congregation is able and willing to erect a church large enough for its own needs... It is the presence of these hundreds of students...mostly from non-Christian homes, which makes a large church necessary.[19]

Manchuria

War and famine brought thousands of immigrants from overcrowded provinces in China to Manchuria. In 1927, the Presbyterian Church in Canada was invited to take up work in Manchuria, the societies already working there realizing that they could never hope to cover this vast field. Dr. Jonathan and Mrs. Rosalind Goforth, Mr. Allan Reoch, Miss Jean Graham and Miss Anna Kok (Cook) responded to the call. They worked in three large cities. Mr. Joseph Koffend and his wife, Mrs. Koffend, came to help the Goforths and Miss Luella Crockett came later. They said that never before had they met with such wholehearted response to the gospel.

Luella Crockett, writing in *The Glad Tidings*, described the homes and told how the missionaries tried to reach the people with the gospel. Their homes were usually small, usually just one room with many families clustered around the small courtyard. The k'ang or built-in bed was the chief article of furniture and occupied a large space on one side of the room. It often served as a table and chairs as well. Upon entering their home you would be invited to "shang k'ang" which meant to get on the bed. The floors were earth or brick and were cold in the winter. By the time the neighbours gathered, the k'ang was pretty well occupied. A hymn sheet would be fastened up and a simple hymn or chant sung over and over again. This helped, said Miss Crockett,

...to distract the attention from your clothing and general appearance and also helps to prevent time having to be spent in relating your family history, the cost of your clothing, the salary you receive, the amount you spend on food and the kind of food you eat, the wages your servants get, and what they eat, and so on indefinitely. It also prepares them for the story. The picture roll is then produced and the old, old story which is ever new, is told. A verse of scripture is taught and tracts and gospel portions given to those who can read and prayer offered that the seed sown may bring forth fruit.[20]

Koreans in Japan

Koreans had been living in Japan for centuries before there was a Christian church there, says Robert Anderson in his book *Kimchi and Maple Leaves Under the Rising Sun*,

> *...while it may be said that the missionary initiative for work among Koreans in Japan began in Korea, it began with the foreign missionaries and the Federal Council there, with the concurrence and co-operation of the Korean Churches. It was thus a reflection of the North American missionary concern which provided both personnel and support funds for the Japan operation.*[21]

In 1914, the work with the Korean Christians in Japan had been turned over to the Federal Council of Churches in Korea. This work was supervised by the joint committees of the Methodist and Presbyterian missions in Korea. They were asked to supply missionaries for work among the Koreans in Japan but none could be found until after church union in 1925, when the Korean field came under the jurisdiction of the United Church of Canada, and the Rev. Luther and Mrs. Miriam Young, who had worked on that field, were free to accept an appointment. In 1928, the Youngs, along with a Presbyterian delegation of three, sailed from Vancouver, arriving in Yokohama in October. The members of the delegation met with Caroline Macdonald who "filled them in on the situation in Yokohama and Tokyo" and introduced them to several prominent Japanese leaders.[22] A large part of the financial support for the Youngs was provided by the WMS(ED). This society also supported a Bible woman, Miss Pak.

The WMS supported several Bible women. Mrs. Suk Kyung Ye, one of the Bible women, was educated at the mission schools in Korea and was a graduate of Pyeng Yang Bible Institute. She divided her time between two congregations in Kobe, in Sunday school work, prayer meetings, night school for women and other activities. She visited in the homes and in the winter collected clothing from the foreign residents and distributed it among the poor.

Mrs. Chong Ai Kim, another Bible woman, was a graduate of Seoul Bible Institute. She had a group of Christians under her care. She not only conducted all meetings, Bible classes and did all the visiting for this group, but she held church services in a nearby city and taught two Bible study classes in other cities. Another Bible woman, Mrs. Em, a teacher, spoke several languages and did valuable work at the industrial school.

Miss Jean MacLean was appointed to the work in 1928. Miss Ethel MacDonald was appointed in 1929. Both of these women were appointed by the WMS(ED). In September 1930, Miss Gladys Murphy from the

WMS(ED) and Miss Mary Ellen Anderson from the WMS(WD) were appointed to serve with the Korean Church in Japan.

One of the most effective forms of outreach, says Robert Anderson, was through Bible women, women lay-workers and women's organizations. He quotes Gladys Murphy who describes the work among the women.

All over this land from north to south the women have had a worthy share in establishing churches. Although scarcely realized, yet in more than one instance groups owe their beginning to the initiative of a woman who, though in a new and strange land and surrounded by non-Christians, lets her light so shine that others were brought to a saving knowledge of the Truth... Thus from the first have women, old and young been used in the establishing of Churches in this land.[23]

The June 1931 issue of *The Glad Tidings* announced that, due to serious illness, Caroline Macdonald had given up her work in Japan and returned to her home in London, Ontario. The October issue brought the sad news of her death on July 18th, 1931. Fourteen pages in *The Glad Tidings* were devoted to the story of her life and the circumstances of her death, including the last article she wrote for the magazine. The funeral service was held on July 20 in St. Andrew's Presbyterian Church in Wingham, Ontario. Memorial services were held in the Knox College Chapel, Toronto and in Tokyo, Japan where among the many floral tributes were two beautiful wreaths sent by thousands of the inmates, men and women, of some of the largest of Japan's prisons.

Rev. D.J. Davidson of India, a classmate of Caroline Macdonald's at the University of Toronto in 1901, spoke at the service.

"The Flower of her class," he called her. "That great internationalist, and, most beautiful of all, 'The White Angel of Tokyo,'" — the term applied to her by a Japanese student who visited Canada.[24]

Caroline Macdonald had received an honorary LL.D. from the University of Toronto in 1925. Mrs. Helen Strachan wrote an appreciation of Dr. Macdonald in the October 1931 *The Glad Tidings.*

I think of her and her life work as I saw it when in Japan. I went with her one morning to one of the large prisons where she carried on her work... When we came back to her settlement I saw her with another piece of work..., the care of the families of prisoners... Then came the evening and the weekly prayer meeting.... To this came the girls from her night school and some ex-pupils. Across from me sat a man just out of prison. There were also present several boys on probation from the juvenile court and other ex-prisoners.

That night she and I lingered for a talk after the rest of the household had retired. When we finally were going upstairs, I remarked that she had not locked the front door. "This door is never locked," she replied, "and if you lock it now you will be locking in the burglars instead of locking them out, for upstairs there are six men sleeping who just came out of prison today. This is the 'House of Friendliness.'"[25]

British Guiana

The Presbyterian missionaries soon realized that, while other churches were ministering to the black people, the large number of East Indians had no opportunity for religious or secular education and no medical help was available to them. Consequently, the East Indians became the focus of the Presbyterian Church in Canada.

After several months of delays and disappointments in securing a principal for the girls' high school at New Amsterdam, Miss Mary Murray of Milan, Quebec, a graduate of McGill University, Montreal and of the Missionary and Deaconess Training Home in Toronto offered her services.

In Miss Murray's first letter, she reported that she had already begun to work at the high school in New Amsterdam. There were forty-one girls enrolled, representing all the different races in British Guiana. Schools were provided by the government. The field missionaries had to supervise the schools in their districts as well as look after church work.

A Flourishing Society!

By 1931, reports indicated that the work of the society was flourishing. The WMS had hospitals in four centres; six school homes in five centres; two residential schools and one improved day school for Aboriginal children; a flourishing Welcome and Welfare Department with a staff of eighteen port and station workers, hospital visitors and deaconesses.

Overseas mission work was carried on in Formosa, India, Manchuria, China, Japan and British Guiana. There were no vacancies in the national work but overseas there was always urgent need: a lady doctor for India; a nurse evangelist for Manchuria; a university trained woman for the principalship of the girls' school in Tamsui, Formosa, as well as two evangelistic workers and a music teacher for Formosa.

At this point the WMS owned the hospital in South Porcupine, the school homes in New Liskeard, Huntingdon and Saskatoon; and the Gonor Mission in Selkirk, Manitoba. (The girls' school home in Canora, Saskatchewan was closed.) $20,000 had been expended on new buildings overseas.

The phenomenal growth and development of the WMS(WD) during this period is well documented in their annual reports, their reports to the General Assembly and in *The Glad Tidings*.

The WMS(ED) After the Disruption

The first annual meeting of the WMS(ED) after the disruption was held October 8-9, 1925. In spite of the disruption of the society, there was a large attendance and intense enthusiasm marked the meeting. Reports from all the auxiliaries were encouraging, particularly since all the presbyterials except two were organized after June 10, 1925, and nearly all the auxiliaries organized later. The society supported the Maritime synod by assuming $5,000 of the budget for home mission work and set aside funds for work on foreign fields. Mrs. McKerroll, president of the western division, attended the meeting and brought greetings from the council executive of the WMS(WD).

WMS(ED) celebrated its 50th anniversary in 1926. Miss Annie Blackadder, the society's first missionary, addressed the General Assembly that year. When she rose to speak, the Assembly stood in her honour. Miss McCulloch and the editor of *The Glad Tidings* were asked to prepare a history of the past 50 years of the WMS(ED).

Chapter 12

The Depression Years

1931-1939

Famine, Pestilence, War and Death

The farmers in the West were having a difficult time in 1931. There were reports from hospitals that they were being paid in produce rather than money. The farmers were still managing to get along as Mrs. Robertson, matron of the school at Vegreville reported, in writing about her visits to some of the Ukrainian families. The homes were picturesque with white-washed mud walls inside and out, thatched roofs and outdoor bake ovens of mud. She adds, however, that although many of these people had plenty to eat, they had no way of making money.

Things did not improve. There wasn't sufficient rain for nearly three years and, by the fall of 1931, the situation was grim. The area affected through crop failure extended from Brandon, Manitoba, westward through Saskatchewan and into Alberta. In this entire area the average farmer had no crop, no feed, no water, no money. In some cases water had to be hauled nearly six miles and water tanks were seen everywhere. That fall many farmers did not even take their binders out since there was no grain to cut. By 1932, the Depression had affected northern Ontario. The lumbering industry in South Porcupine was closed, putting hundreds out of work.

The government and the churches were quick to respond. The government worked through the Red Cross in co-operation with the churches. The General Board of Missions appealed to the churches for relief in money and clothing. A letter was sent to ministers to be read to every congregation. Realizing that it would probably be the women in the congregations who would be responsible for collecting supplies, the WMS sent a letter to the women of the church through the supply secretaries of the WMS. The letter was printed in the January 1932 issue of *The Glad Tidings*. The WMS made it clear to their members that this work must be over and above the regular supply work and, since the need was so appalling, the help of all the women, particularly the Ladies' Aid groups, and of every other organization in the congregation would be required.

The church asked the WMS to take charge of the appeal for clothing. The headquarters for relief work for Ontario, Quebec and the Maritimes was Knox Presbyterian Church, Toronto. Mrs. H.R. Horne of Regina, Saskatchewan was the Presbyterian Church's representative on the Government Relief Commission. WMS members were told that clothing could go direct from the presbyterial supply centres or congregations to Mrs. Horne. Free rates had been arranged with both the Canadian National and Canadian Pacific railways.

Things got worse. By the fall of 1933 apparently what hail, drought and caterpillars had not destroyed, the grasshoppers had. One report said, they crossed the country like solid armies, with a noise like nothing ever heard before. Nothing was left.

Mrs. Horne's husband, mission superintendent for the synod, reported that the need for relief in the southern areas of Saskatchewan, Manitoba and Alberta was greater than ever due to the continuing drought and the scourge of grasshoppers.

The WMS was anxious to help in whatever way they could and, since the people in the West were unable to raise enough money to pay their ministers, the WMS supplemented their salaries. They also appealed once more to the women of the church for warm clothing for both children and adults.

Wiping Out the Deficit

In the early months of 1931 the church held its own.

> *Notwithstanding the stress and strain from what has now become a familiar term, "The Period of Depression," the work of the Presbyterian Church has been carried on without retrenchment in her missionary, educational and administrative departments.*[1]

However, by the end of 1931, the picture had changed and the church was running a deficit of $184,000, and had, consequently, cut the allocation for mission work. The Moderator was suggesting that, if each member of the church gave one dollar, the deficit could be wiped out.

For the year 1932, the WMS had three goals: an adequate budget for the year; making up the deficit; and standing behind the people in the stricken areas of the west.

In 1935, a letter to the WMS(WD) from Dr. A. S. Grant, secretary of the General Board of Missions and of the budget and stewardship committee, acknowledged the part the WMS had played in making up the deficit:

> *...I am writing to convey to you and to your Council Executive and to all those who took part in raising this large sum of money, amounting to $25,000, for the work of the Presbyterian Church in Canada through this period of depression, our sincerest thanks.*
>
> *This in itself is one of the most magnanimous, self-sacrificing things that has come under my observation in the history of our Church. Your Board during this period of depression and with the tremendous volume of work for which you were responsible has made this additional contribution to the general funds of the Church, and as one who made this request of you I wish to convey to you my sincerest thanks....*[2]

Canada

Growing municipalities were gradually taking over their own hospitals and in 1935 the hospital at South Porcupine in northern Ontario was sold to the municipality of Tisdale. The hospital had been built and operated by the WMS as a contribution to the life of the community with the expectation that eventually the municipality would take over the responsibility. Many expressions of thanks and appreciation had come to the WMS from the community of South Porcupine. When the cornerstone for the new Porcupine General Hospital was laid, the hospital board decided that the honour of laying the cornerstone should go to a representative of the WMS(WD). At the ceremony which took place on October 17, 1937, Mrs. Mary McKerroll officiated. The inscription on the trowel presented to Mrs. McKerroll read,

Porcupine General Hospital
Corner-stone laid by
The Presbyterian Women's Missionary Society
October 17th, 1937
In token of appreciation of original
Hospital Service in the Community[3]

In June 1938, after many years of pioneer work, the R.M. Boswell Hospital at Vegreville was closed. *The Vegreville Observer*, after giving a brief history of the hospital says,

> *It is not lack of funds which has led to the decision to close the hospital. At the time it was opened there were no hospital facilities round these parts closer than Edmonton. It was a missionary venture to fill an existing need and that need is now covered by hospitals at...other points, especially the General Hospital here.... Nevertheless, the citizens of Vegreville view with extreme regret the closing... It has been a good hospital...a power for good in the community.*[4]

While some hospitals were closing there were new ones being opened that needed help from the WMS. A new hospital at Rocky Mountain House, Alberta, was in the process of being built. A local business committee was formed to work with the WMS council executive. The new hospital was opened on July 14,1938. The Rocky Mountain House Board of Trade wrote to the WMS council executive expressing their gratitude and deep appreciation as, they said, the hospital would not have been built without the financial aid and co-operation of the WMS. In northern Saskatchewan the WMS undertook to complete the unfinished hospital at Weirdale and maintain it as a nursing home operated by the WMS. The official opening took place in July 1939.

What was happening in the hospitals was also happening in the boarding schools. In 1935, the girls' residence in Prince Albert closed. It had served that part of Saskatchewan for fifteen years, but public schools had opened in the area and there was not the same need for the residence. The girls' residence in Vegreville also closed in 1935. However it was opened again in the fall of 1937 as the demand for accommodation was so great.

Mrs. Robertson reported from Vegreville that several of their pupils had become teachers while others had studied pharmacy. One boy, who had just graduated, planned to study medicine, and one of the girls, nearing graduation, hoped to become a nurse. Two Romanian boys, recently graduated, hoped to become missionaries to their own people but needed financial help. Mrs. Robertson commented that these young people would not have had an opportunity of education if it had not been made possible by these schools. It was gratifying for the WMS to see the good results that were coming from their efforts.

The *Vegreville Observer*, in the same article that reported the closing of the Vegreville Hospital, also spoke about the closing of the boarding schools.

> *The reason for closing the Homes is practically the same as that given for the closing of the hospital, namely the Homes were a missionary*

> *effort, the need for which has largely disappeared. Rural schools are now established in all parts of the district... Many brilliant students, who made their mark later in life, received their first opportunities for education through the medium of the Homes. They were fine institutions, giving boys and girls much more than mere educational chances, in that efforts were made to train the pupils in the amenities of life, moral and spiritual values and the courtesies which arise from culture.*[5]

The residence at New Liskeard was closed in June 1937: pupils were few due to changing conditions and high fees for those who lived outside the district.

At Cecilia Jeffrey the school band was making a name for itself. The band visited Winnipeg in 1933 where the young people were guests of the T. Eaton Company and played for the luncheon customers. While in Winnipeg, they were also invited on a tour of the Winnipeg Free Press and later put on a concert in front of the Free Press building. The band took the highest marks in the Western Music Festival held at Kenora in 1934. High marks were also given at the music festival to a two-part song presented by the pupils of the school bringing to the school the silver shield. This band of Aboriginal boys and girls was honoured to share in welcoming the King and Queen at Redditt in 1939, where thousands from Kenora, Keewatin and other parts of that district of northwestern Ontario gathered when the Royal train stopped for twenty minutes.

Gerald Redsky, a student at Cecilia Jeffrey, carried off the first prize in the art display section of the Brandon Exhibition in 1936 where he competed against school children in the province of Manitoba. At the YMCA hobby show in Kenora in 1938, the Cecilia Jeffrey pupils won over forty awards. Honour also came to the Birtle School when their senior girls' choir won the first prize at the music festival in Winnipeg in 1939.

Two young girls, Mary Begg and Mary Green, graduates of Cecilia Jeffrey School, went to Toronto in 1937 and stayed at the Missionary and Deaconess Training Home while taking vocational courses in household science at the Central Technical School. They also took music lessons in piano and pipe-organ during their stay.

In 1935, representatives of all denominations in Canada that administered schools for Aboriginal people met in Ottawa to talk about their common problems and to speak to the premier. They stated that they had done some investigating and discovered that other institutions in Canada educating white children received per capita grants ranging from $400 to $700, while

Birtle Choir

the average grant per child to the churches was at the present time about $165, which had been reduced further by 15 per cent. The cut, they said, had a serious effect since strict economy had always been practised. Since the 15 per cent cut was put into place, stocks of food, bedding, agricultural implements, and so on, were seriously depleted and deficits were mounting. The premier promised that, beginning April 1, 1935, the government would restore 10 per cent of the cut they had deducted from the grant.[6] In 1939, the full grant was restored.

Mr. Bird of the Mistawasis Reserve was a commissioner to General Assembly in June 1938. He was the first Aboriginal commissioner to attend a General Assembly of the Presbyterian Church. His family was the fourth generation to have been connected with the Presbyterian Church's Mission at Mistawasis. Mr. Bird went to General Assembly with Rev. W.W. Moore, missionary at the reserve.

In 1928, the WMS was able to bring Miss Lilyan Yeung, daughter of Rev. K.H. Yeung of the Chinese mission in Vancouver, to Toronto to complete her secondary education, then to study for three years training in the Women's College Hospital. She was awarded the board of governors scholarship and several other prizes in 1935. She obtained her Bachelor of Arts degree and offered her services to the WMS and then to the Chinese government. Her sister, Pansy, graduated from the University of Toronto and took courses at the Ontario College of Education hoping to work in Free China. Both Lilyan and Pansy helped at summer camps in 1939.

Another successful student, Miss Rosalind Wong of Montreal, was the first Chinese woman to sit the nurses' examination of the Association of Nurses in the Province of Quebec. She left for South China in November, 1936, to fill the position of superintendent of nurses in the Chinese government's Military College for Nurses at Canton.

At the request of the Presbytery of Montreal and the Montreal provincial board, financial assistance was given by the WMS for French work in Montreal. Reports indicate that four or five hundred people were attending the Sunday services in the two preaching places, and 100 to 250 attended the Thursday evening prayer meetings.

The Hungarian Presbyterian Church, Toronto, bought property to build a church in 1938. The WMS assisted with a grant of $1,000. In 1939, the WMS gave a grant of $500 toward the building of the church. Mrs. Beatrice Steinmetz, the wife of the minister, worked as a deaconess among the Hungarian people.

In the 1930s, deaconesses were taking on more and more responsibility in the west. They were much in demand and presbyteries were urgently requesting their services.

Dr. Margaret Strang worked as a medical missionary in Dixonville, Alberta and the surrounding districts. Often travelling on horseback, she covered an area of 600 miles. She conducted services and Sunday school each Sunday and organized a Ladies' Aid. In 1933, she married Mr. Douglas Savage. Dr. E.A. Wright, minister at Grande Prairie, speaking at General Assembly in 1934 of the work of devoted missionaries, noted that Dr. Strang-Savage was a heroic soul.

Rev. W. M. Kannawin, secretary of Sabbath Schools and Young People's Societies, brought news of the work in the west to the members of council executive at a meeting in 1936. He was deeply impressed by the remarkable work accomplished by the WMS during the previous ten years. He mentioned in particular several deaconesses in the western provinces who were building up Sunday schools, organizing women's and children's groups, doing house to house visiting and preaching sometimes two or three times each Sunday: Miss Ruby Walker, Miss Frieda Matthews, Dr. Margaret Strang-Savage, Miss Mary Todd, Miss Margaret Grigor, Miss Roberta Smith, Miss Ruby Blyth. Dr. Kannawin said he believed that there was for our church a great opportunity for service in the western provinces.

There had been no religious gathering at Blueberry Mountain, Alberta, until Mrs. Margaret Macdonald gathered twelve women in her home on February 28, 1936, for the World Day of Prayer. At the close of the service a WMS auxiliary was organized with Mrs. Macdonald as president. Miss Margaret Grigor, deaconess, had been for some time anxious to visit Blueberry Mountain and she made arrangements with Mrs. Macdonald to come on August 13 along with the minister in the area, Rev. Atkinson. Fifty-two miles was a long trip but they reached Spirit River at 12:30, had lunch and rested the horses. When inquiring about the way to Blueberry Mountain they were told to go west and right into the bush. Upon arrival, they stopped to ask the way to Mrs. Macdonald's house. About a mile from their destination they heard singing. Inside the little room they found 25 men, women and children ready to welcome them. Mrs. Macdonald told them she was just getting ready to read the Moderator's sermon out of the *Presbyterian Record* because they had been singing for some time. As far as was known, Miss Grigor said, this was the first Presbyterian service ever held at Blueberry Mountain. They needed Bibles for the Sunday school so she sent some with some text cards.

> *...we are going to try and go once a month. Our other new points are coming along. Services are conducted every other Sunday at Belloy and Fox Creek. Mr. Atkinson has been taking these while I have taken Heart Valley and Westvale, but we are going to alternate. Also I hope to have Mission Bands. Presbytery has promised them every encouragement and will give them dollar for dollar... Presbytery is also sending a request for another deaconess...*[7]

Miss Helen Madill, a nurse-deaconess, went to the Peace River District in April 1936. In order for her to be located in a more central part of the district, the WMS planned to build a little home farther north than Brownvale. Patients would then be able to visit the nurse and benefit from the small dispensary they were hoping to have in the house. Miss Madill reported that, before leaving the east, she thought she had a fairly good vision of the Brownvale mission field,

> *...but not until I was here a while did I realize the vastness of the work, the distances between the districts being so great and the roads so often in poor condition.*[8]

In another report, she said the northern field was difficult

> *...and especially so in nursing; in fact, I am going day and night trying to cover as much as possible...my house will be a godsend... I feel I should be up here where a worker is needed... People will be able to come to me then, instead of waiting day after day wondering whether we will call on them... Really one often thinks people can get sick from loneliness up here, which is quite true, as often I do not give medicine but visit with them, and they do feel so much better afterwards.*[9]

Miss Helen Madill did get her little house and moved from Brownville to Last Lake, where she was closer to the people.

During the summer of 1936 new survey work was done and groups were organized in Algoma Presbytery by Miss Roberta Smith. The church had also ventured into northern Ontario and northern Manitoba. In March 1937, the church opened up work in Kirkland Lake under Rev. C.J. MacKay. Miss Lily Macarthur, deaconess, found the work encouraging. Not long after she began work, they had a Mission Band, a CGIT group and a Ladies' Aid society and were working towards their objective of a church of their own. On October 30, 1938, a large congregation gathered for the dedication of the new St. Andrew's Presbyterian Church in Kirkland Lake.

Miss Lily Macarther was the deaconess sent to the new Val d'Or field in northern Quebec. Rev. J.L. Hughes, Home Mission convener of Quebec Presbytery, spoke of the splendid way she had taken hold of the work in so short a time. She already seemed to know a great number of the women in that stretch of sixty miles which she covered and was gradually working towards forming groups of women in the different parts of the field.

A forward step was taken by the Presbyterian Missionary and Deaconess Training Home when, probably for the first time, provision was made for the training of volunteer workers. They offered a year's tuition to Sunday school teachers, youth workers, leaders in women's and girls' work and any others who desired additional training.

In 1937, the council executive welcomed Mrs. Goldwin Smith, lecturer at the Presbyterian Missionary and Deaconess Training Home, toward whose salary the society made a contribution. After graduating in theology in 1936, Mrs. Smith volunteered her services for the students at the training home. She was appointed lecturer in theology for the session 1937-38. Mrs. Smith declared she was delighted with the great opportunity of work with young women. She said,

> *Deaconesses should receive a training strongly tinctured with theology which would be in line with everyday life.*[10]

Miss Margaret Wong, Christian literature secretary for Africa, wrote to say that a grant from the committee on Christian literature for women and children had made it possible to provide a little magazine, *Listen*, which circulated in east, west and south Africa. Translated in a number of languages, the magazine was especially intended for villages and for schools.

Mrs. Elizabeth MacGillivray of the Christian Literature Society in China was a welcome visitor to council executive in September, 1936. Mrs. MacGillivray and Dr. MacGillivray worked in Shanghai for the Christian Literature Society for thirty-six years. Mrs. MacGillivray continued the work after Dr. MacGillivray's death. The WMS(WD) had always given the grant to the Christian Literature Society in China through Mrs. MacGillivray. In 1936, they doubled the grant.

Mrs. MacGillivray suggested to the council executive that if the society wished to make a special gift to the Christian Literature Society at Shanghai on the occasion of their Jubilee in 1937, money to defray the cost of publication of one or more books written by Chinese authors would be greatly appreciated. It was decided that *The Chinese Mother's Book* would be published as the special gift of the WMS(WD) and any money left over could be used for other publications.

Miss Margaret Brown took over as head of the children's work department of the Christian Literature Society in Shanghai in 1936 and wrote to express appreciation of the interest of the WMS in the work.

By 1935, nearly fifty countries were participating in the World Day of Prayer. The day would begin in New Zealand and the Fiji Islands with a sunrise prayer meeting and would end in Hawaii with evening services for young people.

In 1938, with war raging in the far east, the inter-board committee of the Women's Missionary Societies of Canada added a prayer to the World Day of Prayer program and asked churches and groups to use it with the service on March 4.

> *Almighty God, King of Kings and Ruler of all the world, have mercy on the nations now devastated and perishing by war. Have mercy, O Lord, have mercy. Turn the hearts of their rulers that they may be willing to make peace. Answer the prayers and prosper the counsels of all Thy servants who are working for peace and over-rule the wrath of men to praise Thee. Through Jesus Christ our Lord. Amen.*[11]

The WMS was a corporate member of the League of Nations and felt closely allied with this movement for peace. In 1934, The League of Nations Society in Canada planned a nation-wide effort to give expression to the policy of peace. The aim was to induce every thinking man and woman in Canada who accepted his or her responsibilities as a citizen to consider what he or she could do in the cause of peace.

The Governor-General of Canada, Dr. John Buchan, in an address to the Ontario Provincial Society of the WMS in April 1936 said,

> *If the League of Nations means anything, it means that all civilized governments have to undertake tasks which in the past were left to the Church and to the missionaries. They have accepted a solemn moral responsibility, and Churches and Governments are now united as partners in the same duty. The hope of the world lies in the success of this partnership. But internationalism will not succeed unless it acquires much of the purpose and spirit of the old missionary… For world peace and world prosperity the soul is more important than the body… The League of Nations will only fulfil its task, if, side by side with it, there is another and a spiritual League of Nations, a universal acceptance of the Gospel of Peace.*[12]

In 1937, the annual conference of the League of Nations in Canada, at its meeting in May, decided to set aside one week in each year as Peace Action Week. The week of November 8-14 was to be observed as Peace Action Week to demonstrate Canada's will for effective action on behalf of world law and justice. Mrs. J. R. Hill, president of the Ottawa presbyterial, represented the council executive at the annual meeting of the League of Nations Society in Ottawa.

The Presbyterian Church has always worked interdenominationally with other churches, thus strengthening their witness. The WMS, too, has always looked beyond itself, working in close association with interdenominational women's boards and missionary organizations.

In the anxious times before the Second World War, it was even more crucial for churches and missionary organizations to work together. Several important conferences took place in the late 1930s in which the Presbyterian Church and the WMS were involved. Among them was the World Conference on Faith and Order, which met in Edinburgh in August 1937 and adopted the following resolution:

> *We have met at a time of great strain and distress...in Europe and in the Far East. We watch with sympathy and sorrow the menace and the horrors of war. We are persuaded that war never occurs except as a result and expression of that sin from which Christ came to redeem the world. We therefore call all men, and ourselves before all others, to pray that God may give to us and to all men the love of justice, the readiness to forgive, the knowledge of His will, and the courage to obey it.*[13]

Another important conference was held in January 1938 in Toronto. It was the Foreign Missions Conference of North America and it held its annual meeting in Canada for the first time in its forty-five year history. The two most important matters on its agenda were, first, preparations for the third World Missionary Conference which was to be held in Madras, India, December 1938 and, second, consideration of the tragic situation in the Far East arising from the Japanese invasion of China,

> *...both serving to stress the fact that the concern of the men and women gathered in conference was not only with the Churches of the United States and Canada, but with a world Christian Church, a world Christian community...*[14]

The third World Missionary Conference was probably one of the most important and significant conferences ever held. It took place in December 1938 at Tambaram at the Madras Christian College, sixteen miles from Madras City in India.

The first World Missionary Conference was held in Edinburgh, Scotland in 1910. Representatives from most of the Protestant churches and missionary societies attended. Recognizing that the overlapping of work and the competition among the different sections of the Christian church were stumbling blocks to the proclamation of the faith, delegates at this first conference tried to bring about a true unity of effort and of faith in carrying out the task of the world church.

The second World Missionary Conference was held after the First World War in 1928 in Jerusalem. For the first time, the younger churches of the Orient, Africa, and Latin America were represented. At this conference it was recognized that one of the tasks of missions would be to so strengthen these younger churches that they would be able to undertake more and more of the work of evangelism in their own countries.

At this third World Missionary Conference, a world crisis resolution was passed on Christmas morning. It was a resolution of sympathy with comrades in the universal Church throughout the world in the areas of conflict, and the council pledged itself to use every effort to eliminate the causes of war. The resolution also called upon Christians in all lands to give generously to the work of relief in China, in view of the extensive suffering that had resulted from war in that land.

One of the women delegates at Madras was Miss P.S. Tseng of China. She was the first Chinese woman to graduate with her B.Sc. from London University and was the founder and principal of the I Fang Girls' School in Changsha. She commented that at Tambaran,

> *I began to see new visions and to have new hopes... In these days of mutual fear and suspicion it is not easy for so many nations to come together to discuss questions...it is splendid to see the working together of the older and younger Churches. Here we see the old Churches eager to render all the assistance they can to the younger members, and the younger Churches sending forward keen, earnest and capable leaders. It seems to me the day will not be far when there will be one flock and one Shepherd...*[15]

After the Madras Conference, two teams of representatives of the churches of Asia, Africa and Latin America came to the churches in the United States and Canada to share their impressions of Madras and to bring something of the new vision of the unity of the Christian church throughout the world. These teams spoke at several Sunday services and in Convocation Hall, Toronto, at meetings for various church workers, and at mass meetings, one especially for young people. In addition, two of the women spoke to a large gathering of women under the inter-board committee of the Women's Missionary Societies.

The World Christian Youth Conference was held in July and August 1939 in Amsterdam, Holland. The most important thing about Amsterdam, said Dr. Wilfred Lockhart, general secretary of the Student Christian Movement, was that it did happen.

> *At a time when the rest of the world was literally flying to pieces, the youth of the world came together; Christ was Victor.*[16]

The Glad Tidings had numerous articles about all the conferences that took place in the late 1930s and particularly about the Madras Conference. At their council meeting in September 1939, the program was devoted to Madras and Amsterdam — two world conferences of the utmost importance for the whole Christian church and the missionary movement throughout the world. Of the ten Canadian delegates to the Madras Conference, two were women. One of them was Miss Violet Tennant, Girls' Work secretary for the Presbyterian Church in Canada. Rev. J.H. Arnup, secretary of the Board of Foreign Missions of The United Church of Canada, and Miss Tennant gave some of the impressions of the Madras conference. They also showed how material from the conference could be used with groups. Addresses were given by Rev. Wilfred C. Lockhart, secretary of the Student Christian Movement, and Miss Jessie Storrie, both of whom were delegates to the World Christian Youth Conference at Amsterdam, Holland.

Among the resolutions passed by this council meeting was an offer to help the General Board of Missions.

> *At this time of crisis in our country as in other countries, inevitably a time of crisis in the Christian Church, the Women's Missionary Society is deeply conscious of the heavy burden and responsibility laid upon the General Board of Missions. The Women's Missionary Society realizes that the maintenance of ordinances is of supreme importance to the Presbyterian Church at this time and wish to assure the General Board of Missions that to the utmost of their ability they will stand behind the Board, ready to help as may be required with their organization and with their financial support. To this end the Women's Missionary Society would welcome a conference.*[17]

At the WMS council meeting, Rev. William Barclay spoke on behalf of the budget and stewardship committee of the church, expressing appreciation of the step taken by the WMS in pledging itself to stand behind the church in the difficult days and expressing the hope that a conference might be arranged with representatives of the General Board of Missions, the WMS(WD) and the budget and stewardship committees.

The Glad Tidings, from 1935 to 1939, reported the visits to Toronto by Dr. Conrad Hoffmann and Dr. Conrad Hoffmann, Jr., director and secretary of the International Committee on the Christian approach to the Jews. In an attempt to get the churches to take action, they described what was happening to the Jewish people in Europe. An editorial in the magazine titled, "Work Among the Jews" says,

> *Never before in the history of the Christian world has there been such a critical situation facing the Jewish race. The persecution they have been suffering in Poland, Rumania and Germany has beggared them economically and disfranchised them politically. Every Christian should have a sympathetic understanding of these conditions and we are glad to have, in this issue, considerable information of work being carried on today among the Jewish people.*[18]

The same issue also announces that Dr. Hoffmann, Jr., would be in Toronto in April 1936 and would lecture at the School of Missions.

There are also several excerpts from the news sheet supplied by the International Committee on the Christian Approach to the Jews. One of these, "What Christians Should Remember and Jews Forget," by Rabbi Stephen S. Wise says,

> *The only redeeming hope of the world can be that Israel and Christendom stand together. Christians should remember at this season that nowhere is there to be found the faintest scintilla of evidence that Christ sought to take Himself out of the Jewish people or to create an ecclesiastical organization to supersede the synagogue wherein as a Jewish child he had been reared...*[19]

There does not seem to be a report of Dr. Hoffman's lecture at the School of Missions in April 1936 but the first item under the editorial in the January 1937 issue of the magazine reports on a luncheon meeting arranged by the inter-board committee of the Women's Missionary Societies of Canada at which Dr. Hoffmann reviewed recent activities in his field of work.

At this meeting Dr. Hoffmann spoke of the tide of anti-Jewish feeling that was sweeping over the world, affecting even Great Britain, the United States and Canada. He reminded his hearers that if Gentiles were really Christian there would be no problem. The all-important thing in the situation in Germany, he said, with the movement to eliminate everything Jewish from their religion, was that it is being demonstrated that one cannot "de-Judaize" a country without "de-Christianizing" it. Anti-Semitism and Christianity were irreconcilable. In the face of the present situation, he asked, what were the Christian churches doing?

During one of the visits arranged again by the inter-board committee of Women's Missionary Societies of Canada, he expressed gratitude for the committee's assistance and asked for its continuance. The work, he declared, had become more important than ever. Half the Jews of the world were exposed to the woes of anti-Semitism and there was no place for them to go. He had never seen such human wretchedness. There was no help for them in the existing world, unless God intervened. Dr. Hoffmann urged Christians to pray for the persecuted and the persecutors and to help the Jewish people in Germany and the ones travelling to other countries. Moreover, they could fight anti-Semitism here in Canada.

None of the conferences that took place in the late 1930s seem to express alarm at what was happening in Europe, although, from at least as early as 1935, Dr. Hoffmann had been in Canada speaking to Canadian churches about the horrifying plight of the Jewish people.

India

In spite of political unrest and other problems, work in India was going forward. New buildings were being erected and new staff were arriving on the field. Miss Bertha Robson, who had built up the Helen Macdonald Girls' School and served in India for twenty years, was leaving for health reasons. The Bhils showed their devotion and gratitude by coming long distances, often on foot, to say good-bye to the beloved Miss Sahib.

Dr. Effie Winchester left Montreal for India in September 1936 to serve in the Jobat Hospital which had just opened its new Louise Henderson Maternity Ward and the Mary Broadbent Training Home for nurses and Bible women. Unfortunately, Dr. Winchester's term was short since she had to return to Canada because of illness. Miss Margaret Kennedy was designated at Kensington Presbyterian Church in Montreal to serve on the Bhil Field in India under the WMS(WD).

Miss Christine Maxwell, evangelistic missionary for the WMS among the Bhil people at Sardi, Central India had translated the Gospel of St. John and the First Epistle of John into Bhili. Always an earnest Bible student, Miss Maxwell, when on furlough in Canada in 1933, spent much of her holiday studying Greek and Hebrew in Knox College.

Dr. Mary Mackay Buchanan, wife of Dr. John Buchanan, died on May 15, 1935: She was "a beloved missionary of our church who gave her rich talents

Bertha Robson in India

to the missionary cause." Mary Mackay was born in Stellarton, Nova Scotia, and was a graduate of the Women's Medical College in Toronto. She was designated in Knox Church, Toronto in 1888 and went to India as a medical missionary under the Woman's Foreign Missionary Society. She married Dr. Buchanan shortly after her arrival in India and together they started medical work in Ujain. Seven years later, in 1895, they accepted the charge of opening up the work among the Bhils in the Amkhut valley. Mrs. Buchanan gave herself unreservedly for 47 years. She was a woman of deep and vital faith and found abundant opportunity for the use of her medical skill. Her Bible classes, the teacher's Bible class, and those for the women were a wonderful feature of her work. Preachers, teachers, men and women told how she, from week to week, had opened up the scriptures for them.

Bessie MacMurchy, a nurse, appointed to India in 1932, later recalled how

> *Outside on the verandah, Mrs. Buchanan talked to the women, many of whom were too shy and backward to enter the building, and they listened to her affectionate and compelling voice with the deepest attention as she told them of how much their Saviour, Jesus Christ, had done for women while on earth...*[20]

The Buchanans had one son who was killed while serving in the First Canadian Contingent during the First World War. They had two daughters. Ruth Buchanan served unofficially on the Bhil field, assisting her father and helping the Bhil people in many ways. The other daughter, Edith, was a nurse on the staff of the Lady Hardinge College Hospital in New Delhi.

China

Reports showed that invading armies were in North China and in parts of the south. They occupied the strategic cities and the highways of commerce holding "ribbons" of country along the lines of communication, rivers and railways. All in between was still under the control of the Chinese national government thus exposing the invaders' lines to guerilla warfare. There had been bombing in all parts of the country, and it was estimated that thousands of people had been uprooted, but the atmosphere was quite different in free China. In the rural areas of West China primary education was being carried on as before the war.

It was a dangerous time in China, yet there was not a missionary there who did not feel privileged to serve. Amid conflict and destruction, the Christian church was, they believed, writing one of the most glorious pages of its history. The missionaries were giving protection and service in the name of Christ, bringing together families, helping the wounded and doing all kinds of relief work. The compounds were like little cities of refuge. This service rendered by the Christian church had a profound effect upon the Chinese people.

The church in China issued a call to go forward. The call was issued by the National Christian Council of China on December 29, 1937, and broadcast to their whole church on January 2, 1938.

> *Despite all the black facts of life around us, God calls us not to retreat, not even to stand still and hold on, but to go forward.... In the midst of suffering and loss and national crisis we would call upon the Christian Church to move forward. The Gospel of Christ is not a message of defeat. It is a summons to struggle against the forces of evil in the lives of men and nations. It is the good news of the love of God in action... Many Churches are now suffering from war, with their members scattered and their services disrupted. Many schools and hospitals have been seriously affected... We call upon all Christians to co-operate in relief work and thus to exemplify the Christian spirit in the face of the horrors of war.*[21]

On April 6, 1938, in the name of General Chiang Kai-shek, tribute was made to Christian missions and there was an announcement of an important government change of policy in regard to the teaching of religion in private schools.

> *The Generalissimo wishes me to tell you that he deeply appreciates the fine work which you have been doing to help our people. Please take this as a personal tribute to your courage and self-sacrificing spirit, to your valour and determination to help our people, regardless of the dangers to your own persons and lives... The fact that you not only risked your lives in succouring the wounded, but also helped the destitute, and saved many of our women and girls from a fate worse than death, and gave hope and support to all the refugees, has moved the whole Chinese nation to a sense of appreciation of the true Christian spirit which animated you in your action...*
>
> *Some years ago the Government issued an order which forbade religion to be made a compulsory study in any private school... It gives me very great pleasure, therefore, to-day to tell you that by your work and the spirit that underlies it you have made manifest the meaning of true Christianity. The results of your efforts are so appreciated by the Government and the people that the Generalissimo has now found it possible to have that law forbidding religion to be compulsorily taught in Christian Schools amended, so that religious subjects may henceforth be taught in registered Mission Schools...*[22]

Formosa

The Formosan Presbyterian Church celebrated its diamond jubilee in 1932. The Moderator of the General Assembly of the Presbyterian Church in Canada, Rev. W. G. Brown, and Mrs. Brown, were in attendance. In commemoration of the diamond jubilee, Tamsui Church, the first church to be established by Dr. Mackay, was rebuilt. The WMS(WD) pledged $500 as their share in this memorial.

In Tamsui there were four institutions: the theological college, the women's Bible school, the Tamsui Girls' High School and the Tamsui Middle School.

In Taihoku (Taipei) there was the Mackay Memorial Hospital with a leprosy clinic connected to it. There was also a nurses' home and a kindergarten. The Happy Mount Leprosy Clinic was not directly under the Presbyterian mission but the WMS, through their gift of $5,000, had a share in it. The Formosan Women's Missionary Society supported five of the mission's Bible women who worked in the country, in the hospital and with the kindergartens.

The jubilee services took place April 6-7. A diamond jubilee Mission Band was formed by Mrs. Jean Mackay, daughter-in-law of the founder. It was the first Mission Band in North Formosa and had a membership of about 60 girls and boys.

An interesting feature of the anniversary program was the indigenous folk dances and songs from the Ami tribe from the East Coast who had come to study in Tamsui. There were eight men from the Ami tribe and one from the Tayal tribe in the theological college taking a special course. Five Ami women and one Tayal woman attended the women's Bible school and about ten of their children were studying in the public school and in a special kindergarten prepared for them.

Japanese control was slow but sure. In 1895, at the close of the Sino-Japanese war, Formosa was ceded to Japan. Almost immediately the government began to introduce an educational system for the Formosans and there was a growing interest in education and an increase in the number of schools for both boys and girls. The Japanese system of education had high standards. Their teachers were well qualified and used the Japanese language. The government representatives treated the missionaries with courtesy and the missionaries always tried to meet the requirements of the government.

Nationalism grew rapidly and the missionaries were apprehensive about the effect it would have on their schools. The government demanded that no teacher be engaged or dismissed without its approval, thus making the securing of good, Christian teachers difficult. They also ruled that only two foreign teachers could be engaged in each school, and that all instruction in the schools must be given in Japanese. This meant that missionaries had to study Japanese as well as Chinese in order to carry on the educational work. The government did not allow religious instruction in the schools and had ordered that pupils of all schools must do homage at the shrine. The Japanese Educational Department assured the missionaries that this was not regarded by them as a religious act but as a demonstration of loyalty to the emperor. The missionaries decided it was best to concur and go to the shrine as a gesture of loyalty and homage to the emperor.

The missionaries realized that, for their schools to be recognized by the government, salaries would have to be increased and large sums spent on buildings for repairs and new equipment. It was impossible to compete with the government's fine, up-to-date buildings, modern equipment and well trained teachers.

In 1936, acting on information from the Formosan Christian Council, the General Board of Missions and the Women's Missionary Society, Western Division, gave their schools to the Japanese government and sold the surrounding property. The government was appreciative of the service the missionaries had given in the past and their contribution toward education in the schools. The governor suggested that, if the mission wished to put in some memorial to those who had served in the schools or to the Canadian Presbyterian Mission, he would be glad to agree, if it were not contrary to the government's principles. The governor told the missionaries that, since their schools had so many graduates, out of deep consideration for them, he would keep the schools as an alma mater forever.

In giving up this part of their educational work, the missionaries felt they would be free to devote themselves to the work for which the mission was intended, teaching the gospel and training indigenous workers for that work.

With this decision, evangelistic work expanded rapidly. A revival in Taihoku (Taipei) with three meetings daily had thousands in attendance. The spiritual life of the whole church was quickened. The first Preachers' Wives Conference of North Formosa was held in Tamsui. Christian pupils and their friends carried on their Christian endeavour and other activities in the women's school. The WMS had over 400 members and supported four full-time Bible women. The people of the Formosan churches began to place greater emphasis on Sunday schools and youth work. Several summer conferences and Bible study groups were held and every effort was made to interest the young people of Formosa and lead them to take part in the activities of the church.

Koreans in Japan

Koreans came to Japan in great numbers in the late 1930s. For the most part they were young people coming with hope for the future in a new country. But the country was overcrowded and labour was cheap. There was extreme poverty and sickness was common among the Koreans.

Jean McLean, Kindergarten teacher and evangelistic worker among the Koreans in Kobe, Japan

There were six Presbyterian missionaries on the field. Two of them, Miss Jean McLean (Rumball) and Miss Ellen Anderson, were supported by the WMS. Christian groups sprang up faster than leaders could be found and the most remarkable increase was in the WMS. The Bible women did splendid work.

One of the aims of mission work in Japan was to build up a strong self-supporting church for Koreans in Japan, which led to a growing ability of the church to manage its own affairs. A General Assembly of the Korean Christian Church in Japan was organized in the spring of 1935, and in the fall it was recognized by the General Assembly of the Presbyterian Church in Korea and by the National Council.

Manchuria

Failing health necessitated the return of Dr. and Mrs. Goforth from Manchuria to Canada. The church appointed Rev. E.H. and Mrs. Catharine Johnson to Szepingkai. Manchuria was at war and fighting was taking place near the mission. There was some worry about Miss Luella Crockett working alone in Szepingkai. Miss Errey was a nurse, ready and eager to join Miss Crockett. When the work was temporarily closed in Manchuria, Miss Crockett left and Miss Errey was transferred to the Bhil Field in India.

The policy of the WMS council executive in re-opening the work in Manchuria was that no worker should go there alone. There was no mission hospital, hospital unit or dispensary in connection with the evangelistic work in and around the city of Szepingkai. It was not an easy field and suitable accommodation would have to be provided. Mrs. Mavis Reoch wrote that while conditions made it unsafe to go into the country, they had concentrated on Bible study and intensive preaching.

In spite of all difficulties, Mrs. Laura Davis, wife of one of the missionaries, was enthusiastic about the work.

> *Some of us have enthusiasm for this field, that all the dust storms cannot smother. This is not a land of "balmy breeze" and pleasant prospects. Our busy desert city is built mostly of mud houses. The streets are of deep dust. However, in contrast to all this, we see the Church of Christ taking root in the desert soil...flourishing in spite of all conditions...war, bandits, etc. have been working confusion and distress — still the Church grows and prospers...*[23]

Mrs. Mildred Gehman, a teacher from Ontario and a graduate of the Brantford General Hospital, and Miss Helena Gibbs, a graduate of the Toronto Bible College, were appointed in 1936 to Szepingkai, but their departure was postponed because of war conditions. They finally sailed for Manchuria in August 1938.

British Guiana

In 1937, reports from British Guiana showed that, while in 1934, there had been 3,000 in the schools, now 5,000 children were being educated and receiving religious instruction. There were better buildings, better equipment and better teachers. The church was spending a great deal of money on primary schools but the government had taken responsibility for teachers' salaries and the upkeep of the school buildings. Great encouragement and help was received from the government and from owners and managers of the great sugar plantations. There was religious instruction in all the schools. Two East Indian deaconesses were doing fine work among the women and children, and Christians were increasing in number. Congregations had their own sessions and it was hoped that they soon might have a presbytery of their own with their own ministers.

Chapter 13

Another War to End All Wars

1940-1945

Praying for Peace

A Call to Prayer

> *O God, the Father of us all, Who hast made of one blood all nations of men, mercifully receive the prayers that we offer for our anxious and troubled world. Send Thy light into our darkness and guide the nations as one family into the ways of peace. Take away all prejudice, hatred and fear. Give grace to all who serve and suffer because of war. Strengthen in us the will to understand one another, and forgive us our trespasses as we forgive them that trespass against us. To those who by their counsels lead the peoples of the earth grant a right judgment, that so through them and us Thy will be done. Through Jesus Christ our Lord. Amen.*[1]

The Women's Prayer for Peace originated in October 1936, in a League of Prayer and a call to pledged prayer for peace which went out over the "wireless" from St. Michael's Church, London, England, where many still remembered the horrors of the last war and were beginning to realize that a more wide-spread conflagration might be ahead. The League of Prayer had a membership of 600,000 and their prayer card was translated into twenty-six languages.

An enlarged organization, The League of Prayer and Service, came into being in September 1938. There was a great service of dedication on November 11 around the Unknown Soldier's tomb in Westminster Abbey. By September 1939 war had broken out once more.

In November 1939, many representatives of different women's groups were called together by Rev. Mother Superior of the Sisterhood of St. John the Divine (of the Church of England in Canada). The Women's Prayer for Peace was drafted with slight changes from the original. Small variations in the cards were made for members of Jewish and Roman Catholic gatherings and a French translation issued. The initial supply of 300,000 cards was soon gone.

The prayer was printed in every issue of *The Glad Tidings* from January 1940 to September 1945 and women across Canada were asked to join in daily prayer. A second shorter prayer was printed to be used at twelve noon each day. On the reverse side of the card was printed a pledge that could be signed. It was a pledge to pray and work for peace.

The writer of a report to the annual meeting of the Call to Prayer Committee says,

> *However, there is much more to be done... If we are to pass on to* [our neighbours] *and the younger generation the vital things of reality, we must be on fire ourselves with that light caught from the Eternal God.*

She asks,

> *We do realize, don't we, that the ultimate victory of good over evil will be achieved, not on the field of battle, but in the soul of men... We hope that a deeper understanding of all the implications of this prayer may remove from the minds of all people the prejudices and misunderstandings that form such a serious barrier to world brotherhood and a lasting peace.*[2]

At the beginning of June, 1940, a call of the hour was issued over the signatures of the primate of the Church of England in Canada, the president of the Baptist Convention of Ontario and Quebec and the moderators of The Presbyterian Church in Canada and The United Church of Canada urging all Christian people in Canada, in this hour of stress, to hold fast to their confidence in God and to give themselves to

> *...this sacred cause with singleness of purpose, dedicating to it all their powers, and grudging no sacrifice, whether of comfort, wealth,*

> *or life itself, which will secure for us and our children the precious things won for us by the sacrifices of our fathers.*[3]

On the very day that Paris fell in June 1940, a group of men and women of different denominations and nationalities were gathered in London to discuss missionary work overseas. Dr. William Paton, secretary of the International Missionary Council, spoke of the recent blows to the missionary enterprise caused by the war but he believed that there was still reason for confidence and hope.

> *In the same world we see the rending of the body of humanity by war, and, at the same time, the growing unity of the Church of Christ.*[4]

Dr. Paton pointed out that the council's share in the missionary movement was a protection against the danger of narrow nationalism, offering instead to every church member the sense of membership in the world-wide Church of Christ.

The churches in the United States and Canada responded to a request from Adolf Keller of the Central Bureau for Inter-Church Aid, Geneva, for further grants towards the relief of churches in Middle Europe. The WMS continued the grant it had made in 1939.

The WMS sent a grant of $4,000 to the International Missionary Council for Orphaned Missions and received a letter of acknowledgment from Dr. Paton. He said,

> *An immense and delightful surprise. What I like most of all is your remark that your Society voted this money as a 'thank-offering that we have the money to give.' That seems to me, if I may say so, a very fine spirit.*[5]

By 1943, the WMS had contributed $8,699 to orphaned missions (missions that had been cut off from their home churches). They also made contributions to aid bombed churches in England, Scotland and Ireland. They gave aid to Protestant ministers from Europe who had taken refuge in Britain, many of whom had Jewish wives or relatives. They gave assistance to Chinese War Relief, as well as many other causes, over and above their regular estimates.

The missionary cause suffered severe blows because of war conditions and tense international relations. At the same time, new opportunities for missionary service were opening up. There was a complete withdrawal of all Canadian missionaries from territory under Japanese control — parts of China, Formosa and Korea. This was not just because of danger to the missionaries themselves but also for the protection of indigenous Christians who were persecuted more because of their relationship with foreigners. Although some people seemed to have concluded that overseas mission work was at an end, this was far from the truth.

Work was not interrupted on the fields in India. In fact, it was expanding and could be strengthened if the church took advantage of the opportunity. In British Guiana the work continued. Now as never before came the call from the Chinese leaders for missionary service in West China, where millions moved from the occupied areas of their country.

The council executive knew the auxiliaries would be wondering what was happening and they sent the following message:

> *This is no time to....bemoan our fate; neither is it any time to wonder if the Society can do with less money. Rather is it a time to plan to accomplish many things in Canada hitherto left undone for lack of funds, to strengthen our Church and so strengthen Canada. Of what use will it be to win the war, if victory finds the Christian forces weak in Canada? And what of India, where we are still free to work and where endless opportunities await the Christian Church? So the message we send is: Give as you have always given, work with one mind and one purpose, and, above all, pray without ceasing... It is the intention of the Council Executive to keep each one on our staff, putting them to work in Canada or elsewhere at the type of work suited to them...*[6]

A new sign was prominently displayed in the Women's Building of the Canadian National Exhibition in Toronto in 1940. It read "Church Women at Work" and below that line, "Anglican, Baptists, Church of Christ, Society of Friends, Presbyterians and United." With Christian unity of spirit and purpose Christian women exhibited many branches of their activities. A large stand displayed rows of the monthly magazines of the various women's missionary societies and other interesting books and pamphlets. A wall poster called attention to the first arm of defence, to the source of all power. From the booth 10,000 "Call to Prayer" cards were distributed. Women's work in peace and war was an innovation at the 1940 Exhibition and the church women regarded it as an opportunity for witness.

Canada

It was always the aim of the WMS that the municipalities should take over the hospitals as soon as they were able. After serving the community at Canora, Saskatchewan, and the surrounding districts for thirty years, the WMS sold the Hugh Waddell Memorial Hospital to the municipality. It was then known as the Hugh Waddell Hospital and was transferred on May 1, 1944.

The Weirdale Nursing Home in Weirdale, Saskatchewan, was temporarily closed because there was no doctor available to serve there. The Huntingdon

Residence in Huntingdon, Quebec, closed at the end of June 1942 and the property was sold. It was no longer necessary to maintain such an institution in that district, especially since few of the students were Presbyterian.

The missionary on the Mistawasis Reserve, Rev. W.W. Moore, wrote to *The Glad Tidings* telling of his mother's death on April 21, 1940 and saying that he would much appreciate it if the editor would publish the extracts of her life which he was enclosing since she was "truly one of the most self-sacrificing of the early pioneers."

Indeed she was! Mrs. W.S. Moore was the former Miss Wight of Kirkwall, Ontario. Her story begins in January 1887. She planned to go as a missionary to the foreign field. Instead, she answered the call of the Woman's Foreign Missionary Society to go to work among the Sioux who had escaped to Canada after the Dakota massacre. They settled four miles from the small village of Portage la Prairie. The women from Knox Church in Portage la Prairie formed themselves into a Woman's Sioux Missionary Society and opened a school for the children. Miss Wight was sent by the WFMS to teach in the school. Later, she would say that one of the things of which she was most proud was her recommendation to presbytery to appoint John Thunder as her assistant.

> *A young Indian, John Thunder, a graduate of a college in Dakota, came to visit our Reserve. As he was an eloquent speaker, a good singer, and a devout Christian, I lost no time in applying to the Presbytery to appoint him as my assistant, and so efficient did he prove that he was later appointed as a missionary on another Reserve, where he laboured until his death.*[7]

Miss Wight loved her work at Portage la Prairie. At the end of two years she was transferred to the school built for the children from Muscowpetung's, Passquah's and Piapot's reserves, where there were 60 children in residence and a regular staff of workers. It was here that she met and married Mr. Moore.

In 1895, Rev. and Mrs. Moore, missionary and matron, left the Lakesend Industrial School where they had served for a number of years and went to Mistawasis. After her husband died, their son, Rev. W.W. Moore, became missionary at Mistawasis and his mother continued to work as she always had. She opened a school for the children in her home and, supported by the Mistawasis WMS Auxiliary, convinced the government to make it a day school receiving the government grant. After 1925, the school was put under the care of the Presbyterian WMS.

The Moores had a daughter, Wilma. In a letter to the WMS in 1942, she tells of going to Mistawasis for the Easter services, as was her custom. The church was so full that chairs and benches from the Mission House had to be brought in.

> *One thing that I noticed... was the complete absence of young men. Every young man, physically fit, has enlisted... My heart rejoiced, however, when shortly after the service began, Tommy Muckaloo(Bird), straight and tall...in his soldier's uniform, walked in and came up to his usual place near the organ. He is a beautiful singer and his mellow Indian voice was lovely to hear in the Easter hymns.*
>
> *The text that morning...was: "Why should it be thought a thing incredible that God should raise the dead?" The evidences advanced were the same as always, but somehow seemed to take a firmer grip...*
>
> *It was truly inspiring to see the Indian Elders assisting in that solemn Communion service. Old Thomas, the oldest Indian on the Reserve and a consecrated Christian Elder, did look distinguished.*[8]

In the chapel services and the Sunday school, students of the graduating class at Birtle were given more responsibility. Senior students conducted chapel services, held three times a week and occasionally they took charge of the Sunday service and the Sunday school. The junior and senior choirs added tremendously to the worship services. They were being well trained, they were enthusiastic and their voices marvelously sweet, said the report.

In April 1945, the Cecilia Jeffrey School band went to Winnipeg for the musical festival. They were the guests of the Hudson's Bay Company for a luncheon, of the Sea Cadets for sleeping quarters, and of the WMS provincial for another luncheon. The Young People's Council of Winnipeg organized a concert in First Presbyterian Church to help with their expenses.

The formal opening and dedication of the Chinese Presbyterian Church took place on January 12, 1940. This was an important step for the congregation. The attendance at Sunday school had doubled and from 50-80 attended Sunday services.

There were two Ukrainian congregations, one in Toronto and one in Ottawa. Rev. M. Fesenko in Toronto credited the loyalty of the Ukrainian people in Canada to the missionary work of the churches. He was reaching, he said, about 500 families with his paper, *Evangelical Truth*, the printing of which was financed by the WMS.

The WMS again answered an appeal for help from the French mission work in Montreal and gave a grant to assist the French Presbyterian congregation.

The WMS contributed $1,000 towards the cost of the new Italian church building in Montreal and $500 towards the furnishings. The Italian Presbyterian Church in Montreal was the oldest Italian Protestant mission on the continent. It was begun by Waldensians about 1875. After 1925, they were without a church building until their new church was opened in May 1941. It was called Beckwith Memorial Church in memory of General Beckwith, who was born in Halifax, Nova Scotia in 1789 and died at Torre Pellice, Italy, in 1862. In 1941, the congregation had 250 members and a fine Sunday school.

In the north, progress was being made at Cochrane, Ontario and in January 1940, work was opened up in Timmins, Ontario. The WMS gave a grant of $1,000 towards the building of the church in Timmins. At Geraldton, the number of members had doubled and the church had to be enlarged. For this $800 was subscribed locally and a grant of $750 was made by the WMS.

In April 1940, deaconess Miss Mary Todd reported from the Willowdale field in Alberta that seven districts kept her quite busy. Sunday, she says, was the busiest day of all, as the deaconess preached at four services one week and three the next. She ended her report by saying that she wished there had been more time for visiting in the homes.

The next year, at General Assembly, she reported that in Brownvale, Alberta, with no previous experience with horses, she had to drive a team to

Driving a team of horses

get from place to place and that driving over bush trails at all hours of the day or night was not without difficulty and danger. She told of getting lost one dark night in forty-below-zero weather, then, after getting directions, running into a deep snowdrift; and, another time, of getting stuck with the team in a muskeg and escaping as if by a miracle. She and Rev. J. M. Fraser had nine preaching places. On Sundays she drove forty miles and conducted two, and sometimes three, services, using a little organ which she took around with her. In closing, Miss Todd stressed the need for ministers.

Miss Roy, a nurse at the Last Lake field in the Peace River district, reported that, besides caring for the sick, she had carried on work among women, girls and children, conducted church services, and, by no means least, visited the people in her scattered field. She said that visiting could not be stressed too much, especially in those lonely places where homes were so scattered.

Miss Ruby Walker reporting from Saskatchewan on her summer's work of taking services, attending the Saskatoon summer school, directing the camp and the Rosetown vacation Bible school, said that she travelled about 3,500 miles over good roads and bad, but mostly bad. Miss Elizabeth Walker, reporting on her first three months in the Ferrier district near Rocky Mountain House, said that she needed an army of workers to do effective work. When Miss Mabel Booth was leaving Edmonton, the presbytery's appreciation of the service she rendered was expressed in a letter sent to the WMS in 1945 by Rev. H. Douglas Stewart, clerk of presbytery. He wrote,

> *Miss Booth's duties have been various and numerous. Her work has carried her over many miles. No request has been too great for her. She is a master of church work from the pulpit down to the Mission Band. Her willingness, diligence, and earnestness have been a source of inspiration to us all, and her radiant personality has shed good will in all our churches…*[9]

Miss Iris Munro, deaconess and port worker in Montreal, reported that port work was uncertain. They had an average of one boat a week. Sometimes there would be a spell of no boats at all and then, since the British refugees started coming, there would be several in one week.

From port work, she moved to Kirkland Lake.

> *Miss Iris Munro, after many years' service in Montreal as port worker and deaconess, was transferred at the end of January* (1943) *to Kirkland lake, Ontario, in response to an appeal from the Presbytery of North Bay and Temiskaming for a deaconess to help in the work of that congregation, which has for some months been without a minister.*[10]

Owing to the long illness of Rev. P. W. Graham of Englehart, Ontario in 1944, Miss Monro was responsible for the church service in both Kirkland Lake and Englehart, as well as for visiting and other work during the week. In the first nine months of 1944, before Rev. G. S. Baulch came as minister in October, she took forty-five services in the two churches, made 485 calls in the congregations and attended 194 meetings.[11]

These are just a few examples of the work carried out by deaconesses between 1940 and 1944. There were many, many other deaconesses doing the same kind of work and many other facets to their work besides the children's and women's groups, the visiting and the preaching. They also held vacation Bible schools, directed camps (which were growing in importance), addressed church groups and acted on boards and committees.

At the General Board of Missions meeting in 1943, it was noted that a serious situation had arisen because of the number of ministers who had gone to serve as chaplains, leaving too many congregations vacant. In reporting on the synods, it was mentioned that several new churches were opened during the year and that the work had been strengthened in some areas by the amalgamation of congregations.

> *Laymen assumed responsibility for church services in some places when no minister was available. Deaconesses are doing much to strengthen the work of the Church, especially among the young people.*[12]

In this report, while laymen were credited with assuming responsibility for church services, no mention was made of the deaconesses who took services and preached often two or three times a Sunday. In actual fact, they took over fields, often with several points, and did everything a minister would do and more, except for administering the sacraments.

The 25th anniversary of CGIT was celebrated in 1940. There were almost 4,000 CGIT groups and that summer nearly 3,500 girls gathered in 100 CGIT camps. However, the problem of leadership for both girls' groups and Mission Bands persisted.

Camps were becoming increasingly valued as centres for leadership training and Christian education and were springing up all across Canada. Deaconesses were usually involved in giving leadership at these camps. The WMS made contributions to the establishing of the camps: $800 to Sylvan Lake, Alberta and $2,000 to buy the adjoining property; $1,500 for Buena Vista in Saskatchewan; $2,020 to Christopher Lake in Northern Saskatchewan; $950 to Shoal Lake; $2,500 for property on Lake St. Francis near Lancaster, Quebec;

and $3,150 for a campsite in British Columbia. These were not WMS camps. The society worked with the synod camp committees on which the WMS had representation. The WMS was anxious to do all it could to strengthen the efforts of presbyteries and synods in their work with young people.

Miss Laura Pelton, in addition to her other commitments, was appointed student secretary for the WMS. She attempted to get in touch with Presbyterian students at the University of Toronto and was successful at getting groups of students together. She encouraged students to attend student conferences such as those organized by the student volunteer movement. She initiated the Presbyterian Fellowship, an organization for university students. Miss Pelton urged provincial societies to have student secretaries. She also encouraged the WMS women to help students in any way they could.

While teaching the illiterate and providing suitable literature were not new, illiteracy had come to be recognized as one of the great problems of the world. All too often illiteracy meant poverty, a low standard of living, disease, and exploitation by unscrupulous people.

In connection with efforts to promote literacy in Africa, Asia, and Latin America, no name had become more widely known than Dr. Frank C.F. Laubach, sometimes called the "Apostle of Literacy." His method of teaching was embraced and supported by missionaries in many countries. Dr. Laubach developed a simple method of phonetic teaching. In twelve lessons, he taught people to read in their own language. What one person learned, he or she was told to teach to five other people, and they in turn to teach others.

On a visit to Toronto, Dr. Laubach said that the churches must lead in the task of teaching illiterates to read and write. In making people literate, one can make them Christian. If the world is to be saved from destruction, the Christians of our churches in Britain, the United States and Canada must show forth the love of Christ in service to the peoples of the world.

At the second Inter-Church Conference on Missionary Education held at Alma College, St. Thomas in June, 1942, the principal speaker, Dr. H. P. Van Dusen of Union Theological Seminary in New York, left the delegates with a message of hope. Wartime, he said, left two impressions. The first impression was the profound unity of Christ's church, a unity far greater than the churches themselves had realized. The second impression was the unexpected strength of the younger churches and their ability to assume and discharge responsibility, shown by their capacity for self-government. The great new fact of the time, and the great hope, was world Christian fellowship.

Another conference, the second Inter-Board Conference on Foreign Missions was held in February, 1944 at Wycliffe College in Toronto. Devotions at this conference were led by four men and two women. The two women were Miss Bessie MacMurchy and Mrs. G. E. Forbes, both of the Presbyterian WMS.

Among the special speakers at this conference were Dr. Timothy Lew, formerly dean of the School of Theology in Yenchiang University, China, and Mrs. Lew, a leader in education and religious work. Mrs. Lew said the people of China resisted the invader for more than six years. Large areas of their country had been occupied and towns and villages reduced to ruins. Yet, here and there through the country, in occupied China and in free China, Christians were to be found in small groups, praying to God, the Father of our Lord, Jesus Christ. She concluded her address on an optimistic note.

> *Christian comrades, we ask you to share with us the faith that sustains us. We know that the hour is dark, but we know, too, that the night is already far spent, and we shall soon see the glorious dawn.*[13]

At the annual meeting of the League of Nations Society in Canada, held at the Chateau Laurier in Ottawa in May 1942, the WMS was represented by Mrs. Clarence Pitts and Mrs. Alexander Ferguson of Ottawa. Senator Cairine Wilson opened the meeting and welcomed the delegates; she said she had filled in for the chairman in 1936 and had been there ever since. Mr. Warwick Chipman of Montreal, later elected president, said that the work of the league was to bring races and nations to dwell together in harmony.

> *While we are desperately struggling against the madness of Nationalism now threatening all our hopes of a decent world, let us not find in ourselves any contagion of the same disease.*[14]

India

During the summer of 1941, a cholera epidemic raged in India. In the United Provinces alone, about 1,300 people were dying every week. In many parts of the country there was a shortage of food and water. Gasoline rationing made travelling difficult. As a result, the Jhansi missionaries did more intensive work in nearby villages where there was no lack of opportunity for Christian work. Indian Christians, trained in the Bible schools, went out to work in the villages.

Miss Annie Lee Whatling spoke to council executive in June 1940. She had worked on the Jhansi field since 1926 in and around Baragoan, ten miles from Jhansi. To reach the village folk, she said, it was necessary to go to them. When she first went to live there not a home was open to her. By 1940, not a home was closed. When she left on furlough, she was asked to bring other workers when she returned.

Miss Irene Stringer wrote in August 1942 to say that at the Helen Macdonald School in Jhansi the war had touched them little. The government had asked for accommodation for refugees from Burma. They had been settled comfortably in bungalows.

Before going off to Landour for language study, Margaret Kennedy, in a letter to *The Glad Tidings* printed in the January 1940 issue, tells of her first Sunday in Jobat on the Bhil field. She did not understand a word of the service but found much of interest to note. All the women in their saris were on one side of the church, the men on the other side, with children on both sides. She found the children remarkably well behaved, though it was much more comfortable for them than for children at home sitting bolt upright in pews, not supposed to move. There was a delightful casualness, she said, in seeing a youngster, tired of sitting by his mother, crossing over and squatting by his father for a while, or a little girl pattering over from father to mother. Nearly every woman had an infant or a small child with her. You just could not imagine, Miss Kennedy said, what a comfortable, cozy cradle the crossed legs of a mother made. One corner of the sari made an excellent covering.

Miss Mary Sherrick spoke to council executive at its May 1940 meeting about the educational work on the Bhil Field. The teachers were all Bhils. While the missionaries did some teaching, their work was essentially that of supervision and administration.

Miss Ruth Buchanan, in addition to her other work, had been doing "uplift work" among the Bhils. She had introduced Leghorn fowl there and had been training the people in better methods of work in chicken-raising and gardening, and successful marketing, as well as helping the Bhils in many other ways to a better life.

Miss Margaret Kennedy reports that she too was helping Jobat women to earn a little money. She started sewing classes. The women came to the bungalow three times a week and, besides the sewing, they had good fellowship and regular Bible study.

The cholera epidemic reached the Bhil field in August 1942 and Bessie MacMurchy went to Amkhut to help. The misery and illness she saw there gave some idea of the devastation the cholera epidemic had wrought. It was much worse in the villages, where many families had been completely wiped out.

The Japanese, reported Mrs. Quinn from Jobat, were at the northeastern border. While the monsoon lasted they were unable to advance. Whether they would attempt to invade India after the monsoon no one could tell. The American government was advising its missionaries to go home but most of them decided to stay. She said they were praying that the horrors that were taking place in China would not have to be suffered by the Indian people as well.

Miss Isabel McConnell, writing from Kashmir in the summer of 1945 where she was spending her holiday on a houseboat, tells how she heard the war had ended.

> *We had not been getting papers regularly, nor had we heard any radio for days. We went into Srinagar and saw all sorts of decorations being put up. I asked someone if the war had ended and he said, "Yes, this is 'V Day.'" While waiting for my friend, I heard a radio and stopped to listen; it was the BBC and I heard what was going on in London. It thrilled me through and through. I immediately went to the telegraph office and sent a telegram to Miss MacMurchy and Miss Kennedy in Jobat. I wanted them to know that we were rejoicing here in Kashmir, too. There were great celebrations for two days. Sunday we went to the Thanksgiving service in the church in Srinagar, it was simply packed.*[15]

China

The women's advisory committee of the New Life movement in China served their country during the war in many ways. At the Kuling Conference in 1938, with fifty of China's outstanding women leaders in attendance and Madame Chiang Kai-shek as convener, it was decided that this committee should be the directive body of all Chinese women in war work and reconstruction; other women's organizations were to be affiliated with it. About 20,000 war orphans were under the sheltering care of this committee in the vicinity of Chungking. They were gathered from all over China and taken, after the fall of Hankow, to the safety and liberty of Free China. The war relief department of the committee concerned itself directly with the suffering brought about by war conditions. It maintained five medical units near the front lines, at an expense of $50,000 annually. It was also responsible for the collection of supplies and money for use in war areas. A New Life village was constructed near Chungking to house refugee women.

As the war progressed, large areas of the country were plagued with famine. In South China the situation had become acute with thousands starving to death and many near starvation, moving from place to place looking for cheaper food. The plight of many people became desperate and Madame Chiang Kai-shek arranged for a grant of $3,000 from the Aid to China Fund for the relief of the suffering.

Much of the missionaries' time was given to the relief of human suffering and part of the WMS grant was used to provide food for the orphans. During these war years Christian hospitals laboured day and night to care for the wounded and the victims of air-raids. They co-operated with the Chinese Christian agencies in helping many hundreds of thousands of refugees and providing food for multitudes of starving people. These services made a deep impression on the Chinese people as was shown by an expression of appreciation in a magazine produced by a group of Chinese intellectuals who, in the past, had been hostile to Christian missions.

> *One of the things that have come out of the present war has been the realization that, whatever doubts may have existed in the past the Christian missions in China fully and indispensably justify their existence. How without a moment's hesitation they faced the test and were not found wanting will remain one of the most dramatic and epoch-making pages in the history of Xn missions.*[16]

General Chiang Kai-shek added his words of praise. He said that Christians

> *...had left no stone unturned to show their growing interest in the material, as well as the spiritual, welfare of our suffering people. Missionaries, in particular, have never hesitated to make even the greatest personal sacrifice to heal the wounded and to succour the distressed.*[17]

The great migration of people from the Japanese-occupied east to the free west of China had brought the Chinese church new and unexpected problems and opportunities. The south-west province of Yunnan, which for three centuries had been almost completely isolated from the rest of China, had become a centre of modern industrial development. Thousands of students migrated from occupied China to Kunming, the capital of the province. In the extensive co-operative work planned in South Yunnan by the Christian church in China, emphasis was put on the steadily growing work among the educated Chinese gathered in Kunming and the effort to reach the tin miners in the Kokiu district in the south. In this project sixteen mission boards were co-operating by providing personnel and funds; two of these were the General Board of Missions and the WMS of The Presbyterian Church in Canada. Miss Helena Gibbs was appointed to work in the province of Yunnan under the Church of Christ in China as a representative of the WMS(WD). She arrived in Kunming, Yunnan, China on November 15th, 1941.

> *I found it very much colder here than I expected...we have to be ready any time during the day to leave the city... We don't go out until late afternoon unless we all go together.... The work here is very new, and the mission moved into new premises very recently; the old place was destroyed. Quite near is a University of 3,000 students, all of whom walked or made their way here by some means from occupied parts. It is for these students that the work was opened here...*[18]

In the summer of 1942, word was received that Miss Helena Gibbs left Kunming and was at Chengtu in West China. She wrote a letter from Chengtu explaining that the situation in Kunming was tense and she had to leave for Chengtu or India. She chose to stay in China because she felt that her work was there. Chengtu was also the headquarters for the Christian Church in China.

A letter to the WMS from Mr. E. Bruce Copland, executive secretary of the provisional council of the Church of Christ in China, written from Chengtu on March 5, 1943, expressed thanks to the WMS for making available the services of Miss Gibbs and also for their generous gifts to the work in Yunnan. He quoted a few sentences from the address of the chairman, Mr. W. V. Djang, at the recent annual meeting of the CCC on February 10 who said that the mission boards overwhelmed them with their genuine good wishes and their generous support. Mr. Djang mentioned particularly Miss Helena Gibbs who, representing the Canadian Presbyterian mission, helped in the office at a time when such service was sorely needed. By April, Helena Gibbs had returned to Kunming but must have left as a report at the council meeting in September, 1944 said that although there was no missionary in China, the society contributed $3,700 towards the missionary work that the Christian Church in China was carrying on in Free China. It was not long before another missionary was on her way to serve in Free China.

In November 1945, Mrs. Mildred Gehman arrived in Yunnan, China to serve as a missionary nurse under the Church of Christ in China. (She left Manchuria in 1940.) While she was serving under the Christian Church in China, the WMS supported her and her work.

Koreans in Japan

The year 1940 was remembered as one when many drastic changes were made in the Korean Church in Japan in both mission and church activities. Among these changes was the government-forced amalgamation of the Korean Christian Church in Japan (KCCJ) with The Presbyterian Church of Japan. (After the war, the KCCJ re-formed their own denomination.)[19]

Another change was the adoption by the indigenous denominations of a plan aimed at complete independence of the churches from foreign influence, financially and otherwise. A third change was a determined effort by the government to bring about national unity by the elimination of everything that might tend to interfere with the ways and beliefs of old Japan. There was also an attempt to bring about a union of all Protestant denominations in Japan and the evacuation from the Japanese empire of three-quarters of the missionaries.

In spite of all this, says Miss Mary Anderson, who had returned to Canada, the twenty-eight Bible women continued their gracious ministry of personal visitation and preaching the Gospel.

According to government regulations, all Korean services had to be conducted in Japanese. The regulation proved a real trial to the older women of the congregations who did not understand the Japanese language and who would sometimes be seen sitting with tears streaming down their faces as they listened to the services in a language they could not understand. In some cases the Bible women had the added task of persuading these women to attend the services, even though they could not understand. Some of the Bible women who had to lead services had the added difficulty of preparing sermons not in their first language.

Miss Ethel MacDonald, writing from Canada, said her thoughts turned to those faithful, spirit-filled men and women,

> *...who are carrying on so splendidly in the midst of trying circumstances. The pastors and Bible women know the seriousness of the situation for the church... It is not easy to give encouragement to people who have to give up their language and names for the Japanese language and names, and who have been forbidden to wear their own Korean styled clothing. A few of our Korean women stopped going to church when the services were held in the Japanese language, and it was the Bible women's task to give comfort and encouragement to these souls when they themselves needed comfort and encouragement...*
>
> *All of the Bible women, whether they have the gift of preaching, teaching, or singing, are a blessing to the women and the Church. The personal helper who was with me when I left Japan had refused to bow at the shrine in Korea. She had been called several times and questioned by the authorities, and one day shortly before we left she told us that she might be sent back to Korea before we sailed... Some of the women told us that if the Church compromised too much they would remain at home and live the Christian life....*[20]

Formosa

A 1941 message from the Formosan WMS to the Canadian WMS,

> *Thanks to the Lord's guidance and your past assistance both spiritual and material we have the pleasure to report that this Society has grown larger and stronger year by year and has improved its sphere of activities for the salvation of our sisters.*
>
> *We learn with much surprise and regret of the withdrawal of the local missionaries. But we are praying earnestly that a better time will come when you will find the preaching work much easier for the spread of the Gospel in this island, and that you will always remember us by sending back these old friends of ours at the earliest possible opportunity.*
>
> *Yours faithfully,*
> *Chupo, Secretary, The Formosan Women's Missionary Society.*[21]

The Women's School and Training School in North Formosa was to be brought under the theological college with the same principal but each with its own staff and work. The plan that in ten years all congregations should become self-supporting had already been in operation for three years. This plan was to be continued by the Formosan church, with larger churches helping the smaller ones.

Mrs. Lillian Dickson, on her return from Formosa, writes,

> *We who come from Formosa have already lived many years under the shadow of war... Our freedom to do Christian work had become sharply restricted, our movements from one place to another were subject to suspicion, and often native Christians with whom we talked or had fellowship were detained and questioned by the military police. Despite all this, the church work progressed surprisingly smoothly... Looking back, we realize that our church in Formosa is strong and well established. It has trained, well-educated leadership and we believe...it will not only survive but progress during this time when it must march on alone.*[22]

Manchuria

It was not safe for missionaries to stray far from the main centres in Manchuria but the Bible women in the churches and the Christian women in the homes were faithful witnesses for Christ and little children at an early age were taught to know and to love Jesus.

Mrs. Mavis Reoch told of an old lady in Szepingkai who was always ready to lead the Bible women to new homes. She was no longer well, but formerly she seemed to have tireless energy and led the missionaries to places they might not otherwise have entered. Usually the woman did most of the preaching herself and most effectively, too.

British Guiana

The Dicksons and Miss Margaret Ramsay, having to leave Formosa during the war, were sent to serve in British Guiana. Rev. James Dickson, writing from New Amsterdam in 1942, says that one of the hopeful developments in Berbice was the women's work. There was a fair number of societies, he said, and they were most enthusiastic. At Bohemia, they realized $40 from the sale of tea, candy, and some sewing they had done. They never knew before that they had the power to raise $40 and they declared they were going to start raising money to build a church.

Mrs. Dickson also writes to tell of her busy schedule of evangelistic meetings.

> *We have been having evening out-door evangelistic meetings all over our Berbice district lately… The other night we were far up the Coast in a very lonely village. Miss Martin and Marilyn and I were the only white people present and our group of Christians was very small. The group we faced was large…we will go back, and back again, until we win some of these people for Christ.*[23]

Mrs. Dickson also speaks about the teas and sales but her emphasis was a little different from that of Mr. Dickson who spoke of the women's new-found power to raise money.

> *During December three of the Happy Workers groups had Teas and Sales… The East Indian people do not have any social life, so they enjoy these teas very, very much, and especially the fun of planning for them and giving them…. Last year I had four groups of Happy Workers comparatively near Amsterdam. Now we have eleven and two more are impatient to be organized.*[24]

At the Bethel Theological College there were 14 students in residence, including two young women who were being trained for deaconess work. Some of the students, after their three year course, would be ordained and they would be the first East Indian ministers of the church in British Guiana. A number of churches were already preparing to "call" their first ministers. Seven churches became self-supporting. New churches were built at Palmyra and Albion. Ten women's groups were formed. Membership was on the increase and there were twenty-nine ordained elders. At long last the British Guiana mission stepped triumphantly out of its pioneer stage and was well on the way to achieving, in the name of Christ, great and lasting accomplishments.

In 1945, the Moderator, Dr. John MacGillivray, visited British Guiana for the celebration of the diamond jubilee of the mission. While Dr. MacGillivray was there, a presbytery was set up and three of the first graduates of Bethel Theological College were ordained.

Peace Thanksgiving Fund

The WMS council in 1941, by a standing vote, accepted a resolution authorizing council executive to work on some plan for a fitting thanksgiving by Presbyterian women.

In 1944, a letter to members of the WMS told of the Peace Thanksgiving Fund that was being launched under the auspices of the WMS. It was *Thanksgiving for the many blessings that have been ours in Canada in these war years.* The plan was to raise $30,000 between January 1, 1945 and September 30, 1946. The purpose of the fund was to assist in training those who wished to enter the service of the church but were prevented for financial reasons from taking the specialized training required. The letter noted that *This is an investment by you in the youth of our Church in memory of the sacrifices youth has made for you.*[25]

It was also pointed out that the WMS would join in the interdenominational Peace Thanksgiving Fund in which The Presbyterian Church in Canada was participating.

The War Has Ended!

The September 1945 issue of *The Glad Tidings* begins with words from Psalm 77 and Isaiah 40.

> *Unto thee, O God, do we give thanks, unto thee do we give thanks... Thou art the God that doest wonders: thou hast declared thy strength among the people. Comfort ye, comfort ye my people, saith your God. Speak ye comfortably to Jerusalem, and cry unto her, that her warfare is accomplished, that her iniquity is pardoned. Prepare ye the way of the Lord, make straight in the desert a highway for our God.*

At the council meeting, September 24-28, 1945, much time was taken up discussing post-war opportunities for missionary work which the WMS, along with its own and other churches, would have to meet.

Mrs. Beatrice McLennan, ended her recording secretary's report for 1944-1945 with these words,

> *Now the great thing for which we longed has come. The war has at last been won, and in our deep thankfulness for such mercy let us never forget and teach to our children's children that for each of us there is a mighty part that must be played if the world is to survive...*[26]

Chapter 14

The Aftermath of War

1946-1951

The Devastation

The war was ended and the dancing in the streets was over but the devastation was beyond belief. Much of Europe lay in ruins. In China, ruined buildings were seen everywhere. The world was awakening to the horror of the bombing of Hiroshima and Nagasaki. Any groups that could were asked to send food parcels to individuals in Europe, where *hunger with all it means of bitterness, disease and loss of morale is widespread this winter.*[1] The Council of Protestant Churches of Poland, formed in the autumn of 1945, issued an appeal for help to all the Protestant churches in the world.

A great enterprise of inter-church aid and service to refugees was directed by the World Council of Churches. The churches in the more favoured countries gave millions of dollars in cash and goods for the relief of the needy and for the rehabilitation of church life and work in the war devastated lands.

Widespread concern in Great Britain over Europe's starving millions was brought to the attention of the people at a mass meeting which packed Albert Hall in

London on November 25, 1945. The crowd flowed into the nave and crypt of a nearby church. There were proposals that Britain should send four and a half million tons of food to Europe, and that the government should sponsor a scheme for the voluntary sending of food and clothes.

In June 1946, there was a second national clothing collection in Canada. Great quantities of good, used clothing was sent from Canada in the autumn of 1945 for use in destitute areas. But the need was still great. Many thousands of children in Europe were unable to attend school during the winter because they did not have warm clothes. The situation was desperate.

The 1947 General Assembly of The Presbyterian Church in Canada called upon all congregations to respond to the need of relief for Great Britain and other European countries. A Presbyterian Inter-Board Committee for Relief Abroad was formed to direct the relief work of our church. The great need was for money to buy food, and for clothing. Every congregation was asked to set up an organization for the collection and forwarding of contributions for this relief work.

Mrs. T. L. Haitjema, speaking for the women of Holland at the Conference of the International Women's Union meeting in Geneva in August 1948, told of the hopelessness in the hearts of the people during the war, and added,

> *It would have warmed the hearts of the women of North America had they been able to witness the transformation which took place when the planes bearing food and clothing arrived. These planes were symbols of the outside world's love and concern....*[2]

Changes in WMS

In 1946, in accordance with a notice of motion given at the 1945 council meeting, it was agreed that synodicals be adopted throughout the society, in place of provincial societies.

At the September, 1948 council meeting, the recording secretary's report stated that the WMS, looking to a fuller integration of the work of the WMS with the general work of the church, agreed that the young women's secretary and the children's work secretary should work more closely in co-operation with the Board of Sabbath Schools and Young People's Societies.

In 1925, the WMS had asked General Assembly to have their status changed from an auxiliary to the mission boards of the church to a board directly responsible to the General Assembly. The request was granted. However, it seems there was some problem with this decision from the other boards of the church, probably because the WMS, being a women's organization was not represented in any of the courts of the church. The WMS felt it would improve relationships with the other boards if, instead of a board, they were an organization within the church. In submitting the constitution with this change for the consideration of the General Assembly, they were endeavouring to improve the relationship of the society to the other boards and to the courts of the church. The 1948 General Assembly granted their request.

The Peace Thanksgiving Fund

This fund, set up by the annual meeting in 1944 with the goal to raise $30,000 by the annual meeting in 1946 was to be used to train workers for the church, both women and men, either in Canada or overseas. At the 1946 council meeting, the fund was presented and dedicated. It exceeded the $30,000 and the total amount received by October, 1946, was $34,121. By 1950, the total stood at $40,286.

At the 1950 council meeting, Miss Laura Pelton introduced two young people who were in Canada and were supported by the WMS fund. Miss Katherine Sun from Yunnan, China, had been in Canada for a year, completed a year at university and was taking the course at the Deaconess Training School. Mr. Wenchi Kim, a young Korean from Japan and minister of a church in Osaka, was studying at Knox College, Toronto.

Canada

The Rocky Mountain House Hospital in Alberta had been operated by the WMS for eight years. In June 1946, it was purchased by the municipality and WMS work ended there. This was in accord with what had always been the policy of the WMS in its hospital work — to provide service in pioneer or frontier districts until such time as the municipalities were able to take them over.

In 1949, the WMS purchased a building in Medicine Hat, Alberta, which would be used as the first official Presbyterian Training School to teach church workers. The WMS, together with the Synod of Alberta, made extensive alterations to the building. The school would be under the supervision of the Board of Sunday Schools and Young People's Societies.

Mrs. Héléne Smith of Église St. Luc, Montreal, writes that L'Église des Cantons de l'Est, Melbourne, Quebec, was the baby of the French work in Quebec, but a remarkably strong and independent one. There were, she said, about forty second-generation Protestants who had been neglected for the past twenty years. They asked the minister of Église St. Luc, Rev. Jacques Smith, if he would take occasional worship services. During August 1947, he spent his vacation in the region and held regular worship services at Danville which were so encouraging that a board of managers was named and it was decided to continue during the winter at Richmond twice a month. A women's group was organized and they hoped to have elders and perhaps a WMS.

The meetings at Granby were suspended for a year because no suitable hall was available. A building was purchased and meetings would be resumed when the building was ready.

Mrs. Smith said that there was an immediate need for French students to be able to take theology in their own language and a pressing need for a French school for the children. A radio program would enable them to reach hundreds of people who would not otherwise come to a church service.

The new Chinese Church and Community Centre in Montreal was opened on June 11, 1950. Rev. Paul S. Chan presided at the service in both English and Chinese. The all-Chinese choir of young people of the congregation sang under the direction of Mrs. G. P. Louie, and Miss Muriel Judd (Brown), deaconess, played the organ. The General Assembly was meeting in Montreal at that time and the Moderator, Rev. G. Scott Mackenzie, took part in the service.

Changing immigration laws allowed Chinese families to enter Canada. This had a beneficial effect upon the work of the church among the Chinese. Boys and girls were seeking training in English and finding it at the Chinese centres in Montreal, Toronto, Vancouver and Victoria.

Knox Presbyterian Church in Sudbury had a different approach. They believed in integration and were happy to announce a new auxiliary of the WMS in their church, comprised of Chinese women who had come to Canada within the last year.

The General Board of Missions at its September, 1947 meeting welcomed a minister of the Reformed Church of Hungary, Dr. Bela Vasady, president of the 400-year-old theological college in Debrecen, secretary of the Hungarian Council of Churches, and a member of the provisional committee of the World Council of Churches. Dr. Vasady was the first minister to get permission to leave Hungary after the war. He came to the United States and Canada on behalf of two million Hungarian Presbyterians and other Protestants in Hungary who were in desperate need because of the destruction and loss caused by the war and the occupation. Of the Protestant churches, 200 were entirely destroyed, and 2,000 other church buildings were damaged. Property was taken from them and church colleges endangered. Only with the aid of western churches could their work be re-established.

One specific need mentioned by Dr. Vasady was the restoration of the religious periodical, *Igazsag es Elet (Truth and Life)*, which had to cease publication because of the war. It was a periodical for ministers and students of the

Bible to which nearly all Hungarian Reformed ministers in Hungary and North America subscribed. As part of the society's gift to European churches, the WMS board agreed to give $500 to make it possible to again publish this monthly.

The deaconess of the Hungarian Church in Toronto, Mrs. Beatrice Steinmetz, reported that 1950 was a busy year in the Hungarian Church. Seventy-four new members joined the previous year. These new members were mostly new Canadians who needed assistance to find places to live or places to work.

A letter of appreciation was received from Rev. B. Kusiw who received 324 Bibles sent by the WMS for the Ukrainians in Germany. Rev. Kusiw said that Rev. M. Fesenko wrote him to say the Women's Missionary Society intended to send some Ukrainian Bibles to displaced persons in Germany. These exiles had fled from the Soviet Union and were eager to go either to Canada or the United States. More people were coming from other countries dominated by the Soviet Union. Many lost all their earthly possessions and they preferred to go into exile rather than remain in their native land that *they may still follow the voice of their conscience.*[3]

After the war many deaconesses were employed by the WMS to help rebuild the church. The WMS gave $500 for extension work in Sudbury where Miss Estelle MacCausland made a successful survey early in the summer of 1945. A Sunday school was started, a Mission Band was organized and a vacation Bible school was held. In August, evening services were begun. Everything had to be held in the rented house where Miss MacCausland and another worker lived. With WMS help it was possible to buy the property and have a more permanent centre for church work. In 1946, the WMS also gave $200 towards a new church at Last Lake in the Peace River district where deaconesses opened up the work earlier.

In the fall of 1945, Miss Muriel Judd (Brown) worked in Val d'Or and Perron. At both places Explorer groups were organized. At Val d'Or, a CGIT group, a children's group and a choir were started. Miss Judd held meetings and visited in the homes as well as being responsible for a camp reunion and worship services. She reported that, in the absence of a minister, she would try to keep up the church services.

Miss Athalie Read worked in the Presbytery of North Bay and Temiskaming. Beginning in September, 1945, she was responsible for the church services in Cochrane. In the summer of 1947, as a student, and in 1948, as a graduate,

Hilda Blackwell and Loreen Leatherdale, port workers, Montreal, Quebec

Miss Hilda Blackwell served as port receptionist in Quebec and in her free time as secretary to the director of the Assembly's immigration committee.

A small crowd gathered at Knox College in Toronto in April 1950 for the dedication of two blue panel trucks which were going to northern Alberta and northern Saskatchewan for the use of deaconesses in those areas which were not easily accessible. The Alberta van was in the charge of Miss Agnes Hislop, graduate deaconess, and Miss Agnes McLeod (Conkey), student deaconess. Miss Isabel Scott, graduate deaconess, and Miss Flora Whiteford, student deaconess, were responsible for the work in northern Saskatchewan. These workers carried on vacation Bible schools, made surveys and kept lists of all the families they met and served.

The silent majority in the story of the WMS is, of course, the women in the auxiliaries without whom there would be no WMS. They are usually unnamed, but once in a while a story surfaces that gives us some insight into their dedication and faithfulness.

Miss Margaret Grigor's account of the first church service at Blueberry Mountain and the part that Mrs. Margaret Macdonald played in that story was mentioned earlier. We learn more about Mrs. Macdonald from a personal testimony she wrote for *The Glad Tidings.*

> *When my husband asked me, in 1934, if I would be willing to leave our Saskatchewan home, and go to his homestead in the Peace River, I instantly thought, how wonderful to make a home....where there would be no meetings to attend. I was then President of the Whitewood Auxiliary... I came to Blueberry Mountain and made our home. But I found that a lifetime member of the Missionary Society, cannot throw off the responsibility so easily, and as I thought of my Mother, who had been in the work in Toronto from its beginning, and had in 1886 organized the Brandon Presbyterial, I felt ashamed. So when the World Day of Prayer came I took The Glad Tidings and walked to my nearest neighbour's house, where she, her daughters and I, kept with the rest of the world our hour of prayer.*
>
> *The next year nearly all the women of the settlement came to my house for the meeting and at the close we organized our Auxiliary... Our Peace River Presbyterial was organized last July. We are all looking forward to our first Annual Meeting...*[4]

Susan Gibson and Lois Stewart with the Rocky Mountain House Van, summer of 1956

The Glad Tidings printed the report of Rev. M. A. Mark on the work in western Canada. In the past five years, Mr. Mark said, there was a marked advance in the west, especially in the Presbytery of Red Deer. He mentioned places where new churches had been dedicated, highlighting Red Deer as having emerged as one of the strongest self-sustaining churches in the Alberta Synod.

> *Great credit is due the men who have laboured in this Presbytery to rebuild the Church, and whose faith and sacrifice have led to the gains which have been realized.*[5]

Then Mr. Mark named these men who were "modern heroes of the faith." He mentions that the WMS established the hospital in Rocky Mountain House with Miss Hildur Hermanson as matron and that auxiliaries supplied great quantities of clothing, bedding and so on. He also mentions the new vans supplied by the WMS for work in the west. But there was not a word of the deaconesses who had gone into these areas in the west, visiting homes, starting Sunday schools and women's groups, taking vacation Bible schools, directing camps, and preaching regularly.

This omission was too much even for the Women's Missionary Society and they felt compelled to add an editor's note to Mr. Mark's report to bring to the attention of their readers such an obvious oversight.

> *Mr. Mark has mentioned the men who have done much to make our Church in Red Deer Presbytery what it is today. He mentioned too, that deaconesses and nurses have played their part in that area. We would like to add their names. They are women who have gone to Red Deer Presbytery with deaconess training, who have served either under the Church or under the WMS. You will remember such names as Frieda Matthews, Hazel Macdonald, Hildur Hermanson, Gertrude Rollo, Elizabeth Walker, Ruby Walker, Mary Todd, Kathleen Stewart, Rae Starrett, Athalie Read.*[6]

Frieda Matthews

The board of directors of the Christian Literature Society for China met in Chengtu in September, 1945 and asked the staff committee "to explore the advisability and possibility for an early return to Shanghai" where the staff had its headquarters before the Japanese occupation of Shanghai. Some members of the staff escaped from Shanghai and made their way to Free China where the work had been carried on at Chengtu.

Miss Margaret Brown, writing from Chengtu, said that the magazine *Happy Childhood* continued to flourish and, when they returned to Shanghai, they would probably get thousands more subscribers. She quoted from some letters sent by *Happy Childhood* subscribers,

> *Yesterday I received my constantly-hoped for "Happy Childhood"... From long reading we know that the contents of "Happy Childhood" are of unlimited preciousness... To the Editor of Your Honourable Paper — I am one of your indefatigable readers.*[7]

Miss Brown also said that the *Women's Messenger* had become very popular.

Miss Margaret Wong, secretary of the international committee on Christian literature for Africa, in a series of addresses to the Canadian School of Missions gave some impressions received during her visit to West Africa. Wherever she went, she found that the war created a new desire for literature. What was happening among the men was having a great effect on the women. They wanted to learn to read and write in order to read letters coming from the men who were away and to be able to answer the letters. Gradually, resistance to the education of women was breaking down. It was the Christian church, said Miss Wong, that urged the importance of literacy in the early days. They transcribed unwritten languages and compiled grammars and dictionaries in order that the Bible might be translated into the languages of the people. Miss Wong died of a heart attack in Uganda in April 1948.

> *...the cause of world-wide Christian Literature has sustained a grievous loss, and her place will be hard to fill in connection with one of the most vital movements of present-day missionary endeavours.*[8]

By the end of the war, the World Day of Prayer stretched into eighty-one countries of the world.

> *...on that day the women of this continent who, through no merit of their own, have been privileged to walk but on the fringes of suffering, join with their Christian sisters who, in other parts of the earth, have suffered so grievously.*[9]

Women's Inter-Church Council received two messages in 1948. Each country made its own decision as to where to apply its World Day of Prayer offerings.

From Japan:

Our church will never forget those prompt measures your Women's Inter-Church Council took when the war was over, in sending to our people the Bibles to replace those destroyed during the war. To-day many hundreds of Bible study classes and groups have been organized in schools, factories, hospitals, offices, and farms. We are now eagerly looking forward to the coming of the Japanese Hymn Books as the gift for 1948.[10]

From Germany: (In 1947, for the first time in years, the German women observed the World Day of Prayer.)

Will you please convey to the Women's International Church Council of Canada our heartfelt gratitude for their splendid contribution to the re-education of German Youth. It is good to know that the Commonwealth is with us in our endeavour to give German boys and girls the opportunity to appreciate those values which the National Socialist Regime taught them to despise.[11]

Every year more Canadian churches joined in the World Day of Prayer. A letter from the manse in Smooth Rock Falls, Ontario speaks enthusiastically of their first meeting: *The observance was really a first venture in our little papertown… Twenty-three were present…* The committee in Ottawa, aware of the many hundreds of women who worked on Parliament Hill, approached the government to grant an additional half-hour to all women civil servants who desired to attend the noon-day prayer service. There were more than two thousand present and many had to be turned away. In London, the committee, realizing that in the Christian family the work of women and children had always been closely identified, approached the school boards and won their consent and co-operation to arrange prayer services in both the secondary and primary schools. The service for girls was adapted for use in the secondary schools and a special service written for the younger children.[12]

Conferences galore marked the years following the war. These included the first assembly of the World Council of Churches in Amsterdam in 1948 and the Women's Conference in Baarn, Holland, held in connection with the World Council of Churches. A report of the 1945 student conference in Edmonton, Alberta informed the members that the students raised money for Christian students in Germany and promoted quicker action for aid in Europe.

Many WMS people attended the Presbytery of Toronto's Mission Rally at Massey Hall on Sunday, January 20, 1946. Nearby churches cancelled evening services so their members could attend. The rally was conducted by the Moderator, Rev. James Milroy, and led by a massed choir of 300. Missionaries from British Guiana, India, Formosa, Japan and Manchuria were introduced by Dr. W. S. Cameron, secretary of the General Board of Missions.

The first assembly of the World Council of Churches met in August 1948 in Amsterdam. Moderator Rev. C. Ritchie Bell was one of The Presbyterian Church in Canada's delegates and also a delegate to the World Alliance of Reformed Churches that same month in Geneva. His wife, Margaret Bell, was the WMS representative at the 12th conference of the International Women's Union which met parallel to the alliance meeting in Geneva.

At the Women's Conference in Baarn, Holland, held in connection with the 1948 World Council of Churches, the women called for action: recruit and use the most able women, encourage them to study church work and take full responsibility for tasks to which they are appointed. They also called for a study on the relationship between men and women in church life, and a study of how the power of the Holy Spirit can guide men and women in problems of the day. The 1948 World Council of Churches appointed a committee on the *Life and Work of Women in the Church*. Almost a year later, in the summer of 1949, at a meeting of the Executive of the World Council, held in Chichester, England, the *Commission on the Life and Work of Women in the Church* was set up. Miss Sarah Chakko of the Syrian Orthodox Church of India and Principal of Thoburn College, Lucknow, India, had been a delegate to the World Council of Churches in Amsterdam and a speaker at a plenary session. She was appointed to chair the Commission. She later became the first woman president of the WCC.

Early in 1949, the Women's Inter-Church Council sponsored a meeting at which four of the Canadian women who had been delegates to the 1948 WCC brought reports. Dorothy Young, Youth Secretary for the United Church of Canada, had been appointed at the 1948 World Council to the *Committee on the Life and Work of Women in the Church*. In reporting, she said that the eminent Swiss theologian, Professor Karl Barth, had been appointed advisor to the Committee. He advised the women, said Miss Young,

> *not to be a group of feminists out to fight for their rights — but to remember that men and women do not necessarily have the same ministry, that each group must find the best place in which they can serve and be educated to serve in that capacity.*[13]

A report in 1954 spoke of Sarah Chakko's able chairing of the *Commission on the Life and Work of Women in the Church* and *of her spirited firmness in opposing certain Pauline attitudes on the part of Dr. Karl Barth as to the place of women, of her disarming manner, and her charming appearance in her pink sari, so that she won the hearts of all.*[14]

WMS had representatives at the Missionary Conference of North America, along with 66 other Protestant denominations. As part of the conference's plan for the Missionary Advance movement, they brought together 4,000 representatives including lay leaders from all parts of the United States and Canada.

In November 1950, Laura Pelton attended the Foreign Missions Conference in Cleveland, Ohio. Dr. Sarah Chakko gave the address "The Church in the World." She gently reminded people that western countries do not know everything that God has to say to man and that westerners need to understand the graciousness of receiving as well as giving. Miss Pelton reported,

We inferred from her address that she believes that before the Church will learn its unity the churches of the East and of the West must enter into mutual relationships in a new way...it has never dawned on us that these people had much to say to us; it has never dawned on us that God would speak to us a new word through them. Our senses appear to be too dull to realize that often they could show us new riches of Christian faith which we have never known...[15]

Miss Pelton's remarks were much harsher than Dr. Chakko's. Even if Miss Pelton includes herself, as she seems to do, she certainly misjudges many of the missionaries who went overseas and were not unaware of the 'gifts and graces' of those to whom they ministered.

The 1950 World Convention on Christian Education was held in Toronto with 5,000 delegates from 65 countries. Information coming to WMS noted that Dr. Toyohiko Kagawa, distinguished social leader and author from Japan, spoke of the importance of building a church through the church school. (It seems this is what our deaconesses and missionaries had been doing all along.) He also urged his fellow-Christians in all parts of the world to think more earnestly of the thousands of children in all parts of the world who are "in the street," children who have no parents or whose parents do not care what happens to them. Dr. Paul Vieth spoke of the Christian education of adults. "Elders" are themselves constantly in need of an ongoing educational program, he said. Most men and women know little about the Bible. New insights come with more mature thinking and constant study of the Christian text is essential.

India

Ellen Douglas returns to India and writes:

> *When the wire came from Mrs. Pae asking if I could be ready to sail in about a week's time, my first thought was, 'I could be ready tomorrow.'... The Marine Angel was a troop ship going out to bring home American soldiers from India... What a difference it makes when you feel this is the place God wants you to be, these are your people and here you belong!.... How good, too, to see friends from Amkhut and Jobat... But what was rather a surprise was to find how welcome were even the dusty, narrow bazaar lanes with the old familiar sounds and smells. The jungle, already becoming dry and brown in the approaching hot days, with the flame of the forest a riot of colour on the hills, was, oh, so welcome. Happiest sight of all, however, was the Amkhut valley, the mission compound nestling between the hills and the river, the innumerable brown-faced boys and girls on hand as usual to welcome back their Canadian friends with garlands and such smiles.*
>
> *The week after my arrival the annual mela was held in Amkhut... six days of spiritual food and fellowship.... Some of the older friends, too, were missing. I could not recall a mela without Dr. Buchanan and Naku Padre, but both these grand men had gone on to their rest... How encouraging it was, though, to see the son of Naku, Musa Padre, guiding the affairs of Presbytery so very capably!...the older ones are passing on, but almost every woman at the mela had a baby in her arms. From these arms and from our Christian homes new leaders are coming forward....*[16]

Margaret Kennedy described the reception Miss Isabel McConnell received on her return to Jobat. There were flags all over, an evergreen arch, welcome signs and many garlands! The new shiny station wagon was soon thronged. The barri Miss Sahib was back. She had a special place in their hearts because she had helped to bring many of these young people and children into the world. Miss McConnell said that never in all the years she had been in India had she received such a welcome. Miss McConnell was returning to India to work as a member of the staff at the Vellore Medical College.

Margaret Kennedy also reported on the Bhil Field's golden jubilee in March 1948. Everyone was up by 5:30 a.m. The morning light revealed a circle of people, Bhil Christians, standing on the far side of the river where the first missionary to the Bhils in this area camped fifty years ago. As well as the people from Amkhut, there were people from Sardi, Mendha, Jobat, - Alirajpur, Chicheniya, Barwani, Khalghat and Toranmal. They were all there to give thanks that the light of God's truth broke into the darkness of the Bhililand when Dr. Buchanan of the Canadian Presbyterian mission arrived half a century ago. At the sunrise service they looked back to the beginning and then marched over the river and up the hill to where Dr. Buchanan's bungalow had been built, and where his daughter, Miss Ruth Buchanan, who still served the Bhils, led them in prayer.

An overflowing assembly gathered for a thanksgiving service at 9 a.m., presided over by their foremost Bhil minister, Musa Padre. At this service a tablet on the church wall was unveiled in memory of Dr. and Mrs. Buchanan. In the afternoon they assembled again for a service of consecration. At night everyone's attention was drawn toward the big stretch of open ground where fires were lit and between them was the "stage" where the young people of the Bhil Christian community enacted their part of the program, "The Next Fifty Years."

Miss Kennedy describes the closing ceremony,

> *The Moderator of this our Vindhiya and Satpura Bhil Mountain Presbytery had lighted a candle; then the padres lit their candles from it; the elders followed suit; then the people — men, women and children — until a sea of light showed up the faces of all as they sang. Some of us went up to the bungalow verandah, so that we could watch as the light divided up into rivers and streamlets, following the paths homeward. The darkness had been lightened and the enlightened ones went out into further darknesses, carrying their light with them.*[17]

Through a generous gift from a friend of the WMS in memory of her mother, the WMS was able to send their first mobile clinic to the Bhil field. This meant reaching out to the 275,000 Bhils who could not, or would not, go to the hospital for treatment. Plans were then made to place a second mobile clinic in India.

Miss Bertha Robson died in March 1948. She had served under the WMS in India for twenty-one years and in 1925 was the only WMS missionary left on the Bhil Field. The others had gone into the United Church or retired. It was Bertha Robson who began an organized system of education in Amkhut and the nearby villages. She had a genius for imparting knowledge and training others, so that the Christian education as she planned it flourished and bore lasting fruit on the Bhil field. Among the leaders in the Christian Bhil communities there were many who had been her pupils: Jigiyo Padre, the ordained minister of the Jobat congregation; Tezlo Master, a teacher and

Musa, a pastor; of her two special "wards," Ruth was a nurse in the Jobat hospital and Patsy a successful teacher. There was sadness and mourning in the Amkhut valley when word reached there of her death.

The Vellore Missionary Medical College opened in 1918 by Dr. Ida Scudder, pioneer medical missionary. It was a centre to train Indian women to minister to their own people. During the first twenty years, 250 women obtained the degree of LMP (Licensed Medical Practitioner). In 1938, the government of Madras Presidency abolished the LMP degree and required all medical students to take the full six year course leading to BM (Bachelor of Medicine) and BS (Bachelor of Surgery) degrees. Vellore was unable to finance the necessary training for these higher degrees.

There was no thought of giving up the plan for the "healing" of India's women. A university commission of medical educationalists from all India visited Vellore. They recommended to the University of Madras that on the fulfillment of certain conditions the college be affiliated with the university for the first two years of the Bachelor of Medicine course; the situation to be reviewed again at the end of the two years. Finally, it was decided to make Vellore a college for both women and men.

The WMS gave a grant of $2,000 to the capital account of this college and each year an additional amount of $500 was given towards its maintenance. In order to help still further, they "loaned" one of their experienced nurses, Miss Bessie MacMurchy, to serve on the teaching staff. She later worked as a lecturer in post-graduate studies at the Mid-India Board of Examiners of the Nurses' Auxiliary of the Christian Medical Association of India.

Dr. Hilda M. Lazarus, OBE;BA;BS;MB;FRCS(Edin);MRCOG; FICS;FACS, trailing her impressive list of degrees, visited Canada in 1949. Dr. Lazarus had been recently appointed as principal of Vellore Medical College. She ranked among the outstanding Christian women of India, not only in the service she had given and in the position she occupied but also in the high honours she had won and that had been bestowed upon her, and in her loyalty to the Christian church. Dr. Lazarus spoke in Toronto in November under the auspices of the Canadian Overseas Missions Council, on the influence of Christianity on the New India.

In 1950, the same year as the hospital celebrated Ida Scudder's golden jubilee, the University of Madras granted permanent affiliation for the M.B., B.S. course, a course comparable to the M.D. degree. Vellore, with the support of many countries and many branches of the faith, brought its standard up to that of a class "A" medical school.

Miss Edith Magee writes to say what a tremendous thing the student bursaries are in the context of the backwardness of women's education in India. Two young women, Lajwanti and Viola, could never have gone to school without the bursaries sent from Canada.

In 1951, four denominations, Anglican, Methodist, Presbyterian and Congregational, joined to form the Church of South India. Each individual congregation would maintain its own form of worship.

Rev. Norman Goodall of the International Missionary Council writes of the great movement of people in India that resulted from the August 14, 1947 formation of the Dominion of India and Pakistan. Without any declaration of war, he says, and without serious premeditation and in completely haphazard fashion, from eight to ten million people in one corner of India took to the road. Some of them were accompanied by ox-wagons or camels and with nothing more than they could carry. For weeks and weeks the trek was accompanied by *savageries which scarcely bear talking about.* Floods added their toll. All agreed that the casualty total was comparable to that of a major war. The governments of both dominions worked day and night at the immediate task of relief and resettlement and some progress was made.

> *Apart from the vast and poignant human problem, the economic shock to the new Dominions' economy occasioned by the unplanned transfer of six million people from India to Pakistan and four million from Pakistan to India must have far-reaching consequences. Pakistan has lost the services of most of its professional and commercial classes. India, (or that part of it directly affected), is without many of its artisans and technicians.*

Rev. Goodall adds that there was widespread gratitude for the work of Christian relief agencies during those months.[18]

China

Rev. R.M. Ransom tells the story of Mrs. Wu, a Chinese Quaker Bible woman. She was nearly fifty years old when she heard her call to missionary service. In distant Fukien province, on the south-east coast of China, while she worked at her chores she had a "vision." It was the women of Yunnan calling her to help them. Her own people laughed at her. Even the foreign missionary disapproved, but her vision sent her on a 1,000-mile pilgrimage to remote Yunnan. Gradually she drew a little band of faithful women about her along with some of their families. Most of them could not read, but all could and did pray. She taught them songs and scripture portions. She taught one of them to read. She started a Sunday school. She sold gospel portions in the streets and visited in homes. Leaving a group of about thirty Christians, this fearless, aging crusader pushed on further into the interior with her gospel. For several years the little group continued without their leader, meeting regularly for prayer and Bible reading. Mrs. Wu continued to take a motherly interest in the little cell she had started in Kienshui and, when the Church of Christ in China came into the area, they found this small group of Christians that had continued year after year meeting regularly for prayer and Bible reading. This little group became the nucleus of the church in Kienshui. From this small beginning a splendid congregation developed. The grandmothers' group was one of the most interesting and most enthusiastic organizations in the church.

In February 1950, the material for the World Day of Prayer actually reached the group before the date. About the same time old Mrs. Wu, now nearing seventy, returned to her flock. Immediately, the church organized a five-day conference for women to follow the World Day of Prayer service.

> *They came in from as far as thirty miles, taking two days to make the trip on their little stumps of bound feet and carrying their rice for the week. They slept on the floor of the church and cooked their own meals. Over a hundred attended the Day of Prayer Service and, for the first time, perhaps, caught some glimpse of the World Church and of the women of the world joined in prayer.*[19]

In a letter written November 24, 1945, when Mildred Gehman was en route to Kunming, she tells of how, while waiting in Calcutta, they went to Belvedere, a former residence of the viceroy of India. During the war this residence served as a Royal Air Force headquarters and later a Red Cross centre for the repatriation of children and adults interned by the Japanese. It was a palatial residence with beautiful grounds. There she met and talked with Dr. and Mrs. Goforth's son-in-law, Mr. I. Jaffrey, who was on his way to England. Some of the children at the centre were, she said,

> *...pitiful with their spindly legs. One French couple with five little children who had been interned in Saigon came over and gazed unbelievingly at Janet Leigh, our six-months-old American baby, and looked at the skeleton bodies and sad little faces of their little ones, and we all wanted to cry. Their parents, too, looked starved. I can hardly believe I am so near journey's end. Early to-morrow afternoon we shall be in Kunming...*[20]

Later Mrs. Gehman wrote of her trip from Calcutta to Kunming and of her first days in Kunming, the capital of Yunnan province. She was going to Kienshui near the French Indo-China border to help open a mission hospital there.

In Kienshui, organizing the hospital brought months of frustration and worry. To begin with, there were language problems, but the work left her with little time or energy to do much studying. For the first month she was the only foreigner. Mail service was unreliable which added to her loneliness in a strange, bandit-ridden country where there was considerable robbing and shooting. Mrs. Gehman did not go far outside the city walls. Nevertheless, she worked hard to set up the hospital and a training school for nurses.

Yunnan was the southwestern province of China on the Burmese, Tibetan and Indo-China frontiers. The Yunnan mission with headquarters in Kunming had branches in Kaiyuan, Kochiu, Mentgze, Kienshui and Shihping, all important cities on the South Yunnan railway. In April 1949, communists were within fifteen miles of the railway for over two thirds of its length and the Yunnan Mission Committee with Dr. W.H. Clark as field secretary began forming plans for the continuance of the work under the incoming regime.

The first step, said Mildred Gehman, was to inquire of our Chinese coworkers as to whether they wished the foreign personnel to remain or go, since association with foreign missionaries might jeopardize their own safety. The Kunming church committee wished its foreign missionaries to stay but to live inside the city rather than on the church compound. The general policy of most missions in South China was for women and children to leave and also any who were not in the best of health. Early in April 1949, the missionaries in Kienshui received a letter asking them to ask the opinion of their co-workers and then decide whether they wished to remain. Their coworkers wanted the missionaries to stay and the missionaries wanted to stay. Not long after, for health reasons, Mrs. Gehman left on furlough.

The fifth General Assembly of the Church of Christ in China met in 1949. It was the first Assembly since 1937. The Moderator, Rev. C.C. Chen, emphasized that the Church had not only maintained its life and witness, despite the stress of war, but had also opened three new mission areas, in Kweichow, Yunnan, and among the tribal peoples in south-west China.

Rev. E. Bruce Copeland, who had been executive secretary of the provisional council of the Christian Church in China and was now the missionary liaison secretary in Hong Kong, wrote that 1951 saw the withdrawal of nearly all the Protestant missionaries from China but the Chinese church remained strong. After the standing committee of the General Assembly of the Christian Church in China officially adopted (October 1950) a document which was known as "The Manifesto," a pastoral letter was addressed by the standing committee to members of the Christian Church in China. The manifesto called upon Christians in China to make the church self-supporting, to support the common program of the Peoples' government and to oppose imperialism, feudalism and bureaucratic capitalism. The pastoral letter, while drawing attention to the manifesto and endorsing it, put the main emphasis upon specific Christian tasks and upon universal Christian truth, in the following words:

> *The older churches of Europe and America, inspired by the love of Christ and regardless of difficulties and hardships, brought the Gospel to China. The pioneers of our own Church of Christ in China with well-thought-out plans laid the foundations of a Chinese Church. Today we cannot shirk our responsibility; we must bravely take up the responsibility of the church. We cannot always be dependent upon financial aid and personnel of western missions and throw away the opportunity for growth as an indigenous church… Christ is eternal truth. He is the Gospel for the world. He is the central object of our faith. He is the symbol of justice and peace. By His death and resurrection the barriers between man and God, the hatreds between race and race, the pressures between class and class, can all be removed. He points the true and shining way to "one family under heaven," and one world brotherhood. We worship Him with all our hearts. We would preach Him and manifest Him to the world. This is the greatest contribution which our Church must make in the New Age.*[21]

Soon after this message was issued, said Dr. Copeland, the situation for Christians in China became much graver. The continued presence of the missionaries, the Elders, the Ransoms and Mrs. Gehman had become a source of embarrassment to the Christian church in China, not so much because they were missionaries but because they were westerners, and all such were suspects to the Chinese Communists.

Formosa

The first letters Mrs. Jean Mackay received from Formosa after the war were from Mrs. Bella Koa. It was Mrs. Koa who had

> *…the joy of breaking to us the news that our beautiful schools, taken from us by the Japanese Government, had been returned to us by the Chinese Government towards the end of last November…*

Mrs. Mackay said,

> *I do not expect to have so much of a resurrection feeling again on*

> *this earth...about two thousand aborigines of the Northern and Central East Coast have declared for Christ and during the years of oppression sealed their faith (an undisclosed number of them) with 'their flesh, their bones and their blood.*[22]

The Mackay Memorial Hospital was also returned to the Formosan church, although some buildings were still occupied by Chinese soldiers. The church was free to carry on its work and, after six years, Formosa was once more open to missions. In response to the pressing invitation of the leaders of the Formosan church, the General Board of Missions and the Women's Missionary Society sent back those of the former missionaries who were able to return. The MacKays went in January 1946 and the Dicksons, Miss Dorothy Douglas and Miss Isabel Taylor in February. Miss Hildur Hermanson had been in Formosa since June 1946, having been sent by the China Relief Committee.

During the war Miss Hildur Hermanson went to Alberta to work as superintendent of the Rocky Mountain House Hospital. After the war she returned to Formosa to undertake relief work there. The hospital, she said, was practically empty. What the Department of Public Health did not take away when they came, the soldiers who occupied the place had either broken or sold. Miss Hermanson said she felt quite ill after seeing it. The officials, she said, treated them kindly and sent an officer to the hospital to interview the man in charge. She hoped to see the Out-patients Departments opened in about two weeks, but the wards could not be opened until they got some beds, bedding and supplies. A few of the nurses who were there before were able to come back but most of them were married so it meant starting to teach new ones right away. The WMS sent money to Miss Hermanson to repair and refurnish the WMS bungalow and engage a Bible woman.

Hildur "Hermie" Hermanson

The Mackay Memorial Hospital began training young women from some of the indigenous tribes. These young women would then return to their own villages and help set up some kind of medical work there.

Cave church near Hualien at entrance to gorge where Tayals lived

Chi-Oang, the Tayal woman with the impressive tattoo on her face, who was responsible for bringing the Christian message to her tribe, became the Formosan WMS missionary to the Tayal people. She was highly esteemed by the Japanese authorities for her efforts to bring about peace between them and the Tayal tribe. Mrs. Young writes that on

> *...this delicate and somewhat elderly woman has rested the task of presenting the Gospel to her own people. Her home has been a little church near the entrance to the gorge in which the Tayals live.*

There, some seven or eight years ago, Mrs. Koa and I spent an evening with her. After supper she beat a resonant drum, and many from the village (Pe-po-hoan people) came in for an hour's singing (they have good voices) and worship.[23]

Rev. James Dickson writes of his return to Formosa. The greatest industrial metropolis on the island, Ko-hiong, he reports, was almost completely in ruins. Blocks of buildings had been reduced to rubble. Other streets had empty shells of buildings standing with great ragged gaps in the brick and concrete walls. An American search team was at work recovering the bodies of airmen, and prisoners of war who had died or been killed in Formosa.

In contrast, Mr. Dickson tells of how, looking out of the train bound for Taihoku (Taipei), the peaceful countryside looked the same. There were the rice fields, the fields of sugar-cane, the neat rows of peanuts, and sweet potatoes; the farmers, with their big hats and heavy hoes; here and there a water-buffalo pulling a plow. In the distance were the purple mountains, unchanged. These mountains had a new interest for him for there, in those great mountains, were over 3,000 new Christians, and new believers were being added to the quickly built churches every week.

That night in Taihoku city the news quickly spread that I had come… What a welcome I received!… Some had suffered great hardships. A few of the Christians, including Ministers and Elders, had been put in prison by the Japanese. Others had lost their homes in the bombings raids.[24]

He soon realized that while outwardly there was little change and the church's foundations remained as firm as the purple mountains, the old Formosa was gone. The people now had a freedom which they never knew before. The anti-foreign and anti-Christian feeling which had been worked up by the Japanese was swept away. There had never been a time when the preaching of the gospel had such an opportunity.

When Miss Isabel Taylor was on furlough in Canada, she spoke at WMS council about the singing church.

In our small Island the singing in the church has become a part of our life. People from the mainland, missionaries and Chinese alike are amazed at the singing of the church in general.[25]

How did this come about? Tribute must first be paid to Mrs. Margaret Gauld, most beloved of all missionaries by the Formosans, who taught music to the Formosan church for forty years. Through the years, the theological college students had to know how to sing and play and when they went out into the churches they were the teachers. This was the true reason why they had become a singing church. Everyone sings and loves to sing, she said, from the smallest child to the oldest man or woman.

Miss Laura Pelton, overseas secretary for the WMS, while in Formosa in 1947, was greatly impressed by the witness being made by the Bankah church. She asked *The Glad Tidings* to print an interview with the pastor, Rev. Go Eng-hoa.

> *What do you consider the secret of the congregation's growth?*
>
> *He replied without taking a breath of hesitation — "two words, 'children' and 'youth'. The Sunday School averages 275 to 300."*
>
> *But how do you manage a school so large? I asked. "I don't," he answered modestly with a smile, "that's where the 'youth' come in. Our YPS membership is about fifty and they are nearly all active teachers and helpers. They handle things."*
>
> *And what is the secret of keeping that youth group together? His answer was just as unhesitating. "We have an early morning prayer meeting, sometimes two or three times a week, which twenty to thirty attend. That, together with lots of work to do contain the secret, I think."*
>
> *And what about the congregation of grown-ups? The average Sunday congregation (two services) is about 200 to 250, about all the Church holds, out of a possible 600. We have six elders at present, one a woman; and eight deacons, three of them women. We emphasize giving ourselves lots of work to do in the community that keeps us from idleness, and growing.*[26]

On March 8, 1951, the Formosan church held its first General Assembly in the Siang-lian Church in Taipei. Eighty delegates represented a Christian community of about 60,000 from more than 200 congregations. Representatives of the synods of North and South Formosa met officially for the first time, marking the culmination of a movement toward unifying the two bodies which had been progressing through two decades. The Church of South Formosa was founded in 1865 by a missionary from the Presbyterian Church in England, and the Church in North Formosa was founded in 1872 by a missionary from the Presbyterian Church in Canada, Rev. George Leslie Mackay. Dr. Mackay's son, Rev. G.W. Mackay, and his wife Jean were at the time of the General Assembly on the Formosa field. Under fifty years of Japanese administration, Formosan Christians had few contacts with the western world, but now with freer coming and going there was keen interest in world Christianity, particularly through the World Council of Churches.

Koreans in Japan

In 1948, the Presbyterian Church re-opened the work among the Koreans in Japan from which missionaries had to withdraw in the latter part of 1940 because of war conditions. The General Board of Missions appointed Rev. Luther Young and Rev. Paul Rumball, who had been working in British Guiana, to return to Japan and re-establish the work among the Koreans there. Mrs. Jean MacLean Rumball was for twelve years engaged in that work as a missionary for the WMS. The WMS gave a grant of $1,000 toward the re-opening of the work.

Jean Rumball wrote to tell of their first trip to Tokyo to visit the Christians in that area. They were able to visit most of the districts where the Korean Church had been holding meetings. Mrs. Rumball was able to interpret for her husband.

The society had already sent $1,000 to help rebuild one of the Korean Churches in Japan. An additional $200 was sent to assist in repairing the roof of the church. Four thousand dollars would be sent to help in the church building program. The Korean people believed that they could raise a sum equal to any sum sent from the home church and the money would all go to restore the bomb-damaged churches. The WMS was supporting two Bible women.

The church among the Koreans in Japan was not a part of the Japanese Church and only loosely associated with the church in Korea. Prior to the war there were forty-eight congregations. They had depended upon The Presbyterian Church in Canada for their development. After the war the congregations were small, although the Osaka Church had 200 members. The Korean Church in Japan was left with only four buildings at the end of the war.

This terrible loss, said Dr. J. Alan Munro, secretary of the Board of Missions, could only be understood against the dire poverty of an outcast people. It is inconceivable, he said, that the Korean community of Christians could rebuild these churches, yet here and there through the cities of Japan, brave congregations began the task of rebuilding. One of the three congregations in Osaka was rebuilt. It was the only congregation which The Presbyterian Church in Canada had helped to rebuild. No other building aid was given. Dr. Munro said,

> *The Presbyterian Church in Canada has been generous in its aid to Europe in the matter of rebuilding bombed churches and in the supply of clothing. Surely, we should feel some responsibility for our own infant mission amongst the Koreans in Japan. The ranks of their ministry has been hopelessly depleted. There are only three ordained ministers and five non-ordained pastors. The encouraging*

thing is that there is, since the war, a fine group of young men entering the ministry. A strong appeal has been made to the mother church in Canada to send out missionaries to give leadership, instruction, and encouragement to the local congregations and to act as liaison with the Japanese and occupying power. The Korean Christians knows that the lure of Communism is strong. The church must be strong if it is to survive the years ahead.[27]

Manchuria

The story of the churches in Manchuria during fourteen years of Japanese occupation and some eighty days of Russian occupation is a story of hardship, danger and suffering but it is also one of endurance, courage and triumphant faith. The women's work suffered heavily. Christian education was suppressed except for a few kindergarten schools. The Japanese demanded attendance at the Shinto shrines and, rather than submit, the schools were closed. The theological college carried on all through the period of occupation and was never closed. Some Japanese Christian pastors ran risks to help the Chinese churches. Now it was the turn of the Chinese Christians to help their Japanese brothers and they were doing it. The church in Manchuria was very much alive and was not dependent on any mission for its life.

Mr. Allan Reoch went back to Manchuria while he was doing relief work in North China after the war. Before the missionaries left, fifty churches had been established and a presbytery had been formed. Forty-four of the churches were still carrying on after the war. Szepingkai had been shelled for fourteen days and the church and the missionaries' houses had been burned but services had begun again. The Chinese Christians could carry on, said Mr. Reoch, as they could not if foreign workers were there with them. Even if they were scattered, he said, the Christians would carry the gospel with them.

Miss Luella Crockett died in New Glasgow, Nova Scotia on March 19, 1950. She was appointed to the WMS staff in 1919 and went out to South China that fall. When that field was given to the United Church in 1925, she returned to Canada and worked for the society with the Chinese in Canada. In 1929, she was appointed to Manchuria, the first person to be appointed to that field by the WMS. She resigned in 1931 when the country was at war and the missionaries were forced to go home. She closed the mission alone and saw that all of value was sent away for safe keeping. She went to Peking where she carried on a fine work among the rickshaw men and their families and also helped many Chinese boys and girls with their English. When war came she was interned for two and a half years. In 1946 she was released and returned to Peking where she worked until war again forced her home.

British Guiana

Miss Margaret Ramsay wrote telling of the harvest services conducted and the schools visited in Essequibo County where she and Miss Sarah Cameron had been working since Miss Cameron arrived in late September, 1946.

> *So far this year we two have officiated at ten Harvest services and concerts, and when the Moderator was here we attended four other Harvest services with him. Next Sunday we plan an all-day trip up the coast for three more services… We are really doing the work of the Field Missionary, without the authority that his position carries. Mr. Dickson is very busy…so that we try to relieve him of as much as possible. Of course, we cannot take Communion services, or baptisms and weddings, but for the ordinary services we are acceptable apparently….*[28]

Chapter 15

Changing Times

1950-1972

Missions are Changing

Doors were being closed to missionaries in many countries but still the younger churches were calling to the older churches for help. They needed assistance in money and personnel. This was the conclusion drawn by the delegates to the International Missionary Council which met in Willingen, Germany on July 5-18, 1952.

Council delegates concluded, however, that assistance must come in a different spirit from that given in the past. Help must come from one equal partner to another equal partner. Above all, if the church was to speak effectively and authoritatively, it must be a church witnessing in unity, a church that was one in Christ Jesus, not a church tragically divided.

Laura Pelton, executive secretary of overseas missions for the WMS, was a delegate to the Willingen Council. She reported in *The Glad Tidings* in November, 1952:

> *Implicit throughout the discussions* [at Willingen] *was the question of unity. The results at Willingen...have moved me to make some comments on the matter of unity. It is not clear to*

me...what is meant by many who talk so much today of unity. If they mean that the churches should make their witness in a spirit of "oneness"... I am for unity. On the other hand if these pronouncements on unity envisage ecclesiastical organic union, I, for one, predict that the ecumenical movement will be retarded indefinitely...

In her report, Laura Pelton mentioned phrases used by the delegates at the conference that indicated the impatience many of them felt with the ecclesiastical divisions within the Protestant church. She quoted some of these phrases: *the scandal of the divisions of the Church; the Church's witness on the mission fields is made ineffectual by its divisions; the divisions of the Church are a sin against God*. She said she could understand the difficulty which members of the younger churches had in appreciating the historic fact of denominational divisions. However, she added,

Willingen **was** *unity. Transcending all our differences of race, nationality, tradition, theological expression...was our oneness in Christ... To me Willingen demonstrated that much of our discussion about unity is premature...*[1]

Dr. David W. Hay, Professor of Systematic Theology at Knox College, was prompted to take up his pen and, in an article appearing in *The Glad Tidings* of February, 1953, he challenged Miss Pelton on her views on church union.

Dear Miss Pelton,

"Ecumaniacs" have been raising a howl of disappointment because divisions seem to be harder to deal with. But actually the situation is a far more wholesome and promising one, provided we "stay together," as Amsterdam vowed we would. I say more wholesome, because theological differences are being courageously met head-on, and not covered up by false prophets crying, "Unity, unity" where there is no unity. (There is another kind of false prophecy which says that unity is "spiritual" and therefore we can remain happily in our divisions)... It is a fallacy to assume that theological enquiry is necessarily divisive... the World Council of Churches — and that means we and the other Churches meeting in council — have officially declared that the Council exists "not to negotiate unions between Churches...but to bring the Churches into living contact with each other and to promote the study and discussion of the issues of Church unity." To evade these issues is to evade the call of Christ Himself. I profoundly agree with you that it is He Whom we are meeting in the ecumenical movement...and we dare not turn away from the claim that He makes upon us there. It is He Who refuses to accept disunity among His followers.[2]

"Acting Together" is Laura Pelton's follow-up article on the issue of unity in April, 1953.

> *As we consider the Church's mission in unity, one thing is clear: whatever may be the final manifestation of the Church's unity the churches must act together in a spirit of understanding and sympathy.*

The most important consideration for all mission boards, she said, was to discover where their witness could be more effective by acting together. One of the difficulties about co-operative work for many people, she suggested, was that the work tended to become depersonalized. For example, when a grant was given in the estimates, it seemed to mean more if we could say that it was going for Miss McConnell's work on the Bhil Field. A question asked at Willingen, said Laura Pelton, was, *Are we prepared to make the necessary sacrifice for the initiative and mobility required for the new missionary era?* Perhaps, she said, we have depended too much on the personal element in our missionary work. Whatever would advance the mission of the church should be our first concern. The International Missionary Council, she pointed out, was the channel through which the churches communicated with one another across the barriers of war.[3]

In her report on the Willingen Council to the Board of Missions in September, 1952, Laura Pelton spoke about factors that weaken the church's mission which had been discussed by the delegates at Willingen. An era in mission work had ended, she said, and the church must be prepared to conduct missionary work in a way appropriate to the needs of the day.

The council at Willingen had some harsh words for the churches in the West. It concluded that God had spoken to the church through the failures of the past. Examples of this failure were the half-hearted efforts of prosperous churches in the West in sending the gospel and the unwillingness on the part of many missionaries to hand over control of church affairs to the younger churches. Other examples were the extravagant expenditure of money on large institutions which the younger churches were unable to maintain, and the failure by Western churches to give an effective witness in their own countries and communities.

Some vocal Christians from the younger churches attending the third World Conference of Christian Youth, meeting in India, also voiced their criticisms. Miss Helen Bricker, Girls' Work Secretary for The Presbyterian Church in Canada, serving both the Board of Christian Education and the WMS, attended the conference. She spoke at the WMS annual meeting in May, 1953. Many of the thinking and vocal Christians in the younger churches, she said, felt there was an unnecessary identification between mission work and the Western way of life. She quoted the Ceylonese theologian teacher, Rev. D. T. Niles.

> *The gospel is a seed that is sown in the soil of a culture. The plant bears the marks both of the seed and of the soil. In Asian countries Christianity is a potted plant which needs to be rooted in the cultural soil of their own countries.*[4]

Bricker said that Christians in the young churches felt a deep-seated gratitude for the work of the Christian churches which had enabled them to hear of Christ. But they wondered why Christian churches in Canada were not trying to reach out to the people around them who were not Christian.

Margaret Kennedy, on her way home from India, attended a study conference for missionaries on furlough at Bossey, Switzerland, where questions about Western missions were also expressed. The whole conference was led into a study of Romans 12 to 15 by Suzanne de Dietrich, a prominent theologian, and then went into small discussion groups.

> *To hear those missionaries, especially the Dutch and German theologians, dig deep into each verse to find Paul's vital meaning and application was an inspiration to me.*[5]

Regarding the question of genuine love for the brethren as applied to the mission field, Miss Kennedy said, they asked how our attitude towards Christians of other nations, those of the younger churches, measured up. Was genuine love expressed in "all give and no take?" What of the unconscious superiority of Western culture that caused decisions to be made for others instead of allowing the gospel message itself to leaven its way through another culture towards new standards?

A World Mission Consultation was held from June 17-22, 1971, at Waterloo Lutheran University, Waterloo, Ontario. In his theme address, Rev. Harold Sitahal, moderator of The Presbyterian Church of Trinidad and Grenada, said that overseas churches were no longer content to play a subservient role to Western churches. They wanted to be equal partners. Bishop Bhandare, deputy moderator of the Church of North India said that the time had come for us to stop saying 'mission', 'missionaries', 'sending' and 'receiving', 'developing' and 'non-developing', because these terms create misunderstanding.

> *No longer is mission work a one-way street. The whole world is the mission field. Churches in India and Japan are sending out missionaries to other countries.*[6]

Were these criticisms of Western Missions well deserved? We know, of course, that there is some truth in them but, in light of the dedication and self-sacrificing devotion of the missionaries, these allegations do seem to be rather super-critical, and not altogether true. Often our own church people were the most critical. In 1955, Laura Pelton says,

Much of our missionary response smacks of nineteenth century consciousness rather than mid-twentieth century.[7]

In 1970, Rev. H.T. Ellis writes,

Why all the doubt and confusion and loss of confidence? Why? — because of past paternalism, insensitivity to local customs and culture,…the dissimilarity between church and Christ, and lack of confidence in the Gospel itself…[8]

In the beginning of mission work the missionaries had to assume leadership. Yet we know from their reports that the intention was always to have the people take ownership of their own churches as soon as they were able. There were training schools for evangelists, Bible women, nurses and doctors, and there were schools for children. Comments like the following were common.

One of the directions in which we are endeavouring to move on all our overseas fields is more responsibility on the part of nationals.[9]

To be sure, the missionaries brought with them Western culture, which was all they knew, but many of them did attempt to let the truth of the gospel speak to the people in ways that were meaningful to them. Yes, they taught them Western hymns but what else could they do until the churches were able to raise up musicians who could write their own hymns? Miss Isabel Taylor said in May, 1957 that there was much work waiting for someone with the necessary talent to develop music which was indigenous to the Taiwanese church. *This is work for a Formosan to do and we are praying for just the right one.*[10] By 1963, the Formosan General Assembly was working on a Formosan hymn book.

Missions did change, of course. The women and men who worked on the mission fields could see with thankfulness and joy the fruits of their labours as the people assumed leadership over their own churches. Surely, the fact that the churches overseas survived the war after the missionaries left was a tribute to the training they had received from the missionaries.

A kinder, gentler approach was taken in 1964 by Kathleen Moody, a missionary of the Presbyterian Church in England who attended a meeting of council executive with Isabel Taylor, with whom she worked in Taiwan. She addressed the executive in a gentle manner, speaking about what the changes taking place in missions would mean to those concerned about following Christ's call to share the good news of the gospel. She used the words of Jesus to his disciples before his arrest and crucifixion. He was trying to tell them that life was changing, that "it is different now." What does this mean for us? she asked.

It means learning a new relationship; learning to work together, sharing ideas and plans. It means…a willingness to see that God is

> *acting and speaking in Asia... It means giving up the comfortable feeling we sometimes have, of a richer nation helping a poorer. It means a new respect for one another; it means accepting the leadership and direction of Asian Christians...if we believe in the world Church, we must share with the Churches in other lands.*

She added,

> *And this is a tremendous privilege — a gift from God to our generation. Our forebears went because they were sent; we go because we are invited. In this day, when nationalism is so strong; when white faces and white attitudes are resented and rejected, surely it should be our joy, that, within the Church, the barriers are broken down, and that East and West, white and brown, work together as one... Yes — it is different - but one thing is* ***not*** *different. It is, and always will be, the same — the command of God to go to all Nations. The times are different, the work is different but the Call is the same.*[11]

1964 — The 100th Anniversary

In 1964, the WMS celebrated its 100th anniversary and its 50th anniversary, 100 years since its beginning in 1864 and 50 years since the amalgamation of the three branches in 1914. Almost 1,500 women came

100th anniversary

> *...to honour and remember those stalwart women of our Church who, in 1864, planted so truly and so well, the first small, vital seeds from which has grown the Women's Missionary society(WD) in its broad outreach of today.*[12]

The celebration was held in the Church of St. Andrew and St. Paul in Montreal. Amid all the events that took place the theme of change in missions could not be avoided.

"The Anniversary Corner," appeared in each issue of *The Glad Tidings*, usually written by Jean Stewart. In the May issue, Stewart quoted Alice Inkster, a past president of the WMS, who wrote these words to the anniversary committee:

> *We look back with gratitude and pride upon the achievements of the WMS pioneers of our first century. They were women of foresight, initiative, and courage. Are we of today showing the same characteristics? Surely they are needed in these changed and still changing times. I hope that this Anniversary will not close merely with praises for the past, but with a definite challenge for the future — no matter what the cost — of change perhaps?... My hope is that the Anniversary will close with a mandate for the 2nd century of our WMS.*[13]

Jean Stewart, in her article, quotes from the Foreign Mission Committee of the Church of Scotland in "Mission for This Day," a 1958 account of the mission work of The Presbyterian Church in Canada.

> *How many still think in terms of so many Fields, Mission 'Stations' with familiar names, and Missionaries marked out as 'our own'? It is a formidable task to help ministers and congregations...to realize that the mission as a separate entity is lost in the Church, that the denominational loyalty gives way to co-operation and that the frontiers of Missionary service are always changing and expanding.*

Then Stewart asks,

> *Do we, as a Women's Missionary Society in 1964, understand these changes, and how are we meeting them?*[14]

The theme of change was emphasized in Dr. Kenneth McMillan's address on the opening night of the anniversary celebrations. He spoke about our inheritance — our inheritance being those early missionaries who had pioneered work in education and medicine. *These pioneer missionaries wrote one of the most blazing chapters in the history of the church.* They were, he said, our inspiration for the future. He went on to say that the world had changed more in the past century than in the thousand years before 1864. When we remember, Dr. McMillan said,

> *that a century ago…women did not have the vote; higher education was all but denied them; women in politics was practically unheard of; women had little to say in the leadership of the church, …we can appreciate something of the revolutionary character of the movement launched by Presbyterian women when they founded a missionary society.*

Dr. McMillan added,

> *I would emphasize that we are now living in a brand new age of history, and that God is calling us to act now in this new age, and not to pretend that the new age does not exist. We are now witnessing the dawn of Universal history…. The world is becoming one…*

Dr. McMillan spoke of "The Revolution of Rising Expectations," where dispossessed people were no longer content to accept famine, sickness and illiteracy as their way of life.

> *The VISION and the FAITH and the ACTION of our ancestors is needed today. The temptation to retreat into the past must be resisted… The greatest peril faced by the Christian Church today is not that it will suffer, but that it will fail; not that it will be persecuted or crushed, but that it will be ignored… It is true that Jesus Christ is the same yesterday, today and forever. But it is also true that the world to which we are called upon to witness, is not the world of the past. It is not the world of 1864 or of 1914 but the world of 1964.*

Dr. McMillan concluded his address by saying that in celebrating the two anniversaries, 1864 and 1914, the WMS was passing two significant milestones and he reminded the women of the original purpose of the milestones that were set up along the famous Roman roads of the ancient world.

> *Those milestones were placed, not for people to sit on, and not as places to stop and rest, but that the traveller might know how far he had come, and how far he had yet to go.*[15]

At the conclusion of the 100th anniversary celebrations in Montreal, a dinner was held in the Chinese Presbyterian Church. As an expression of gratitude to the WMS, the Chinese Presbyterian congregation presented a Chinese banner to the national president of the WMS, Agnes Curr. The banner bore the inscription "Love Knows No Boundaries" (OY MO YUEN NAY) and was presented by Mrs. James S. Lee, honorary president of the Chinese WMS Auxiliary. The minister, Rev. Paul Chan, expressed the appreciation of the Chinese people for the long years of understanding and encouragement given by the WMS to bring the gospel to the Chinese people through financial support and Christian interest.

Canada

In 1954, all the teachers in the residential schools had become employees of the Department of Indian Affairs. Denominations still had the privilege of nominating qualified teachers. In 1958, the government assumed full financial responsibility for the operation of the schools. The denominations retained the responsibility of administering the institutions.[16]

Mr. Steve Robinson, principal of the Cecilia Jeffrey School in Kenora, reported in May, 1960 that he was pleased to see that ten of their former students were continuing their education and were attending high school in Sault Ste. Marie and in North Bay.

In December, 1960, Frieda Matthews, director of National Missions, reported that the Indian Affairs Branch had arranged for all pupils of the Cecilia Jeffrey School beyond the grade four level to attend a district public school in a nearby municipality. However, when August came and the new district school had not even been started, plans had to be changed. Where would the children of the district attend classes until the new building was erected? The only possibility was the classroom block in the Cecilia Jeffrey School. Integration for the Aboriginal children took place in their own school. This was a new venture. For a few days, said Miss Matthews,

> *...the Indian children stood by, while the non-Indians monopolized the playground equipment. But that did not last long and in less than a week they were playing happily together. Forty of the Indian children were invited to have Thanksgiving dinner in the homes of their newly-found non-Indian friends. It appears the easy approach to integration has been found — through the children who have accepted each other.*[17]

In 1969, the Department of Indian Affairs took over the operation of the residence. A celebration to honour students and staff of Cecilia Jeffrey School was held on May 30, 1971. It was the first of the Presbyterian functions held to mark the closing of the schools. At the morning service at First Presbyterian Church, Kenora, Ontario, a memorial window was dedicated. The window, depicting St. Peter, also bore several Aboriginal motifs, the thunderbird, a teepee and a birch-bark canoe. The beating of drums and the sound of singing heralded the start of the pow-wow that took place on the afternoon of May 30, and a large crowd gathered outside the Kenora Fellowship Centre. Men, women and children were dressed in their colourful indigenous dress and performed their indigenous dances. The pow-wow was followed by the dedication of the addition to the Kenora Fellowship Centre.

Built about 1930 by the federal government, Birtle School, Manitoba, was turned over to the Women's Missionary Society to operate as a mission school for Aboriginal children. It replaced an earlier building, owned and operated by the WMS, to serve the educational needs of the children from the Presbyterian missions on the Birdtail Sioux Reserve, the Waywayseecappo Reserve, the Keeseekoowenin Reserve and the Rolling River Reserve. For a time, some of the children from the Mistawasis Reserve in northern Saskatchewan were brought in as well. In the late 1940s the half-day system was abolished and the pattern of the provincial schools followed. There was an emphasis on religious training. It was also the era of Aboriginal teams in various sports, choirs and bands. The Christmas concert was the highlight of the winter.

As time went on, an increased interest in education brought an increase in attendance and children had to be refused due to lack of accommodation. The need for greater educational facilities saw the introduction of day schools on the reserves.

Birtle was the first residential school in Manitoba to introduce high school education. At first the courses were added to the residential school curriculum but, as the numbers increased, the Birtle High School opened its doors to Aboriginal students. As accommodation in the public schools in Birtle permitted, the elementary school students were accepted in the classes until all students became integrated into the town schools. This was the end of federally operated classrooms in the residential schools. The residential schools became residences and the names of the schools were changed. They were then used for children who were orphans, children from broken homes and children who lived too far away from schools in their home area.

On April l, 1969, a major change took place at Birtle when the Department of Indian Affairs took over the complete operation of the residence. The staff became civil servants and the institution was then operated on federal government policies and procedures.

A special service of worship was held at Birtle on Sunday evening, June 8, 1969. The senior girls of the residence formed the choir. Rev. Gordon Williams, a graduate of Birtle and the first Aboriginal Canadian Presbyterian minister, preached the sermon. In addition to the student body and staff of the residence, many persons from the area, as well as some from farther afield, were in attendance. The service was a fitting climax to the eighty years in which the society had served the Aboriginal children who had come to the residence on the hillside overlooking the town of Birtle.

That year marked the end of an era in the WMS ministry to Aboriginal students. The takeover date of the residences by the Department of Indian Affairs and Northern Development was set for April 1, 1969. It was the end of an era but, as we shall see, not the end of the church's involvement with residential schools.

A dedication service to mark the re-opening of Presbyterian Fellowship House in Winnipeg was held on April 16, 1971. The house was first opened in 1960 to provide a Christian environment and a wholesome recreational centre for young people of all races who came to Winnipeg to continue their studies or to find employment. The first residents were largely Aboriginal young people. As more provision was made for them by the Department of Indian Affairs, the ministry of the Fellowship House was then directed to young people from overseas countries studying in Winnipeg. When space permitted, transient residents were accommodated. In September, 1969, the house became home to teen-age boys on probation, there being a tremendous need for such accommodation. An addition to the building was made so this work might be continued more effectively.

One of the outstanding and encouraging changes in connection with Chinese residents in Canada in 1974 was granting them the rights of Canadian citizenship. Naturalized Chinese could now bring their wives and families to this country. This was a tremendous step forward for the Chinese people. It allowed them to have proper homes and family life. Many of the newcomers went to the missions where they had the opportunity to learn English and where they were also taught the Christian faith.

Grace Lee, who had worked at the Chinese Mission in Victoria for many years, went to Hong Kong in August, 1952. Her letters told of her great joy in being with her family again. She said that churches were well attended and that there was greater interest than twenty-five years before when she had last been home.

One of the highlights in 1958 was Ron Con's graduation from Knox College. After his ordination, Rev. Con went as minister to Emmanuel Presbyterian Church in Sudbury. In his childhood, he had attended the Chinese kindergarten and church school and was a member of the Chinese church in Vancouver.

In October, 1956, chiefly through the efforts of Rev. André Poulain of Église St. Luc, the French Protestant School, Peace Centennial, was established in Montreal. In September, 1961, the Protestant School Board of Montreal agreed to start a grade 8 French class and promised to start a new class each year until a regular secondary school was established. At the time, it was government policy that French children went to Catholic schools and English children went to Protestant schools.

In the summer of 1958, the WMS provided two leaders for Le Camp d'Action Biblique, Dorothy Lukes (Nekrasoff) and Frances Clark (Nugent). This camp, for French-speaking Protestant children from 7 to 15 years of age, was situated about five miles from Richmond, Quebec. The camp was started by Rev. Jacques Smith.

Tyndale House in Montreal had been established in 1927 by The Presbyterian Church in Canada and by the Church of St. Andrew and St. Paul in Montreal. From dingy, inadequate quarters on Seigneur Street East, it moved in 1951 to a beautiful new building on Richmond Square. The nursery school was the greatest source of potential church members in the community. It was also popular, the demand far exceeding its capacity. Tyndale had Explorers, CGIT and a choir. An evening department of the WMS was organized and Sunday school and church service attendance increased. In 1948, Margaret MacKenzie left Tyndale House to take up an appointment in Formosa, leaving Tyndale in the capable hands of Margaret Boyd.

The Peace River van began operations in the summer of 1951. In 1952, for the first time, vacation Bible schools were held at maintenance camps on the Alaska Highway. In the summers of 1954 and 1955, Muriel Judd (Brown), with the help of Lauraine Elder and Joan Fryer (Murcher), conducted eight vacation Bible schools in various places along the highway. In the early days, valuable work had been done by Dr. Alexander and Mrs. Agnes Sorrell Forbes, Dr. Margaret Strang Savage and Margaret Grigor.

Presbyterian training institutes, sponsored by the WMS(WD) and the Board of Christian Education, were arranged by joint committees of presbytery Christian education committees and WMS presbyterials. They were launched at the end of September, 1953, with the purpose of strengthening all branches of the work — training leaders of youth groups, assisting officers of auxiliaries and presbyterials, and giving missionary information and inspiration. Sixteen workers participated in the project during the ten weeks. They set out in teams of four. Each team included a national organization secretary, regional secretary, missionary and a lay expert. One member of the team was a specialist in children's work, another in girls' work, and a third in the work of adult groups. Each team stayed a week in a presbyterial. Every evening during the week a missionary spoke and training sessions were held for leaders and officers. The institutes were held in 43 of the 44 presbyterials in the Western division with over 5,000 people registered. A significant factor in the success of the institutes was the outstanding contribution made by the lay members of training teams. These men and women (chiefly women) left their homes or jobs for one to five weeks each to work with a team.

Students at WMS Training School, Belleville, Ontario

In 1954, plans for adult conferences were made. These were held right across the country. A national missionary, an overseas missionary and a regional secretary or some representative of that part of the society's work would go to each conference.

The 1969 WMS annual report comments on the close co-operation that continued through the years between the WMS(WD) and the Board of Christian Education.

The WMS had helped with Christian literature in India but said that the Christian church was not yet producing and circulating nearly as much literature as it should, whereas Communist literature from Russia was constantly flooding India and the whole East with expertly prepared reading material which came into India tax-free as educational literature. If, the WMS pointed out, the church recognized the urgency of this challenge and was able to provide the literature in quantities wherever people had learned to read and write, it would have a great Christian impact in India.

The people of Africa were becoming increasingly conscious of the lack of adequate reading material written in their own languages. The majority of the population was still illiterate. Mr. G . R. Katongole, on a scholarship awarded by the National Council of Churches, who had studied in Syracuse, majoring in religious journalism, said that Africa needed a spiritual revival, as well as a social revival in which her writers would play a most important role.

The World Day of Prayer Service for 1957 was prepared by a woman who lived in Hungary during the Second World War. The theme was "Who Shall Separate Us?" and was written by Serena Vassady on behalf of all Christian women who were living behind the Iron Curtain. Mrs. Vassady came to live in the United States at the end of the war. She had lived through the miraculous awakening of the church in Hungary, which sprang out of the depths of suffering.

Mrs. Vassady said that during the three month siege of Budapest they lived in unsanitary cellars while bombs burst over their heads. It was still winter when they first emerged from the darkness to pale daylight. They saw shattered streets covered with melting ice, blood and dead bodies. And ruins, blackened ruins were everywhere. Mrs. Vassady went on to tell of how, in those devastated countries of eastern and central Europe, God started an awakening unlike any since the Reformation.

> *The Bible ceased to be a two-thousand-year-old book. It became the practical guide of our daily existence…peasants, nobility, factory workers, socialites and professors sitting side by side around the Bible.*
>
> *It would not be true to say that the Christians of those countries, because they are Christians, are actually persecuted today. But to say that they are not under pressure would be equally untrue… But the proclamation of the gospel is permitted and for them attending church services is no longer a Sunday routine but a priceless privilege. Huge historic churches that had been half empty in the era of ease are now packed to their utmost capacities… Their freedom may be crippled according to the world; but there is a freedom even "in chains," according to the Word.*[18]

The day dawned dark and dreary in Wonju, Korea, but the tent church in the village of Kyung Chun was well filled by 10 o'clock in spite of drizzling rain, the leaky tent, and the fact that few of the worshippers had either umbrellas or a change of clothing if they got wet. Almost as many men as women were in attendance for this was a great occasion in the village. It was the first time they had ever observed the World Day of Prayer. They had never heard of it before. They could not unite with other Christians in the same church building for they were people apart, outcasts from society, shunned and feared by all. They were victims of leprosy. Here they were, though, joining with other Christians around the world. Few had any education and none any experience in public speaking.

> *Shyly they took their places, and read their Scripture passages and responses with increasing confidence. Special music had been prepared, and their prayers were not for themselves, but for all the people of the world. Even in the semidarkness of the tent, their faces, scarred and twisted as some of them were, shone with an inner light as they realized that, though outcasts from society, they were still part of the family of God, and worshipping that day in unity with Christians all over the world.*[19]

India

By 1950, the WMS had been associated with the work in the Vellore Christian Medical College in South India for about ten years. The society contributed an annual grant of $1,000 toward college maintenance. It also had missionaries who served on the nursing staff: Bessie MacMurchy, Isabel McConnell and Mildred Gehman.

Although many people knew the story of Dr. Ida Scudder and the hospital at Vellore, perhaps not so many had heard the story of Edith Brown and Ludhiana. Both hospitals, the only two Christian medical colleges in India at the time, were founded by women. Miss Brown, in 1895, almost single-handedly conceived the idea and then developed the first school for the training of Indian women in the art and science of medicine at Ludhiana in North India. The hospital grew along with the medical school and, although it was officially named Memorial Hospital, to friends and the Indian people of the city it was affectionately known as "Miss Brown's Hospital." For her service to India, Dr. Edith Brown received many honours. In the year following the 50th anniversary of her work in India, she retired from active direction of the medical college.

Isabel McConnell, RN, Superintendant of the Presbyterian Hospital, Jobat, India

A letter, written November 30, 1954, from the Christian Medical College at Ludhiana, Punjab, thanking the WMS for its gift of $2,000, reported that the decision made to go ahead with the building of a new hospital. By 1955, the diamond jubilee year of the college, great projects were planned. In order to meet government requirements for the full degree course in medicine and surgery, a new 500-bed hospital was built.

Dr. Pushpa Lall was the daughter of Rev. Moti Lall, who was pastor of the Jhansi congregation and then on the staff of the Bible school at Jhansi. Pushpa graduated from the Helen MacDonald School and entered the pre-medical year at Ludhiana with financial assistance from the WMS Peace Thanksgiving Fund. In the spring of 1956 she graduated with the degree of MBBS, the equivalent of a Canadian M.D. She began her work at the Presbyterian Hospital at Jobat.

Ruth Buchanan writes from the Bhil field.

> *I don't want to tell you of the horrors of famine, the tragic little families and broken bits of families at my door morning, noon and night. But I do want to thank you with all my heart for the way in which you have come to our help in the Bhil country with your prayers and your money.*[20]

It was a phony famine, Miss Buchanan said, but a famine just the same. The government grain shops were well stocked but the poor subsisted on weeds and roots since many of the people had no money and nothing to sell to buy food.

Marion Williamson, another worker on the field, said that one of the great difficulties was that the Bhils had nothing to work at and no way to earn any ready cash.

> *The very poor are selling all they have to buy a handful of grain, a meagre supplement to their diet of roots and leaves and grass seed.*[21]

What gave the missionaries the idea of doing something to help the people, said Marion Williamson, was sitting down in the mud one day, when the car got stuck and some holes had to be filled with stones to get free. They decided to get people working on the road. They figured out a rate for small stones that would be fair, and by giving contract work they did not have to supervise the workers. The response was beyond their wildest dreams. But when the road work closed, the situation got worse. Then the money arrived from Canada.

> *They've sent you this money,* Ruth Buchanan told the people, *those Canadian women, to tell you that God does care and that for Jesus' sake we care, too.*[22]

In 1951, Bessie MacMurchy reports that the major part of her time was spent in travel. On January 2 the new program for district work had been inaugurated with the employment of a nurse and a student driver. The new car, sent out especially for this mobile unit, arrived in April. MacMurchy said she felt that the minimum number of units needed for effective work was four and even that would only touch the fringe. She was hoping that the government would soon be able to make plans for more medical relief in remote places.

MacMurchy, who left on furlough after setting up the mobile unit, was invited to become director of post-graduate studies for the Mid-India Board of Examiners at Indore. She held this post from 1955 to 1961. She was still on the staff of the WMS and was their contribution to co-operative work.

She returned to Canada to complete her studies and was awarded the Master of Science inNursing degree from the University of Western in London, Ontario. She was looking forward to resuming her task as director of the graduate school of nursing in Indore, India, but this was not to be. She died on June 16, 1963, in London, Ontario.

Bessie MacMurchy served in the Jobat Hospital and had helped establish the mobile medical unit. She also made great contributions in her teaching at Vellore Christian Medical Hospital and in the Indore Hospital. She came to be recognized as an influential force in the development of professional nursing in India.

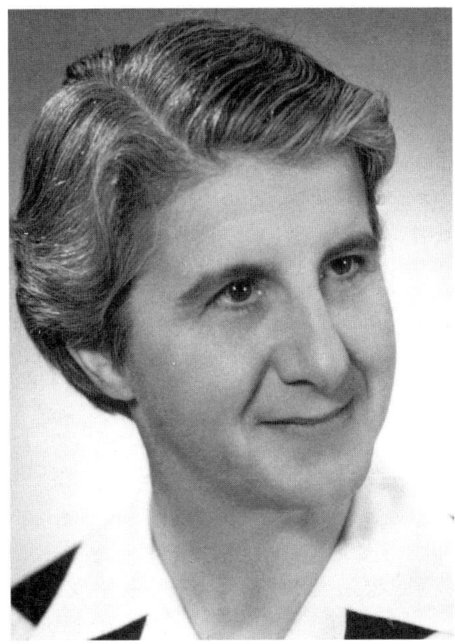

Bessie MacMurchy R.N.

A memorial fund was established by the WMS council executive to commemorate the life and work of Bessie MacMurchy, R.N., M.Sc.N. It was decided that the money obtained for this fund would go as a bursary to bring to Canada an Indian woman who would be trained to succeed Miss MacMurchy as director of the graduate school of nursing. The first beneficiary was Sushila Patras who worked with Bessie MacMurchy in the graduate school. It had been Bessie's hope that some day Sushila might be brought to Canada to complete her studies. Sushila received the Master of Science of Nursing degree from Western University, London, Ontario in 1967 and returned to India to take over the position of director of the graduate school of nursing in Indore, India.

The school of nursing at the Jobat hospital had been closed in 1948 due to difficulties within the administration. In 1963 a new school of nursing was begun and plans were underway to make additions to the nurses' residence. The WMS (WD) contributed $10,000 to the school of nursing and residence project as part of the special anniversary projects.

After India became an independent nation in 1948, the missionary picture changed. Nevertheless plans were afoot to celebrate the Golden Jubilee of Amkhut school in 1964. But what about the future? The government was steadily pressing forward with its educational program and it could well be that the days of private schools were numbered. It may be, said Mary Sherrick, one of the missionaries on the field, that in future the educational contribution will be more through hostels than through schools. In hostels the missionaries could provide a Christian home life and Christian nurture for boys and girls attending government schools and for Christian young people working away from home.

In 1966, the missionaries on the Bhil field were preparing for another famine and were planning how they could provide some work and give enriched meals as part of the remuneration.

> *People in Canada are being asked to help,* said Margaret Kennedy. *This is the price of being affluent! Yet, forgive us, we must put this situation before you, as the people in this area have known Canadians, as their Christian brothers and sisters, for many decades now. We have told of the love of God — now, more than ever, we must show this love, not only in word, but in deed.*[23]

A major step forward was taken in the search for Christian unity at the Third Assembly of the World Council of Churches, which met in New Delhi, India in 1961. It was here that plans were approved for the integration of the World Council of Churches and the International Missionary Council. This merger would indicate to the world that evangelism must always be an integral part of the life of the church, and never a mere "extra."

The Church of North India (CNI) was born on November 29, 1970 in Nagpur. Some 3,000 people sat silently, worshipping God and giving thanks. Six banners indicated the groups as they walked up the red-carpeted aisle under the huge, gaily-striped canopy — Baptist, Church of the Brethren, Disciples of Christ, Church of India (Anglican), Methodist Church of Britain and Australasia, and the United Church of North India (Presbyterian). When the service ended, the procession began to emerge: first the Bible, then the cross, then those who represented the Church of North India, coming out as equals under the one large banner of the new church. Women representing the various fellowships and societies of the uniting churches had also been invited to Nagpur and they met as a group to become better acquainted and to procure copies of the proposed constitution for the CNI Women's Fellowship for Christian Service. Women would be voting members on the pastorate committee (similar to session), on the diocesan council and on the synod (highest court).

> *What a joy,* said Margaret Kennedy who was present at the event, along with Irene Stringer, *to see the fine quality of leadership, the keenness of these Indian women, and among them is our Bhil area President, Mrs. Louise Jalal Masih.*[24]

Formosa (Taiwan)[25]

During February, 1952, a series of meetings took place in Formosa to commemorate the 80th anniversary of the beginning of missionary work by The Presbyterian Church in Canada in Formosa. The celebrations were held at Bankah Church, Taipei, the first church organized in North Formosa under the Presbyterian church. In 1952, it was one of the largest on the Island. Laura Pelton, executive secretary for Overseas Missions for the WMS(WD), Rev. G. Deane Johnston, chairman of the General Board of Missions, and Rev. W. A. Cameron, executive secretary for Overseas Missions, represented The Presbyterian Church in Canada at the celebration and took part in the services.

The Mackay Memorial Hospital was located in the heart of Taipei, a bustling metropolis of 1.5 million people. Each year this hospital sought to reach out to Taiwan's millions in a creative way. In 1968, they opened a burn centre and also conducted burn clinics for local doctors in order to teach proper care of burned patients. The Mackay Hospital reached the mountain people of Taiwan through mobile medical clinics. With the help of Church World Service, clinics were set up in many slum areas throughout Taipei.

Dr. George Gushue-Taylor, instrumental in having Happy Mount Leprosy Colony established, although retired from active service, worked for the lepers again in Formosa in 1952. The WMS sent $1,000 to help build a church at the Government Leprosarium at Lok-seng-i in Sin-Chng. The sod for this church had been turned in 1939 but the construction was stalled during the war.

Eleven years later, on October 5, 1952, with Dr. Gushue-Taylor, Lillian Dickson, and many of their old patients in attendance, the dedication of the Church of the Lepers took place. These Christians in the leprosy colony had waited many years for a church. They had met regularly wherever they could and waited and prayed. On Oct 5, they saw the culmination of their prayers and hopes.

Just before she went home on furlough in 1954, Hildur Hermanson (affectionately known as Hermie) was able to put into practice an idea she long had held concerning health education. Her plan was to go among women's groups delivering health lectures to help Formosan women understand basic rules to improve their health and that of their families. With the use of a projector, her health lectures were so popular that, instead of giving her six lectures to a group of women, she found herself faced with men, women and children. She realized something must be done for all these people. The children needed stories told and songs taught, while their parents studied. The young people wanted to learn English. With the help of Gordon and Hazel Macdonald, Hildur Hermanson attempted to meet the needs of the crowds of people who gathered each night.

In 1955, after attending a conference for women on the east coast, Hildur Hermanson, Hazel Macdonald, Grace (her interpreter) and Pearl Wong went to hold meetings in some churches Pearl had visited.

> *When we got to the first church,* Hildur Hermanson reported, *we found great numbers of people needing medical attention… In all the time I've been here I have never seen so many horrible wounds and abscesses, most of them caused by just uncleanliness… We worked all day and then had a long evangelistic session in the evening… we went to five churches altogether and more or less repeated the same programme.*[26]

Hildur Hermanson continued her travels on the east coast and in the mountains among the tribal people in 1957. Climbing mountains, wading through streams and hitching terrifying rides down mountains in lumber trucks were all part of the job.

Mary Whale tells of a visit she made to Taiwan in 1957. She attended the General Assembly of the Taiwanese church and the women's council meeting. Approximately twenty women had gathered at 'The Hermitage' where

Hildur Hermanson and Hazel Macdonald lived when they were in Taipei. The women who attended the women's council meeting were expected to go back to their own churches to lead Bible study groups, assist in home visiting and in work with children and youth. The aim was to develop a lay leadership among the women.

Kong-kean was a small Taiwanese village about sixty miles south of Taipei in the Hakka country. Hildur Hermanson held one of her four-day classes in the small church. The women slept in the church. Usually Hermanson would stay with the women but since the village was just a short distance from the home of George and Margaret Malcolm (Canadian missionaries), she stayed there. Mary Whale joined them for the last day. There was a great need, Mary said, for help in training leaders for the mountain people.

Later in 1957, Hildur Hermanson reports that, on a Monday they started off for a mountain village where women from eight churches met together for daily studies and fellowship. This was the first time classes like this had been held. On their last evening, they met in the local schoolhouse and were entertained with songs and dances and tea. The following week was spent in a small Taiwanese church near the edge of a mountain district where women from five villages came down and had a four-day session.

After attending the 1958 General Assembly in Taiwan, Hildur Hermanson and her team started back to Taipei, stopping at several places on the way. In one village there were many cases of trachoma.

> *We did eyes all day long, and such terrible cases of Trachoma I have never seen...the whole village needs extensive teaching in Hygiene. We saw almost blind mothers wipe their own infected eyes, and then wipe their children's faces with the same towels! Many of these children had sores all over their heads... Olive Oil, followed by a good washing with soap and water was most effective.*[27]

In the late 1950s, a department of Christian education was established at Taiwan Theological College in Taipei. It was a four-year course. The purpose was to train young women to give leadership in local churches.

In 1958, the WMS(WD) gave $10,500 to build a dormitory for women students at the Taipei Theological College. The Formosa church raised $3,500. Margaret MacKenzie (McCutcheon) lived on campus and conducted classes in Christian education. She also had a share in the teaching program in the schools in Tamsui but it was expected that her work would gradually move in the direction of training young women students.

A large part of the missionary work done by the WMS(WD) in Taiwan was done in the Tam-kang Middle Schools. Four WMS staff people were stationed in Tamsui and associated with the school through several of their departments. Besides the services of these missionaries, the WMS gave a $3,000 grant to assist in operating costs of the school. Many Tam-kang graduates, girls as well as boys, decided to enter the ministry and continue their education in the Taiwan Seminary in Taipei, both in the three-year Christian education course and in the six-year theological course. Many theological students married Christian education students and provided an active team ministry. There have always been ordained women ministers and elders in the church in Taiwan.

Mrs. Ena Hong Mar, one of the leaders of the women's organization in the Presbyterian Church in Formosa, tells of the dedication of the women in Formosa. They served cheerfully, she said, and were willing givers of their time. They regularly attended church services and meetings, usually four times a week. They also paid all their own travel expenses. The women were willing givers of money, even though they did not control the family treasury. When the opportunity to re-open the women's Bible school was laid before them, they lost no time in helping it to materialize. They decided not to write to the mother church for help because, they thought, since the former had helped the Formosa churches for so long, now they should stand on their own feet. They tried hard to win pledges, and within two months more than three-quarters of the goal was reached. The school building was repaired and plans for other equipment were made. When the need to help the poor patients at the Mackay Memorial Hospital increased, the women organized a social welfare department.

On Easter Sunday in 1962, a new church was opened in north Formosa. It was built by the Formosan Women's Missionary Society, whose members had been working toward this end for several years. They had originally intended to build a place at the old peoples' home where the patients could meet for worship. They then decided they would build an extension of the home not far from Tamsui where those people who could look after themselves would live. They built the church nearby. Beside the church, there was a small house for the Bible woman who worked in the district as well as in the home. Future plans included a home for the minister.

Grace Keh Tsai was the daughter of a Formosan minister. She was a graduate of the Taipei Theological Seminary and since graduation she worked closely with Hazel Macdonald among the women of Formosa. She reported on the work among the mountain people.

During the Second World War, she said, the Christian movement was begun by a woman, Chi-Oang, in the Hualien area, under circumstances of terrible persecution by the Japanese government. This church has seen phenomenal growth.

> *Quite a few women's auxiliaries had been already started before we began our work with them, but they did not have much organization, or plan, to their work. In four districts on the East Coast, out of 200 churches 144 were ready to be organized, so the WMS Council started to work with them. We meet with them twice a year, having their Annual Meeting and election of officers in May, and inspiration and training in October. They meet three days each time, and each time the attendance has increased… It was a wonderful thing when the Pi-nan tribe joined the Ami in their Regional meeting…though they don't speak the same language. Isn't it amazing that a weak woman with a baby on her back, carrying many pounds of rice, wood, Bible, Hymn book and her clothes wrapped in a faroshki, will walk four to eight hours in order to attend the conference, or to visit and help other Women's Auxiliaries?*[28]

It was in the 'silent years' after the missionaries were compelled by the Japanese to leave Formosa in 1940 that this wonderful movement began. For years the missionaries had wanted to go beyond the plains, up into the mountains to carry the news of Jesus Christ to the people there but they had been forbidden by the Japanese authorities. Then the missionaries had to leave Formosa. On their return in 1946, they discovered that the gospel had been carried to the mountain tribes by one or two of their own people. Outstanding among them was Chi-Oang, a woman of the Taroko tribe. Chi-Oang was the first tribal person to become a Christian. Yet, before her death in 1946, more than 4,000 tribal people belonged to the Christian church due to her fearless witness. The Chi-Oang Memorial Church, dedicated in 1962, was one among almost 400 tribal Presbyterian churches in the mountains of Formosa. It stands at the mouth of the famous Taroko Gorge, built on a hill, just beside a cave in the rocks where Taroko Christians used to meet secretly at night for worship. By Japanese decree, it would have meant death had they been discovered. Many Christians cherished earth-stained, battered Bibles that had been buried or hidden in the thatch of a home to save them from discovery.

The Presbyterian Church of Formosa was made up of presbyteries on the plains (Taiwanese) and two in the mountains (tribal). The work among the tribes of Taiwan was under the guidance of the mountain committee of the General Assembly. In 1962, the first tribal presbytery was formed, the Taroko. This had been Chi-Oang's tribe. The second tribal presbytery, the Ami, consisting of one hundred churches, was received into the General Assembly in 1963 at Kuang-fu on the eastern coastal plain of Taiwan. Even as Chi-Oang was the mother of the Taroko Tribe, so Kho Liam-bian, one of her contemporaries, was the father of the Ami Tribe. Rev. Kho Liam-bian was a member of a small, almost extinct tribe, but his wife was Ami. When they were first married, they prayed that someone might be sent to bring the gospel to Mrs. Kho's tribe. No one came. Finally, in 1931, Mr. and Mrs. Kho sold their water buffalo and went to the Tamsui Bible School — the same school where Chi-Oang was studying. When the Khos returned to the east coast, they began preaching among the Amis working from Kuang-fu. They worked for three years with little success. As the Second World War progressed, they became more and more oppressed by the Japanese. Preachers and Christians were threatened, beaten or imprisoned and tortured. Their Bibles were burned.

Thirty years later, in 1963, the cross of the new Kuang-fu Presbyterian Church could be seen etched against the dark green mountains and the clear blue sky. It was at this church, on April 29, 1963, that one hundred churches became a presbytery of the Presbyterian Church of Formosa. The 800 seats were filled and many people stood at the back of the church, in the doors and windows, and many more sat outside on the grass. The 83-year-old Kho Liam-biam and his wife were prevented by illness from attending.

Two foreigners were highly honoured by the city of Taipei. They were among 70 persons selected by the Committee on Good People and Good Deeds. In 1963, for the first time two foreigners were included in the list of 60 men and 10 women. They were Hildur Hermanson, an employee of the WMS, and Lillian Dickson, missionary for The Presbyterian Church in Canada. Both were chosen because of their long and dedicated service to the people of Formosa.

The Korean Church in Japan

After the war, Dr. Luther and Mrs. Miriam Young returned to Japan and found that only two buildings and a few Christians had survived the war. However, by the anniversary year in 1952, there were twenty-two congregations and fourteen church buildings. Both the WMS and the General Board of Missions helped the Koreans in Japan to rebuild their churches and congregations. Dr. W. A. Cameron, secretary for Overseas Missions, went to

Japan for the celebrations. Commenting on the anniversary service, Dr. Cameron said,

> *The people were poor. There were 32 at the service. There was one chair and they gave that to the guest. It was an impressive service for the poverty of the people did not hinder the richness of their devotion to their Lord.*[29]

Jean Rumball, who also attended the celebrations, reported in a letter to the WMS that she had the privilege of saying a few words on behalf of the Canadian WMS. The WMS had contributed $600 towards the building of the Yokohama Church. It had arrived, she added, at one of the most difficult times in the building of the church and was gratefully received.

> *Yokohama has now not only a pastor and a Church but also a Bible Woman, Mrs. Moon from Korea.*[30]

In the autumn of 1957, Miss Jean Brown (Sonnenfeld) went to Japan, the first missionary of the WMS(WD) to the Koreans in Japan for a number of years.

Rev. In Ha Lee wrote to the WMS to say that he was pleased to see that Jean Brown was welcomed at the General Assembly of the Korean Church in Japan. In his letter he also thanked the Christian Literature Secretary of the WMS for the gift of $500 to help provide Christian literature for the women and children in the Korean Churches in Japan. In Ha Lee studied at Knox College, Toronto. On his return to Japan he became assistant minister in the Tokyo Korean Church in Japan. He later became minister of the Kawasaki congregation which began as a Sunday school outreach program after the Second World War.

Mavis Hyndman

Because of the expressed need for assistance in the administrative office of the Korean Christian Church, Mavis Hyndman was appointed by the WMS to serve in the Korean Christian Church in Japan (KCCJ). She was designated on December 29, 1963 and arrived in Japan on January 6, 1964. An experienced office administrator and secretary, Mavis was administrative assistant in the office of the Korean Christian Church in Japan, secretary to the general secretary of

Tamiko Nakamura (Corbett)

the KCCJ, treasurer of the Japan Canadian Committee and worked with Korean people in Tokyo, particularly in Bible classes. While her appointment was intended to be for three years, an appeal came to the WMS asking that she be reappointed to the General Assembly office. She returned to Japan after her furlough in 1966-67 and served until September 1977.

By 1966, the Korean Church in Japan had moved into a program of Christian education. Miss Tamiko Nakamura (Corbett) worked with the Korean Church for three years. She acted as executive secretary for the assembly's committee on Christian education. At the completion of her term of service in Japan, the Korean Assembly appointed two women workers to serve as regional education leaders.

The sum of $15,000 from legacy funds was approved by the 1971 WMS council for the Sakuramoto Nursery in Kawasaki, Japan. This brought the total WMS contribution to $30,000 because $15,000 was approved in 1970.

British Guiana[31]

In the mid-1940s, the Canadian Presbyterian Mission was started at Bartica, a fast growing town, described as the gateway to the interior. A beautiful church, St. Paul's, was built and was soon the leading church in the Essequibo area. A manse was built and dedicated in February, 1951. With so many church activities and organizations there was need for a hall. Plans for the manse had included room for a hall and minister's study. When the manse was completed, the congregation turned to the hall project and on Sunday, October 14, it was dedicated to the glory of God for religious, social and cultural work in connection with St. Paul's Church.

On the first Sunday of the month, Miss Ellen Anderson and an East-Indian deaconess made a round trip of thirty-six miles into the country. They would have four meetings under houses. Guianese houses were built on stilts and the space beneath afforded a comfortable place for a meeting, with protection from rain or the hot sun. In the evening they attended a service in Burns Church, Georgetown. On the other Sundays of the month, Miss

Anderson visited Sunday schools in the country. On the last Sunday of the month they held a women's service after Sunday school. The other days of the week they had women's meetings, teaching periods in schools, Bible class meetings, and Sunday school teachers' meetings. On Thursday evening, Miss Anderson said, there was always an open air service in New Town Kitty.

A new building was dedicated on May 4, 1952 at Uniform. This was made possible by gifts from the General Board of Missions and a legacy from the WMS Senior Auxiliary of Knox Church in Toronto and other donations.

The first colony-wide conference was held in Georgetown at Burns Memorial Church in August, 1958 with over 100 women in attendance. The plan was to have another in five year's time, in 1963. Unfortunately, political unrest in the country made it impossible to even have the committee meetings. In 1964, however, the committee began meeting again and the second colony-wide conference was held in April, 1965, and the third in 1968. It was the hope that the women's groups in the two churches would work in closer cooperation and become one integrated organization known as the Guyana Presbyterian Women's Organization. On October 12, 1968, the proposal for working together was brought to the women at the rally. The national executive of the Guyana Presbyterian Church's women's group and seven women designated by the Presbyterian Church of Guyana became a planning committee for the new National Organization of Presbyterian Women.

In 1965, the Presbytery of Guyana appointed Merle McGowan, a deaconess working in British Guiana, to an executive position in Christian education. She was asked to survey the needs of the presbytery and to develop a pattern of leadership training, both for St. Columba's House, the leadership training centre, and the parishes.

Merle McGowan

The aim of the Presbytery of Guyana, said Merle McGowan, was to place one trained deaconess in every parish to promote and build up a Christian education program. The presbytery was divided into ten parishes, and four trained deaconesses worked in the presbytery. In the fall of 1961, under the leadership of Margaret Ramsay, eight young Guianese women took a training course to equip themselves for the role of leaders in Christian education in the Guyana Presbyterian Church. The young women were sent out in 1962 to do practical work under the guidance of the four graduate deaconesses.

Athalie Read, in her 1963 report, said that the presbytery had authorized the publications committee to write and produce vacation Bible school material to be used in August. She and Margaret Ramsey, with the help of Elaine Zingg, undertook this task.

> *It was a lot of work but it also was rewarding to find that it...was successfully used.*[32]

In spite of continuing difficulties in 1964, the church in Guyana began using a curriculum in the church schools that was truly Caribbean, written by churches in the Caribbean for life in the Caribbean.

Mabel Booth, national children's secretary, went from Canada to share in the planning for curriculum with representatives from other churches in the Caribbean, including the Presbytery of Guyana Presbyterian Church.

Louise Reith, executive director of organization, spent four weeks in Guyana in 1969, the major part of her program being with the women's organization. Helen Tetley, secretary for lay ministry and youth, travelling via Trinidad and Jamaica spent three months in Guyana to do a survey of Christian education work at the request of the Guyana Presbyterian Church.

Africa

At the 1954 General Board of Missions meeting, members listened with interest as their chairperson, Rev. G. Deane Johnston, related the steps which led to the General Assembly's acceptance of an invitation to share mission work in Nigeria with the Church of Scotland.

The WMS(WD) had been in correspondence with the Church of Scotland with a view to co-operating with that church in one of their missions in Africa, if the General Assembly of The Presbyterian Church in Canada should approve. This matter was brought before the WMS council meeting in London, Ontario, in May, 1953. At the request of Mr. Johnston, no action was taken until the General Board of Missions and the WMS could make this a joint effort. The General Assembly in 1954 agreed to accept the invitation of the Church of Scotland to co-operate with them in their mission field in Nigeria. This action of the General Assembly, said Mr. Johnston,

> *authorizes the General Board of Missions in co-operation with the WMS(WD) to enter upon a new phase in the missionary expansion of our Church.*[33]

Joan Rochemont (Kristenson)

Agnes Gollan and Joan Rochemont (Kristensen), who were studying at Selly Oak in England, left for Nigeria in September, 1954, the Scottish church making all arrangements for their passage. In Calabar, they were engaged in evangelistic work and Christian education, giving leadership to Nigerian women. They worked as partners, not only with the Scottish missionaries who were there but also with the Nigerian church workers.

Evangelistic work among women and girls was always an important part of the Scottish Mission's work in the Calabar field. Ever since the days of Mary Slessor, a missionary who served there from 1876-1915, there were women district missionaries who visited villages and conducted various classes for women and girls.

In 1951, seven African women were trained for full-time church work at the Hugh Goldie College and later appointed by synod to work under different African pastors. At the end of their probation they were dedicated as church sisters and given a uniform. Their work was strenuous; each of them in charge of a large district and each had many miles to cycle and walk to her various classes. As well as conducting classes for women they preached in the village churches. They were paid from synod funds and were under the care and supervision of the women's work committee of the synod.

Agnes Gollan

There was a women's conference at synod every year with delegates from all over the mission fields. Nearly every congregation had its own women members' meeting. These women were not yet formed into a women's guild but the plan was to unite them under one organization which would strengthen women's work.

Agnes Gollan wrote from Nigeria that the main news on the mission field was the 1957 arrival of Rev. Earle and Dorothy Roberts with their son Bruce. Earle engaged in youth work among the boys. Agnes worked with the girls' groups. The teaching in the primary schools was all done by Nigerians. Agnes said,

> *I hope that you are still trying to find someone to help me … If I had a colleague, we could really get going on it.*[34]

By this time, Joan Rochemont had left the field to be married.

In March, 1958, it was announced that Dorothy Bulmer would soon go to the Calabar Mission in Nigeria. Dorothy speaks about her first look at Nigeria in the September, 1959 issue of *The Glad Tidings.*

> *How pale they* [the missionaries] *seem, among the deep, rich browned Africans! I still find myself gazing at the graceful walk of the women; which comes from carrying headloads and 'junior' tied on her back.*

Dorothy, with her expertise in music and the arts, appreciated the graceful walk of the women carrying heavy loads on their heads. What she would not be able to see would be the crushed discs caused by carrying such heavy loads. Dorothy, naturally, mentioned the Nigerian dancing.

> *The footwork is most intricate, with body movements emphasizing the atmosphere of the dance, and hands clapping a syncopated rhythm…. Usually a native instrument, such as a drum, shaker, two-holed pot…accompanies the dancers.*

She said the Nigerians hesitated to use their own musical instruments in worship because they were used by pagans and by some sects.

> *Understandably, this matter must be handled with care. We must…introduce to them the good points of using their own instruments, and not the asthmatic organs and pianos, coughing in the Nigerian humidity, and then finally folding up under an onslaught of white ants….*[35]

When Civil War broke out in 1967 in Nigeria, the Presbyterian Church and the WMS were anxious about their missionaries in the break-away Nigerian state of Biafra. Elsie Taylor went to London, England and then to Canada in late August. Agnes Gollan remained in Biafra along with Dorothy Bulmer. A Nigeria-Biafra negotiated peace was urged by the Vatican and the World Council of Churches in a joint statement issued simultaneously in Geneva and at the Vatican.

The Canairelief Super-Constellation plane, provided through the initiative of The Presbyterian Church in Canada and Oxfam of Canada, was in full operation as part of the joint church aid airlift into Biafra. While the original initiative was taken by the Presbyterian Church in cooperation with Oxfam, other churches and organizations had joined to provide financial support. The venture was truly ecumenical with support coming from the Jewish community, Roman Catholic and Protestant churches and from church groups in Europe and the United States.

Dorothy Bulmer reported that refugees were being moved to their area from areas where local food was scarce. Dorothy ran a sewing factory and when they ran out of imported cloth, they used corn meal and flour bags. She said it was surprising how good they looked. Reports indicated that the tons of protein food airlifted into Biafra by relief planes had had a tremendous effect on the health of the Biafrans.

In March, 1969, the General Board of Missions agreed upon a resolution reaffirming their concern and dismay at the prolonged suffering of men, women and children on both sides and said they would do all in their power to bring relief and peace. They also expressed their solidarity with the missionaries and workers of The Presbyterian Church in Canada who were involved in this tragic conflict.

After the war, help was needed to rehabilitate the Nigerian people. The Christian Church of Nigeria was responsible for an extensive emergency relief program during the war. Rev. Earle Roberts was relief administrator under the church from 1968 to 1970. One million people were treated at hospitals and sick bays. Without the feeding stations many would have starved. At the same time, help was given to farmers to help them get started farming again and to reorganize community life. The priority after medical facilities and feeding programs was education. A great many schools and hospitals were destroyed during the war. These were being restored and maintained by the Christian Council.

South America

During 1953, many WMS auxiliaries concentrated on South America with particular interest in the Student Christian Movement (SCM). The WMS had contributed to the work of the SCM in South America ever since 1943. At a meeting of the Women's Inter-Church Council of Canada in September, 1953, Philippe Maury, secretary of the World Student Christian Federation, described the work. In South America there was a complete spiritual vacuum in university life. The teaching was entirely secular and the final test of success was material advancement. Frightened by this spiritual vacuum the students easily turned to communism. Mr. Maury expressed appreciation for the steady help given by Canadian mission boards towards the work of the SCM in South America and told of the development of the work since 1939 at which time there had been only a few contacts with a group working among high school students in Brazil. Now there were strong groups in Brazil, Uruguay, Chile, Argentina, Puerto Rico, and beginnings in Peru, Paraguay, Bolivia, Mexico and contacts being made in other areas. Mr. Maury referred to the work being done in Brazil by the part-time student secretary, Jorge Cesar Mota, towards whose support the WMS gave a grant of $500. It was his responsibility to keep in touch with about fifty local groups, edit books and magazines, keep up the work in the office and travel as much as possible.

Changing Times for Women in The Presbyterian Church in Canada

For all the women who, over the centuries, accepted without question the decision that women could not be ministers of word and sacraments, there were always those thoughtful few who asked, "Why not?" However, even those who did not question went ahead and prepared themselves for the ministry to which they believed God was calling them. Deaconesses in Canada carried out pastoral ministries. Women missionaries overseas were evangelists. They preached, they taught, they visited. They were ministers in every sense of the word except for administering the sacraments and speaking or voting in the courts of the church.[36]

The question of whether women should be ordained in The Presbyterian Church in Canada came up as early as 1876, the year after Presbyterian churches across Canada joined together to form The Presbyterian Church in Canada. It came up again in the early 1920s when the question of church union was being debated and again in 1953 through an overture from the Synod of Manitoba. At the 1953 General Assembly, the Committee on the Place of Women in the Church was formed to deal with the issue.

In 1954, the committee asked the General Assembly to grant permission for women to serve as consultants and six women were added to the committee. They were reminded often that they were consultants only and, although they could speak, they could not vote.

In 1955, a questionnaire was sent to all presbyteries and WMS presbyterials asking whether or not they favoured the ordination of women as elders and as ministers of word and sacraments. Although responses indicated that the presbyterials were more favourable to the ordination of women than were the presbyteries, the majority of both were opposed. On the basis of the results of this poll, the committee recommended that the 1956 General Assembly declare that the church was not ready to ordain women and that specific action be deferred. The recommendation was approved.

It was a sad day for those who had hoped to see some progress on behalf of the women who felt that God was calling them to the ministry of word and sacraments. At the request of the committee, Margaret MacNaughton, one of the six women consultants on the committee, was given permission to address the General Assembly on behalf of the committee. She begged the Assembly to continue its study in order that it might respond — not to the pressures of the people — but to the guidance of the Holy Spirit leading the church into the future.

Finally, a dramatic change took place. In 1958, a new committee was appointed with Rev. Eoin McKay as convener. The new membership included nine women. This time, the women were appointed as full voting members. In 1960, a motion was passed to remit the question of the ordination of women to presbyteries under the Barrier Act. It failed to win a majority.

In 1961, the Presbytery of Montreal overtured the General Assembly, claiming that presbyteries had not had sufficient time to consider the question and asking that any decision be withheld for at least two years, during which time a full study could be made. Putting Woman in Her Place was the title of an excellent study guide published in 1963 and widely used throughout the church.

In 1966, the questions on the ordination of women went down to presbyteries once again under the Barrier Act. This time the response favoured the ordination of women and a motion was passed and carried at the 1966 General Assembly, allowing women to be ordained to the ministry of word and sacraments and to the eldership. Twenty-four commissioners recorded their dissent from the decision to ordain women to the ruling eldership. Thirty-two commissioners recorded their dissent from the decision to ordain women to the ministry of word and sacraments.

Were women who worked for the WMS seeking ordination? Although deaconesses and women missionaries carried out their ministry which often included leading worship services several times on a Sunday, it would seem that most of them did not feel a call to the ministry of word and sacraments. But some did.

Marion Webster (Ballard), a student in 1955 at the Presbyterian Missionary and Deaconess Training School, applied for a summer field, as did many student deaconesses. It was possible to apply for such a position under the General Board of Missions or under the Women's Missionary Society. Marion Webster, feeling a strong call to ministry, applied to the General Board of Missions, asking if it would be possible to have a summer charge in some vacant church. Dr. J. Alan Munro, Secretary for Home Missions at the time, conceded that such positions were, in fact, available but said that if a male student minister became available for the position, she would have to be removed. He reiterated this, Marion said, in order to be sure she understood the condition under which she would be assigned to such a summer charge. After thinking it over, Marion decided not to accept any such position and instead happily worked for the Women's Missionary Society in both her summer appointments.

On completing her three years at the Presbyterian Missionary and Deaconess Training School, Marion entered Knox College in Toronto in 1961. Oddly enough, for women to engage in theological studies was not a problem for the male students and faculty. Several women had, over the years, graduated in theology from Knox College. But for a woman to presume that God had called her to the ministry of word and sacraments was another matter. When Marion graduated from Knox College, the church had not yet made the decision to ordain women. Marion went on to exercise her ministry as a parole officer.

What was the involvement of WMS in the ordination issue? We know that many members of the Women's Missionary Society were involved in the issue of women's place in the church. Several of the women on the Committee on the Place of Women in the Church were WMS staff or members of the WMS. Maydae Pae was a past president of the society. Margaret MacNaughton was a graduate of Presbyterian Missionary and Deaconess Training School and had worked as a congregational deaconess and regional secretary in Manitoba until her appointment in 1955 as National Girls' Work Secretary for the Presbyterian Church. Hughanna Ralston was an active member of Regina Presbyterial in Saskatchewan until her appointment as principal of the Missionary and Deaconess Training School in 1940.

Throughout the 1950s and 1960s many articles and reports on the subject of women's place in church and society appeared in the pages of *The Glad Tidings*. For example, in the June, 1953 issue, editor Mary Whale, says,

> *The eyes of the world will be focused on one young woman June second of this year of our Lord… It seems significant for these times that the ruler of the British Commonwealth is a Queen; a woman, a wife, a mother. In a day when much is being said about the place of women in all walks of life, we realize that one cannot, and will not evade her calling. Nor can any woman who believes she is a Christian…the time has come for us to leave the security we Canadian women have built around us and take our place in the world of affairs. This is a call for Christian women to share in the political*

> *life of our nation, in the business, professional and vocational life of Canada — and most important — in every phase of the Church's life....*[37]

Just in case women in the WMS did not notice the above editorial, Mary Whale added, in large letters, YOUR ATTENTION PLEASE. In this issue of *The Glad Tidings*, she said, appearing in the month of the Coronation of our gracious Queen Elizabeth, there was an attempt to place a little more emphasis than usual upon the place of women in the world today. She pointed out that three articles in the June issue were by well-known Presbyterian women, Agnes Roy, Donalda MacMillan and Leeta McCully Cherry which, she said, directed our thoughts to three important places in which women served today. There followed three articles: "The Church Woman and Immigration;" "Women in the Church and in the World;" "The Church Woman in her Home."

Donalda MacMillan, missionary to Taiwan, wrote an article about women in the church and the world. In her article, she quoted Madeline Barot, secretary of the World Council of Churches' Commission on the Life and Work of Women in the Church, who recently visited North America.

> *A few years ago the question of the ordination of women was generally regarded as the most important one in regard to women in the Church. Now, it is seen as only part of a more general question... Within the Church, women have felt imprisoned by structures they have had no part in creating. They have come to realize that the real question for them is: What is the will of God for His Church on earth? And this involves the question of what is the will of God in man-woman relationship with the Church?*[38]

Madeline Barot reported that Christian women in Europe became convinced that they must re-study this relationship in the light of the Bible, the doctrine of the church and sociological developments in the modern world.

In the summer of 1954, Margaret Webster, director of organization for the WMS, represented the women of The Presbyterian Church in Canada at the meetings of the World Presbyterian Alliance in Princeton, New Jersey. She attended the final meeting of the Women's International Union which had been founded at the time of the World Presbyterian Alliance in 1892. At the Princeton meeting, the Women's International Union was replaced by a Department of Women's Work. Lady Louise P. MacDermott of Belfast, Northern Ireland, honour graduate in modern history and political science from Trinity College in Dublin and officer in several women's and youth organizations in the British Isles, was elected the first chair of the department. Lady MacDermott was the sister of Rev. G. Deane Johnston, who was minister of Central Presbyterian Church in Brantford at the time.

After the Alliance meeting, Margaret Webster said she became more strongly convinced about the place of the laity — and particularly the place of women — in the life of The Presbyterian in Canada. In her address to the WMS council in 1955, which contained a report of the meeting of this World Presbyterian Alliance in the summer of 1954, Webster quoted one study commission report,

> *The human situation in our day lays demands upon the Church for the full utilization of the gifts of all its members and therefore, the status of women in the Church must be restudied. Many of us feel strongly that all fields of Christian service should be open to all members without distinction as to sex, so that the best talents wherever found can be fully utilized.*[39]

Some of the delegates at Princeton felt this statement was not strong enough and one of the Canadian Presbyterian delegates moved that they go on record as favouring the ordination of women to the full ministry of the word and sacraments. The motion was passed by a small majority and the Alliance established a commission to formulate afresh the reformed doctrine of ordination with particular reference to women. The constitution of the Alliance was changed to allow women to be full delegates.

Margaret Webster was not a delegate when the World Presbyterian Alliance, European area council of the alliance, met in Emden, Germany in August, 1956, but she went anyway. She was travelling in Europe at the time and received special permission to attend. She said that there was great interest in the churches there in regard to the place of women in the church, and particularly the opening of the ministry and eldership to women.

Margaret Webster wrote an article for the June, 1957 issue of *The Glad Tidings* on the North American area council meeting of the Alliance which met in Atlantic City, New Jersey in March, 1957. At this conference, she noted that Dr. Rachel Henderlite,, member of the World Presbyterian Alliance Commission on Ordination, reported on progress to date in studies undertaken by this commission. In her article, Margaret Webster quoted at length from the paper given by Dr. Henderlite.[40]

Helen Turnbull, associate secretary of the Department on the Co-operation of Men and Women in the Church and Society of the World Council of Churches, and Hans Reudi-Weber, secretary of the Department of the Laity of the World Council of Churches, visited Canada in December, 1956. A conference was held, which members of the Presbyterian Committee on the Place of

Women in the Church attended with representatives from similar committees of the other member churches of the Canadian Council of Churches. The Committee on the Place of Women in the Church was fortunate to have Miss Turnbull spend an afternoon with them while she was here.

At the 1957 annual council meeting, Agnes Roy, past director of the YWCA of Canada, was guest speaker. The title of her address was "Women Are People," an obvious allusion to the women are persons decision made by the Privy Council of Great Britain in 1929. She said,

> *As Christians there never has been any question that women are persons, with the right and ability to develop the capacities within them… Our countries have not given recognition to the fact of the equality of men and women in the sight of God…*[41]

She might have added "neither has the church."

Takuko Inagaki was an ordained minister of the United Church of Christ in Japan (a union of all Protestant Churches in Japan). She was in charge of the church at Shiba, Tokyo. In a *Glad Tidings* article on the ordination of women in Japan, she says that the first ordination of a woman as a minister took place in 1933, although her actual ministry had preceded the ordination. The second was in 1934 and she herself was ordained in 1939. By 1956, out of a total of 929 ordained ministers in her church, 58 were women. She said there had never been any objection to the ordination of women in her church and the main points for the church affirming the ordination of women, were:

> *There is no teaching in the Bible that forbids or negates it. The divine call is absolute and above any rules…nothing may hinder anyone from responding to it and submitting his or her whole life to full ministry. And full ministry requires ordination….*

As a practical matter, she added, the full ministry of women was needed and urged in her country. There were more women missionaries than men there and they had worked together with men missionaries. She said,

> *How much greater the fruit is when men and women thus co-operate, when all the members of His body work together for the Lord with their God-given gifts of grace! (Eph.4:7-16) We thus affirm the ordination of women on the basis of the Bible, and by the urgence of the need.*[42]

Mary Whale reported, after her 1961 visit to east Asia, that in the Formosan Church, the ordination of women, both as ministers and elders was allowed. There was a women's committee of General Assembly. In

Mary Whale

working and talking with the women themselves, she said, one realized that the machinery had been established but the ordination of women to the ministry was not encouraged. Only one or two women had persevered to become ministers of word and sacraments. A few were elders.

Mary Whale reported further that the women in the Korean Christian Church in Japan (KCCJ) seemed to be better off than their Formosan sisters. Although their women's committee of General Assembly was run by men and the women had no votes on it, there was acknowledgment among the men that this could not continue. The Korean men, Mary thought, were prepared to see the women achieve a more responsible place in the life of the church.

In spite of the fact that the World Council of Churches set up a Commission on the Life and Work of Women in the Church in 1949, just one year after the WCC was organized, it would seem that change did not happen quickly. In an interview that appeared in the April, 1962 issue of *The Glad Tidings*, Teça Coles, who accompanied her husband, Rev. Stuart Coles, to the 1961 World Council of Churches in Delhi, responded to several questions.

> *In the Assembly's Work Book, there is only one item referring to women… Does this mean that women played a minor role at New Delhi?*

Her response was 'Yes.'

> *To begin with, women were outnumbered by men, abut ten to one, in the delegations appointed by the churches. Madeline Barot is the lone woman among the senior Executive Staff of the Council; she is the Director of the Department on Co-operation of Men and Women in Church, Family, and Society. In a panel of seven commentators on the question "Why Must we Speak?", one was a woman: Dr. Mary B. More of the Church of Scotland. Lady Olayinka Ibiam read her husband's hard-hitting speech to the*

> *Assembly, because he was a day too late in arriving. Out of some sixty addresses on the Assembly agenda, only one was assigned to a woman. She was the extremely able E.M.("Mollie") Batten, Principal of William Temple College, Rugby, England. She shared with two men…in the major presentation on the Laity as the Church in the World. Batten said, in part, the Christian Church was and is a revolutionary movement. When it came into being, men and women found themselves, for the first time, equal members of a society called into existence not for its own ends but for the purposes of God in the world….*[43]

It is clear that the WMS was aware of and involved in the issues of the day concerning women and the church's decision in 1966 to ordain them. However, you will search in vain through the pages of *The Glad Tidings* in 1966 for any mention of the decision that was to come before the General Assembly in June, and, more surprising, no mention in the months after the momentous decision was made.

In the annual reports, there were few references to the issue and these references were in connection with the effect the General Assembly's decision would have on the consolidation of the mission work of the WMS and the General Board of Missions.

The silence was broken after 1966. In April 1967, *The Glad Tidings* announced that

> *…among those ordained to the eldership of their respective Churches since the 1966 General Assembly of the Presbyterian Church authorized the ordination of women elders are two of our Executive Directors — Miss Giollo Kelly in St. John's Toronto and Miss Mary Whale in the Presbyterian Church in Erindale, Ontario.*[44]

The magazine also announced in 1968 that, although Shirley Jeffrey was not the first woman to graduate from Knox College, she was the first to be ordained to the ministry of word and sacraments in The Presbyterian Church in Canada and took up duties at St. Paul's Presbyterian Church in Englehart, Ontario.

We can only speculate why the issue was given such short shrift by the WMS in 1966. Perhaps it was because this Committee on the Place of Women in the Church had met for thirteen years and interest had waned. After all, the question had already gone down to presbyteries under the Barrier Act in 1960 and had not passed. Or was it because the society had always been a lay women's organization? Most of its workers were single women, graduates of the deaconess training school, often with nursing or teacher training, who felt their calling was to diaconal ministry. Of course, the choice had not been theirs to make. Or perhaps the society was preoccupied with other things. After all, 1964 was the 100th anniversary (or 50th since amalgamation) of the society with almost 1,500 women descending on Montreal with all that involved in planning and carrying out that great celebration.

Surely, all these things must have had some effect on the society's silence. However, a far more likely explanation was that the over-riding issue that occupied the minds of the executive and staff was their involvement in the forthcoming "integration" of the work of the WMS with the work of the General Board of Missions. The major changes that would occur because of that integration caused fear and uncertainty over what would happen to the WMS when all was said and done.

Changing Times for the WMS

Until 1925, the WMS, both before and after the amalgamation in 1914, operated as an auxiliary of the mission boards of the church. After 1925, it asked for, and received, permission from the General Assembly to become a board in its own right directly responsible to General Assembly. Later, due to questions regarding its right to be a board of the church, the WMS went back to the General Assembly requesting that it be a society within The Presbyterian Church in Canada responsible to General Assembly.

It is important to say that the WMS, from the beginning, wanted to work closely with the church in its mission work both at home and abroad. The church was not always so co-operative. A report in 1924 stated that

> *...some years ago the WMS, anxious for closer co-operation and better understanding approached the General Assembly asking for representation on its Home and Foreign Boards — a request that has not yet been granted.*[45]

In 1948, a close working relationship was developed between the WMS and the Board of Christian Education. In 1959, a joint board was formed to integrate the work overseas of both the mission board and the WMS.

The WMS saw itself as a society within the church that worked with and through the other boards and committees of the church in many areas of the church's outreach in Canada and in other lands. Hildur Hermanson, writing from Formosa in 1960 said,

> *All of our work is so closely integrated here that it is difficult to draw a line between the work of our WMS Missionaries, and that of those sent out by the Mission Board. We all work together, in an effort to strengthen and help the Formosa Church, wherever they feel we are most needed.*[46]

In 1958, four separate overtures were presented to the General Assembly, all indicating dissatisfaction with over-spending and deficit financing on the part of the church. The General Assembly appointed a special committee with authority to investigate and to engage business consultants to examine the financial structure and administrative organizations and procedures of assembly boards and committees. As a result of reports and recommendations of this special committee, the 1960 General Assembly established the Administrative Council. This council was to be the chief administrative body of the church, reporting to and responsible to the General Assembly.

After careful study, the council recommended various changes which the General Assembly adopted. Among them was utilizing all the resources of the church for the whole program of the church and enabling the Administrative Council to allocate available funds to meet approved expenditures.

Closer co-operation was achieved, said Laura Pelton, overseas secretary for the WMS, between the Women's Missionary Society and the General Board of Missions through the leadership of the WMS president, Maydee Pae, and the chairman of the General Board of Missions, Dr. G. Deane Johnston. They

> *...brought us together in fruitful consultation and creative action in the Overseas work of our Church... Mrs. Pae and Dr. Johnston demonstrated how the Overseas Mission of our Church could be amicably, and with advantage, much more closely integrated.*[47]

Mrs. Maydee Pae went further in this direction than any previous president. There were those who believed that Mrs. Pae wanted to move too fast while others feared an eclipse in the society, if cooperation went too far. Mrs. Pae, lacking a background in the WMS, found it difficult to understand those whose long attachment and deep loyalty to the society made them fearful of what appeared to be a threat to the society's independence. Laura Pelton expressed her own opinion of the situation.

> *I believe that the future will vindicate Mrs. Pae's vision of an integrated Overseas mission.*[48]

Some might agree with Laura Pelton, while others might think that what the future did show was that the fears of those women who saw integration as a threat to the independence of the society were well-founded.

At the 1961 annual council meeting of the WMS, Dr. J.L. King of Galt, Ontario, chairman of the Administrative Council, explained the purpose of the Administrative Council to the delegates. The chief duty, he said, was to seek to integrate and co-ordinate all the work of the church and ultimately to present to General Assembly short- and long-term plans, financial needs and policy. The chairmen of all committees were members of this council. He stressed the point that, while women never before were represented on the higher councils of the church, on this committee there were six women, with power to vote.

Many in the WMS were keen on integration. A resolution from the Montreal and Ottawa synodical to the 1964 council asked that an investigation be made into the cost of administration, especially of work carried on jointly by the General Board of Missions and the Women's Missionary Society (WD) with a view to bringing about closer co-operation between these two bodies. It was believed this would lead to a reduction in administration costs.

In 1965, a more radical overture went to council from the Red Deer presbyterial of the Alberta synodical.

> *Whereas there is constant need for unity within the family of the Presbyterian Church in Canada; and*
> *Whereas it is advisable to have one missions policy, one missions department and one missions staff; and*
> *Whereas some economies might be achieved in administration costs, and*
> *Whereas the Presbyterian Record could be enlarged to include the material of The Glad Tidings magazine, to the mutual advantage of all readers; and*
> *Whereas there are several recommendations in the report of the Management Consultants that point to the need for consolidation along these lines; and*
> *Whereas the Committee on the Place of Women in the Church in its report to the General Assembly (Minutes 1964 – Page 387 – Paragraph 3) has enunciated a guiding principle for the unifying of both men's and women's activities in the Church; and*
> *Whereas it is widely agreed that the time has come to bring all women's work together in the total life of the Church,*
> *Therefore be it resolved that the Red Deer Presbyterial of the Alberta Synodical of the Women's Missionary Society request Council of the Women's Missionary Society that in its Annual Report to the General Assembly they recommend a special joint-committee be appointed to make a study of the problems and possibilities of consolidating the total work of men and women of the Presbyterian Church in Canada; and that this special joint-committee report to next year's meetings of both Council of the WMS and the General Assembly.*[49]

Edna Henry of the Alberta synodical indicated that there was a feeling prevalent among the women of the synodical that there was much confusion and over-lapping of work between the men and women of the Presbyterian Church. It was explained to the delegates that all workers were appointed jointly by boards of the church and the WMS(WD) but that following their arrival on a designated field, they were under the direction of the presbytery of that area.

Much discussion followed. As the recommendation concerned the place of women in the church, it was suggested that it be tabled until the progress report on the survey of the work of the women in The Presbyterian Church in Canada was presented. This survey, made by the WMS in 1964 at the request of the Administrative Council, was separate from the work of the General Assembly's Committee on the Place of Women in the Church and should not be confused with that committee's work.

In 1965, council received the report of the survey but, since the findings had to be reported first to the organization and planning committee of the Administrative Council, the WMS had to wait for the results.

The WMS had sent questionnaires to all synods, ministers and clerks of session, with copies for ladies' aids, women's auxiliaries and WMS groups. From the responses it would appear that the purpose of the questionnaire was an attempt to encourage the integration of all women's groups in the churches and that the reason for wishing to do so was financial.

A large majority surveyed favoured continuing two women's organizations. Many expressed the opinion that it would be unwise to change the present organization and that any amalgamation of the two groups would be a detriment to the total work of all women in the church. There were those who were keenly interested in mission work, but not in aid-type work while others were solely interested in aid-type work. There was also the feeling that the church would be irresponsible if it made a change in the organization of women in the church merely to gain more money and to bail the church out of debt in regard to missionary work. The general feeling was that the women's organizations worked happily together. Some said they would support amalgamation of groups if the church felt it was for the good of the church but there would be problems.[50]

An article that appeared in *The Glad Tidings* by Rev. D. T. Evans, chairman of the General Board of Missions, explained to the WMS the close relationship between the General Board of Missions and the Women's Missionary Society. When committees of the board were named, explained Mr. Evans, care was taken that they be composed of representatives appointed from all three divisions, the Women's Missionary Societies (Eastern and Western) and the General Board of Missions. No action was taken, he said, without consultation or review by all the missionary agencies of the church. In an obvious attempt to woo the women, Mr. Evans continued on a more persuasive note,

> *Over the years, there has been a steadily growing co-operation between these three missionary agencies. The future holds promise that this will continue. Can we see a day when the three will be one rather than the one, three? Tis a question which is being talked about in many sections of our land and our church. Indeed, it is fair to say, that apart from the Finance Budgeting and receiving of funds, the three are now almost one. Many concerned people trust that this question will not be ignored. This concern is shared by members of the WMS as well as the male members of the Church.*
>
> *This summer, the New Church Offices are to be opened. Here all our Administrative Offices will be under one roof. There is an interesting symbol involved in that, is there not? In a day when we are growing accustomed to changes, we need not be surprised at what can happen. The mobilization and deployment of the resources for Mission is a challenge. Would that this could be done under one administration wing, shared fully and freely by the men and women of our Church.*
>
> *The women of the Presbyterian Church have given prophetic leadership in the field of Missions in the past. Their influence has had a profound effect in the Missionary policy of our Church. They will be the ones who will lead us into the new day of an even more meaningful relationship between the Women's Missionary society and the General Board of Missions.*[51]

The recording secretary's report for 1965 begins,

> *During the year 1965, we have endeavoured to continue and to extend the work of our Society, within the total Mission of the Church. In this ever-changing world, we have been faced with adversity, we have been challenged with problems and difficulties, but with faith and under God's guidance, we have been enabled, in wisdom, to find solutions…*[52]

The 1966 council responded to the Red Deer resolution in the following manner,

> *In view of the fact that the General Assembly's Commission on the place of women in the Church has presently under consideration the status of the women in the Presbyterian Church in Canada, and that a Committee on the Vocation of the Church is giving thought*

to Christian Vocation, and since this is basic to the overture presented by the Alberta Synodical in 1965 re consolidation of work of the Presbyterian Church in Canada, therefore be it RESOLVED that the Council appoint a Committee to ascertain the thinking of the women of the society as to our special mission in the Presbyterian Church in Canada and that the Committee report back to the 1967 Council Meeting.[53]

It was agreed that further discussion was needed and the motion was tabled. This response indicated that the women of the WMS certainly believed that the General Assembly's decision about the ordination of women would have some bearing on the future of the WMS. Perhaps they thought that if women were allowed a voice in the courts of the church, closer integration would not pose such a threat to women's work. However, the crux of the matter comes out later in one of the questions asked in a panel discussion conducted at the 1969 council meeting.

How would the integration of the WMS(WD) with the General Board of Missions affect the financial support now given to the WMS(WD) by the women of the Church?

In other words, would women continue to give their generous financial support after the Board of Missions took over the mission work?

The new president, Laura Burnett, in her president's message in the *Glad Tidings* after the annual meeting in 1970, spoke of how many had expressed the desire for a closer relationship with the various boards of the church and how this would now be possible in some measure as a result of the action taken at the annual council meeting in May. There would now be a unified budget for the administration of all overseas mission work.

In the same issue, Mrs. Edith Keefer, secretary for friendship and service for the WMS, wrote glowingly of how a giant step forward had been taken by the 1970 council when it approved the recommendations made by the WMS reassessment committee regarding the integration of certain areas of administration. Many questions were asked. However,

...by the end of the day, small lingering doubts had vanished, and we looked to the future with enthusiasm for the part our women would play in this greater field of endeavour...

Mrs. Keefer explained that the reassessment committee was formed at the request of the 1966 council to more closely integrate the work of the WMS(WD) and the boards of the church.

Where two units are — to all intents — carrying out what appears to be the same type of work, it is assumed that unnecessary time and money is expended.

Although this point was debatable, she admitted that it was the reason to form this committee.

Mrs. Keefer further explained that the 1967 General Assembly had appointed the Committee on Overture 10 with Dr. G. Deane Johnston as chair. This overture from the Synod of the Atlantic Provinces asked the General Assembly in 1967 to

> *...take immediate steps to integrate and unify the administration of the Mission work of the Church under one General Board of Missions of the General Assembly...*

This committee was asked to investigate the possibilities of integrating the administrative and missionary functions of the WMS (WD and ED) with the General Board of Missions.[54]

Mrs. Keefer continued,

> *After much deliberation we agreed to approach the changing times first as Christian women, then as members of the Presbyterian Church in Canada, and THEN as members of the Women's Missionary society. Our only concern being the Mission of the Church and how we may continue to be involved.*
>
> *Somehow, this put our whole plan into proper perspective. First as Christian women — when we remembered this, other things fell into place. Now came the time for joint meetings with the General Board of Missions Committee on Structure and the General Assembly's Committee on Overture 10. Soon we found that where our original plan called for the integration of our work overseas, that there were other areas where we might also work together more closely, although the overseas fields were the logical place to start — much of our work there being already integrated.*[55]

After going over several points that had to be considered, Mrs. Keefer said that if the Women's Missionary Society and the General Board of Missions could come together confidently in a step towards the future, it would be a good thing for the church as a whole. Then, in a seeming attempt to calm fears, she added,

> *One thing must be made clear, however. The Society will continue to exist — groups, Presbyterials, Synodicals and Council UNTIL such action is taken by Council (not Council Executive) to change it. We hope there will be many areas of integration, but Council will still be asked to carry out such work as does not come within the scope of the new Board which may be formed and we think of as the Board of World Mission.*[56]

The proposed Board of World Mission would be set up at the 1971 General Assembly. On this board would be representatives from the WMS(WD and ED). The guidelines were outlined, among them, one that said the WMS council would notify this board annually of the amount of money which it could make available for the Board of World Mission. This board would then administer these funds together with the funds provided by the General Assembly. The new board would have a chair and a vice-chairperson. If the chairperson was a man, then the vice-chairperson would be a woman, and vice-versa. For a period of two years all secretaries and assistant secretaries of the current General Board of Missions and Women's Missionary Societies would be continued at their existing rates. Staff serving under the national and overseas departments of the WMS (WD) would become part of the staff of The Board of World Mission.

Dr. G. Deane Johnston, chair of the Committee of Overture 10, spoke to the delegates at the 1970 WMS council meeting regarding the work of his committee and the proposals his committee planned to take to the General Assembly in June. He emphasized that the WMS(WD) was, unlike the WMS(ED),

> *...an autonomous society, which while brought into existence by the General Assembly raises its own money, spends its own money, and sets its own policy.*

He said that it was apparent that one could not integrate or unify a board with a society but that one could, and his committee felt should, unify certain aspects of operations that fell within the same field of endeavour. He mentioned that the WMS was an organization deeply interested in and vitally concerned with the outreach of the church but spent a good part of its time, effort and money in youth work through its association with the Board of Christian Education. What Overture 10 referred to, he said, was the outreach of the church, the extension of the church both at home and abroad. There was a feeling throughout the church, Dr. Johnston said, that the present structure led to a duplication of staff with an attendant unnecessary spending of money, although what was actually the case was that for many years there had already been a wide area of co-operation. The final step in the integration, however, had still to be taken. In his concluding comments, Dr. Johnston said,

> *A great responsibility rests with the women to make a substantial financial contribution each year to the new Board of World Missions that the total mission of the Church may go forward. Presbyterials, Synodicals and Council will continue to have their place in bringing women together for inspiration, fellowship and planning that women may take an ever-increasing part in the mission entrusted to the Church.*[57]

All this appeared in *Glad Tidings* in August/September 1970. Copies of reports that were given at the council meeting in May were given to delegates and synodical presidents. Any member of the society could borrow the reports from a delegate or contact the office for further information. The WMS executive seemed anxious to make sure the information got out to the auxiliaries and that all the women would have the opportunity to get the picture of what was happening. On the other hand, it seems they might have hoped that the picture would not be too clear. They wanted to assure the women that nothing would change.

> *One thing must be made clear... The society will continue to exist — groups, presbyterials, synodicals and Council...*[58]

The Montreal-Ottawa synodical informed their presbyterial executives that it was their responsibility to impress upon group members that this change would not affect their work as a group and that they would be operating on the present basis until 1972.

Nothing had changed. At least, not until 1972. The WMS executive seems to have worked hard to maintain the status quo. They needed to pacify the troops. After all, if the women in the local groups thought their mission work had been taken over by the church, they might stop putting their money in those little mite boxes!

The WMS executive must have done a good job of keeping down the level of alarm. In the September, 1970 issue of the magazine, Betty Kilgour, president of the Red Deer presbyterial and the only woman elder in the presbytery, gives her "Impressions of Council 1970." It was a wonderful experience, she said. She came away with the impression that she belonged to a truly wonderful body. She goes on to describe the highlights of council and ends by calling it a wonderful eye-opening week. She makes no mention at all of the integration issue. Her "Impressions" appear in the *Glad Tidings* after five pages of the president and Mrs. Keefer explaining the major changes about to take place in the society. These changes would include the transfer of 33 national staff and 18 overseas staff from the WMS to the new Board of World Missions. The "giant step forward" taken by the 1970 council was the approval of the recommendations of the reassessment committee regarding the integration of the mission work of the WMS, as well as certain areas of administration, with that of the General Board of Missions. Yet this delegate does not even mention these changes as part of her "eye-opening" experience!

It would seem that it could not have been too clear to the ordinary delegate what the momentous decision they had voted on at council would mean for the society. Did the executive downplay what was happening, fearing what it might do to their finances if the women in the auxiliaries knew that they would no longer have responsibility for their own workers? Perhaps the executive did not have too clear a picture themselves. Perhaps they thought the integration would just be an extension of the kind of integration they already had. Maybe they hoped it would be like the integration described by Hildur Hermanson of Formosa where all the work would be so closely integrated that it would be difficult to draw a line between the work of the WMS missionaries and that of those sent out by the mission board. They would just all work together. They may have hoped but they were not sure. In the reports there is an air of uneasiness. They were not sure what to expect. But did they really have a choice?

In the June/July, 1971 issue of *Glad Tidings* we read,

> *By the time this issue of the Glad Tidings arrives in your home the General Assembly will have met and made a decision regarding the question of the Integration of Overseas and Home Mission Work of the WMS, W.D., and the Board of Missions of the Presbyterian Church in Canada.*[59]

Lydia Child, a nineteenth-century American author and abolitionist, used the old story of the sorcerer's apprentice to illustrate the expansion of women's involvement in society. The apprentice bewitched a broom into a living being but was unable to change it back into a broom.

> *Thus it is, with those who urged women to become missionaries and form tract societies…they have no spell to turn it into a broom again.*[60]

One is tempted to wonder if, perhaps, the church, after all those years, had finally found the formula for turning the WMS back into a broom. Or was it, as Mrs. Keefer said, "A giant step forward"?

PART III

What Next?

1972-2002

Chapter 16

New Ways

1972-2002

New ways for new days[1] was the challenge with which Laura Burnett, the president, ushered the WMS into 1972. Her words came in the wake of a significant shift by The Presbyterian Church in Canada in its policy and practice of mission.

The Board of World Mission (BWM)[2]

As already noted, the church had contemplated for some time the administrative integration of its mission work, which up to that point had been carried out by a number of agencies. A report of the joint General Board of Missions and Women's Missionary Society committee, mandated to discuss the integration of the mission work of the church, identified the "three sovereignties" in that work — the Woman's Missionary Society, Eastern Division, the Women's Missionary Society, Western Division and the General Board of Mission.[3] The discussion was carried on over several years and by several bodies — the organization and planning committee of the Administrative Council, the committee on Overture No. 10, the WMS(WD) executive and sub-executive and organization committees among others.

Initially, some of the discussion had to do with the possibility of having just one missionary society, perhaps reaching out to include men.[4] A major part of the discussion focused on better implementation of the church's mission program, both at home and overseas, and whether or not administrative integration would be a benefit. Representatives of both missionary societies were involved in the discussion and planning, and in June, 1970 the committee on Overture No. 10 (1967) reported to the General Assembly that,

> *In view of the evident desire for integration in the administration of the missionary function of the WMS (W.D. and E.D.) with that of the General Board of Missions, and in view of the very real structural and procedural problems which such an integration would entail, the Committee on Overture No. 10, having conferred repeatedly with the parties concerned over the last three years, recommends as follows:*
>
> *That the present General Board of Missions be dissolved and that a new Board to be called, "The Board of World Missions" be formed. This Board to consist of forty members, all to be appointed by the General Assembly, twenty-seven on Nomination of the Committee to Strike Standing Committees, ten to be nominated to the Assembly by the W.M.S. (W.D.) and three by the W.M.S. (E.D.)...*[5]

The General Assembly agreed with the committee's recommendations, and, after due Presbyterian process, The Board of World Mission became a functioning reality in 1972.

Its mandate was

> *...to give leadership to the whole Church in all its structures for mission responsibility and vision, as authorized by the General Assembly, to plan and administer specific mission work throughout the world.*[6]

As a result, overseas and national mission work, previously administered by the General Board of Missions and the WMS (WD and ED), was transferred to The Board of World Mission. Missionaries who had been appointed and financially supported by both missionary societies were now the responsibility of the new board. Thus the operation would be streamlined and simplified. National field workers and many of the projects they worked with were likewise now under the supervision of the board rather than of the societies and there were also some staff transfers. Giollo Kelly, for example, moved from being executive director of national missions of the WMS to being assistant secretary of The Board of World Mission, and Mary Whale, executive director of overseas mission for the WMS (WD) became secretary for mission personnel for the board. Only in the area of education did the

Giollo Kelly

WMS retain its role. Field workers of both missionary societies with responsibilities primarily in Christian education, mission education and organization of the societies remained in place.

The two missionary societies were to notify the board annually how much money they could provide for the work of the board but would cease to have any further direct control over that money. One of the terms of the new board reads as follows:

> *That the Councils of the W.M.S. (W.D.) and (E.D.) notify this Board annually the amount of money which these Councils feel they can make available for the work of the Board of World Missions in any given year. The Board of World Missions would then proceed to administer the funds provided by the General Assembly and by the Councils of the W.M.S. (W.D.) & (E.D.) without further reference to these Councils except for purposes of consultation and information.*[7]

The money would be collected through the societies, forwarded to the treasurer of The Presbyterian Church in Canada and then disbursed at the will of the board.

Reaction

All of this looked good on paper. Initial reaction, however, was often one of uncertainty. The WMS (ED), reporting to the General Assembly in 1970, speaks of a year of

> *...work, anxiety, frustration and introspection for* [the] *society as...for other branches and organizations of our church.*[8]

Mary Whale writes in her diary of May, 1971 about the annual meeting of the WMS (WD) council. She comments on the apparent calmness with which the society accepts the demands of the new integrated system but adds,

> *There is a sort of unreality about it all — we really do not know what we are doing. Hopefully we are in God's way.*[9]

However good a face the WMS (WD) tried to put on the "new way," it is clear that the society, as it had been conceived and had existed for so many years, was dealt something of a body blow. Its *raison d'etre* of working hands-on in mission fields at home and abroad had been radically altered. There was still to be a role but its shape and focus were to be different.

Concerns

Some members of the society saw the whole operation as a takeover on the part of the church with the main advantage going to the church. Many felt angry and threatened by a plan which they did not understand. May Nutt, then secretary for adult work with the WMS (WD), and Helen Tetley, consultant in leadership development for the Board of Christian Education, recall being sent out west to interpret the new directions the church was taking in mission and in Christian education with instructions to concentrate on the latter and downplay the former. It was a rough ride. They remember encountering outrage and opposition in the matter of The Board of World Mission and their efforts to stay low key almost cost them their jobs. Some people felt that May and Helen were avoiding the issues and demanded that they be replaced!

The key anxiety, they reported, was that of losing direct responsibility for the missionaries. By virtue of the society's early work *with* women *for* women, especially overseas where often male missionaries were prohibited from approaching potential women converts, the WMS had established a close bond with its women workers. Under the new arrangement this would come to an end. Margaret Kennedy, missionary in India, wrote in 1972 to council executive, expressing

> *...concern as to who will now pass on personal information between the workers on the field and the women who raise the money.*[10]

This anxiety was dealt with in the short run by agreeing to ask The Board of World Mission to pass on to council executive for information minutes from the overseas mission councils. Miss Kennedy's letter, however, points up one aspect of the sense of loss experienced by many throughout the society, members and workers

Margaret Kennedy

alike. It was a sense of loss that encompassed loss of identity as an autonomous missionary-supporting organization, loss of "ownership" of projects and personnel and loss of significant relationships.

Another concern had to do with finances. Would the society simply be regarded as a money-generating agency? This was not a new issue. It has already been indicated throughout its history, that WMS' usefulness to the church was measured in terms of dollars. In a discussion about the proposed new board, the question was raised at the annual meeting of the WMS council in May, 1971. Following a report by Rev. Robert Carter (secretary of the committee on organization and planning) on the progress toward amalgamation, concern was expressed by the delegates about the status of the WMS. Would it become merely a 'cash cow' for The Board of World Mission?

Rev. George Malcolm, chairman of The Board of World Mission, addressed this issue in an interview with the editor of *Glad Tidings* in February, 1972, implying that the solution lay in the hands of the society itself. In Mr. Malcolm's opinion, the role of the WMS would increase under the new arrangement and if the society became merely a money-making organization, it would be failing in its particular calling as a missionary society.[11] To give money without that sense of dedication would be to betray the calling and purpose of the society. Mr. Malcolm also reminded the WMS that it was represented on the new board. In his opinion this would provide opportunities to contribute the society's interest, concerns and expertise, as well as allowing it to share in determining how and where the money for mission would be spent and the form that mission work should take.

Missionaries who worked for the WMS faced problems of adjustment under the new regime. There was a feeling in some quarters that the psychological impact of the changes was not sufficiently addressed. One missionary described the transfer of administrative responsibility from the WMS to the BWM as being unwelcome and traumatic. Field staff, especially overseas, often felt left out of the debate and simply confronted with the *fait accompli* of integration. For some there were issues over pensions which were not always portable. Solutions were not always satisfactory.

The Positive Side

Whatever was happening in the field or at the grass roots level, however, official response to the new situation was to put a positive spin on it. Mrs. Burnett says,

> *In our relationship with the new Board of World Missions, as women of the Presbyterian Church and as representatives appointed to that board by the Women's Missionary Society, many*

> *exciting things already have happened. We have been challenged to enlarge our missionary family and to accept a share in the total mission program of the Church at home and overseas; to have a closer relationship with the Missionary and Christian Education Departments of the Church and participate in a "team Ministry."*[12]

Rev. Robert Carter in answer to the question "Is the WMS on the way out?" declared,

> *Only if it loses its vision, vitality and the will to serve…the WMS, at its best, represents that concern for mission outreach, which is the very essence of the Church's life… If the Church is coming alive to mission in a new way, surely the WMS can and should be on its way in, not out… You have not lost your mission program — you have opted in to the whole mission operation of the Church.*[13]

The WMS might have been forgiven for believing that was what the society had been doing all along!

Mr. Malcolm, in the interview already noted, spoke of a new flexibility and unity and suggested that with both missionary societies and the former General Board of Missions

> *…all putting their people who are doing mission work into the Board of World Missions,* [it] *can't help but strengthen our use of corporate resources.*[14]

This idea was reinforced in a 1972 article, "The Ongoing Responsibilities of the Women's Missionary Society," written to help the WMS membership understand the "new way."

> *Our women are now faced with the challenge, not only to continue* [their financial and prayer] *support, but to widen their concern to encompass the entire mission staff serving our Church under the Board of World Missions.*[15]

Working It Out

This they did. With regard to finances, the needed money continued to come. Although the society no longer had direct responsibility for sending out or maintaining overseas and national missionary personnel, it continued to raise money for mission. This money went into a common church pool from which the salaries and expenses of mission workers were paid. In its 1974 report to the General Assembly, The Board of World Mission thanked the WMS for its support of the board and the church in prayer, mission service and financial assistance. In 1973, the WMS (WD) had contributed $360,000 and the WMS (ED) $26,000, representing 20 per cent of the board's budget. In 1977, the society's treasurer, Clara Hogg, noted that the largest item in the WMS(WD) budget was the grant to The Board of World Mission, representing approximately two thirds of the society's budget.

With regard to the issue of personnel support, old contacts were retained and new ones made through the exchange of reports and letters between the society and the mission fields. Many of these were published in *Glad Tidings* and read at meetings or used as study material. Other correspondence was maintained on a one-to-one basis by individual members of the society. In addition, people visited missionaries, either as representatives of the society or on their own, to get a feel for the work. Also, missionaries, when home in Canada, frequently did deputation work, taking their stories out to WMS groups and to congregations. Although many of the programs and projects, formerly either initiated and/or supported by the WMS within Canada — for example, work with Chinese Canadian women and children, fellowship houses for young Aboriginal people, hospital visitation — were now administered by The Board of World Mission, the society continued to be interested in and informed about them. Thus, bonds were forged and strengthened.

Verdict

Rev. Louis de Groot, chairman of The Board of World Mission, writing for *Glad Tidings* in 1973, asks,

> *What does it mean for the Presbyterian Church in Canada to have this new Board, the Board of World Mission? Many people in our congregations, especially women, are asking this question quite frequently. Our women have been long used to the WMS directing its own missionary activities. That has now come to an end... Did the women gain or lose in the setting up of the Board of World Mission?*[16]

Thirty years or so after the event some of those intimately involved in it offer their opinions on the matter. Giollo Kelly, May Nutt and Helen Tetley see the amalgamation as *a job that had to be done, so we did it.* They speak of the good cooperation that took place, especially in the matter of mission education under the guidance of Rev. Malcolm Ransom. They also speak of loss, that previously noted loss of contact with missionaries, which affected the local auxiliaries, taking away their sense of responsibility for the work. Knowledge and information were harder to come by. Contact and communication were broken. And in the end, not much money may have been saved.

Louis de Groot answers his own question by saying,

> *It is the opinion of the writer of this article that the whole Presbyterian Church has gained in the new setup.*[17]

In 1977, a report on budget estimates for the coming year notes that,

Five years ago the Women's Missionary Society (W.D.) and the Board of World Missions were integrated at the administrative level, amid predictions that "it will be wonderful!" "it will be disastrous!" Five years later — have things changed so much?[18]

Thirty years later, have things changed so much? There are still those who say it was wonderful! (or at least, if not wonderful, then good, successful) and those who say it was disastrous! The jury would still appear to be out.

The Board of Congregational Life (BCL)

Another new entity, the Board of Congregational Life, appeared on the scene in 1974 as the result of an earlier General Assembly decision to integrate the services of existing agencies into one. This was done in order to encourage and enable congregations in their delivery of programs and in leadership development. Existing boards and committees and both missionary societies were involved in discussion of the proposal.

The mandate of the new board was to include helping congregations in their work of evangelism, social action, Christian education and the production of church school curricula. As well, the board would work with churches in the areas of education for mission, stewardship, planning and leadership development for mission in local congregations. The WMS (WD) would be represented on the board by two members, the WMS (ED) by one, and so both would participate fully in planning and decision-making. For example, a joint committee on Christian education was established, consisting of representatives of the two missionary societies, the Board of Congregational Life and The Board of World Mission. The committee's function was to ensure the continuity of the work of education in all its aspects.

Some reservations about the proposed board were recorded. From the beginning there was concern about developing the relationship between the Board of Congregational Life and the WMS. The society's report to the General Assembly of 1972 notes the strong cooperative links between the missionary societies and the Board of Christian Education (one of the components of the new board) but refers to the need for

...full and frank discussion with the W.M.S., so that suitable working relationships can be established, and the fullest coordination achieved in serving the needs of congregations and local groups.[19]

The report further states that,

...the present cooperative relationship between the WMS and The Board of Christian Education could provide a good basis on which to initiate...consultation... Both the Societies and the Board need

to look for the most effective ways of serving the congregations of the Church in the years ahead…it is of the greatest importance that there be full cooperation, communication and fellowship between the WMS and the Board of Congregational Life. Many questions remain to be resolved. Clarification and interpretation will be needed on many matters.[20]

History and personal testimony, however, indicate that these issues were worked out. The relationship was good and productive and brought benefits to the church as a whole. A WMS report to the General Assembly in 1974 states that,

For many years National and Area Educational Staff have worked in close cooperation with the Board of Christian Education as they represented both WMS and BCE…We are assured that WMS Staff, National and Area will be considered as Associated Staff with the Board of Congregational Life. Joint planning has begun through Joint Task Forces on Field Services and Continuing Missionary Education.[21]

For the most part the advent of the Board of Congregational Life seems to have caused fewer problems for the WMS than that of The Board of World Mission. Perhaps this was because there was less direct sense of loss. The work of the new board reaffirmed much of what was already being done by the society in the field of education and offered the opportunity for some regrouping and redirection. It also acknowledged the importance of the connectedness of the WMS at the local level. Rev. Robert Carter, speaking to the annual council meeting in 1972, noted that the Board of Congregational Life would affect the WMS at all levels of church life.

Because W.M.S. members are an important element in the life of the congregations, in every respect congregational life is their concern.[22]

The WMS consistently made a significant contribution to the work of the new boards through the women who represented the society on them. These women brought to the affairs of the church their experience in speaking, praying, organizing and teaching. The high quality of leadership, provided by both missionary societies, continued over the years of the existence of The Board of World Mission and the Board of Congregational Life and their successors and has been no small factor in bringing about the integration of women into all aspects of the work of the church and their acceptance as co-contributors to its life and purpose.

Educating in Mission

In 1999, the WMS set itself three priorities for the following three years — promotion, education and finances. Writing about these priorities, Margaret Robertson, program secretary for the society, notes that,

> *Frontiers may be on our doorsteps... In order to reach those frontiers, we need to be organized and informed.*[1]

As already noted, in the wake of the creation of The Board of World Mission the major role left to the WMS(WD) was that of educator. The informing and educating of people about mission and missions has always been important to the society. In "The Ongoing Responsibilities of the Women's Missionary Society"[2] the writers refer to the educational program of the Foreign and Home Missionary societies, two of the three missionary societies which came together in 1914 as the Women's Missionary Society, Western Division. This program was begun to inform and update local groups, leaders and officers and to help them feel a part of the whole. Field secretaries were appointed to visit and encourage groups (children, youth and adult). Committees prepared and sent out resource materials, some of the earliest of which were letters from missionaries. Over time a series of magazines came into being, culminating in the creation of *The Glad Tidings* in 1925. The magazines contained educational and inspirational material, aimed at keeping the membership informed and connected. The annual report for the WMS in 1923 notes that,

> *A woman having any contact with missions needs information to develop capacity for service, whether she be member, giver, active leader, or just able to serve by the "hard and happy work of prayer." Intelligence concerning the work and its needs is essential to efficiency in every line of service.*[3]

In 1948, the organization department was set up. Among other things it enabled the WMS to

> *...continue to be a key interpretative channel for the mission of the Church through its study programmes.*[4]

In 1972, this department became the education committee because it was felt this name better reflected the committee's work. This work consisted of preparing study materials, providing leadership training and assistance to groups and overseeing the WMS Book Room and *Glad Tidings*, as well as publishing the annual report and other educational literature.

After 1972, therefore, the WMS simply kept on doing what it had been doing for so many years. In the August/September, 1972 edition of *Glad Tidings*, a page is dedicated to answering readers' questions. In answer to the query,

> *What does the Women's Missionary Society, WD, continue to administer?* the editor replies that...*the WMS, WD, continues to administer and be responsible for the educational programs of the society, which includes the Glad Tidings, the WMS Book Room, the educational resource people serving in the western and east central regions, and the resource materials for study in adult, teen-age and children's groups.*[5]

Thus the mandate for education is worked out in a variety of ways.

Glad Tidings

It would be difficult to over-emphasize the importance of the role of *Glad Tidings* in the life and work of the WMS, particularly in the society's role as educator. In her book *A Lively Story*, Jean Campbell says *Glad Tidings has been referred to as "the arterial system that carries life to every part of the body."*[6] Under the guidance of a series of editors the magazine has kept the society informed of mission happenings within the church and beyond. It has kept the membership up-to-date on activities within auxiliaries, presbyterials and synodicals, provided financial reports, marked important milestones and challenged its readers with articles on faith, the practice of Christianity and the issues of the day. Writers have come from inside and outside the church and the society and have provided a wide spectrum of views and opinions.

Although the material in *Glad Tidings* was often fairly predictable and "safe" in nature and content, it sometimes ventured into controversial topics, which nonetheless could point to new avenues of mission. In 1974 and 1975, for example, the issues of drugs, abortion, apartheid and racism were discussed. As might be expected, this drew responses from both ends of the spectrum, ranging from support for the "new and improved" magazine to rebuke. One reader writes to the editor:

> [I] *wonder if you are aware that the Glad Tidings is a Missionary Magazine and that the total purpose of it is to bring the news from our many areas of work at home and abroad in to the homes of WMS members. This issue* [November, 1972], *appears to be an advertisement for Women's Lib.*[7]

Similar opinions and responses are found in the 1980s and 1990s. While continuing to include traditional mission-oriented material and news, *Glad Tidings* was aware of the need to reach out to, and meet on its own ground, a constituency that was breaking away from the traditional. It chose, therefore, to confront its readers with some of the less comfortable questions of the day. It presented material about women and poverty, about homosexuality, about spousal abuse and incest. It ran a series on Christianity and its response to other faiths. It told the story of the church, the society and the residential schools. It challenged people to think about inclusive language.

Responses were not long in coming. Some subscriptions were cancelled. An April, 1992 article on homosexuality, for example, brought the following,

> *Please cancel further copies of Glad Tidings. I found that I only enjoyed missionaries' letters; stories of missionary work in times of early Canada. Heartily disliked the abhorrent emphasis on feminism; homosexuality.*[8]

On the other hand, one reader expressed appreciation to the editor for her *courage and wisdom*[9] in printing the material, while another spoke of *the fine April issue with* [its] *thoughtful and sensitive articles.*[10]

In order to continue to present material, which could cause offense to some but which allowed *Glad Tidings* to pursue its policy of confronting the questions of the day, the 1990 WMS council authorized the publishing of a disclaimer at the beginning of each issue. It reads:

> *Glad Tidings provides a forum for a broad spectrum of opinion and information, thus the views expressed in features, news reports, letters and book reviews are not necessarily endorsed by the WMS (WD) or by the editor.*

Not only has *Glad Tidings* moved with the times in terms of content but it has also streamlined its operation with a view to reducing costs and improving both production and circulation. In February, 1958 there was a proposal for the magazine to carry paid advertising but it was not until 1995 that the proposal became reality, providing much-needed extra income. In the late 1800s missionary letters were copied by hand and sent out to the auxiliaries. Today, *Glad Tidings* is produced on computer and is distributed throughout the world. It is available six times a year in regular format, as well as in large print or on cassette tape. This is a far cry from the 1920s, when missionary books and papers were sometimes given to the Canadian Pacific Railway engineer to *throw out to waiting hands along the line!*[11]

Glad Tidings has a loyal following within the society but would, of course, like to expand its subscription list. Like the society itself, it seeks ways to grow. In the 1990s, the WMS undertook an internal restructuring with a view to changing its image and way of doing things so as to connect with a new generation of women who often see and do mission differently. This was not a new idea. Laura Plummer, a former editor of the magazine, writes with prophetic vision in the early 1970s.

> *We are trying to interest people (men and women) throughout the whole church in the on-going mission story. The evidence is, however, that the magazine, a main source of mission information, has*

an almost totally private readership, that readership being found largely within WMS groups... Does the magazine need a fresh start as a magazine for everyone to read? Does the name "Glad Tidings" confine the message it brings [because of] *the long-established connotations built into the name?*[12]

(In 1999, however, based on an overwhelmingly negative response to the issue from the grassroots, the WMS council voted against a name change, at least for the time being.)

Laura Plummer continues:

We want to establish a new image for the magazine, that image saying "This is a magazine for everyone, and what it has to say is in the now and is about the happenings of today!" The magazine...must reach present-day readers. The language, including its name, should relate to and be their language. It must be in terms they know. It can't use words which for many years have ceased to have meaning.[13]

This is what *Glad Tidings* strives to do. It has received awards from church press associations both for features and format. In 2000, the magazine marked its 75th anniversary. The *Glad Tidings* report that year to the annual meeting of the WMS council notes that,

Glad Tidings greeted the 21st century with optimism and anticipation... We look forward to the challenges of the new millennium.[14]

The WMS Book Room

Another channel for communication and education is The Book Room, formerly known as the WMS Book Room (see also the section "Lean and Accountable"). For many years the WMS acquired and distributed mission- and study-oriented materials. Jean Campbell notes that, in 1967,

...the Book Room got its own office, a Book Room Committee was established and a Manager appointed. The continuing task of filling requests for study resources and other materials was housed with the Book Room.[15]

Since then there have been five managers of The Book Room and its operation has expanded extensively.

The role of The Book Room has always been less to make money than to educate, though profit is always welcome! It fulfills the educational mandate by providing a wide range of materials for all ages — books, magazines, music, video tapes etc. — and making this accessible, not only to members of the society but to the church at large and to the general public. Displays are made available at all levels of the society, often through literature secretaries. The book table is a feature of General Assembly and, if requested, can be provided for meetings of synods and presbyteries. Book reviews appear in *Glad Tidings* and in the PCPak, an information package which goes primarily to the congregations but is available to individual subscribers. Through marketing its resources, both on and off site, The Book Room makes an important contribution to the ongoing educational role of the WMS.

Study Materials

The Women's Missionary Society defines itself as a "community of Christians," whose purpose is, among other things, to encourage people to be involved in mission "through prayer, study, service and fellowship."[16] Study has always been an important part of the life, work and purpose of the society. Annual reports refer to pamphlets and books which were used by groups as a basis for information, study and discussion. In 1931, for example, 2,800 copies of the study *The Tide of Opportunity* were issued, along with 1,200 copies of *Big Ships and Little People* for children's groups and 1,000 copies of *Council Fires*, intended for girls' groups. In addition, 1,000 copies of *The Lectures of Laura K. Pelton* and 1,000 copies of *Three Services of Devotion* were published.

There were visual aids as well. Mollie Harback, reminiscing in "Decisions Over Teacups," remembers lantern slides as part of the mission studies of earlier years. The exchange and literature secretary was

> *...custodian and distributor of the various sets of lantern slides, the most advanced contribution to visual education at that time.*[17]

Not everybody was impressed, however. The article continues,

> *One of the faithful used to complain about "the missionaries and their darn lantern slides" — strong language for that generation!*[18]

This emphasis on informing and educating has remained central to WMS philosophy and policy. Louise Reith, at one time literature secretary and later executive secretary of the society, says in an interview for *Glad Tidings* in November, 1974,

> *To begin with, the WMS had as its educational responsibility the providing of information "about missions" for groups related to it... When CGIT was recognized by the Church as a recommended group for teen-age girls, the Board responsible for Christian Education asked the WMS to provide suitable mission study programs. Gradually the need for coordination of Christian Education and Missionary Education became obvious. Information "about" missionary work meant little unless there was an understanding of "Why Mission?" which called for an understanding of the Christian faith. The cooperation between the WMS and the Board responsible for Christian Education, which began with teen-age work, extended to Children's Work*

> — *COC* [Children of the Church], *Explorers with sharing of staff, joint sponsorship of groups and production of materials...*[19]

At the time when The Board of World Mission and the Board of Congregational Life came into being, the study material used throughout the church was the result of teamwork between staff of the national church and of the WMS, powered as much by fellowship as by agenda. Helen Tetley, at the time a joint appointee of the WMS and the Board of Christian Education, comments, for example, on the production of mission studies for children.

> *Mabel* [Booth] *and I worked through the committees to prepare materials... The meetings were held in living rooms, kitchens etc. and were great fun but hard work. Mabel and I edited and produced the final packet. Many of the packets were supplementary materials for the books that came from the U.S. but which we (staff) had worked on there (creating outlines), but members of the committees reviewed outlines and manuscripts.*[20]

The mission study materials distributed by the WMS set out to inform readers of mission activity in a specific area, either at home or abroad. When the area was overseas, background material on geography, culture, dominant issues, etc. was made available. From the beginning, efforts were made to ensure Canadian content. The material often came from offshore sources — the United States and Great Britain, for example — and from other denominations. Provision, therefore, was made for the Canadian — and Presbyterian — perspective by turning to writers within the WMS and/or the church itself. In 1920, for example, the annual report notes that

> *Plans are in operation for issuing a study book for 1922 on the WMS work, the different chapters being prepared by those most conversant with the subject or country.*[22]

In the 1926 report, reference is made to the book *New Ontario*, by Rev. J. A. MacInnis (later a moderator of the General Assembly), telling the story of the school home in New Liskeard and the Presbyterian hospital in South Porcupine. In 1945, the literature department issued *Listening In!* by Margaret Webster, stories of mission work through the years. Miss Webster later became principal of Ewart College, the training school for deaconesses.

This emphasis on 'things Canadian' kept surfacing over the years. For many years the WMS has been a participating member of the Program Committee on Education for Mission (PCEM)/Friendship Press, a committee of the National Council of Churches of Christ (NCCCUSA). Barbara Woodruff, at one time program secretary for the WMS, outlines the history of the relationship in the article "Mission Education" in the *Presbyterian Record* of October, 1997. She tells of the formation in the early 1900s of the

Young People's Missionary Movement of the United States and Canada (YPMM). Women's foreign mission boards also operated in both countries and formed a committee to publish study materials. In 1911, the YPMM joined with the women's committee, and the publishing part of the merger became Friendship Press which published materials for PCEM until the spring of 1998, when the two were legally separated. PCEM no longer produces resources. Instead it works to encourage and enable the commitment of member denominations and their congregations to partnership in God's mission and provides opportunities for study of mission trends and the developing of education resources. Both the WMS and The Presbyterian Church in Canada are connected to the Program Committee on Education for Mission of the NCCCUSA and contribute financially to its work.

Representatives of the church and the WMS have had input into the materials produced by Friendship Press. They helped select the study themes and also contributed to the actual writing. Often, however, reports from the WMS auxiliaries would indicate a need for more attention to the Canadian Presbyterian experience and expression of mission. As a result, in 1997, The Presbyterian Church in Canada began to write its own study materials. This was a joint venture for the WMS, along with Education for Mission, Justice Ministries (departments of the Life and Mission Agency of the church) and Presbyterian World Service and Development. Together they produce and promote an annual study for the whole church. In recent years studies have covered topics such as Loaves and Fishes, Cuba, Mission Partnerships and The Presbyterian Church in Canada, Living as a Jubilee People, and God's People, God's Planet, Living Lightly on the Earth.

Evelyn Murdoch, Dorothy Ruddell, Helen McLeish, Hamilton-London Synodical, 1988

Resource People

Margaret Boyd

Educational resource people have played an important role in the life and work of the society. Over the years they have been known by different titles — field secretaries, regional secretaries, educational resource persons (ERPs) and area educational consultants (AECs). Many of the educational staff were diaconal ministers, earlier known as deaconesses, and, as such, were well-equipped for the work.[23]

Margaret Boyd, with many years of experience as an AEC, defined that work as

> *...being of assistance to Church School teachers in becoming familiar with resources, helping in training events, referring them to available resources, being a listener to concerns and problems, not only of teachers and leaders but also of WMS people. An important part of the work is assisting in planning and implementation of programs, particularly with Presbyterial executives and Synodical executive. Officer training is also a part of the responsibilities.*[24]

This pattern was the norm for many years.

The WMS had always striven to maintain educational staff in all the synods/synodicals within the bounds of the society. Sometimes the work was done by teams. Sometimes freelance consultants were employed to help out where necessary. Often there was just one person serving a large geographic area. In the early 70s, educational resource staff were associate staff of the Board of Congregational Life. Their salaries were paid by the WMS, with the board contributing toward travel expenses. By the mid 90s, however, the pattern began to change. The concept of regional staffing emerged. Detailed discussion of this follows in the next section.

Christian Literature Fund

In *The Glad Tidings* of 1937, Mrs. D. Strachan, treasurer and vice-president of the WMS, presents the estimates for 1937. She notes that,

> *a separate estimate has been made for that most important field of service, Christian literature.*[25]

The amount budgeted is $745 and is earmarked for grants to

> *Christian Literature Societies in China, Manchuria and Korea, to*

> *the Committee on Christian Literature for Women and Children, and for Literature for Hungarians in Canada and for Chinese in Saskatchewan.*[26]

Prior to 1937, the provision of this kind of material was reported under 'miscellaneous' but from that year on it became, and remains, a special focus for the society. In recent years the amount budgeted for Christian literature has remained around the $10,000 mark.

This is another aspect of education. It is education 'outside the bounds' of the society, so to speak, and not always exclusively mission-oriented education, at least in the traditional sense. It is, however, education undertaken 'because' of faith with a view to 'promoting' faith. Money is allocated to a variety of projects. In 1982, for example, $500 was sent to the All Africa Conference of Churches to help with a program of study and research. Two hundred dollars went to supply material for a reading room near a bus depot in Jobat, India. The Costa Rica Literary Centre for Caribbean and South America used their $500 to set up "wall libraries" in outlying villages. Canadian projects included the Canadian Bible Society and *La Vie Chretienne*, a publication of The Presbyterian Church in Canada. In 1997, grants went to The Presbyterian Church of East Africa for HIV/AIDS education materials and to Mayan Ministries in Guatemala for Bibles and study materials, as well as to work in ten other countries. Within Canada, two of the projects were *Evangelical Truth*, the publication of Christian literature in Ukrainian, and the North Peace River Territorial Presbytery's purchase of church school materials.

The Christian literature report to the annual meeting of the WMS in 1999 noted that the Christian literature committee had not been receiving many direct requests, which perhaps indicates a need to re-evaluate this aspect of WMS work. Other sources of funding for the projects have opened up and are being supported by church members at large. Nonetheless, the society continues to set aside a significant amount of money for Christian literature, still seeing it as an important part of the mandate to educate.

Why Education?

Louise Reith was once asked to define the greatest challenge of the future for women in the area of missionary education and the total mission of the church. She replied:

> *...it is fitting that women of the Church think of the heritage that is theirs in the mission begun and carried forward by women... Women are challenged to share their knowledge of mission work with others... Women are challenged to always keep in mind that "Every land is a mission field and every Christian a missionary."*[27]

Lean and Accountable

Recommendation No.1

That the present status of the WMS(WD) as an autonomous organization within the structures of The Presbyterian Church in Canada be reaffirmed, noting the society's willingness to co-operate with the agencies of Assembly in the life and work of the Church.[1]

This was the request brought to the 117th General Assembly by the president of the WMS in her annual report. The notion of autonomy has been an important element in the self-understanding of the society. In reality the autonomy can never be total. The WMS exists by the will of the General Assembly of The Presbyterian Church in Canada and, as the society has on occasion been reminded, may be eliminated at any time by that same body. However, the degree of autonomy permitted to it has enabled the WMS to control its own finances, appoint its own executive and support staff and, until 1972, its own missionaries, design its own programs and determine its own goals and priorities. Autonomy is seen as an asset to be protected and this "declaration of independence" was just such an act of protection. The body of the report containing the recommendation noted that

The mind of the 1990 Council Meeting reflected their determination that the society continue to function independently within The Presbyterian Church in Canada.[2]

The recommendation was adopted.

Working Out the Vision

This issue arose in the face of yet another upheaval in the structure of the church. After the reconfigurations of the late 1960s and early 1970s, that led to the establishment of The Board of World Mission and The Board of Congregational Life, the life and work of the church continued to evolve in new directions. In 1989, the General Assembly adopted a nine point vision (see Appendix E) for the church, which included emphases on growth, mission and outreach, community building, communication, Spirit-led ministry, revitalized courts and a lean and accountable administration. This vision was the work of the executive planning and coordinating committee, appointed by the Administrative Council to lead the church in a strategic planning exercise. Out of the exercise came a plan for restructuring. The General Assembly appointed a task force, which included representation from the two mission societies, to

...recommend to the 116th General Assembly a detailed proposal for

> *restructuring the way the General Assembly fulfills its responsibility through boards, committees and agencies*[3]

Further, the task force was to examine the financial implications of such action and solicit responses from the presbyteries. The ultimate aim of restructuring was to help the church carry out its work more effectively and more efficiently through an administration

> *...stripped of redundancies and overlapping jurisdictions and functions and made more responsive to the call of the Spirit* [through] *a model that is less cumbersome* [and] *which will be able to respond more flexibly to God's call.*[4]

Consultations were held with the two missionary societies concerning the effect of church restructuring on their structure and work. The issue of the relationship between the societies and the church emerged in the report of the task force on restructuring agencies of the General Assembly in 1990.

> *The place of lay organizations within the Church has a long and honourable history. Within The Presbyterian Church in Canada, two such societies have been given special status and recognition by General Assemblies, which continue to hold the societies in esteem and accountable. They are the Atlantic Mission Society and the Women's Missionary Society (Western Division).*
>
> *The Task Force has spent considerable effort in reviewing the unique place and contribution of the two lay mission societies... Their role and status within the Church is unprecedented among voluntary associations. Moreover, their contribution to Christian education and to mission at present as in the past, is largely unheralded and may well be crucial to key aspects of our collective life as a community of God's people. Their financial contribution (between the two societies) to the general coffers of the National Church is in excess of $1.3 million annually.*[5]

This was good to hear. Too often the WMS experienced or automatically assumed, perhaps not always with adequate foundation, a lack of appreciation on the part of the church. Nonetheless, it had concerns about some of the proposed recommendations in the report. These recommendations had to do with the status of area education consultants, with financial grants and with possible new directions for the society in terms of membership and stewardship. At its annual meeting in May, 1990, the WMS council authorized a supplementary report to the General Assembly which included the following statement:

> *It is clear that these recommendations have serious repercussions for the life and identity of the WMS (WD) and its contribution to the*

work of The Presbyterian Church in Canada but those present at the Annual Meeting feel that the proposed recommendations have been drawn up without sufficient input from, and consultation with, the society. It is also felt that adequate consideration has not been given to the psychological effects of such restructuring on the members and staff of the WMS (WD).[6]

These comments, along with others made by different bodies and interest groups across the church, had an effect. The report of the special committee on restructuring to the General Assembly the following year notes that it planned to reconsider in detail several elements of its proposal. One of these was

...the relationship of the mission societies to the new structures. There has [sic] *been consultations with both the AMS and the WMS as part of our general consultation. We welcome the WMS (WD)'s initiatives to assert their autonomy as a separate society and look forward to next winter when discussion will take place with both societies about ways in which they can play vital roles in the life of the whole Church.*[7]

Restructuring, as finally approved by the General Assembly in 1991, called for the establishment of the Life and Mission Agency (responsible for Christian education and nurture, mission and outreach), the Service Agency (responsible for matters of finance, resource production and distribution, personnel and administration)[8] and the Assembly Office which would oversee the work of the courts of the church. Existing standing committees on Doctrine, History, International Affairs and Ecumenical Relations were to remain as before. The Administrative Council would be replaced by an Assembly Council, of which at least one third of the members were to be women. The presidents of the AMS and the WMS would be members of the council. The missionary societies would also have representation on the various committees associated with the agencies, though not to the extent of their earlier representation on The Board of World Mission.

Several times the WMS raised concerns about loss of representation. It was felt that, given the financial contribution of the society to the work of the church, the WMS was entitled to a greater voice. In 1992, the special committee on restructuring recommended that the WMS have an ex officio voting member on the committees of the Life and Mission Agency and the Service Agency. In return the general secretaries of the agencies would become ex officio, non-voting members of the WMS council executive and of the council itself, and the conveners of the two agency committees would become ex officio voting members of council. The society also had the opportunity to be represented on support committees for program staff. Similar arrangements were put in place for the AMS with regard to the Life and Mission Agency. However, the matter has never really been resolved to the satisfaction of the WMS.

Restructuring proved to be a difficult and often painful experience for the church, at least in the transition period. While the new ways, methods and schemas were challenging and opened the door to new possibilities, some people were hurt in the process as positions were redefined or eliminated and personalities clashed. In addition, what the church had hoped to save in terms of money was often eroded, at least in the short run, by the compensation that had to be paid out in severance packages and litigation settlements. Over and above the general fallout from restructuring, which affected all who worked for the church, the WMS experienced a particularly direct impact from three proposals emerging from the process. One was the matter of regional staff.

Regional Staffing

In its report to the General Assembly of 1990, the task force on restructuring agencies of the General Assembly spoke of assessing the needs of synod and regional staff over a period of three years. The hope was that some programs (especially those related to education, nurture and mission) could be implemented at the synod rather than at the General Assembly level. It was suggested that there could be a team of staff persons at the regional/synod level to provide program leadership to presbyteries and congregations. This could potentially involve a staff executive officer, an area education-nurture consultant and a youth director working together as a team.[9] Needs and bounds of synods and presbyteries would be studied over a period of three years before such a plan would be implemented. The missionary societies were to be consulted as to how they could best support such a scheme. It was proposed that the support come through representation on supervising bodies and ongoing financial contributions.

In its report to the General Assembly of 1991, the special committee on restructuring acknowledged changes in the proposals for restructuring, noting that the committee

> *...has received no positive reaction to the idea of a new regional system to facilitate the delivery of programme.*[10]

Some synods were not particularly enthusiastic about the plan, perhaps because they felt ill-equipped to carry it out or were happy with the way things were. "If it ain't broke, don't fix it," was the philosophy.

Nonetheless, the concept persisted and a task force on regional structures was appointed in 1992. The mandate of the task force was to consult with the synods and synodicals, presbyteries and presbyterials, congregations, WMS and AMS among others and, through the Assembly Council, bring in a final report on regional structures and staffing to the 1994 General Assembly. As a result of the consultation, the task force affirmed a need for regional staff in the areas of leadership training, provision and recommendation of resources, pastoral care, conflict management, the revitalizing of congregations, communicating and interpreting information and new church development. It also noted that needs differed from region to region.

The task force now felt that the church was committed to strong regional staffing which would respond to regional needs. It acknowledged a diversity of opinion as to how this might be organized. It emphasized the need for partnership, cooperation and joint accountability between national and local levels of the operation and called for strong regional support groups.[11]

In its recommendations, the task force report called attention to the problem of lack of funds for the proper implementation of its proposals. It noted that

> *The Women's Missionary Society (WD) has committed funds for seven staff positions (at 1993 levels), while the Life and Mission Agency has budgeted funds for five positions...*[12]

It then proposed a configuration for staff positions, according to the needs of each individual synod, and requested ongoing WMS financial support. The report was adopted by the General Assembly and regional staffing became a reality.

The whole concept of regional staffing caused the WMS, in the words of the president, Joan Sampson, *some uncertainty and much confusion,*[13] though later she spoke hopefully of *a challenging and exciting time.*[14] It also presented the society with another perceived erosion of its role and sphere of influence. The restructuring of the early 1970s, which had brought into being The Board of World Mission, expropriated some major areas of the society's work but left in place the task of education, an important part of which had been carried out by AECs, appointed by the WMS (see Educating in Mission). In 1990, the task force on restructuring acknowledged the importance of the AECs.

> *An issue...is the crucial role, mandate and deployment of the area education consultants who have been key among the roles in which the* [missionary] *societies have been involved in Canada. The Societies are naturally anxious to preserve the mission/Christian education focus of the AECs work, and they recognize the importance of maintaining a sense of ownership to ensure financial and personal support for the programme.*[15]

In 1992, the WMS council reaffirmed the status of the AECs as employees of the society and in 1994 reiterated

> *...the determination of the Society to continue to provide the services of the Field Workers to the Presbyterian Church in Canada* [along with] *the absolute necessity to continue the employment of the present workers...*[16]

The problem was how to do this. The AECs were already in place in synodicals, and had been for many years, educating, informing, and providing leadership. Would they now be redundant? With the arrival of regional staffing, the parameters of the work were to be much broader. Workers were being called to serve as

> *...consultants for mission, education, youth ministry, pastoral care and congregational life.*[17]

Would existing workers need further training? To what body would regional staff be accountable? What would the WMS role be in the new configuration?

Efforts were made to address this last concern by ensuring WMS participation in the regional committees, which became the overseeing bodies for the new structure. In some instances this worked well, in others less so. Sometimes the issue was one of authority — who was answerable to whom? Whose was the final decision? Sometimes it was a matter of poor communication or groups that simply did not work well together. A council sub-executive meeting in September, 1994, noted that the WMS representation in the various regions needed more support and encouragement to stand up, speak up and be counted.

Another concern for the WMS was that of funding for regional staffing. The General Assembly had approved involving the WMS in ongoing financial support of the plan. How much money could the WMS realistically provide and for how long? Regional staffing required long-term commitments so that budgets could be worked out and long-term contracts drawn up. The society, faced with shrinking funds, felt it could only commit on a year-to-year basis. However, given its belief in the importance of the work, the WMS gave first priority to upholding it. At the annual meeting of the council in 2000, it was noted that the society was seeking to guarantee until 2003 its grant of $390,000 toward the support of regional staff.

In 1998, the Life and Mission Agency reported to the General Assembly on a review of regional staff and their work. While most synods and synodicals were positive about their experience of regional staffing, not all needs were being met. The report identified concerns about grants, accountability, ongoing funding, communication and the willingness of synods to carry their share of the load. The Life and Mission Agency recommended continuing consultation among the agency, the missionary societies and the

Regional staff
Back: Anne Yee Hibbs, Wayne Stretch, Kathy Ball, Gwen Brown, Wayne Menard, Spencer Edwards, Anita Mack, Keith Boyer
Front: Christine Ball, Margaret Wilson, Colleen Smith, Sidney Chang, Pat Allison

consultative committees with regard to vision, priorities and finances. A further review was slated for 2001.

While the WMS continues its financial support for regional staff, there is a growing concern about the ongoing function of the society in this area. Due to changing priorities, there appears to be less stress on, and less time for, traditional WMS emphases, such as educating in mission and support for auxiliaries. There is also no longer direct accountability to the society. This leads to a feeling of powerlessness in terms of decisions and outcomes. The society is left to wonder what connectedness or involvement it can realistically continue to have.

"One Stop Shopping"

A second aspect of the church's restructuring that had a direct and visible impact on the WMS had to do with resources and their distribution. As noted earlier, the WMS had for many years provided books and materials for its members through the WMS Book Room. The church had its own channel for producing and distributing materials, known as the Resource Distribution Centre. As early as 1985, there was dialogue between the two agencies about some form of joint operation. Under the guidelines for restructuring, it was proposed to amalgamate the two, in the hopes of streamlining the process and procedures.

In its report to the General Assembly of 1990, the task force on restructuring the agencies of the General Assembly noted that *some marginal gains might be made by integrating the...sales and distribution operations* and proposed consultation with the WMS on the matter.[18] Discussion continued over the next few years. In 1994, at the request of the Service Agency, Dorothy Ruddell, then manager of the WMS Book Room, undertook for a limited time to manage the Resource Distribution Centre as well. In 1996, the society discontinued the arrangement because of a drain on finances and also staff time and energy. By 1998, however, the two agencies were working toward a fully amalgamated operation.

Agreement to this idea had not come easily to the society. There was the inevitable suspicion of yet another takeover by the church, of loss of control by the society of its own operation and a recognition of the need for careful and unhurried negotiations. One comment was that the WMS often seemed to be picking up things that the church couldn't handle! The society was happy to co-operate with the church but not to do its work. It was also felt that, if the partnership were to succeed, the church needed to get its own house in order, in terms of how the distribution of resources could best be done. As well, issues of staffing, inventory and accountability needed to be addressed. However, in 1998, at the annual meeting of council, the following motion was proposed,

> *That there be a partnership between the Women's Missionary Society and The Presbyterian Church in Canada in order to provide One Stop Shopping...*[19]

This proposal had been under review for some time. The intention was to provide a consumer-friendly operation, which would be *efficient...economical and courteous.*[20] Existing personnel, from both WMS and the Resource Distribution Centre, would be brought together into a single unit, supervised by the manager of the WMS Book Room. Operating procedures would be simplified. A joint committee from the WMS and the Life and Mission Agency would supervise the process, with a review to take place at stated intervals. The new creation would be known simply as The Book Room.

The motion was carried and, after further negotiations with the Life and Mission Agency and approval by the General Assembly, One Stop Shopping became a reality in 1998. Naturally, there were, and are, inevitable hitches and glitches in the working out of the new system. The WMS personnel have been faced with a heavier workload than anticipated. Adjustments in the disposition of staff have sometimes caused resentment. Keeping all the customers happy is a perpetual challenge. Few people, however, would deny that there has been a change for the better. The Book Room moved to a new and better location. The resources, both church and WMS, are more readily available to a wider clientele. Sales have increased. A report from the Assembly Council notes that *the comments on The Book Room/Resource Centre were glowing.*[21]

The pros would seem to have outweighed the cons.

Children and Youth

A third impact of restructuring was felt in the area of work with children and young people. This had always been a primary focus for the WMS. As noted in Educating in Mission, an earlier form of the society's purpose spoke of

> ...[uniting] *the women, youth and children of the Church, in prayer, study and service for the advancement of the Kingdom of God at home and abroad.*

The first children's work secretary, Ada Adams, was appointed in 1940 and the first youth secretary, Grace Irvine, in 1953.

The WMS had involvement in Mission Bands, still remembered fondly by many for whom it was their first introduction to the idea of mission. When the older Mission Band children switched to being Explorers, the younger ones joined Children of the Church. The two groups were involved in mission studies and related activities. In addition, the WMS was involved with CGIT, many of whom became junior members of the society.

Programming for children and youth followed this predictable pattern for many years but with the changes in Canadian society as a whole the pattern inevitably faced challenges. Reports to the WMS council in the 1980s, for example, speak of fluctuating numbers and a membership that now goes beyond the four walls of the church. Lois Powrie, who became national secretary for Teenage and Children's Work for the WMS in 1979 and who was a powerful advocate for young people, spoke of the need for good leadership in the face of the challenge. In 1988, she writes,

> [There is] ***an urgent need to reassess what we are doing... AS A SOCIETY, we need once again to define what OUR goals are in terms of the growth in faith we want to see happen.*** *Adult members, Kirk Sessions in Congregations, Boards and Committees, and the Women's Missionary society, W.D.,* ***need to restate their reason for existence in terms of their responsibility for the growth and development of the children and youth with whom they come in contact every day.***[22]

In 1992, the WMS held a forum on ministry with children and youth. Out of this came a recommendation, presented to the General Assembly later the same year. It requested that

> *...the Life and Mission Agency, in consultation with the Women's Missionary Society(WD) and the Atlantic Mission Society, be asked to review the manner in which children's and teenage work within the Church is carried out, determining the future of mid-week groups, study the way this ministry will be carried out in the future and establishing policies and priorities.*[23]

The recommendation was adopted but there was a sense of frustration about the slow pace of the discussions. The Children and Teenage Working Group, reporting to council executive in 1994

> ...[makes] *a strong case for Children's work to be intentional about meeting the needs of children/youth or there will be no future for them. We have to be committed to be responsible and work in co-operation with L&M* [Life and Mission Agency] *in providing staff for C/Y* [Children and Youth] *programming.*[24]

Two motions came out of this meeting:

> *...that we reaffirm the WMS, WD's historic and continuing commitment to ministry with children and youth.*[25]
>
> *...that we endorse the creation of a position within the Life and Mission Agency that will focus on Ministry with Children and Teens and will be a shared responsibility of the WMS and the Life and Mission Agency.*[26]

In June, 1994, the Life and Mission Agency reported to the General Assembly on the work of a consultation on Ministry with Children and Youth. The goal of the consultation was

> *...to have at the end of its work a policy and priorities for children and youth ministry that have grown out of theological reflection, and that are functional and action oriented.*[27]

One part of the report speaks of work already in progress.

> *The WMS has had a contract person working in the area of ministry with children and youth one day a week. This person maintains some contact with and limited servicing of those involved in ministry with children and youth in our congregations. The WMS supports six Area Educational Consultants in various regions from Quebec to British Columbia. A part of their work is with children and youth.*
>
> *The Atlantic Mission Society employs an Executive Secretary. She has written resources for use with children and youth and provides support to group leaders. A diaconal minister is working in the Presbytery of Pictou. Her responsibilities include support for ministry with children and youth.*[28]

The report also notes the work of the Education for Discipleship team of the Life and Mission Agency whose task was to provide services for older youth and sustain the development of curricula, worship resources and leadership in church schools.

The consultation proposed the establishing of a working group for ministry with children and youth. This group was to include representatives of the mission societies and local congregations and work under the umbrella of the Life and Mission Agency. The 1994 General Assembly approved this as an interim solution, pending the appointment of Life and Mission program staff with responsibility for children, youth and families in the Education for Discipleship team. This was to take place *when funds are available.*[29]

As always, the issue of funding was crucial. In 1996, the WMS, still concerned about the delay in establishing a ministry for young people, designated $50,000 to be used to assist the Covenant Community for Children and Youth or CCCY (so named for the first time in 1996) to implement its program. Through this gift, the Life and Mission Agency was enabled to appoint an associate secretary with responsibility for Education for the Faith. 60% of the secretary's time would go to youth and camping programs and 40% to the CCCY. The WMS money ensured two years of this latter part of the work.

In 1998, a report to the WMS outlined the work of the CCCY. It *continues to support leaders in children and youth ministry in a variety of ways.*[30] These include the production of an annual learning/sharing project, which educates young people about specific mission areas and projects and encourages them to raise money for the projects. As well, the CCCY produces written material and videos and supports major youth initiatives, such as Triennium and Youth in Mission (YIM).[31] The society continues to co-operate with the Life and Mission Agency in the work with children and youth and provides ongoing financial support. In this way, it remains faithful to its historical commitment to the young people of the church.

Internal Affairs

Restructuring was not an exercise confined to the church. Over the years, the WMS also felt the need to reorganize. In the early days of the society, the council executive met weekly. Later that became monthly and then, in 1981, it was agreed that there would be three meetings of the executive between annual meetings. Membership on council executive was at one point redefined in response to financial constraints. The cost of travel to and from meetings and/or necessary accommodation came to determine the number of representatives from the more distant synodicals. Recognizing, however, that these areas had the right and need to be heard, the council made certain that they had adequate and ongoing representation at all meetings through their president or an alternate delegate. In 2001, Joanne Instance became the first westerner to be elected to the office of president of the society.

Some positions on council executive disappeared. In 1982, for example, the society discontinued the office of supply secretary at council level. As already recorded, in the early years WMS groups put together and shipped bales of clothing and other supplies to people in need. With an increase in transportation costs it was thought better simply to send money directly to the areas where the need was. After 1972, this money formed part of the WMS contribution to the work of The Board of World Mission and was intended to provide program materials for missionary staff as well as medical supplies and clothing for the people they served. Time made the office of supply secretary redundant and it was phased out.

The work of executive and support staff also changed over the years. In the regrouping of the society after 1925, there were four organization secretaries. As noted, a secretary for children's work was added in 1940. The first executive secretaries were appointed in 1947, one for national and one for overseas work. Later came an executive director of organization and a secretary for adult work. Sometimes the titles of the positions changed with the times.

After the retirement of Lois Powrie in 1992, no immediate replacement was sought. Ultimately, the position of secretary for teenage and children's work was eliminated and the work was then largely carried out through the Life and Mission Agency. In 1995, further streamlining took place. There were reductions in support staff and a new approach to the work of executive staff. The personnel committee reported to council executive in October, 1995, that, with regard to executive staff, it was endorsing *shared responsibility, team concept, and parity of stipends.*[32] The team consists of the executive secretary, program secretary, manager of The Book Room and editor of *Glad Tidings*, and provides the infrastructure for implementing the work of the society.

Changing Times

It is interesting to note the difference in response by the WMS to the upheaval in the 1970s, generated by the formation of The Board of World Mission, and to the upheaval caused by the restructuring of the agencies of the church in the 1990s. In the former instance, the society clearly had its doubts and problems but for the most part these were muted. There is little in the written records that expresses the dismay and confusion which were felt and are vouched for today by those who lived through the experience. The written records, for the most part, merely list the ultimate decisions. Faced with the challenges of the 90s, the WMS becomes far more vocal. It makes clear and unequivocal statements. It asks for explanations. It voices concerns and reservations. It negotiates terms. Ultimately, of course, it gets on with its accepted task of *cooperat*[ing] *with the agencies of Assembly in the life and work of the Church,* but not before making its point. Women are to be counted!

The Amount Available

For generations many women in The Presbyterian Church in Canada have felt led to give in a special way to the work and witness of the Women's Missionary Society. For most women, this is "second mile giving," over and above the support they or their families give to their local congregation and the outreach of the national church.

> *In the past, women of the Presbyterian Church gave to the W.M.S. to support "women's work" — work by women who sought primarily to assist other women and their children.*
>
> *Our mothers and grandmothers gave so that the knowledge of God's love...could reach people around the world who had never heard the Gospel; through their sacrificial giving many thousands were brought new life and hope...*
>
> *As members of the Women's Missionary Society today, we give — to support the work of men and women, ministers and lay people who are called to serve the Church through the Board of World Mission in Canada and throughout the world...to support our staff...*[and] *to support our society* [in its goals]...
>
> *As members of the Women's Missionary Society, we give of what God has given us, as good stewards of His bounty, as a symbol of the ties that unite us in mission with our sisters and brothers in a worldwide family, and as a reflection back to God of our heartfelt response to His overwhelming love for us, and all Creation, revealed in Jesus Christ our Lord.*[1]

This could well be called the "financial mission statement" of the WMS. Written in the mid-1980s, it provides an acceptable rationale for the steady flow of givings down the years. In many instances these givings truly were sacrificial, often going beyond what was required or expected.

Commitments

In its early days the WMS responded to immediate needs with an appeal to its membership for money, to be dedicated to those particular needs. As time passed, the structure of the society became more complex, involving administrative costs and a larger salaried staff, as well as responsibility for various missionaries and mission projects. Money continued to be raised, and still is raised, through voluntary contributions on the part of the members. This money, together with undesignated legacies and interest earned on investments, represents the society's only source of revenue. Official policy was, and is, that all monies raised by the auxiliaries should be forwarded to the general fund of the society to provide for its various commitments.

As of 2001, these commitments include a grant to *Presbyterians Sharing...*(the budget of the General Assembly) and a grant of up to $390,000 towards the funding of twelve regional staff positions across the country.[2] It is sometimes forgotten or ignored that the WMS contribution includes these two components. To this end delegates to the 2001 annual meeting of council recommended to the Life and Mission Agency that the annual statement of revenue and expense in the Acts and Proceedings acknowledge the amounts separately. This had not been the practice but the requested acknowledgment appeared in the 2002 Acts and Proceedings.

In addition, the WMS finances the provision of Christian literature to individuals and institutions throughout the world and of mission education resource personnel and materials to all parts of the church. It must also cover its administration costs, although these are kept as low as possible. In 1998, for example, only 13.1 per cent of the total income was applied to administration. Each year council executive presents budget proposals for the upcoming year, which are then approved, or not, by the WMS council at its annual meeting. In 2002, the society approved a budget of $1,070,550 for the following year.

Concerns

During the 1990s, finances became an urgent concern for the WMS. Like its parent body, The Presbyterian Church in Canada, the society faced the problem of declining membership and, consequently, shrinking revenue. There was a growing struggle to balance vision with reality and promised commitment with actual resources.

In 1972, under the terms of the setting up of The Board of World Mission, the councils of the WMS(WD) and WMS(ED) were asked to

> *...notify* [the] *Board annually the amount of money which these Councils feel they can make available for the work of the Board of World Missions in any given year.*[3]

During the 1970s, the WMS (WD) givings to the board went from $345,000 to $385,500 and by 1981 had reached the $400,000 mark. Clara Hogg, treasurer of the society, noted in 1979 that

> *The B.W.M. is very appreciative of the support we render, not only by our grant, but also by our prayers and concern that no urgent work will be withdrawn or curtailed due to insufficient support from us.*[4]

In the 1980s the grant to the board at one point went as high as $488,000. In the following decade, however, it fell dramatically. In the first instance this was due to the council decision to raise WMS staff salaries to a level closer to that of workers in other church agencies, a matter of no small importance. The amount of the grant was also often affected by the fiscal policies of the General Assembly in terms, for example, of certain mandatory benefits and allowances to be paid to church workers. Also, as noted above, falling revenue played a part.

The allocating of the society's money, therefore, had to be adjusted accordingly. In 1995 the amount of the grant to *Presbyterians Sharing...* was reduced to $200,000. In 1996, there was a further reduction to $150,000. Since then the amount of the grant has remained constant.

The Grant

The downsizing of the grant provoked much unhappiness among the membership. Some saw it as sacrosanct, something to be protected at all costs. To fail to meet that commitment would be to fail in the missionary purpose of the society. Indeed, in 1991 the council decided that, even faced with economic woes, the society should commit to raising the money needed for the total work, rather than *trim our work to fit the projected income.*[5]

From time to time it was suggested that any shortfall might be made up through tapping into the investments. A letter to *Glad Tidings* in 1993 notes that

> *I am deeply disturbed at the decision of the WMS Council Executive to reduce our commitment to BWM budget by $150,000 this year... Since we have assets in the General Legacy Fund well in excess of one million dollars, I strongly recommend that these funds be used as required to maintain the BWM budget at $400,000.*[6]

This was not an uncommon reaction. Many people in the society felt that a lot of money was simply lying fallow and unproductive in the bank. In reality, whatever of the investment money was available was already being used. The interest it earned was, for example, an essential part of the budget. As well, much of the investment money was inaccessible. Many of the legacies and endowments contributing to it had riders attached, which kept the money tied up.

Another suggestion was that the destination of the givings become more 'personalized.' In the early years, there was a strong sense of ownership on the part of WMS members. After the deduction of necessary administrative expenses, money raised went to a specific person or project. This generated interest and promoted relationship, which in turn had the potential to increase givings. When The Board of World Mission was formed, it received money from the WMS to finance salaries and grants, which were disbursed through the treasurer of The Presbyterian Church in Canada. Under the restructuring of 1991, WMS monies went into *Presbyterians Sharing...* from which is funded the work of the Life and Mission Agency. This work includes support of mission programs and personnel.

This arrangement caused confusion. Many WMS members believed that their givings were going directly to the missionaries and their work. This was the way it had been. This was the way they wanted it to be. The reality, however, was that, while some, if not indeed a large part, of the money might now still go directly to missionaries and their work, a part of it might equally well go to fund other aspects of the work of the church. The special committee on restructuring in its report to the General Assembly of 1992 stated:

> *The WMS representatives agreed to recommend to the WMS Council that it continue to contribute to the general funds of the Church.*[7]

These general funds could be used to cover everything from the purchase of computers to the wages of the company that cleaned the church offices to staff salaries.

What is Mission?

At issue was the definition of mission. In 1990, a resolution was sent to the WMS council annual meeting. It argued that WMS members were already supporting *Presbyterians Sharing...* through givings as members of a congregation. Since the purpose of the WMS was to be involved in local and world mission, the resolution proposed that

> *...the monies contributed by the Women's Missionary Society (WD) to The Presbyterian Church in Canada do not form part of the General Assembly Budget but be designated for and available to Mission Projects at home and overseas and guaranteed in total to the Agency of the General Assembly responsible for such projects.*[8]

The church's position was that everything that the church does can be defined as mission (including administration) and therefore, by implication, the WMS money was really going to mission. This was not how many in the society understood things.

The resolution was later withdrawn but the issue surfaced again in 1992. At the annual meeting of council resolutions were presented from the presbyterials of Winnipeg and Montreal. Winnipeg Presbyterial referred to the autonomy of the WMS (WD) in raising and spending its own money and flagged concerns about WMS givings in past years disappearing into the total budget of the church, rather than being designated exclusively for The Board of World Mission. The presbyterial proposed that

> *At this time of restructuring, we, as members of a Mission Society, wish to ensure that our monies go to specific Mission Projects and recommend that the Council Executive discontinue immediately the grant to The Presbyterian Church in Canada, and set up a policy whereby the Life and Mission Agency identify specific Mission Projects to the WMS (WD) Council, these to be considered annually at the Council Meeting. Only those accepted will be our obligation, and no lump sum grant be approved without identification of how it is to be spent.*[9]

Montreal Presbyterial had a similar argument based on

> *...an increasing desire among members of the Women's Missionary Society (WD) over the past several years to have more ownership of the funds raised by our groups and given as a grant to the budget of our national church...*[10]

The presbyterial asked that agencies of the church be invited to submit projects annually, a number of which the council would choose and recommend to the auxiliaries for direct support. Neither of the resolutions was approved.

However, in an effort to address the concern about ownership it was decided in 1994 to provide a new face for mission so that people could picture where their money was going. This would not take the form of 'designated giving,' by which money would be sent for specific people and/or projects, but it would be an educational process. The WMS would identify projects within the mission portfolio of the Life and Mission Agency, provide information about them and encourage the membership to relate to them. By such methods the WMS council hoped to meet the need for more personal involvement. It is interesting to note, however, that while many groups still obediently send the bulk of their donations to the General Fund, at the same time they may also support some extra project, which provides the personal touch and is often on the local level. The voice of the people speaks![11]

Creative proposals notwithstanding, however, the larger issue seems not yet to have been satisfactorily resolved for in 2001 a motion was passed at the WMS annual meeting,

> *...that the Women's Missionary Society petition the General Assembly, 2002 by an overture to designate the grant presently given to the General Funds of the Presbyterian Church in Canada to go directly to the Life and Mission Agency.*[12]

Looking Ahead

Despite these efforts, however, the problems of finances continue. This is due not to a failure in generosity but to shrinking membership. In 1997, the treasurer, Irene Nesbitt, noted that contributions to the society had declined each year by three percent. She identified the need to reduce expenditures and balance the budget. The society, however, tries hard to hold the line. The amount budgeted for *Presbyterians Sharing...* for 2002, and the support of regional staff amounted to $540,000. In addition, the society committed $10,000 toward the Life and Mission Agency's work with children and youth.

Of the three priorities targeted in 1999, one was finance. A task force was appointed to research how WMS givings should be allocated for local and national missions. Its report recommends ongoing review of the grant to the Life and Mission Agency and of the society's financial situation as a whole.

Landmarks

The story of the WMS from 1970 to 2001 has not been solely one of *angst* over identity or the struggle to reconstruct and reconfigure according to the decisions of the General Assembly, nor the effort to right the wrongs of the past. The life of the society has also been distinguished by innovations, achievements, celebrations and farewells.

75 Years Plus

In 1989 the society marked its 125th and its 75th anniversaries. It was 125 years since the formation of the Ladies Auxiliary Association in Montreal in 1864, and 75 years since the amalgamation of the three founding groups into the WMS in 1914. A celebration was held in London, Ontario with 400 women — not counting the men! — in attendance. The focus of the celebration was

- *to join together in worship and thanksgiving to God for seventy-five years of service through the Women's Missionary Society (WD);*
- *to celebrate our past and seek God's direction for the future;*
- *to learn about changes and developments in Mission and in the world to which we are commissioned to go and tell the Good News of our Lord Jesus Christ;*
- *to provide opportunities for fellowship, growth, challenge and encouragement.*[1]

Communion Cloth handwoven by Ernestine Allan of Vancouver, a special anniversary gift to WMS on behalf of the BC Synodical

Dr. Mary Malone, associate professor of religious studies at St Jerome's College in Waterloo, Ontario, was keynote speaker. The fact that Dr. Malone is a Roman Catholic theologian raised some eyebrows but her presence was symptomatic of the new spirit emerging in the society, a spirit which was trying to discard some of the limitations of the past and open the society to new possibilities. Dr. Malone's message was described as *empowering and liberating…to the men and women who gathered* [to hear it].[2]

To mark this anniversary the society launched a special project in support of a Presbyterian World Service and Development program in Lahore, Pakistan. The main purpose of the project was to provide health services for mothers and children. By the end of the campaign across the society more than $15,000 was raised. This was over and above the regular contributions to ongoing WMS commitments. *A Lively Story*, a history of the society was also published, written by Jean Campbell of Winnipeg with input from the synodicals and other contributors.

Two visual mementos of the anniversary were produced. One was a logo, designed especially for the occasion and based on the theme of the celebration Go and Tell. The other was a poster, portraying WMS women over the years and intended as a tribute to their Christian service and devotion. An editorial on the poster by June Stevenson perhaps embodies the "new spirit" that was a part of the celebration in London and also coloured some aspects

of the life of the society in the 1990s and beyond. The WMS was not immune to the influence of feminism!

> *No picture...can capture what the Women's Missionary Society is and has been through the years. At best it is a reflection of the intrinsic nature of a group...*
>
> *We are, and have been, women of humility and subservience. For this we need not apologize. We have often been perceived as being weak in our position but strong in our determination. In our naivete we have not always recognized or used our power and influence. Pushed into these roles by patriarchal structures and the role of women through the various eras, we have nevertheless had a strong presence in the Church... Certainly we have always sought to be faithful and consistent in carrying out our purpose.*[3]

Gathering to Learn

There were other conferences through the years which promoted fellowship, discussion and the opportunity for personal growth. These were held across the country and attracted both members and non-members of the WMS, men and women alike. Speakers included missionaries, theologians, clergy and laity and, on one occasion, a clown! Some WMS members also participated in conferences outside of the society. In 1982, for example, the society was represented at a gathering called The Female Connection, held in Thunder Bay, Ontario under the sponsorship of the Women's Inter-Church Council of Canada. The goal of this conference was to *educate participants in the women's experience — non-Canadian, multi-generational, immigrant Canadian and native Canadian women...*[4]

A conference in Minneapolis in 1996, The Third Re-Imagining Community Gathering, created much controversy in both WMS and church circles. Two WMS members attended this event and the society supplied a small

Guests and executive stand in front of the River of Faith: Joan Parajon, Grace Jess, Norah Masopha, Deborah Tezlo, Joan Sampson

grant to help with their expenses. In an article, "Biting the Apple," they describe the main thrust of the program as the encouraging of women

> *...to claim* [their] *power and to use it — not to exploit or dominate, but as power shared in the work of justice.*[5]

The article also refers to the conference's emphasis on Sophia as *a new and liberating image of God in the feminine*[6] and to the use of a ritual of milk and honey which would promote healing of the heart through the gospel message. Many people found these ideas disturbing. One reader wrote on the subject to *Glad Tidings*, saying *'Biting the Apple' is NOT Glad Tidings!*[7]

The Ecumenical Decade

The Re-Imagining Gathering was organized by a coalition of churches in the United States in connection with the Ecumenical Decade of Churches in Solidarity with Women. This was a World Council of Churches project, spanning the years between 1988 and 1998. The goal was to identify the obstacles to women's full participation in church and society, remove such obstacles and affirm the vision and contribution of women, thereby sharing in God's world-transforming activities.[8]

The WMS was supportive of the ideals and work of the Ecumenical Decade. Its issues and progress were given wide coverage in *Glad Tidings*. Although the society did not organize events or programs on its own, it did uphold the efforts of others. A mid-decade event was one such effort. This was held at Ewart College in 1994 and had as guest speaker Dr. Vera Chirwa, at that time the longest serving political prisoner in Malawi. In 1995, a World Council of Churches team visited The Presbyterian Church in Canada and met with Canadian Presbyterians, including Barbara Woodruff, secretary for adult education for the WMS. The focus of the visit was to assess the response of churches to the Decade's vision. Margaret Robertson, program secretary of the society, attended the 1998 Decade Festival in Harare, Zimbabwe, organized to mark the end of the Decade. Delegates participated in preparing a letter to the Eighth Assembly of the World Council of Churches dealing with, among other things, gender issues, the impact of war and violence on women and children, sexual exploitation and debt cancellation. Margaret notes that

> *The end result was stronger than we expected. Could this be* [a] *miracle? It was definitely the work of God's hand.*[9]

Peaks and Valleys

Important milestones were marked by the society in the decades between 1972 and 2002. In that period some auxiliaries celebrated their 100th birthday,

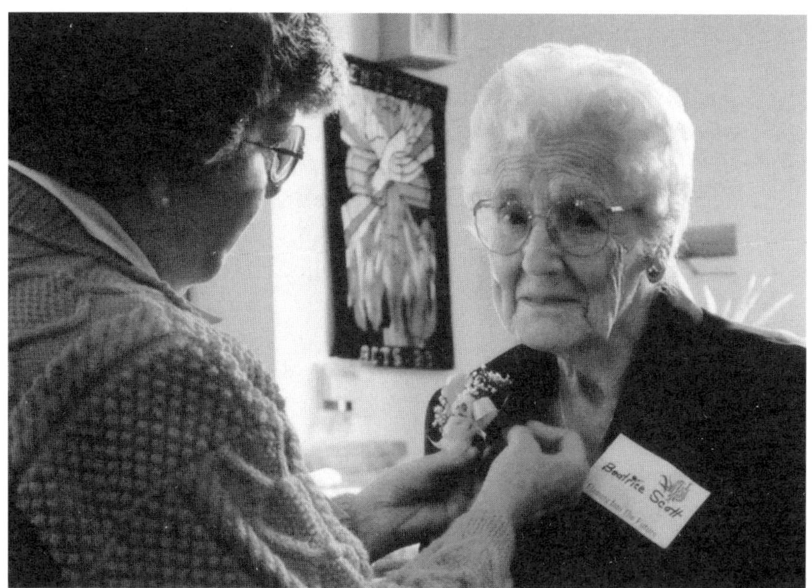

Eleanor (Knott) Crabtree and Bea Scott celebrating the 60th anniversary of Bea's designation, 2000

while some achieved their 110th. There were retirees to honour. There were the deaths of many faithful workers to record, often marking the end of an era. To name only a few — Margaret Kennedy, Irene Stringer, Margaret Leask, Mavis Hyndman, Ellen Douglas, Beatrice Scott, Mary Sherrick, Margaret Ramsay, Mildred Gehman and Hildur Hermanson were overseas missionaries. Louise Reith, Mabel Booth, Laura Pelton, Mary Whale, Barbara Woodruff, Lois Powrie and Ada Adams served as executive staff. Ruby Walker, Loreen Leatherdale, Lillian Reay and Margaret Boyd worked in the national mission field. All these and many other workers and members across the country are remembered with love, respect and gratitude for their commitment to the society, the church and the gospel.

In the same period, the WMS chalked up some interesting firsts. In the 1990s it elected as president two women who worked outside the home — Joan Sampson, who worked part-time, and Rosemary Doran, who worked full-time. This was a departure from tradition and practice. However, it aligned the society with the world of many of its members — or those whom the society wanted to attract as members — a world where women had to juggle many roles and many tasks, balancing the demands of career, family and church. Rosemary was also the first ordained minister to be president. The society had, of course, for some time supported ordained ministers as regional staff and many of its workers over the years have been deaconesses/

Pauline Brown

diaconal ministers. Several of these have gone on to become ministers of word and sacraments.

Another milestone for the society was the election of Tamiko Corbett as moderator of the 122nd General Assembly in 1996. Tamiko, a diaconal minister, had served as regional secretary for the WMS in British Columbia and also worked with the Korean Christian Church in Japan. She was executive secretary of the society from 1993 to 1996. The WMS presented Tamiko with her moderatorial robe, and Rosemary Doran, president at the time, took part in the installation.

In 2001, the WMS shared in the celebrations for Pauline Brown on the occasion of her receiving the Order of Canada. At that time, Pauline was the longest serving missionary of The Presbyterian Church in Canada with 50 years of service in India.

The history of any society or organization is not only a record of dates and decisions. It is, more importantly, the story of people and how they live out the principles and values and vision of their group. The WMS has much to celebrate in this respect.[10]

Residential Schools

I'm bloody tired of having to absorb guilt for the mistakes of the Church in the past in relation to native peoples, said a church delegate.

We know we made mistakes and I want to redress them; otherwise I wouldn't be here… I guess we just have to learn to trust you again, quietly answered an elderly Aboriginal person from the Northwest Territories.[1]

The speakers were attending a unique get-together in 1976 when, for the first time in their history, The National Indian Brotherhood, The Native Council of Canada and the Inuit Tapisirat of Canada met with representatives of the major Christian denominations in Canada to explore

> *…native issues ranging from spirituality to the rights of Indian women*[2]

and to find ways for the Christian church to stand beside the Aboriginal people in their struggles and journey.

The words and sentiments — expressing frustration, guilt, regret, betrayal, perhaps the beginning of hope — could have been repeated in a 1990s scenario. At issue was a specific struggle, a specific part of the journey, that of the impact of residential schools on the children who had been sent there and on the Aboriginal community as a whole. It was a scenario which involved several of the major denominations, including The Presbyterian Church in Canada and the Women's Missionary Society, Western Division, as an agency of that church.

In the Beginning...

The basis of the work of both the church and the society in the early years was the idea that if Aboriginal people were exposed to Gospel teachings, their lives must improve. One way to accomplish this was simply to preach and teach in the customary mission tradition and this, indeed, did produce converts. The gospel message was embraced. Churches were established. Children were baptized.

As part of the policy of the government of the day, which called for the "civilizing" and assimilating of Aboriginal people into the mainstream of society, children from Aboriginal families were placed in residential schools. The churches were given the responsibility of overseeing the schools. From the perspective of the churches this provided yet another opportunity to fulfill Christ's mandate to "go to all peoples everywhere and make them my disciples" (Good News Bible, Matthew 28:19). The children were exposed to the ways and beliefs of Christianity, albeit a Christianity as understood and practised by a largely Eurocentric church. The intention was to create "indigenous missionaries," whose task it would be to carry the message back to family and community.

The WMS has a long history of involvement with Aboriginal people, as is outlined in earlier chapters. After 1925, The Presbyterian Church in Canada retained responsibility for Birtle School in Manitoba and Cecilia Jeffrey School in Ontario. The WMS provided whatever financing was not covered by government grants and was also involved in administering the schools. Changes in government policies over the years led to the closure of many schools and residences so that, by 1964, both the church and the society were no longer directly involved in the work. This was not, however, the end of the story. What had begun as a vision for mission became a nightmare of allegations of wrongdoing, exploitation and abuse. Where people believed they were sowing in love, later generations found themselves, often in bewilderment, reaping a harvest of anger and despair, of hatred and shame.

The Up Side

For some, the system brought positive results, as earlier chapters of this story relate. Steve Robinson, principal at Cecilia Jeffrey School from 1958-1966, comments that many Aboriginal people who speak out today would not have the ability to do so if it were not for the residential schools.[3] At the Sacred Assembly of 1995[4] a few Aboriginal speakers acknowledged the benefits of their education in such schools. One Aboriginal delegate sought out the Presbyterians in the assembly and was happy to reunite with Rev. Jim Marnoch and his wife, Irene, who had been associated with the Cecilia Jeffrey School in the late 1950s and early 1960s. Others have also, over the years, publicly recognized a good outcome from their education at the schools, an education which was, in fact, actively pursued by some of the Aboriginal communities for their children. A report to the WMS council executive speaks of those

> *...who, in spite of having some unhappy memories, in retrospect expressed very positive appreciation of the school experience. They now recognize the value of the care and discipline given in love.*[5]

Kay Blake, a teacher and nurse at the Cecilia Jeffrey School, recalls some of the drawbacks of the situation — persistent disease, cockroaches, inadequate staffing — but notes good relations with the local band chief.[6] She also has a positive perspective on her work.

> *In my 18 years' experience at the residential schools, I never encountered a problem arising from discipline.*[7]

Another Kay, Kay Rusaw, talks of the successes of students from the Birtle school, some of whom became teachers, nurses, administrators, lawyers, artists. She specifically refers to Colin Wasacase who *was one of our best supervisors* and later principal of the Cecilia Jeffrey School, Gordon Williams who became a Presbyterian minister, and Stanley McKay who became a United Church minister and moderator of the United Church of Canada.[8] Gordon Williams, in telling his own story, refers to the encouragement he and other students received from Kay Rusaw and her husband, who was principal at Birtle School.[9]

The Down Side

On the other hand, Rev. Stanley McKay has reservations about his experience. He acknowledges that the churches acted out of love but is critical of the results.

> *The place was well intended,* [he says,] *but it was devastating for native children to be pulled out of their culture and away from their language for the purpose of 'making them human beings.'*[10]

Thus, for too many, the system became a horror story. Children were taken from the reserves and often found themselves far from home and cut off from tradition and language. An Aboriginal woman says

> *The disadvantages of my experience* [were] *the loss of my heritage, my culture and the way of life of my ancestors, and most of all my identity as a once proud First Nation Ojibway woman.*[11]

In a report to the 120th General Assembly entitled "Reconciliation with Aboriginal Peoples,"[12] the Life and Mission Agency notes that the children were also exposed to a discipline far different from what they were accustomed to, one based on punishment and enforcement (which tended to be the norm in the European-settled society) rather than on mediation and conciliation (which was practised by the Aboriginal people). This approach was to have disastrous consequences for all the denominations which had agreed to administer the residential schools. In 1991, The Presbyterian Church in Canada was directly implicated in allegations of abuse at the Birtle School during the 1950s. The allegations were made devastatingly public on a television interview show. The age of innocence, for the church at least, was over. Too many Aboriginal people felt they had lost their innocence long before.

Dealing with the Fallout

In the report mentioned above, the Life and Mission Agency speaks of cultural norms, which change from one generation to the next, from one place to the next, and comments that

> *...nevertheless, Aboriginal peoples hold us accountable for the words and actions of our predecessors, even though they might have been within accepted standards of behaviour for that time.*[13]

This accountability has led the church into doing damage control, presenting a confession, defending itself in lawsuits, and working toward the healing of both church and Aboriginal communities. The WMS has actively participated in this process.

Damage control became necessary in the wake of the flood of accusations about neglect, abuse and exploitation that began to come from Aboriginal people in the early 1990s. It was hard for many in the church and the WMS to accept the claim that bad things had been done in their name. There were expressions of anger as well as concern for faithful workers through the years. The report to council executive in October, 1992 (referred to above) defended the actions and reputations of

> *...those who, by their very nature as Christians, gave loving care to their young charges. It does not say much for us as a caring Christian*

community if we repudiate those faithful servants, allowing their memory to be besmirched by that of those who acted otherwise. While not denying that some abuse took place, we wish to note that there is a distinction between the actions of faithful, trustworthy individuals and the actions of those who were guilty of reprehensible behaviour.[14]

In response to articles on the issue in both *Glad Tidings* and the *Presbyterian Record*, one person wrote,

I agree that many mistakes were made but the situation was entirely without precedent. There was no pattern to go by. The church was confronted with an entirely new situation and they did what seemed to be for the best at considerable expense and effort on their part. Apologize? For doing one's best? Over my dead body![15]

In October of that year another correspondent said

I am still very upset about your desecration of the dedicated people who gave their heart and soul to serving in Indian Residential Schools…[16]

The church, recognizing this genuine pain, included in its confession a section which recognized the

…many members of The Presbyterian Church in Canada who, in good faith, gave unstintingly of themselves in love and compassion for their aboriginal brothers and sisters. We acknowledge their devotion and commend them for their work.

At the same time, the document opens the door to the legitimacy of the Aboriginal claim by noting that

…we recognize that there were some who, with prophetic insight, were aware of the damage that was being done and protested, but their efforts were thwarted. We acknowledge their insight…[17]

With Hindsight

Some of this insight came from staff in the field. Sheina Smith, for example, working for the WMS at Shoal Lake, Ontario, writes in May, 1973 about the church's approach to Aboriginal people, and sees wrongs done in the name of assimilation and Christianization.

We never recognized that [the Aboriginal people] *had something to give. We judged them by our own needs and desires; in other words,expected them to be like us.*[18]

This is a theme which surfaces repeatedly. Rev Florence Palmer, appointed to the Fellowship Centre at Kenora, Ontario, addressed the WMS(WD) council meeting in 1985 and said,

While most missionaries went out to serve among Canadian Indians in…a manner of love and caring, they did not always approach their work in this spirit. Among non-native people little or no effort was made to understand Indian cultures and heritage. The innate spirituality of many tribes was either ignored or condemned… As a result, there was little attempt by non-native people in general to "sit where they sat." Rather there was an insistence that the Native People must learn to sit where **we** *sat — that they must become carbon copies of us and mould their lives after ours.*[19]

Marjorie Ross, member of The Board of World Mission, writing in 1981, quotes from an article by Rev. Zander Dunn in the *Presbyterian Record*. Mr. Dunn notes that

…we have talked to Indians over the years earnestly, but without perceiving that they really didn't understand…we talked down to them, seldom recognizing their basic human dignity and equality with us, unless they consented to becoming "white" Indians…[20]

Mrs. Ross suggests that this last phrase is the key to understanding the communication gap between the church and the Aboriginal people.

…we assumed that their hope was to become like us. We thought that with enough education they would become first 'white Indians', and later dark-skinned 'Canadians', just like us.[21]

She adds that, since Aboriginal people see themselves as community rather than as individuals, they are suspicious of those who would draw individuals out of that community. With hindsight it is easy, then, to have some idea of the resistance of many Aboriginal people to the whole idea of residential schools and their hostility toward them.

The Church Confesses

The Presbyterian Church in Canada came to its confession out of a sense of the need to try to set things right. The final format came into being after much soul- and mind-searching (See Appendix D). There was the need to say what could be, and ought to be, properly said while allowing for changes in attitudes, philosophies, policies and values over the years. In the end, the confession was issued in response to…*the Holy Spirit, speaking in and through Scripture,* [and] *call*[ing] *The Presbyterian Church in Canada to confession.*[22]

The confession spoke to perceived errors in government policies and church attitudes in pursuit of assimilation. It acknowledged arrogance, paternalism and an unwarranted sense of superiority on the part of the church in relation to Aboriginal peoples, their beliefs and culture. In addition, the confession deplored the mistreatment of Aboriginal children with the subsequent loss of cultural and personal identity for those children. The confession ends with expressions of regret and a prayer for forgiveness from Aboriginal people and from God.

In 1992, the WMS was invited to discuss the proposed confession with the right to concur or not. The delegates to the annual council meeting eventually gave their agreement to the statement, though one member of council executive resigned over the issue. In 1994, the president of the WMS, Kay Cowper, was present in Winnipeg, when the Moderator of The Presbyterian Church in Canada, Dr George Vais, presented the confession to Phil Fontaine, Grand Chief of the Assembly of Manitoba Chiefs. The WMS delegation included Tamiko Corbett, executive secretary, and June Stevenson, editor of *Glad Tidings.*

Mrs. Cowper spoke of the society's long association with Aboriginal peoples and of the contribution of the workers who had given so much of themselves in the work at the residential schools. She also said

> *Our ministry with you was given in love and with the best intentions, to share God's love... We are truly sorry for the hurt that was inflicted on some of your people. It was not our intention to hurt but to love.*[23]

The confession was accepted by a former student of the Birtle School on behalf of other former students. Grand Chief Fontaine acknowledged the difficulties in the situation, both for the church and for his own people, reminding those present that it was still early in the journey but noting that the confession was an important step towards healing and represented *the hope of a brighter future.*[24]

Practical Steps

Some steps in the healing process were initiated by the church. The Journey to Wholeness campaign was set up by the General Assembly in 1994 to facilitate healing experiences. Part of the campaign involved a Healing Fund. The fund finances projects and processes which aim at repairing damaged lives and relationships and are in keeping with Aboriginal thought and tradition. In 1997, the WMS made a one-time contribution of $30,000 to this fund and provides personnel for the committee overseeing grants.

In a letter to congregations in November, 2000 pertaining to the church's ongoing involvement in healing and reconciliation, Rev. Stephen Kendall, Principal Clerk of the General Assembly, noted the work at Anamiewigummig in Kenora, at Flora House and Anishinabe Fellowship in Winnipeg and with the Saskatoon Native Circle Ministry in Saskatoon. He also referred to an examination of the church's work among Aboriginal people, being undertaken by the National Native Ministries Committee of Canada Ministries. The WMS supports these initiatives. It is also represented on the Residential Schools Working Group, which continually monitors the issues, and from time to time the society provides money to help in various related projects. One of these, for example, is the production by Interchurch Communications of a series of videos, designed to create awareness and discussion of the residential schools question. A small sub-committee of the council executive was involved, at the invitation of the Life and Mission Agency, in planning a healing event, which was held in April 2002, for church workers who had been hurt and distressed by the accusations against the work they undertook in residential schools on behalf of the church and the society.

On the down side of the issue, The Presbyterian Church in Canada finds itself the defendant in several court cases connected with the Birtle and Cecilia Jeffrey schools, though none, at time of writing, has gone to trial.[25] Mr. Kendall in his letter notes that

> *All* [cases] *allege cultural abuse, all are civil suits and a few allege physical and/or sexual abuse. No criminal charges or convictions have been present with respect to these suits or related to our schools.*

Right or Wrong?

In the article "No Clean Hands," Rev. Ray Hodgson, then general secretary for Church and Society of The Presbyterian Church in Canada, Rev. Ian Morrison, then general secretary of Canada Operations for The Board of World Mission, and June Stevenson, editor of *Glad Tidings*, tell of their encounters with Aboriginal people in the context of the residential schools situation. They met with people on both sides of the question, staff members and former students. The stories were often quite different. Regarding who is right and who is wrong in the recounting of such stories, the editor of the *Presbyterian Record* comments that both sides can believe they are right.

> *One side downgrades what happened. The other side embellishes what happened. The truth is somewhere in between.*[26]

"*I guess we just have to learn to trust you again,*" said the old Indian. It is in the areas of truth and trust that the church and the WMS continue to work, striving to come to terms with the missionary endeavours of the past and the opportunities of the future. Having acknowledged mistakes, they are committed to correcting them where possible and to rebuilding a right relationship with Aboriginal people.

Bishop Gordon Beardy of the Anglican Church of Canada, addressing the General Assembly in 1999, told of his own experience at the Cecilia Jeffrey School. It was a story of a child's loneliness, of anger and brokenness and of

Bishop's Beardy's struggle, as an adult, to come to terms with his emotional pain. In his conclusion he said,

> *I have had very mixed emotions coming here. One side of me was telling me to run. This is the first time I have met the people who ran the residential school of Celia* [sic] *Jeffrey School.*
>
> *The other side of me said it is time to come to meet you, to speak about hope, walking together, grieving and healing together, and journeying together toward wholeness.*
>
> *I have come, though it is hard, and often difficult…*
>
> *I extend my hand to those who meant well and grieve today. Both of our people need healing…*
>
> *My hope is that we will journey together…*[27]

Today's Missionaries

Bob Stinson was an elder in Westminster St. Paul's Church in Guelph, Ontario. His story appeared in the February, 2001 issue of the *Presbyterian Record*. After retiring from his teaching career, Bob volunteered to teach in a secondary school in Livingstonia, Malawi, introducing computer technology to staff and students alike. Bob's home congregation became involved with the school, providing a computer and printer to complement his teaching and setting up a scholarship fund for needy students. The article noted that *Bob gained much from his experience.*[1] So, no doubt, did the people he met in Livingstonia.

Bob Stinson's story illustrates a new way of doing mission. Perhaps, of course, in some ways mission never changes. For the Christian it is always a response to the call of Christ to share the gospel, as she or he understands and experiences it. In 1972, with the formation of The Board of World Mission, the WMS ceased to have direct responsibility for appointing missionaries. Nonetheless, the members of the society continued to foster personal relationships with the missionaries of the church, often through letter-writing. Many missionaries have spoken of the great sense of support this gave them, especially when they were serving overseas. Cathy Victor, for example, in her paper on "The Women's Missionary Society, Past, Present and Future" notes that

> *In a conversation with Linda Inglis, who is now serving in Malawi with her husband Glenn, she made it very clear that the support of the WMS made all the difference for them.*[2]

The Church at Work

During the 1970s, much of the international mission work of The Presbyterian Church in Canada took place in India, Taiwan, Japan and Nigeria. There was also a limited presence in Jamaica and Malawi. In the 1980s work was continuing in India, Taiwan, Japan and Nigeria but there had been expansion in Africa into Mauritius, Cameroon, Malawi, Kenya and Lesotho. Missionaries also served in Nepal and Guyana. By 2000, while work was ongoing in India, Nepal, Japan and Taiwan, as well as many parts of Africa, The Presbyterian Church in Canada had become more involved in Central America and the Caribbean. Missionaries were working in Cuba, Granada, Nicaragua, El Salvador and Puerto Rico. There was also an opportunity to be active to a limited extent in the People's Republic of China, and there were projects in Europe, in Romania and Ukraine.

Nationally, mission work over the three decades took the form of ministries to ethnic groups — Chinese, French, Hungarian, Italian, Korean and Ukrainian. Toward the end of the period the church was also working with people of Portuguese, Ghanaian and Spanish-speaking origins. There was also ministry with Aboriginal people, or 'Indian Work', as it is termed in a 1972 list. In addition, the church worked in the inner city, provided hospital visitors, chaplains on university campuses and in the armed forces, and established programs to assist refugees and immigrants. Some of these latter programs were discontinued in the 1990s, when the national church experienced funding problems. In some cases, the projects were picked up by local congregations or presbyteries. The work of Christian education and education for mission was also important in this period and was often carried out by area educational consultants (or their equivalents) with WMS input (see previous chapters).

It might then be said that between 1970-2001, the mission work of the church was 'business as usual,' and this clearly is true to an extent. The church continued to operate in areas where, for the most part, it had established roots. In another sense, however, the statement is not true. While the 'where' of mission may have remained fairly constant, the 'how' did not.

Bob Stinson is a case in point. He was a volunteer on a short-term appointment. Volunteers are not new on the mission field. A 1972 list of church workers overseas names three volunteers — but their numbers have grown. While many missionaries chose, and do choose, to spend long years in their given field, others, no less inspired and dedicated, may feel called to a shorter time commitment. Those who go as volunteers receive travel expenses to and from the field of service and a minimum living allowance instead of a full-time salary and benefits.

The International Scene

Bob Stinson went to Malawi primarily as a teacher, rather than as an evangelist or 'missionary' in the conventional sense of the term. This change in designation has been a response to political situations. In many countries today the missionary is *persona non grata*. Many governments do not welcome missionaries and some forbid open missionary activity. Writing in *Glad Tidings* in 1973, Louis de Groot, chairman of The Board of World Mission, identifies the problem in terms of India.

> *Some of* [the states in India] *have passed legislation which is very restrictive regarding conversion from one religion to another. Heavy fines and imprisonment may result from non-observance of these restrictions.*[3]

Later that year, Jean (Brown) Sonnenfeld, a diaconal minister, who served in Japan, said

> *The United Mission in Nepal* [in which Canadian Presbyterians have served] *is made up of representatives of thirty-three different Churches from eighteen different countries. As foreigners, they do not try to incur the wrath of their host country, by preaching their religion. They do, however, obey Christ's injunction to heal the sick and feed the hungry.*
>
> *Nevertheless, each foreigner coming to Nepal to work with the United Mission must settle for himself the problem of demonstrating his love and concern without mentioning Christ, his motivator.*[4]

Demonstrating that love and concern brought Dr. Jack McIntosh into conflict with the authorities in Japan. Jack and his wife, Beth, served for many years with the Korean Christian Church in Japan. The Alien Registration Law in that country requires Koreans (classified as aliens although many were born in Japan) to be fingerprinted. This law is not applicable to Japanese citizens and is viewed as discriminatory by many people.

In order to identify with the cause of their Korean colleagues and friends, Jack McIntosh refused to be fingerprinted. His application for a visa extension was rejected and, knowing that if he left Japan, he could not return, he simply opted not to leave at all. His decision was to stay and, through the courts, fight the ruling. The case dragged on for many years. Writing in 1990, Jack said,

> *Sometimes I feel like shouting to heaven, "How long, O Lord?"... One body, one life is all I have, so the long race demands my careful choice of the times and places when I stand with friends and neighbours for real fairness and responsible change at public forums.*[5]

Although the case was eventually dismissed, some changes have been made in the fingerprinting laws as a result and the cause of human rights has

Jack and Beth McIntosh

been advanced. The McIntoshes eventually returned to Canada. At the 2001 General Assembly, the Moderator of the Korean Christian Church in Japan made a presentation to them in tribute to their long years of service among his people. Less than 48 hours later, Jack died. His long race was over.

The Missionary Today

In those countries where 'the missionary' is no longer as welcome as she or he once was, or is actively excluded, there is often still the need for people with specific skills in traditional and developing fields, such as technology, medicine, industry, agriculture etc. The *Presbyterian Record* of January, 2001, for example, carried this advertisement,

> *Are you an accountant in retirement looking for a challenge? Blantyre Synod, Malawi, is in need of your expertise for three years...*[6]

As a result, Christians with experience in many different fields are able to share their expertise in a significant way and, if circumstances permit, also witness openly to their faith. Today, The Presbyterian Church in Canada helps to support a veterinarian and a nutritionist in Nicaragua, a music consultant in Malawi, a doctor in Kenya who focuses on HIV/AIDS prevention, and a professor of humanities/bioethics in Taiwan. Where possible, the more traditional work of mission — in hospitals, schools, communities, seminaries and congregations — is also encouraged and supported. It is, thus, both 'business as usual' and 'not business as usual.'

A New Relationship

There has been another significant shift in the 'how' of doing mission. In earlier days it is probably fair to say that churches and missionaries, afire for the cause, took the Christian message into areas previously unaware of that message and vigorously persuaded people into faith. There was an urgency about their task, a conviction about its innate rightness and its superiority to other forms of belief. Changing times and philosophies have necessitated a new approach.

John Congram in *This Presbyterian Church of Ours* notes that

> *...in the 1960s...the way mission was done began to undergo a radical shift.*[7]

Speaking of the work of Rev. E.H. (Ted) Johnson, well-known for his passion for mission, Mr. Congram writes

> *He* [Ted Johnson]*...sensed the direction in which the world was moving and the opportunities it presented to the church. He encouraged the development of indigenous churches and a changed position for the missionary to a supportive role to leaders in the indigenous church.*[8]

Rev. Agnew Johnston, writing in 1973, said

> *Most of us know that many of the old mechanics of mission must be greatly altered in these seventies, and perhaps, many of the old and once effective Church missionary structures must be completely restructured, or better still, quietly dissolved.*[9]

In the same issue of *Glad Tidings* another writer affirms that mission remains what it has always been but also identifies a new element in the situation. In many cases the churches planted by the first missionaries grew into self-sustaining institutions with indigenous leadership. This inevitably altered the relationship between the "planter" and the "planted." Pauline Brown highlighted the change in an interview for *Glad Tidings* in 1977. She said

> *When I first went to work in India the Medical officer at Jobat Hospital was a foreigner, the Director of Nursing was a foreigner and there were foreigners among the nursing staff. Now all of these positions are held by Nationals. Expatriots* [sic] *serve only in these positions in a temporary capacity to enable Indian staff to upgrade their qualifications...*[10]

The churches, aware of this challenge, had been at work on it for some time (see Changing Times). Over the latter half of the 20th century and into the 21st, the key word in mission has been "partnership." In her article "Mission in the Context of Relationship," Clara Henderson, who works with the

Church of Central Africa Presbyterian, discussed this in connection with The Presbyterian Church in Canada.

> *Relationship or Partnership, as our Church calls it, is at the heart of the present mission activity of our church. All of the churches we are involved with overseas are mature autonomous Christian churches which are under indigenous leadership and which may have a history of Christian witness spanning three or four generations...*[11]

Partnership results in mission which is a two-way street. Churches help one another, sharing vision and experience. 'Missionaries' and/or 'experts' in any given field are available on a reciprocal basis. This can be challenging. In inviting visitors from a daughter church, The Presbyterian Church in Canada has sometimes found itself on the receiving end of the gospel message and been forced to confront some hard truths about itself and the society in which it operates. At the same time, the church has experienced the love of the 'daughter' for the 'mother.' In 1998, a letter was received from the Presbyterian Church in Taiwan. It said in part,

> *We have heard that many people in Canada are suffering from the effects of a terrible ice storm... On behalf of the Presbyterian Church in Taiwan, I am pleased to send the enclosed cheque for US$7,700. Please use it to help bring relief to people whose daily lives have been dislocated by a lack of electricity and water, and who are waiting for help in the deep cold conditions of a Canadian winter. Your Christian brothers and sisters want to be of help, as your church has always been ready to help when we in Taiwan have needed it.*[12]

The Home Front

On the national front, changes in the 'how' of mission are less obvious, perhaps because of the difference in context. National mission work is not subject to the regulations of foreign governments and so, for the most part, there is freedom to preach the gospel in word as well as in deed. There has been, however, a heightened sensitivity to the character of different groups from diverse ethnic and cultural backgrounds and perhaps here the partnership model is at work. Such groups are recognized and celebrated for what they can bring to the existing church, rather than being seen as targets for assimilation. The partnership model has also had an impact on the relationship between the church and the Aboriginal people. In light of the issue of the residential schools, the church has had to take an especially long, hard look at earlier missionary motivation and methods. As a result, there has been a move toward dialogue and co-operation as a way of promoting the necessary healing and reconciliation for both sides.

Many national mission staff work in congregations, providing, for example, pastoral care, education in the faith, leadership training and developing new churches. A new venture in mission has been the establishing of house churches in the Cariboo region of British Columbia. Another initiative is the developing ministry to those who live in boarding homes. Begun in Toronto in 1996 in response to community needs, this ministry is now spreading to other cities. There is also a growing involvement in the field of parish nursing which reaffirms the healing ministry of the church and its concern for the whole person.

A new program, which applies to both national and international settings, is Youth In Mission. This had its beginnings in 1983. Its purpose is to inspire and equip young people to become involved in mission opportunities.

> *Volunteers serve as short-term volunteers in many areas — from leading a Vacation Bible School to building a house, from cutting grass to leading a youth group, from making beds to teaching a musical.*[13]

The WMS provided $8,000 toward the initial funding of YIM.

The Role of WMS

WMS involvement in the new ways of doing mission is less hands-on than it once was. The society provides funding for the work through its contributions to *Presbyterians Sharing…* and also sometimes through direct grants to people involved in specific projects. However, WMS members remain informed about, interested in and concerned for all of the church's missionaries, whether old-style or new-style.

Who Are We?

O wad some power the giftie gie us To see oursel's as others see us!

So wrote the Scottish poet, Robert Burns, in the 18th century. It is wise, however, to be careful what one wishes for. The story is told of a minister asking some children what the letters WMS meant. Back came the reply "Women Making Sandwiches!" This is not exactly how the WMS wants to be seen, even if there is some truth in the perception. WMS members on occasion do make sandwiches in the course of their community outreach.

Through a national survey which it organized in 1993, the society was brought face to face with this kind of communication gap, of failure in public relations. The goal of the survey was to find out what people really knew and thought about the WMS. Those surveyed included clergy, lay people, men and women, members and nonmembers of the society. About 1,065 replies were received and analyzed. The results of the survey were, to say the least, disconcerting in light of the society's 80 or so years of amalgamated existence and its long record of service to the church. Some 41.8 per cent of the non-members who responded did not know what the WMS does locally and 47.5 per cent did not know what the WMS does nationally. Rev. George Johnston and his wife, Mickey, who collated the results of the survey, note dryly in their conclusions that

> *This points to a poor effort in communication and promotion of missions and provides the opportunity for questions to be raised about the society's need to exist.*[1]

Compliments

It is not that the WMS has not been truly appreciated through the years in certain quarters and by specific people. Dr. Kenneth McMillan, for example, Moderator of the General Assembly in 1979, noted the positive contribution of the WMS to the life and work of the church, emphasizing its commitment to prayer, fellowship and faithful giving in support of mission. Dr. McMillan also spoke positively about the WMS role in missionary education.

> *I know and you know that over the years by far the best informed people on church life in the world have been the members of the Women's Missionary Society. A lot of women have been remarkably well-informed even sometimes much better than their ministers...*[2]

The importance of the role of women all across the country in the history of the church is underlined by Dr. Donald C. MacDonald in an address to the WMS in 1983. He said

> *I believe there is reasonable amount of doubt whether our church would have survived the crisis of 1925 without the support of the women of our church.*[3]

This theme was picked up by Rev. John Congram, Moderator of the General Assembly in 1997, in his message to the annual meeting of the WMS council. He quoted from the book *Why I am a Presbyterian* by Walter Bryden, at one time principal of Knox College, Toronto. Dr Bryden, speaking about the WMS, said

> *Perhaps the most satisfying aspect of our whole Presbyterian Church life, during the last eight years* [after 1925], *has been the*

> *direct result of the sustained efforts of our Women's Missionary Society. To this work more than to anything else can be attributed the preservation of a true missionary spirit in the church.*[4]

Although in his 1995 history of the denomination, *This Presbyterian Church of Ours*, Mr. Congram makes no reference to the role of the WMS in that history, in his 1997 address to the council he was happy to echo Bryden's words and even to add to them. As Moderator, he chose to emphasize the importance of evangelism, ministry to children and the challenge to the church of Canada's multiracial, multicultural society. Mr. Congram noted that these were also central concerns for the WMS.

> *Sometimes, it has seemed the society was the only group within the church keeping these matters alive…*[5]

Going on to speak of the new missionary spirit in the church, Mr. Congram acknowledged the role of the WMS in helping to bring it to birth.

> *Sessions and congregations are gradually understanding that they are the primary units of mission… In part this is possible because the Women's Missionary Society would never let the church forget that mission is the life-blood of the church…*[6]

There are those who would argue, perhaps with some truth, that moderators *in their official capacity* could be expected to do no less than to speak in positive terms about the WMS! Others, however, have also had good things to say.

Rev. Rick Fee, director of Presbyterian World Service and Development, sees the WMS as

> *…the most knowledgeable arm of the church.*[7]

Cathy Victor defines the society as

> *…the grass roots organization — the hands on, home based group.*[8]

A writer to *Glad Tidings* notes that

> *The WMS has much to hold lovingly in front of women today. Those attributes and gifts so freely given to me by the members of my WMS group must be extended… Wonderful things are being accomplished, people sent forth in Jesus Christ's name, our persons enriched, and our faith nourished through the Women's Missionary Society.*[9]

For another writer, the WMS is

> *…the soul of the Presbyterian Church.* [In her experience,] *Nowhere in our Presbytery and Synod is there a stronger feeling of fellowship and collegiality… Nowhere is there more knowledge of the history of our Church in mission. Nowhere is there a greater demonstration of stewardship of time, talent and treasure.*[10]

Margaret Greig (Robertson), in the article "Called to Make Justice," observes,

> *As I travel throughout my Synodical, I find WMS members in every corner of the churches...on Sessions, in Choirs, CE* [Christian Education] *Committees, Bd* [Board] *of Managers...you name it... everywhere.*[11]

Criticisms

The WMS has also inevitably had its critics, both inside and outside the society. Rosemary Doran, in the article "Where are we going?" quotes the words of Dr. Agnew Johnston, Moderator of the 1973 General Assembly.

> *One of the grievous weaknesses of the church, at both national and parish level, is that we never seem to find the courage to end something, which, once successful, has now lost its effectiveness and relevancy.*

and goes on to say,

> *Many will feel that this is rank heresy — especially in the WMS! What was good enough for our grandmothers, is good enough for us. But is it? It is not always enough to perpetuate the past for its own sake.*[12]

Eileen Parish, WMS president from 1981-1984, notes that the society needs to look beyond itself to the issues of the community and the world. Recognizing the importance of enhancing the image of the WMS and enabling people to understand its purpose, Mrs. Parish points up the need

> *to make its work more appealing and eye-catching — to keep the issues in front of people.*[13]

In 1989, the newsletter *From a Woman's Perspective*, a publication of the Board of Ministry of The Presbyterian Church in Canada, dedicated its May issue to the WMS, in celebration of the society's 75th anniversary. Having solicited material from the WMS itself, the editorial committee expressed disappointment that little of import (at least by the committee's definition) emerged.

> *Somehow we are not hearing the message or the WMS is not saying it.*[14]

The editorial committee saw issues which it felt were not addressed. These included the relationship between the society and the church and the problem of establishing a new and younger membership.

In her article "What is Missing from this Picture?" Rev. Diane Strickland pulls few punches. The picture in question was the poster designed specifically for the anniversary. Showing women in a variety of costumes, it was intended to represent the historical evolution of the society and to express the purpose of the society. Not all WMS members liked the result. The

Poster designed for WMS anniversary

stylized portrayal of the women was seen as unflattering and many thought the poster projected a negative image of the society. Diane asked

*Does the WMS know how to project who they are? Do those who "Go and Tell" Christ's story know how to tell their own story? Even more fundamental, what **is** their self-image?*[15]

She also perceives a lack of the symbolism of discipleship in the poster and wonders what this says about the self-understanding of the WMS.[16]

Rev. Linda Bell, another Moderator of the General Assembly, in "New Partnerships in Mission" reiterates the theme of image and projection.

The Women's Missionary Society groups must be intentional and committed to sharing every part of their work and studies with the congregations. Often this does not happen and our WMS groups seem to work in isolation, apart from the rest of the congregation, with much of their activities hidden and unknown and consequently unrecognized.[17]

As Others See Us

The seeming invisibility of the WMS has not always been due to the society's poor self-image (if such it was) or to the inability to project an image. External factors and expectations also played their part. Before the ordination of women by The Presbyterian Church in Canada in 1966, many people believed that the WMS provided an outlet, a means of fulfillment for those women who aspired to a leadership role in the church, similar to that of the men, but without the means of attaining it. When the ordination of women became a reality, it was assumed by some that the WMS had no further need to exist. It became an anachronism which did not need to be taken seriously.

Another factor was the attitude of some clergy and, on occasion, courts of the church. Various WMS groups and individual members have had to deal with being put down by the minister of their congregation or by presbytery or synod, and/or denied the opportunity to present their message. There has been indifference and disinterest and sometimes downright hostility.

In *From a Woman's Perspective*, Kathleen Gibson recounts her enthusiasm for the WMS. Since her mother was involved in the work of the society, Kathleen, as a child, appreciated the opportunities to meet missionaries and hear about the life and work of the church. She talks of attending one General Assembly and waiting eagerly for the WMS report to be presented. She paints a telling picture of men getting up and leaving the gathering at that point.

I was shocked, hurt and angered by what I saw. That moment was a turning point in my life, for it showed my [sic] *the truth about the value given to the work of women in our church.*[18]

It would be good to be able to say that this was a once-only happening. Regrettably, that is not so. It still happens from time to time, even if not in so blatant a form.

It is hard to understand the reason for this. Given that The Presbyterian Church in Canada, to say nothing of the whole Christian church, is committed to the preaching and practice of mission, it is difficult to see why the WMS, which has preached and practised mission for so many years, has sometimes deliberately been deprived of a piece of the action. It may be that in some places and for some people the WMS is perceived as a threat to the power of the minister and his or her priorities and style of ministry. It may be a failure to acknowledge that women have something valuable and precious to offer to the church, something legitimate to say. It may simply be lack of knowledge of the society's history and aims. Whatever the cause, for some people the outcome has been bewildering and hurtful.

To Change or Not To Change?

In the responses to the 1993 survey, a key word was 'change' — change of name, focus, structure, image, of potential market. The society was seen as a clique, an 'old girls' club', a secret society. Said one respondent,

> *To an outsider* [the WMS] *appears to be an exclusive little old ladies' group that in some way is interested in foreign missions but no one really knows what they are up to.*[19]

Said another,

> *The salt of the earth needs to come out of the salt shaker to flavour the community.*[20]

A WMS member commented

> *The WMS should stop whining about loss of members ...*[21]

while another claimed

> *This survey may be the start of some new life and new thinking — but only if we endeavour to* **react** *to the comments which we receive — and then to* **act** *on those we can address.*[22]

This was what the society then began to do — react and act. In 1994, survey results in hand, the WMS council at its annual meeting set itself the goal of creating a five year plan.[23] It did this under the guidance of consultants. The council spelled out the strengths of the society, as seen by the society. These included prayer, study, service and fellowship. In addition, it named weaknesses in the organization — an aging membership, gaps in communication, reduced finances, the inability to 'sell' the WMS successfully and attract new members, a burdensome structure, to name a few.

Strategy

In a creative response, council put together a set of action plans, each with an accompanying timeline, designed to address concerns and incorporate new ideas, giving the society new hope and vision. Each set of actions had a specific focus. Some dealt with the work of the AECs, others with programs and resources. Better public relations were emphasized. Priorities in work with children and youth were examined. All of this resulted in a document called *Threatened with Resurrection*. In the words of one of the action statements, the society then prepared to "Stand Up, Speak Up and Be Counted," as it moved ahead to grapple with the challenges of the survey and the five year plan, under the guidance of a task force called Focus on the Future.

Did it succeed? Yes and no. Creative new ways of presenting programs, deliberate experimentation with new structures to meet the needs of the membership (especially in some Western synodicals), brighter and bolder dissemination of material and information emerged here and there across the society and were well-received and successfully implemented. In the spring of 2002 a video — *Still Moving* — was released, giving a well-presented overview of the life and work of the society.

Unfortunately, however, many of the fundamental problems still remain. Many of the changes effected have been cosmetic, altering the appearance but not the substance. The state of membership and financial resources has not improved significantly. In the eyes of some, the society has failed to acknowledge or adequately own the changes taking place in the church at large with its new policies and strategies of mission. In addition, a stubborn attachment to existing patterns and structures can thwart new proposals. For example, over the years efforts have been made to change the name of the society to something more comprehensive and inclusive, such as Presbyterian Missionary Society (though this would have created an unfortunate acronym!), or World Missionary Society. Such efforts, however, came to nothing. *What part of the word 'No' do you not understand?* was one comment at the time of the most recent debate in 1999.

In part of her book *Naomi's Daughters*, Alyson C. Huntly presents an insightful appreciation and analysis of the United Church Women of the United Church of Canada. She says,

> *I have tremendous respect for the UCW and for the wonderful work it has accomplished. I know that nowhere else in the church has there been such dedication and commitment, such deep faith and faithful service. I have long known that if you want something done, and done well, in the United Church, you can count on the UCW to do it. They have been our financial backbone, our conscience in the*

> *concerns of the world, our mission and outreach worker…our eyes and ears open to study and reflection… All this I have received as a legacy and an inheritance. All this I value and respect.*[24]

It would be no stretch of imagination or truth to apply all of the above to the WMS.

The WMS rightly sees itself as a community of women of faith, committed to going and telling the good news in a variety of ways, either in person or through the providing of funds for others to go and tell. It has a long and honourable history of doing this. It has an excellent record of networking and fellowship. Given a task, it can be depended on to get things done. As one reader wrote to *Glad Tidings* in 1998,

> *I think God and us old ladies have been doing a pretty good job for these sixty years and more, and I expect we're good for a few more yet!*[25]

Alyson Huntly goes on to say,

> *The UCW continues to be a vital and important organization… However, there are signs that many UCW groups are struggling to maintain themselves. The organizational structures of the UCW — presbyterial, conference and national levels — also have had a difficult time. There just aren't as many women willing to take leadership, and women who have been in leadership roles are often tired and burnt out, or overloaded with many responsibilities at many different levels of the structure.*[26]

Here, too, for UCW read WMS. Through force of circumstances, the WMS in recent years has had to depend too much on the 'old ladies' referred to above. Their devotion to what the society stands for is unquestionable but they are finding it harder and harder to keep going. With age comes reduction of energy and, often, resistance to change as well as the inability to cope with it. Some groups, seeking help, have been presented with options that might enable them to grow. They have, however, been unwilling or unable to deal with the necessary restructuring and have chosen to stay with the *status quo*. Others, out of necessity, have simply moved their executive officers from one position to another and try to carry on as before. Some, at both local and presbyterial levels, have folded entirely, going with sadness but at the same time with grace, dignity and celebration. It should be noted that where auxiliaries have disbanded, members have been concerned about the finances and have tried to ensure that their individual contributions still go to the ongoing work of the society.

In addition, there is the generation gap. In its efforts to provide for the future, the WMS has often worked hard to 'bring the young women in' to existing groups but without marked success. Daughters and granddaughters have a different lifestyle and work commitment. They also often 'do mission' differently. The issue is one of differing viewpoints which are hard to reconcile. The older generation would like the younger to embrace its vision and values and may be disappointed when that does not happen. The younger generation, while respecting the accomplishments of the older women, reserves the right to do its own thing.

The Challenge

It may be that the WMS, however willing, is simply not able in its present form to make the enormous change required to maintain its viability. And, in fact, it must address the question of whether it should maintain that viability or whether the time has come to face the real implications of "resurrection," namely that death must precede new life. The wording of the theme Threatened with Resurrection may indeed have been prophetic.

Still Counting the Women

A former president of the WMS once made a heretical statement. One of her long-term dreams, she said, was that in the best of all worlds there would be no need for a WMS, because the whole church would be involved in mission! It is possible that The Presbyterian Church in Canada at the start of the 21st century has arrived, or is in process of arriving, at that point. Although in theory, mission has always been the task and calling of every Christian, in practice the implementation of mission has often been regarded as the prerogative or responsibility of certain groups, like the missionary societies. Today, thanks to modern technology, people are better and more quickly informed about needs and issues. Today, whole congregations, as well as individuals in those congregations, are taking on mission projects and organizing hands-on experiences in those projects. Young and old, women and men alike, are involved in long-term and short-term projects, on both national and international levels. Mission is alive and well and living wherever people want to make it happen. Is there then anything left for the WMS to do?

The WMS national survey asked the question: *Can a women's group play a useful role in the Presbyterian Church in Canada?* Eight-five per cent of the respondents answered yes. It was not suggested that the group be a WMS group, but simply that a women's group has a definite role in the church, even though that role may not yet have been precisely envisioned, let alone given tangible form. In the early years of the society's history, the founding groups — the Woman's Missionary Society, Women's Home Missionary Society and Woman's Foreign Missionary Society — had to die to themselves so that the new entity — the WMS — could be born. The process no doubt brought its measure of soul-searching, sadness and pain but the end result was the society as it is known and respected today by many throughout the world, a society with a strong record of good and faithful service in the cause of mission.

Perhaps now history must repeat itself, so that another new entity may be born — born of WMS experience and giftedness and a *willing new breadth of vision.* Perhaps the WMS should aim to say with the late Dag Hammarskjold

'For all that is past, thanks; for all that will be, yes.'[1]

Appenxix A: Mission/Mission Societies in The Presbyterian Church in Canada

Atlantic Mission "Eastern Division"	Quebec to British Columbia Mission "Western Division"	Other Notes of Interest
1825 First women's group noted — PEI		
	1833 — earliest groups form in Ontario	
	ca 1841 — Montreal — *Ladies Society*	
1846/48 John and Charlotte Geddie go to the New Hebrides		
	1864 —Montreal, *Ladies Auxiliary Association* — later becomes ***Woman's Missionary Society, Montreal***	
1875 Presbyterian Church in Canada — Home and Foreign Mission Committees		
1876 *Halifax Woman's Foreign Missionary Society of the PCC(ES)*	1876 — Toronto — ***Woman's Foreign Missionary Society (WFMS)***	
1885 *Woman's Foreign Missionary Society-WFMS(ED)*		1885 WARC recommends to PCC to set up an Order of Deaconesses
	1890-91 WFMS(WD) appoints a committee to confer with theological colleges — re training for missionaries 1897 — Ewart Missionary Training Home opens —TO	
	1898 *Atlin Nurses Committee* 1903 — ***Women's Home Missionary Society (WHMS)***	
1905 add home missions 1910 —becomes *Women's Foreign and Home Missionary Society (ES)*		
		1908 PCC forms Order of Deaconesses. Ewart becomes Presbyterian Missionary and Deaconess Training Home
	May 15, 1914 ***WMS(WD)*** — 3 become one	

<table>
<tr><td>1915 WF&HMS adds social service dept and changes name to Woman's Missionary Society, Eastern Division — WMS(ED)</td><td></td><td></td></tr>
<tr><td colspan="3">1925 — Church Union/Continuing Presbyterian Church
General Board of Missions formed (no longer missions boards-east and west)
WMS (WD) no longer auxiliary to the mission boards of the PCC but an independent organization within the Church</td></tr>
<tr><td colspan="3">Missionaries relocate from East Asia during WWII — Overseas churches begin to become independent — post-war</td></tr>
<tr><td colspan="3">1965 GA considers paper The Place of Women in the Church
1966 GA agrees to ordain women
1966 First woman elder ordained in Arthur, Ontario — Joan McInnis, June 12
1968 First woman ordained to word and sacraments in Appin, Ontario — Shirley Jeffrey, May 29</td></tr>
<tr><td colspan="3">1972 Integration of Mission
WMS(ED) and (WD) keep "education staff"
Board of World Mission and Board of Christian Education are formed</td></tr>
<tr><td></td><td></td><td>1982 name change —
Order of Diaconal Ministries</td></tr>
<tr><td>1987 WMS (ED) becomes AMS</td><td></td><td></td></tr>
<tr><td></td><td>1991 GA agrees to reaffirm WMS(WD) as autonomous organization within the structures of The Presbyterian Church in Canada (A&P p. 473)</td><td>Sept 1991 — Ewart College amalgamates with Knox College
1992 — GA — first diaconal minister commissioners to General Assembly</td></tr>
<tr><td colspan="3">1992 PCC Restructures at National Level
Life and Mission Agency replaces BWM</td></tr>
<tr><td colspan="3">1995 Regional Staff Restructuring
(WMS transfers "education staff" to Synodicals/Synods — WMS provides 7/12th grant towards salaries)</td></tr>
<tr><td></td><td>1999 WMS votes not to change name and not to talk about it for five years</td><td></td></tr>
</table>

Appendix B:
Presidents

Woman's Missionary Society, Montreal: organized 1864
Woman's Foreign Missionary Society: organized 1876
Atlin Nurse Committee: 1898
  becomes Women's Home Missionary Society: 1903
Amalgamated as Women's Missionary Society: 1914

Presidents

Woman's Missionary Society, Montreal 1864-1914

Mrs. Andrew Paton
Mrs. Colin Russel
Mrs. Jane Redpath
Mrs. John Campbell
Mrs. W. J. Day
Mrs. Archibald Campbell
Mrs. Robert Campbell
Mrs. G. A. Grier
Mrs. I. C. Sharp

Woman's Foreign Missionary Society 1876-1914

Mrs. Marjory MacLaren
Mrs. Catherine Ewart
Mrs. Marjory MacLaren
Mrs. T. Shortreed
Mrs. Emily Steele

Women's Home Missionary Society 1903-1914

Mrs. R. S. Smellie
Mrs. William Cochrane
Mrs. A. L. McFadyen
Mrs. John Somerville

Women's Missionary Society, Western Division (Since 1914)

1914-1920	Mrs. Emily Steele
1920-1925	Mrs. Janet MacGillivray
1925-1928	Mrs. Mary McKerroll
1928-1932	Mrs. Helen Strachan
1932-1935	Miss Bessie MacMurchy
1935-1939	Mrs. Beatrice McLennan
1939-1944	Mrs. Muriel McMurrich
1944-1948	Mrs. Alice Inkster
1948-1953	Mrs. Maydee Pae
1953-1957	Mrs. Ethel Adamson
1957-1961	Mrs. A. Glenn Thompson
1961-1966	Mrs. Agnes Curr
1966-1970	Miss E. Luzetta McClelland
1970-1974	Mrs. Laura Burnett
1974-1978	Mrs. Christina Newstead
1978-1981	Miss Isabella T. Hunter
1981-1984	Mrs. Eileen Parish
1984-1987	Mrs. Clare Ellis
1987-1989	Mrs. Grace Jess
1989-1992	Mrs. Joan Sampson
1992-1995	Mrs. Kay Cowper
1995-1997	Rev. Rosemary Doran
1997-1999	Mrs. Esther Powell
1999-2001	Mrs. Mary Moorhead
2001-	Mrs. Joanne Instance

Appendix C:
Financials

Women's Foreign Missionary Society, Reserve Fund

Receipts and Payments Account, June 16th, 1914, to January 31st, 1915

Receipts

Cash in Metropolitan Bank, June 16th, 1914			$58,194 66
Subscriptions:—Missionaries' Salaries	$243 61		
Montreal, for South China	3,763 79		
Do., general subscriptions (see contra)	659 18		
		$4,666 58	
Loan Interest	$913 96		
Bank Interest	639 29		
		1,553 25	
Refund from Women's Missionary Society (as per separate statement)		3,942 31	
			10,162 14
			$68,356 80

Payments

Dr. Somerville for Formosa		$4,500 00	
Loan, Women's Missionary Society (as per separate statement)		50,000 00	
General Subscriptions transferred to Women's Missionary Society (see contra)		659 18	
			$55,159 18
Annual Reports	$1,062 00		
Postage on Reports	89 60		
		$1,151 60	
Sundry Expenses:—General	$6 17		
Missionary Conference	17 70		
Interest W. M. S.	4 15		
		28 02	
			1,179 62
Balance:—Cash, Bank of Nova Scotia, 31st Januray, 1915			12,018 00
			$68,356 80

Auditors' Certificate.—Audited and found correct,

CLARKSON, GORDON & DILWORTH,

Toronto, March 15th, 1915. Chartered Accountants.

Women's Missionary Society of the Presbyterian Church of Canada

Receipts and Payments Account, June 16th, 1914, to January 31st, 1915

Receipts

Loan, Women's Foreign Missionary Society Fund			$50,000 00
Subscriptions:—			
Manitoba Provincial Society		$10,886 15	
Ontario	$44,112 58		
Bequest late Mary Grass, transferred from W.H.M. Acct	500 00		
		44,612 58	
Saskatchewan		4,186 75	
British Columbia		752 33	
Quebec	$7,390 82		
W. F. M. S. transferred	659 18		
		8,050 00	
Alberta		911 55	
		$69,399 36	
General Subscriptions	$1,789 78		
Subscriptions for Missionaries' Salaries	1,901 97		
Home Missionary Society for Missionaries' Salaries (as per separate statement)	810 56		
		4,502 31	
			73,901 67
Bank interest		$155 15	
Interest W. F. M. .S		4 15	
			159 30
			$124,060 97

Payments

Rev. Dr. Somerville, Church Treasurer, for Salaries to Home and Foreign Missionaries			$59,362 34
Vegreville, Home Hospital		$2,338 40	
Quebec, Rev. J. U. Tanner, St. Phillips de Chester, Namur		969 33	
Canora, Hospital Expense		666 34	
Deaconess Training Home, Subscription		500 00	
Supplies:—West	$300 00		
India	27 16		
China	57 60		
		384 76	
Missionaries' Travelling Expenses		345 12	
Teulon, Hospital Expense		129 15	

16

Sifton:				
Hospital Home:				
Real Estate.....	$105 00			
Travelling......	4 90			
		$109 90		
Freight on Goods to China........		66 78		
Bibles for presentation............		41 59		
Jewish Mission..................		30 00		
			$5,581 37	
				$64,943 71
Expenses:				
Rent.......................		$469 23		
Printing and Typewriting......		116 10		
Engraving and Lithographing..		85 73		
Telegrams and Telephone......		3 60		
Advertising..................		2 84		
			$677 50	
Management:				
Postage and Stationery:				
" Treas. & Assist............		$10 00		
" President.................		25 60		
" Corres. Sec'y..............		17 83		
" Strangers.................		8 50		
" Educational...............		5 00		
" N. W. Secretary...........		4 50		
" Secretary.................		3 83		
" Hospital..................		3 25		
Travelling Expenses for Board.................		97 30		
			$175 81	
Salaries:				
Sec.-Treas. Publication........		$508 33		
Ass't. Treas. Publication.......		450 00		
Asst. Treas. Board............		395 00		
Field Secretary......	$375 00			
Travelling Expenses....	369 85			
		744 85		
Assistant Board.............		75 00		
		$2,173 18		
Special: retiring allowance.........		78 75		
			$2,251 93	
Interest on Loan, W. F. M. S................			555 60	
Provincial Societies, Expense.................			150 00	
Women's Foreign Miss. Soc. refund as per separate statement..........................			3,942 31	
Office Equipment, furniture and typewriter......			134 55	
				$7,887 70
Balance: Cash in Standard Bank........................				51,229 56
				$124,060 97

Individual subscriptions..................................	$210 70
Sunday Schools, Bible Classes, Y.P.S., Guilds, etc.............	826 90
L. M. Fee for Miss Hall, Glanford...........................	25 00
W.M.S. Centre Nappon, N.B................................	18 00
Callender M.B..	50 00
Montreál M.W.S..	659 18
	$1,789 78

Receipts for Missionary Salaries

For Miss Sykes, China	$300 00
" Miss Drummond, India	730 00
" Miss Edna McLellan, Korea	450 00
" Miss D. Kilpatrick, India	121 97
" Substitute for Mrs. McClure, China	300 00
	$1,901 97

Auditors' Certificate.—Audited and found correct,

CLARKSON, GORDON & DILWORTH,

Toronto, March 15th, 1915. Chartered Accountants.

EXPENDITURES IN FOREIGN FIELDS FOR THE YEAR, 1914

INDIA

Salaries:

Misses White, Duncan, Thompson, Robertson, Cameron, MacLean, Weir, Brebner, Grier, Drummond, Manarey, Campbell, McHarrie, Herdman, Coltart, Goodfellow, Robson, Drs. MacKellar, O'Hara, McMaster, each $730.00	$14,470 00	
Miss Sinclair, January 1st to May 20th	283 89	
Miss Kilpatrick, Nov. 7th to Dec. 31st	109 50	
Miss Gardner, "	109 50	
Miss Smillie, "	109 50	
Dr. Moodie, "	109 50	
Dr. B. C. Oliver, furlough and salary	558 90	
Miss Clearihue, furlough and salary	534 49	
Miss Glendinning, furlough and salary	559 92	
Mrs. Menzies, furlough and salary	541 67	
		$17,386 87

Evangelistic:

Indore	$373 57	
Mhow	320 17	
Ujjain	274 09	
Neemuch	451 03	
Dhar	167 03	
Kharua	906 29	
		$2,492 18

Medical:

Indore	$2,499 91	
Neemuch	1,838 56	
Dhar	1,247 07	
		$5,585 54

18

Educational:		
Indore	$4,421 07	
Mhow	287 46	
Ujjain	167 64	
Neemuch	1,982 38	
Dhar	106 97	
		$6,965 52
Miscellaneous:		
Indore	$966 01	
Mhow	39 71	
Ujjain	12 41	
Neemuch	89 40	
Dhar	27 50	
Kharua	26 03	
Amkhut	7 15	
		$1,168 21
Travel:		
Home—Misses Glendinning, Oliver, Sinclair, and Mrs. Menzies	$825 99	
Outward—Miss Clearihue, Gardner, Smillie, Kilpatrick and Moodie	1,568 48	
		$2,394 47
Outfits:		
Misses Gardner, Kilpatrick, Moodie, Smillie		$600 00
Medical Examination Fees	$6 00	
Freight and Insurance on Goods	63 82	
Bungalow Furnishings	238 14	
Treasurer's Expenses	79 68	
Scholarship, Ludhiana School	100 00	
Grant, Ludhiana School	240 67	
Hat Piplia Wall	259 55	
Bank Exchange	1,315 01	
		$2,302 87
		$38,895 66

Receipts

Grants, Donations, etc	$261 98	
Fees, Sales, Rents, etc	3,064 89	
Over Allowed in 1913	121 65	
Bank Interest	41 10	
		$3,489 62
Total		$35,406 04

CHINA

Honan

General:		
Tientsin Agency	$177 82	
Registration of Passports	47 48	
Insurance	39 76	
Office Expenses, Treasurer	24 30	
		$289 36
Travel:		
Miss M. E. McNeely (to China)	$261 85	
Miss Shipley "	271 06	
Miss Lethbridge "	257 05	
Miss Cameron (to Canada)	201 19	
Dr. Auld to meet incoming missionaries	21 30	
		$1,012 45

Outfits and Examinations:		
Misses Shipley, Lethbridge, Ross (each $150)	$450 00	
Miss McNeely (part)	100 00	
Medical Examinations (4)	12 00	
		$562 00
Furnishing, Freight, etc.:		
Organ—Wei Hwei Boarding School	$42 00	
House Furnishings	194 00	
Freight and Insurance to Tientsin	114 10	
Freight and Duty	39 60	
Freight and Duty (omitted 1913)	7 73	
Miss Brown—Moving to Hwai King	5 15	
Miss Walks—Moving to Hwai King	4 83	
Misses Gay and Sykes to Wu An	22 44	
		$429 85
Salaries:		
Misses Brown, Dinwoody, Dow, Gay, Hodge, Logan, Macdonald, I. McIntosh, M. I. McIntosh, McLennan, O'Neill, Sykes, Walks, each $600	$7,800 00	
Miss Cameron	498 08	
Miss Lethbridge	41 10	
Miss M. E. McNeely, $447.12 less fees for nursing $102	345 12	
Miss Shipley	108 49	
Miss Pyke	678 50	
Miss McLennan—Balance 1913	2 74	
		$9,474 03
Buildings:		
Wei Hwei—		
Hospital, Materials and Payments on Land	$742 98	
Girls' School, Class Rooms	98 66	
Balance on City Buildings	37 18	
Bell for "	75 00	
Changte—		
Hospital, Building Materials $300.48, less Material sold, $252.10	48 38	
		$1,002 20
Current Expenses:		
Changte—		
Evangelistic	$165 68	
Boarding School	278 17	
Hospital, $83.94, less receipts, $62.20	21 74	
Language Teacher, etc.	76 52	
		$542 11
Wei Hwei—		
Evangelistic	$46 67	
City Work	109 82	
Boarding School	344 65	
Kindergarten (partly for fitting up rooms)	52 92	
Bible School	8 66	
Language Teachers, etc.	138 18	
		$700 90
Hwai King—		
Evangelistic	$161 34	
Boarding School	165 49	
Miscellaneous	48 83	
		$375 66

Item			
Tao Kou—			
Evangelistic		$68 90	
Educational		4 94	
Fitting up Chinese house for Misses Macdonald and Dinwoody, Language Teacher, etc.		171 22	
			$245 06
Wu An—			
Evangelistic		$5 78	
Miscellaneous		1 34	
			$7 12
Married Women's Work:			
Changte		$148 29	
Wei Hwei		66 67	
Wu An		47 38	
Siu Wu		5 31	
Tao Kou		3 40	
			$271 05
			$14,911 79

SHANGHAI

Item			
Miss M. V. McNeely, salary		$525 00	
Miss M. V. McNeely, rent		51 56	
Cost Remitting		0 30	
			$576 86
Native Assistant, Mrs. MacGillivray			37 50
			$614 36

SOUTH CHINA

Item			
Salaries:			
Misses Dickson, Langrill, MacBean and Reid, each $600		$2,400 00	
Miss McLean, salary	$217 74		
Miss McLean, furlough	318 70		
		536 44	
Evangelistic		230 50	
Educational		956 50	
Medical		1,681 25	
Miscellaneous		558 10	
			$6,362 79
Less:			
School Fees		$322 77	
Medical Fees		804 15	
Exchange and Interest		183 74	
			$1,310 66
			$5,052 13

FORMOSA

Tamsui

Item			
Salaries:			
Miss Connell, salary	$162 73		
Miss Connell, furlough	375 00		
		$537 73	
Misses Adair, Clazie, Elliott and Kinney, each $700		2,800 00	
			$3,337 73

Travel:		
Miss Connell to Formosa	$275 00	
Miss Kinney to Japan	19 92	
		$294 92
Evangelistic:		
Bible Women	$44 33	
Travel on Field	49 78	
		$94 11
Educational:		
Girls' School, Food and Maintenance	$711 69	
Women's School	212 92	
Salaries of Teachers	373 29	
Water Works	50 24	
		$1,348 14
Medical:		
Nurses' Salaries, Food, etc.	$256 76	
Hospital Supplies	96 01	
		$352 77
Miscellaneous:		
Language Teacher	$77 68	
Stove for W.M.S. House	51 17	
House Furnishings	17 41	
Building Road	19 92	
Postage	3 53	
Repairs to W.M.S. House	30 04	
Insurance	17 43	
Bank Commission	69 74	
		$286 92
Buildings:		
W.M.S. House, Taihoku		654 00
		$6,368 59
Less:		
Girls' School Fees and Sale of Books	$412 09	
Women's School Fees and Sale of Books	66 69	
Donations	105 00	
Sale of Produce	39 75	
Interest	49 31	
		$672 84
		$5,695 75
New Building for Girls' Boarding School at Tamsui (This amount was taken from the W.F.M.S. Balance)		$5,000 00

KOREA

Salaries:		
Misses M. E. McFarlane, Ethel McLellan, Ethel McEachren and Esther Smith, each $600		$2,400 00
Travel:		
Miss E. McLellan, balance	$115 80	
Examination Fee	3 00	
House Furnishings	78 98	
Freight	27 70	
		$225 48

22

Hoiryong:		
Evangelistic Work	$160 00	
Educational, Girls' School	450 00	
Miscellaneous	158 03	
		$768 03
Yong Jung:		
Evangelistic Work	$100 00	
Educational, Girls' School	200 00	
Miscellaneous	100 73	
		$400 73
Wonsan:		
Miscellaneous		$109 50
Exchange on Drafts		26 12
Buildings:		
Hospital	$2,000 00	
Yong Jung W.M.S. House	970 57	
Hoiryong W.M.S. House	1,029 43	
Materials	197 70	
		$4,197 70
		$8,127 56

CHINESE WORK IN CANADA

Toronto:		
Miss Robson, salary	$150 00	
Expenses	15 00	
		$165 00
Vancouver:		
Miss Stuart, salary	$650 00	
House Rent	96 00	
		$746 00
Cumberland:		
Miss Walker		30 00
		$941 00

INDIANS IN WESTERN CANADA

File Hills Boarding School:		
*Rev. H. C. Sweet, Principal (9 months)	$300 00	
Mrs. H. C. Sweet, Matron	400 00	
Mrs. McRae, Matron	66 65	
Miss C. McDonald, Assistant Matron	275 00	
Miss M. E. Riggs, Assistant Matron	114 50	
Miss F. Ross, Assistant Matron	91 00	
Miss E. Lavallie, Assistant Matron	35 00	
Miss Morrice, Teacher	450 00	
Farmer	80 00	
Labourer	35 00	
Travelling Expenses, Miss M. E. Riggs	55 20	
Travelling Expenses, Miss Stratton	15 00	
Travelling Expenses, Miss Morris	44 55	
		$1,961 90

Round Lake Boarding School:

*Rev. H. McKay, D.D., Principal	$400 00	
Miss F. Munro, Matron	400 00	
Miss B. Read, Assistant Matron	240 00	
Miss F. McKay, Teacher	450 00	
Miss J. Munro, Seamstress	180 00	
Insurance	36 60	
		$1,700 60

Hurricane Hills Reserve:

Insurance		$29 10

Moose Mountain Reserve:

Miss Innes, Reserve Worker	$37 50	
Insurance	13 00	
Repairs to Mission House	75 00	
		$125 50

Cecilia Jeffrey School Boarding:

*Rev. T. F. Dodds, Principal	$400 00	
Mrs. C. C. Kay, Matron	450 00	
Miss T. L. Fraser, Assistant Matron	197 50	
Miss Cormie, Assistant Matron	102 50	
Mrs. D. Phillips, 2nd Assistant Matron	135 40	
Miss C. Brodie, Teacher	450 00	
Engineer	128 33	
Insurance	200 54	
Insurance "The Wanderer"	21 00	
		$2,085 27

Portage la Prairie Boarding School:

*Rev. W. A. Hendry	$400 00	
Miss A. B. Bannerman, Assistant Matron	100 00	
Miss R. Tomlinson, Assistant Matron	287 50	
Miss Gardner, Assistant Matron	114 60	
Miss W. Henderson, Teacher	570 00	
Insurance	12 50	
		$1,484 60

Birtle Boarding School:

*Rev. D. Iverach, Principal	$400 00	
Miss A. B. Folliott, Matron	400 00	
Miss B. Murchison, 1st Assistant Matron	300 00	
Miss B. Henderson, 2nd Assistant Matron	243 05	
Miss E. McCurdy, Teacher	450 00	
Insurance	170 00	
		$1,963 05

Crowstand Boarding School:

*Rev. W. McWhinney, Principal	$400 00	
Miss A. McLaren, Teacher	432 90	
Miss S. A. Windel, Seamstress	250 00	
Insurance	36 00	
		$1118 90

Pipestone Reserve:

Repairs (one-half)		$11 50

Buildings:			
Birtle	$3,881 29		
C. Jeffrey	219 47		
		$4,100 76	
Less:			
Dominion Government Grant.		2,050 97	
One-fifth held for Building Fund.			$2,049 79
			$12,530 21

British Columbia

Alberni Boarding School:		
*Rev. H. B. Currie, Principal	$400 00	
Mrs. H. B. Currie, Matron	400 00	
Mrs. J. Stevens, Assistant Matron	350 00	
Miss E. M. Wright, Assistant Matron	300 00	
Miss V. M. Trew, Teacher	117 50	
Miss B. McMillan, Teacher	255 50	
Travelling Expenses, Miss B. McMillan	73 75	
Insurance	134 95	
Repairs	1,203 75	
		$3,235 45
Ahousaht Boarding School:		
*Rev. J. T. Ross, Principal	$400 00	
Mrs. J. T. Ross, Matron	400 00	
Miss I. McIver, Assistant Matron	300 00	
Miss L. McIver, Teacher	187 50	
Substitute, Teacher	75 00	
Travelling Expenses, Miss L. McIver	98 00	
Travelling Expenses, Mrs. D. B. Millard	14 25	
Travelling Expenses, Miss O. Arbuthnot	14 25	
		$1,180 00
Dodger's Cove Reserve:		
Mr. T. Shewish		$165 00
Ucluelet Reserve:		
Repairs to Roof		$60 00
		$4,949 45

* Where the Principal of a boarding school is also responsible for evangelistic work on the reserve $500 of his salary is paid by the Home Mission Board.

W.M.S. ESTIMATES FOR 1926

NATIONAL MISSIONS

SCHOOL HOMES

New Liskeard, Ont.—		
Matron's Salary	$616.50	
Assistant	300.00	
Taxes	167.48	
Repairs	100.00	
Insurance	60.00	
Contingency	100.00	
		$1,343.98

HOSPITALS

South Porcupine, Ont.—		
Superintendent's salary	$1,080.00	
1st Nurse	900.00	
2nd Nurse	780.00	
Insurance	60.00	
Coal	300.00	
Alterations and Furnace, etc. (still to be paid)	4,500.00	
Maintenance, not yet known	......	
Contingency	300.00	
Drug Contingency	200.00	
		$8,120.00

ORIENTALS IN CANADA

Chinese Work—		
Toronto—Miss Dickson, salary (part time)	$1,000.00	
Contingency	350.00	
Montreal—Miss Mary Hugill, salary	1,100.00	
Expenses	120.00	
Victoria—Mrs. McQueen, salary	600.00	
Contingency	300.00	
Persian Work—		
Mr. Eshoo, (part salary)	650.00	
		$4,120.00

SOCIAL SERVICE

Toronto—	
Miss M. C. Murray, salary	$1,135.00
Expenses	155.00
Miss McDonald (honorarium)	250.00
Expenses	36.00
Miss Gunn, Salary and Expenses	1,080.00
Hamilton—	
Miss Margaret Allen, salary	900.00
Expenses	120.00
Montreal—	
Miss Lily MacArthur, salary	1,088.00
Expenses	120.00
Quebec—	
Miss Scott, salary (part time)	300.00
Gonor (Selkirk), Man.—	

Mrs. MacKenzie, salary (part time)	$600.00	
Assistant	800.00	
Incidentals and taxes	200.00	
		$6,784.00

OVERSEAS WORK

Gwalior, India—		
Two salaries for four months	$ 400.00	
Travelling expenses	1,000.00	
Outfits	400.00	
Contingencies and expansion	500.00	
		$2,300 00
Bhil Field, India—		
Miss Robson, salary	$1,000.00	
Expenses	200.00	
		$1,200.00
South China—		
Miss Reid (on furlough)	$1,000.00	
Miss Dulmage, loaned to The Diocesan Girls' School, Hong Kong	1,000.00	
Dr. Jessie MacBean (salary, at Hackett Medical College, Canton)	1,000.00	
Unit of Support, Hackett Medical College	1,000.00	
Miss Crockett (on furlough)	900.00	
		$4,900.00
Tokio, Japan—		
Grant to Miss Caroline Macdonald for Night School for Factory Girls		$2,000.00

PUBLICATIONS

Editor, salary	$1,500.00	
Secretary-Treasurer of Publications, salary	1,200.00	
Office rent (partial)	540.00	
New publications	500.00	
Contingency	1,300.00	
		$5,040.00

CHRISTIAN LITERATURE

Committee of Interdenominational Christian Literature—		
Miss Kyle	$300.00	
Literature (French)	100.00	
		$400.00

ORGANIZATION

Field Secretary, salary (voluntary)	......	
Expenses	$600.00	
Missionaries' deputation work	300.00	
		$900.00

STUDENT

Expenses		$150.00

MISCELLANEOUS

Pensions	$ 340.00	
Renewals and Furnishings	8,000.00	
Library grant	250.00	
Education of medical and other workers	325.00	
		$8,915.00

ADMINISTRATION

Office rent, (partial)	$ 540.00	
Book Keeper's salary	1,200.00	
Postage, printing, telegrams, stationery, office expenses	800.00	
Fee, Federated Boards	50.00	
Bonding and Auditing—	150.00	
Council Executive members' attendance at Federated Board meetings and deputation work, etc	500.00	
Annual Meeting of Council Executive	......	
Annual Report and report forms	1,500.00	
		$4,740.00

PROPOSED NEW WORK

Hospitals	$10,000.00	
School Homes (2)	15,000.00	
Indian Work	10,000.00	
Orientals in Canada	1,000.00	
Social Service—		
Deaconess (2)	2,000.00	
Welcome and Welfare	1,000.00	
Field Secretary	1,200.00	
		$40,200.00

And such other work as may be given to us by the commission. All these estimates are necessarily approximate only.

SUMMARY

National Missions—		
School Homes	$1,343.98	
Hospitals	8,120.00	
Orientals in Canada	4,120.00	
Social Service	6,784.00	
		$20,367.98
Overseas' Work—		
Gwalior, India	$2,300.00	
Bhil Field, India	1,200.00	
South China	4,900.00	
Tokio, Japan	2,000.00	
		10,400.00
Publications		5,040.00
Christian Literature		400.00
Organization		900.00
Student		150.00
Miscellaneous		8,915.00
Administration		4,740.00
Proposed New Work		40,200.00
General Contingency		8,887.02
		$100,000.00

FINANCIAL STATEMENT — 1964
WOMEN'S MISSIONARY SOCIETY (W.D.) OF THE PRESBYTERIAN CHURCH IN CANADA

STATEMENT OF RECEIPTS AND DISBURSEMENTS FOR THE YEAR ENDING DECEMBER 31, 1964

GENERAL FUND

Receipts:		
Synodical givings:		
British Columbia	$ 15,375.98	
Alberta	15,132.28	
Saskatchewan	10,688.29	
Manitoba	13,298.81	
Hamilton and London	121,933.47	
Toronto and Kingston	138.919.76	
Montreal and Ottawa	56,225.91	$371,574.50
Individual gifts	$ 18,397.16	
Less Individual gifts held for 1965	1,951.15	16,446.01
Church assessment for Indian work in Canada		$ 481.40
Interest		$ 147.58
		$388,649.49
Disbursements:		
National	$111,949.07	
Overseas	163,407.02	
Organization	45,005.45	
Publications	22,614.95	
Administration	26,076.50	
Loss on sale of bonds	922.50	
Synodical grants	951.26	
Grants	2,310.00	
Students	2,575.00	
Christian literature	7,007.00	
Council meeting	4,940.22	
Insurance and taxes	1,691.00	
Medical insurance for staff	2,447.50	

6 THE GLAD TIDINGS

General contingency ....$	165.00	
Visual education	34.21	
Payments from special gifts	10,173.02	$402,269.70

SUPPLY FUND

Receipts:

Synodicals:

British Columbia ....$	655.40
Alberta	665.00
Saskatchewan	610.00
Manitoba	602.60
Hamilton and London	5,939.16
Toronto and Kingston	7,214.32
Montreal and Ottawa	2,926.93
	$ 18,613.41

* * * * * * * * *

SYNODICAL GIVINGS

January-February 1965

	1964	1965
British Columbia		
Alberta		
Saskatchewan ....$	385.00	
Manitoba		
Hamilton and London ....$	6,335.00	$ 3,237.76
Toronto and Kingston	3,000.00	1,500.00
Montreal and Ottawa	1,812.57	2,000.00
	$ 11,532.57	$ 6,737.76

* * * * * * * * *

AN OLD CHINESE PROVERB

If there is righteousness in the heart
There will be beauty in the character.
If there is beauty in the character
There will be harmony in the home.

If there is harmony in the home
There will be order in the nation.
If there is order in the nation
There will be peace in the world.

WMS ESTIMATES FOR 2002

MISSION EDUCATION		ADMINISTRATION	
Salaries	$283,000	Salaries	$37,000
Benefits	39,000	Benefits	6,000
Health/Dental Plan	17,000	Health/Dental	3,000
Travel exp/deputation	8,000	President's expenses	7,000
Program expenses	2,500	Annual Council Meeting	28,000
Glad Tidings	10,000	Annual Reports	12,000
Training events	1,000	Executive / Com. Expenses	15,000
Overseas Travel	2,000	General contingency	2,000
Resources - staff	750	Life membership/youth pins	3,000
	$363,250	Office equipment	8,000
		Office expenses	16,000
		Audit/Legal fees	10,000
GRANTS		Insurance/taxes	4,500
		Continuing education	3,000
PCC General Fund	150,000	Consultative travel/Reg. Staff	10,000
Regional Staff	390,000		**$164,500**
Children/Youth	10,000		
Outside organ. mem. fees	2,000		
Christian Literature	10,000	**Total Estimates - $1,089,750**	
	$562,000		

July/August 2001 **23**

Appendix D: Our Confession

The Holy Spirit, speaking in and through Scripture, calls The Presbyterian Church in Canada to confession. This confession is our response to the word of God. We understand our mission and ministry in new ways, in part because of the testimony of Aboriginal peoples.

We, the 120th General Assembly of The Presbyterian Church in Canada, seeking the guidance of the Spirit of God, and aware of our own sin and shortcomings, are called to speak to the Church we love. We do this, out of new understandings of our past, not out of any sense of being superior to those who have gone before us, nor out of any sense that we would have done things differently in the same context. It is with deep humility and in great sorrow that we come before God and our Aboriginal brothers and sisters with our confession.

We acknowledge that the stated policy of the Government of Canada was to assimilate Aboriginal peoples to the dominant culture, and that The Presbyterian Church in Canada co-operated in this policy. We acknowledge that the roots of the harm we have done are found in the attitudes and values of western European colonialism, and the assumption that what was not yet moulded in our image was to be discovered and exploited. As part of that policy we, with other churches, encouraged the Government to ban some important spiritual practices through which Aboriginal peoples experienced the presence of the creator God. For the Church's complicity in this policy we ask forgiveness.

We recognize that there were many members of The Presbyterian Church in Canada who, in good faith, gave unstintingly of themselves in love and compassion for their aboriginal brothers and sisters. We acknowledge their devotion and commend them for their work. We recognize that there were some who, with prophetic insight, were aware of the damage that was being done and protested, but their efforts were thwarted. We acknowledge their insight. For the times we did not support them adequately nor hear their cries for justice, we ask forgiveness.

We confess that The Presbyterian Church in Canada presumed to know better than Aboriginal peoples what was needed for life. The Church said of our Aboriginal brothers and sisters, "If they could be like us, if they could think like us, talk like us, worship like us, sing like us, work like us, they would know God as we know God and therefore would have life abundant." In our cultural arrogance we have been blind to the ways in which our own understanding of the Gospel has been culturally conditioned, and because of our insensitivity to aboriginal cultures, we have demanded more of Aboriginal peoples than the gospel requires, and have thus misrepresented Jesus Christ who loves all peoples with compassionate, suffering love that all may come to God through him. For the Church's presumption we ask forgiveness.

We confess that, with the encouragement and assistance of the Government of Canada, The Presbyterian Church in Canada agreed to take the children of Aboriginal peoples from their own homes and place them in Residential Schools. In these schools, children were deprived of their traditional ways, which were replaced with Euro-Canadian customs that were helpful in the process of assimilation. To carry out this process, The Presbyterian Church in Canada used disciplinary practices which were foreign to Aboriginal peoples, and open to exploitation in physical and psychological punishment beyond any Christian maxim of care and discipline. In a setting of obedience and acquiescence there was opportunity for sexual abuse, and some were so abused. The effect of all this, for Aboriginal peoples, was the loss of cultural identity and the loss of a secure sense of self. For the Church's insensitivity we ask forgiveness.

We regret that there are those whose lives have been deeply scarred by the effects of the mission and ministry of The Presbyterian Church in Canada. For our Church we ask forgiveness of God. It is our prayer that God, who is merciful, will guide us in compassionate ways towards helping them to heal.

We ask, also, for forgiveness from Aboriginal peoples. What we have heard we acknowledge. It is our hope that those whom we have wronged with a hurt too deep for telling will accept what we have to say. With God's guidance our Church will seek opportunities to walk with Aboriginal peoples to find healing and wholeness together as God's people.

Acts and Proceedings, 1994, p. 376-377.

Appendix E: Nine Point Vision

It is our VISION that:

1. **We will grow in our relationship with Jesus Christ.** Discipleship will become the way of life among our members. We will be a people who pray for others and for ourselves, as we grow toward oneness with Christ, and deep commitment to him. We will seek God's help in becoming a more spiritually-aware people. Guided by the Holy Spirit, we will grow in our knowledge and understanding of the written word of God, as we subject ourselves to the Lordship of the living Word, Jesus Christ. We will seek to be changed, to be reformed, to take whatever risks are necessary as we learn to obey God's will. Our emphasis will be on learning and action in small groups. This spiritual growth is more important than, and is also a prerequisite for, growth in numbers.
2. **We will reach out in mission, proclaiming the Good News of Jesus Christ with relevance and power.** We will be able to share our faith with those around, to speak about our discipleship in the work-place and in the community as we serve Christ in the world through love. As well as living out our own mission, we will, as we are able, share with other churches around the world in their discipleship. A part of the outreach will be to help build communities of faith in newly-developed areas, and in places where resources are limited.
3. **We will integrate evangelism, social action, and justice ministry.** Each of these ingredients will be essential to the others. Our goal will be to serve as witnesses to the transforming power of Christ in our society, beginning with the communities in which we live. We will promote world peace by living at peace with each other and with our neighbours. Our theology will teach the stewardship of all creation, and it will be expressed through our concerns for our immediate environment. We will develop new, creative forms of ministry to the society around us, thus freeing ourselves to respond to the guidance of the Spirit. We will not be afraid to provide moral leadership to society and also to the Church in ministering to new and emerging conditions and issues in society.
4. **Our congregations will be alive.** Worship services will be joyful and full of meaning, aware of the world in which we live, and work, and seek to do

God's will. The forms of worship and the music used in worship will be lively and varied. Congregations will be clear about themselves and their purpose, and will have developed vision and direction about their specific service to God in their communities. Stewardship will no longer mean just money, but a creative, effective, and intentional use of all resources: people, buildings, and technologies, as well as dollars. We will be intentional about the ministry of youth and young adults, recognizing their value in the life and work of Christ's Church. It will be important for us to be aware of being part of the whole Body of Christ in the world. We will be an ecumenical people, one with the other Christian denominations in seeking God's will for the Church, and contributing to that wider work of service and obedience as we are able, beginning in each local community.

5. **We will be a loving, inclusive community — truly God's family.** We will not simply be a club for "nice" people. The use of the word inclusive opens up the Church to take seriously the presence and needs of people of all ages, and of many different cultural backgrounds other than the Scots-Irish out of which this Church sprang in past centuries. We will take seriously the wide ranges of economic and social status within the Canadian population, as well as the presence of races and peoples from all parts of the world. We will take seriously the special needs of disadvantaged people, and we will be intentional about seeing that those needs are met. We will use inclusive language as we learn to be inclusive. Our congregations will be a family for those who have no other family, and an extended family for those who do. We will be a people who practise love, as we have met and experienced it in Jesus Christ.
6. **We will be effective communicators.** We will use contemporary, inclusive language and learn to use metaphors sensitively. Our communication will convey our essential unity, vision, and sense of identity, as we continually witness to the Lordship of Christ over all life. Technology will be a benefit, but will not be allowed to become intrusive. It will provide tools for the service of Christ which will not become barriers between Christ's people. We will learn the effective use of a variety of contemporary media, and all this we will discuss in plain words, trying to avoid speaking in a technical jargon. We will be aware of the tremendous power of technologies as carriers of culture, and molders of morals.
7. **We will have a Spirit-led ministry by the whole people of God.** More patterns of mutual support will be developed for the ministries of the Church. We will seek to mobilize ourselves, the members of The Presbyterian Church in Canada, and to equip ourselves for ministry within the Church, our homes, our communities, and our places of work. We will all

live out the challenging words used at the Ordination and Induction of a minister of Word and Sacraments: "it is the calling of all...to share the Gospel with the whole world, and through Christ the only Mediator to represent the world before the Father in worship and service, until Christ comes again." Within the ministry of the whole Church there will be effective recruitment and screening of candidates for the ministry of Word and Sacrament and the Order of Diaconal Ministries. Their education for a servant ministry will be practical. Pastors and teachers will continue to approach their work of ministry from differing perspectives, but will also show the essential unity which comes through commitment to Christ and his people.

8. **The Courts of the Church will be vital and compassionate.** We will discover our fundamental role in discerning the mind of Christ, in conciliation, and in inspiring and challenging the Church. There will be a spiritual deepening of the life of the Courts through prayer, fellowship, and study. We will learn to function pastorally toward congregations and toward those engaged in the ministries of the Church. There will be positive and compassionate response to crises and conflicts. There will be review of the optimum size of the Courts, including the geographical factors which so affect the life of the Canadian Church. The Courts will be careful not to exclude members and interested persons in such simple ways as scheduling the time of meetings. Priority issues will be given adequate time on the agenda, and less time will be given over to the purely administrative business of the Courts. There will be less desire to escape into legalistic debates over procedures.
9. **The administration of the Church will be lean and accountable.** It will aim at supporting the spiritual development of the people of God within The Presbyterian Church in Canada. The hours involved in administration in the Church will be reduced. We will reclaim the time needed to care for each other as sisters and brothers in Christ, and to fulfill our mission. There will be time to read and reflect upon Christ's call to us. The paralyzing disease of organizational overload will diminish, from the pastor's study as from the General Assembly offices. The Agencies of the General Assembly will do only what cannot be done at the local level, and their mandate will be to serve the congregations, Presbyteries, and Synods. The function of these Agencies will be to provide resources for the programmes of the Church, and to share in the development and training of leaders.

Acts and Proceedings, 1989

Bibliography

Anderson, Robert K., *Kimchi and Maple Leaves Under the Rising Sun.* Belleville: Guardian Books, Ontario, Canada, 2001.

Anniversary Celebration Material (100th Anniversary) 1964.

Annual Reports of St. Paul's Presbyterian Church, Montreal, 1891-1918.

Annual Reports of the Women's Home Missionary Society, 1907-1911.

Annual Reports of the Women's Missionary Society, 1914-2001.

Brouwer, Ruth Compton, *New Women for God: Canadian Presbyterian Women and India Missions, 1876-1914.* Toronto: University of Toronto Press, 1990.

Bush, Peter, *Western Challenge: The Presbyterian Church in Canada's Mission on the Prairies and North, 1885-1925.* Winnipeg: Watson Dwyer Publishing Limited, 2000.

Call and Response: A History of the Women's Missionary Society, W.D. of The Presbyterian Church in Canada. Toronto: Women's Missionary Society, Western Division, 1964

Campbell, Jean, *A Lively Story: Historical Sketches of the Women's Missionary Society (Western Division) of The Presbyterian Church in Canada, 1864-1989.* Toronto: Women's Missionary Society, 1989.

Channels, Winter 2001. Special History Edition: Presbyterian Missions, Vol. 17, #1, The Renewal Fellowship Within the Presbyterian Church in Canada, 2001.

Clare, Roberta, "The Role of Women in the Preservation of the Presbyterian Church in Canada, 1921-1928". *The Burning Bush and a Few Acres of Snow: The Presbyterian Contribution to Canadian Life and Culture*, editor, William Klempa. Ottawa: Carleton University Press, 1994.

Clifford, N. Keith, *The Resistance to Church Union in Canada, 1904-1939.* Vancouver: University of British Columbia Press, 1985.

Congram, John, *This Presbyterian Church of Ours.* Wood Lake Books, 1995.

Cook, Ramsay and Mitchinson, Wendy, editors, *The Proper Sphere: Women's Place in Canadian Society.* Toronto: Oxford University Press, 1976.

From a Woman's Perspective. Women In Ministry, The Presbyterian Church in Canada, Issue 17, May 1989.

Goforth, Rosalind, *Goforth of China.* Toronto: McClelland & Stewart, 1937.

Graham, Elizabeth, "Church Union: Dissenting Presbyterian Women and the Continuing Presbyterian Church". unpublished paper, March 1994.

Gray, Muriel, editor, *The Royal Road.* Toronto: Women's Missionary Society (WD), Presbyterian Church in Canada, 1927.

Hacker, Carlotta, *The Indomitable Lady Doctors*. Toronto: Clarke, Irwin, 1974.

Historic Sketches of the Pioneer Work and the Missionary Educational Benevolent Agencies of the Presbyterian Church in Canada "Twentieth Century Fund". Toronto: Murray Printing Co. 1903.

Hocking, William Ernest, *Re-Thinking Missions: A Layman's Inquiry after 100 Years*. The Commission of Appraisal, New York & London: Harper & Brothers, 1932.

Huntly, Alyson C., *Naomi's Daughters: Bridging the Generations*. Toronto: United Church Publishing House, 2000

Inkster, Alice, *Retrospect 1874-1967*. [Memoirs] unpublished.

Johnston, George and Johnston, Mickey, *Women's Missionary Society National Survey*, 1993-1994. 1994

Kannawin, W.M., *Since 1761*. Toronto: Women's Missionary Society (W.D.) of The Presbyterian Church in Canada, 1937.

Laing, Elizabeth, editor, *Our Jubilee Story, 1864-1924*. Toronto: Women's Missionary Society of The Presbyterian Church in Canada, Western Division, 1924.

MacBeth, R.G., *The Burning Bush and Canada*. John M. Poole, Toronto and Westminster Press, 1926.

MacGillivray, Janet T., editor, *The Planting of the Faith: A Further Story of our Missions*. Women's Missionary Society (W.D.) Presbyterian Church in Canada, 1921

MacGillivray, Janet T., editor, *The Story of our Missions: Women's Missionary Society of the Presbyterian Church in Canada*. Toronto: Women's Missionary Society, Western Division, 1915.

McCarroll-Butler, Pam, "The Impulse for Social Service at the Presbyterian Missionary and Deaconess Training School: 1930-1939". unpublished paper, April 1998.

McGill, Grace, *The Path of Life: Memoirs of Clare and Grace McGill*. Belleville, Ontario: Guardian Books, 2001.

McNeill, John Thomas, *The Presbyterian Church in Canada, 1875-1925*. Toronto: General Board, Presbyterian Church in Canada, 1925.

McPherson, Margaret E, "Head, Heart and Purse: The Presbyterian Women's Missionary Society in Canada, 1876-1925". *Prairie Spirit: Perspectives on the Heritage of the United Church of Canada in the West*, editor, Denis L. Butcher et al. Winnipeg. University of Manitoba Press, 1985.

Miller, J.R., *Shingwauk's Vision: History of Native Residential School*. Toronto: University of Toronto Press, 1996.

Milloy, John S., *A National Crime*. The Royal Commission on Aboriginal Peoples: The Canadian Government and the Residential School System, 1879-1986. Winnipeg: University of Manitoba Press, 1999.

Minutes, Montreal Ladies' French Missionary Association in connection with the Church of Scotland, 1864-1871.

Mitchinson, Wendy, *Canadian Women and Church Missionary Societies in the Nineteenth Century: A Step Toward Independence*. Atlantis (Canada), A Women's Studies Journal, Vol.2, #2, Spring 1977.

Moir, John S., *Called to Witness: Profiles of Canadian Presbyterians*. Committee on History, Toronto: The Presbyterian Church in Canada, 1999.

Moir, John S., editor, *Gifts and Graces: Profiles of Canadian Presbyterian Women*. Committee on History, The Presbyterian Church in Canada, Burlington: Eagle Press, Volume 1, 1999, Volume 2, 2002.

Morton, Sarah E., editor, *John Morton of Trinidad: Journals, Letters and Papers*. Toronto: Westminster Company, 1916.

Poulain, Andre, translated by Evelyne Poulain, "French Protestants and the Foundations of Canada". *Presbyterian History: A Newsletter of the Committee on History, The Presbyterian Church in Canada*, Vol.44, #1, May 2000.

Presbyterian History. In Mary Whale's *Laura K. Pelton, Architect of Mission*, A newsletter of the Committee on History, The Presbyterian Church in Canada, , Part One, Volume 33, No.1, May 1989 and Part Two, Vol.33, No.2, October 1989.

Presbyterian Record. The Presbyterian Church in Canada, 1972-2001.

Reid, Priscilla Lee, "The Role of Presbyterian Women in Canadian Development". *Enkindled by the Faith, Essays on Presbyterianism in Canada*, editor, Neil G. Smith. Centennial Committee of The Presbyterian Church in Canada, Toronto: Presbyterian Publications, 1966.

Ruether, Rosemary Radford and Skinner, Rosemary Keller, general editors, *Women & Religion in America, Vol.1, The Nineteenth Century, A Documentary History*. San Francisco: Harper & Row, 1981.

Still Moving… Popular reports of the Women's Missionary Society, Western Division, 2000-2002.

Strung, Trish, "The World for Christ: Reconstruction, Social Welfare and Evangelism in the Women's Missionary Society of the Continuing Presbyterian Church in Canada, 1925-1930". unpublished paper, April 1998.

The Acts & Proceedings of the General Assembly. Toronto: The Presbyterian Church in Canada, 1876-2001.

The Bulletin, The Continuing Presbyterian Church. WMS issue, Toronto: May 16, 1925.

The Foreign Missionary Tidings. Toronto: 1897-1914.

The Glad Tidings. 1925-1967, Glad Tidings. Toronto: 1968-2002.

The History of our Society, 1864-1934. Toronto: Women's Missionary Society (W.D.) of The Presbyterian Church in Canada, 1934.

The Home Mission Pioneer. 1903-1914.

The Missionary Messenger. 1914-1925.

The Monthly Letter Leaflet. publication of the Woman's Foreign Missionary Society, 1884-1897.

Threatened with Resurrection. Five Year Plan of Women's Missionary Society, Western Division, Toronto: Women's Missionary Society, 1994.

Tucker, Ruth A., *Guardians of the Great Commission: The Story of Women in Modern Missions.* Grand Rapids: Zondervan Publishing House, 1988.

Victor, Cathy, "The Women's Missionary Society, Past, Present and Future". unpublished paper, 1998.

von Wartenbery-Potter, Barbel, *We Will Not Hang Our Harps on the Willows: Global Sisterhood and God's Song.* Oak Park: Meyer Stone Books, 1988.

Whale, Mary E., *Diaries.* Presbyterian Church Archives.

Whale, Mary E., *Women Who Witnessed, Go and Tell.* Oshawa: Tern Graphics, 1988.

WMS Council Executive minutes and files.

WMS Council Sub-Executive minutes.

Endnotes

A& P — The Acts and Proceedings of the General Assembly of The Presbyterian Church in Canada. Before 1938, the church is written 'the Presbyterian Church in Canada.' For 1938 and later 'the' is capitalized to read 'The Presbyterian Church in Canada.'

Introduction

1 Barbel von Wartenberg-Potter, *We will not hang our Harps on the Willows: Global Sisterhood and God's Song* (Oak Park: Meyer Stone Books, 1988.)

2 Elisabeth Schussler Fiorenza, *But she said: Feminist Practices of Biblical Interpretation* (Boston: Beacon Press, 1992), p. 167. She is quoting E.M Broner and Nomi Nimrod, "A Woman's Passover Haggadah," *Ms.*, April 1977, 53-56.

Chapter 1
How Did It All Begin?

1 Luke 24:22 (RSV).

2 Louise Reith, *Historical Skit Prepared for Anniversary Celebration*, 1964.

3 Ramsay Cook and Wendy Mitchinson, editors, *The Proper Sphere — Women's Place in Canadian Society*, Toronto Oxford University Press, 1976, p. 199.

4 ibid., p. 200.

5 ibid., p. 199.

6 Ruth Compton Brouwer, *New Women for God, Canadian Presbyterian Women and India Missions, 1876-1914*, University of Toronto Press, Toronto, 1990, p. 20. Dorcas tradition, see Acts 9:36. Letter from John Thunder, Pipestone, Manitoba, March 31, 1898, p. 55. *Foreign Missionary Tidings: ... The Indian women love to hear the story of Dorcas, so full of good works, making coats and garments for the poor. they will afterwards gather round Mrs. Thunder, asking her questions, which gives her the opportunity of talking more earnestly to them.*

7 Cook and Mitchison, p. 218. Marjory MacMurchy was one of three daughters of Archibald, lawyer and businessman and Marjory (WMS executive member) MacMurchy. (see *Missionary Letter Leaflet 1889*). Their daughter Marjory was the journalist who became Lady Willison. Their other two daughters, Bessie and Helen, followed their mother into the WMS holding a number of executive positions. Helen was one of the first women doctors in Canada and her career is well documented in *The Indomitable Lady Doctors* by Carlotta Hacker (p. 53, 141-142, 171, 211, 224). Bessie, Corresponding Secretary of the WMS at the time was one of the four women (including Mrs. Henry Horne, Mrs. Daniel Strachan and Mrs. D.T.L. McKerroll) who 'saved the Society for Presbyterianism' at the time of Church Union. Bessie later became president of the Society. Bessie MacMurchy, nurse and missionary to India was not, as far as we can ascertain, any relation to the above mentioned MacMurchys.

8 Ruth A Tucker, *Guardians of the Great Commission, The Story of Women in Modern Missions*, Zondervan Publishing House, Grand Rapids, 1988, p. 9-10.

9 Rosemary Radford Ruether and Rosemary Keller Skinner, general editors, *Women & Religion in America, Vol. 1, The Nineteenth Century, A Documentary History*, San Francisco: Harper & Row, Toronto, 1981, p. 243.

10 *Threatened with Resurrection, WMS Five Year Plan*, Women's Missionary Society, The Presbyterian Church in Canada, 1994.

Chapter 2
In Search of Our Roots

1 John Thomas McNeill, *The Presbyterian Church in Canada, 1875-1925*,Toronto, General Board, Presbyterian Church in Canada, 1925, p. 142.

2 *Historic Sketches of the Pioneer Work and the Missionary Educational Benevolent Agencies of the Presbyterian Church in Canada Twentieth Century Fund*, 1903, p. 62
The Edict of Nantes: In 1598 a decree was issued by King Henry IV to restore internal peace in France, a country that had been torn apart by wars of religion. The decree defined the rights of French Protestants (Huguenots) giving full liberty of conscience and private worship and liberty of public worship with full constitutional rights. Huguenots were guaranteed that their rights would be respected. Louis XIV persecuted the Protestants and revoked the Edict of Nantes in 1685. Thousands fled to England, the Netherlands, Germany, Switzerland and America.

3 Janet T. MacGillivray, editor, *The Story of Our Missions*, The Women's Missionary Society of the Presbyterian Church in Canada, Toronto, 1915, p. 227

4 ibid., p. 229.

5 André Poulain, "French Protestants and the Foundation of Canada," translated into English by his daughter Evelyne Poulain, *Presbyterian Newsletter*, History, vol. 44, #1, May 2000, p. 1.

6 ibid., p. 2.

7 *Historic Sketches*, p. 62.

8 Helen Fairburn, "Pointe-aux-Trembles, The Story of its Founding," *The Missionary Messenger*, 1914-1916, November, 1914, p. 111. The School had its origin in the French Canadian Missionary Society formed in Montreal in 1839. Two missionaries, Mr. and Mrs. Amaron, were sent to the Belle-Riviere district where Mrs. Amaron opened a school for boys in her house. The Society bought a farm suitable for a school and the Ladies' Auxiliary Association of the French Canadian Society paid for it. The Belle-Riviere Institute was transferred to Pointe-aux-Trembles where a boys' school was erected in 1846. Rev. J.E. Tanner was first principal. Mrs. Tanner opened a school for girls in Montreal and in 1847 it was transferred to Pointe-aux-Trembles. In 1853 a girls' school was built — a large part of the funding being provided by the Ladies' Auxiliary.

9 Minutes, Montreal Ladies' French Missionary Association in connection with the Church of Scotland, 1864-1871, p. 28.

10 ibid., p. 3.

11 We have tried, where possible to give the women's first names. However, as it was customary at the time to identify women by their husband's names, this was not always possible. We have also discovered that some of the women had university degrees although this was seldom indicated.

12 Minutes, Montreal Ladies' French Missionary Association, p. 30.

13 ibid., p. 42.

14 *Call and Response, A History of the Women's Missionary Society W.D. of the Presbyterian Church in Canada, 1864-1914-1964*, p. 1.

15 Elizabeth Laing, editor, *Our Jubilee Story, 1864-1924*, The Women's Missionary Society of the Presbyterian Church in Canada, Western Division, Toronto, May 1924, p. 20.

16 Alvyn Austin, *Saving China, Canadian Missionaries in the Middle Kingdom, 1888-1959*, University of Toronto Press, 1986, p. 43.

17 Rosalind Goforth, *Goforth of China*, McClelland & Stewart, Toronto, 1937, p. 313.

18 Austin, *Saving China*, p. 127.

19 Edith Creelman, secretary, WMS Annual Report, St. Paul's Presbyterian Church Annual Report, 1917, p. 36-37.

Chapter 3
Women's Work for Women

1 Ruth A. Tucker, *Guardians of the Great Commission*, p. 117.
2 MacGillivray, *The Story of Our Missions*, p. 65.
3 Tucker, p. 61.
4 ibid., p. 155.
5 Brouwer, *New Women for God*, p. 21.
6 Elizabeth Laing, editor, *Our Jubilee Story*, 1864-1924, p. 39.
7 ibid.
8 ibid., p. 40.
9 Brouwer, p. 23.
10 Laing, p. 41.
11 Laing, p. 45.
12 *The History of Our Society, 1864-1934*, The Women's Missionary Society (W.D.) of The Presbyterian Church in Canada, 1934, p. 4.
13 The structure of the society corresponds to the Presbyterian Church's court system. At the congregational level are the auxiliaries; the presbyterial corresponds to the presbytery which consist of a number of congregations within a certain area; the provincials, later to be called synodicals, correspond to synods, which take in a larger area consisting of several presbyterials; and finally the Council, corresponding to the General Assembly which is the national body of the church.
14 Laing, p. 52.
15 Brouwer, p. 37.
16 Laing, p. 54.
17 *Foreign Missionary Tidings*, Vol. 27-30, 1911-1914, April 1914, p. 192.
18 MacGillivray, *The Story of Our Missions*, p. 33.
19 Carlotta Hacker, *The Indomitable Lady Doctors*, Toronto: Clarke, Irwin, 1974, p. 69.
20 MacGillivray, p. 49.
21 Brouwer, p. 144.
22 ibid., p. 135.
23 ibid., p. 142.
24 ibid., p. 143.
25 ibid., p. 148.
26 ibid., p. 152.
27 WFMS Annual Report, 1913-14, p. 25-26.
28 Brouwer, p. 159.
29 Tucker, p. 9.
30 Tucker., p. 10.
31 ibid.
32 ibid.
33 Brouwer, p. 16.
34 John S. Moir, *Called to Witness, Profiles of Canadian Presbyterians*, Committee on History, The Presbyterian Church in Canada, 1999, Vol 4, p. 21-22.
35 MacGillivray, p. 302.
36 *Foreign Missionary Tidings*, Vol. 27-30, 1911-14, June 1911, p. 42-43.
37 ibid., September, 1912, p. 51-52.
38 Rosalind Goforth, *Goforth of China*, Toronto: McClelland & Stewart, 1937, p. 188.
39 Goforth, p. 156-157.
40 *Foreign Missionary Tidings*, June 1914, p. 232. The address of the residence is not given in this article.
41 Mary E. Whale, *Women Who Witnessed, Go and Tell*, Oshawa: Tern Graphics, 1988, p. 29.
42 Muriel Gray, *The Royal Road*, Women's Missionary Society (WD), The Presbyterian Church in Canada, 1927, p. 29.
43 *The Monthly Letter Leaflet*, 1891, p. 187.
44 *The Royal Road*, p. 29.
45 ibid., p. 32.
46 ibid., p. 33.
47 MacGillivray, *The Story of our Missions*, p. 270.
48 ibid., p. 282.
49 J. R. Miller, *Shingwauk's Vision, A History of Native Residential Schools*, University of Toronto Press, 1996, p. 239.
50 ibid., p. 238.
51 MacGillivray, p. 277-278.
52 ibid., p. 293
53 *Foreign Missionary Tidings, Vol. 27-30, 1911-1914*, June 1911, p. 44.
54 ibid., January 1911, p. 35-36.
55 ibid., April 1912, p. 204-205.
56 ibid., June 1911, p. 35.
57 ibid., February 1913, p. 161.
58 ibid., July/August 1913, p. 54.
59 ibid., March 1914, p. 182-183.
60 ibid., February 1912, p. 159.
61 ibid., February 1913, p. 160-161.

62 ibid., April 1913, p. 191.
63 Laing, 1924, p. 59.
64 *The Monthly Letter Leaflet*, December 1889, p. 9-15.
65 Brouwer, p. 50.
66 Laing, p. 62.
67 *Foreign Missionary Tidings, vol. 27-30, 1911-1914*, March 1911, p. 178.
68 ibid., March 1911, p. 181.
69 ibid.
70 ibid., December 1911, p. 131.
71 ibid., December 1911, p. 132.
72 ibid., July/August 1912, p. 33.
73 ibid., July/August 1913, p. 34.
74 ibid., p. 40.
75 ibid.
76 ibid., p. 41.
77 ibid., p. 35-37.
78 ibid., July/August 1914, p. 233-234.

Chapter 4
Winning the West

1 MacGillivray, *The Story of Our Missions*, p. 190.
2 Laing, *Our Jubilee Story*, p. 66.
3 Laing, p. 68.
4 Laing, p. 68-69.
5 Janet T. MacGillivray, editor, *The Planting of the Faith, A Further Story of Our Missions*, Women's Missionary Society, Presbyterian Church in Canada, 1921, p. 222.
6 Laing, p. 72-73.
7 MacGillivray, *The Story of Our Missions*, p. 198.
8 ibid., p. 199.
9 ibid., p. 201.
10 ibid., p. 203.
11 The factor was likely a merchant or land agent.
12 Laing, p. 85.
13 MacGillivray, *The Story of Our Missions*, p. 208.
14 ibid., p. 208.
15 ibid., p. 209.
16 ibid., p. 211-212.
17 ibid., p. 212-213.
18 ibid., p. 248.
19 Gray, *The Royal Road*, p. 54.
20 *The Home Mission Pioneer*, June 1914, p. 235.
21 ibid., p. 225-227.

Chapter 5
Eastern Sunrise

1 Neil G. Smith, editor, *Enkindled by the Word, Essays on Presbyterianism in Canada*, compiled by Centennial Committee of The Presbyterian Church in Canada, Toronto: Presbyterian Publications, 1966. Priscilla Lee Reid, *The Role of Presbyterian Women in Canadian Development*, p. 112. Priscilla Lee Reid states "the society formed in Princetown is the first women's missionary organization of which there is a record anywhere in the world." However, see Reuther & Skinner, *Women and Religion in America*, p. 244, "Antecedents of these organizations went back to the beginning of the century, when the Boston Female society for Missionary Purposes was created in October 1800."
2 Eastern Section was changed to Eastern Division in 1885.
3 WMS (ES) minutes, 1884. There was a children's mission group in New Glasgow in 1847, the first known in Canada.
4 John S. Moir, *Enduring Witness*, p. 147.
5 *Foreign Missionary Tidings*, Vol. 27-30, November 1911, p. 115.
6 *The Glad Tidings*, February 1945, p. 51.
7 MacGillivray, *The Planting of the Faith*, p. 157.
8 ibid., p. 159-160.
9 ibid., p. 164-166.
10 ibid., p. 167.
11 MacGillivray, *The Story of Our Missions*, p. 180.
12 ibid., p. 182.

Chapter 6
The Three Become One

1 Laing, p. 94.
2 The motto appears on the cover of *The Story of Our Missions*, printed 1915.

Chapter 7
The War Years, 1914-1918

1 *The Missionary Messenger*, July/August 1914, p. 4.

2 ibid, March 1915, p. 69-70.
3 ibid., September 1914, p. 40.
4 ibid., October 1914, p. 88-89.
5 ibid., July/August 1915, p. 198.
6 ibid., December 1915, p. 326.
7 ibid., January 1916, p. 2.
8 ibid., July 1916, p. 198.
9 ibid., October 1918, p. 273.
10 ibid., July/August, p. 208.
11 A memorial is a written representation of facts made to a court, and may be the ground of, or embody, a petition. *Book of Forms*, #66, p. 8.
12 *The Missionary Messenger*, July/August 1918, p. 208.
13 ibid., December 1918, p. 330.
14 ibid., January 1919, p. 3.
15 ibid., p. 18.
16 ibid., April 1919, p. 104.
17 ibid., February 1919. p. 34.
18 ibid., p. 138.
19 ibid., January 1919, p. 2.
20 ibid., July/August 1919, p. 198.
21 ibid., p. 209.
22 A&P, 1919, p. 221.
23 *The Missionary Messenger*, December 1919, p. 329-330.
24 ibid., p. 330.
25 Laing, p. 52.
26 *The Missionary Messenger*, June 1921, p. 177.
27 WMS Reports, 1914-1917, 1st Annual Report 1914, p. 32.
28 2nd Annual WMS Report, 1915, p. 75.
29 *The Missionary Messenger*, December 1918, p. 349.
30 ibid., May 1916, p. 151.
31 ibid.
32 WMS 2nd Annual Report, 1915, p. 100.
33 WMS 1st Annual Report, l914, p. 65.
34 ibid., p. 60.
35 MacGillivray, *The Planting of the Faith*, p. 266.
36 *The Missionary Messenger*, December 1915, p. 335-336.
37 ibid., December 1918, p. 350.
38 ibid., November 1918, p. 312-313.
39 ibid., February 1915, p. 52.
40 ibid., April 1915, p. 118.
41 ibid., March 1916, p. 72.
42 ibid., June 1919, p. 172.
43 ibid., January 1915, p. 21-22.
44 *The Royal Road*, p. 126-127.
45 *The Missionary Messenger*, October 1915, p. 264.
46 ibid., December 1919, p. 342.

Chapter 8
After the War — Changing Times for Women

1 Janet T. MacGillivray, *The Planting of the Faith*, Foreword, p. vii-viii.
2 ibid., p. 4-5.
3 ibid., p. 10.
4 ibid., p. 11.
5 Brouwer, p. 170-171.
6 ibid., p. 171-172.
7 William Ernest Hocking, *Re-Thinking Missions; A Layman's Inquiry after 100 Years*, the commission of appraisal, New York & London: Harper & Brothers, 1932, p. 257.
8 *The Missionary Messenger*, July 1920, p. 215.
9 ibid., January 1920, p. 3.
10 ibid., February 1920, p. 40.
11 ibid., March 1920, p. 79.
12 A&P, 1920, p. 22.
13 *The Missionary Messenger*, April 1920, p. 110-111.
14 ibid., April 1921, p. 114.
15 John Thomas McNeill, *The Presbyterian Church in Canada, 1875-1925*, p. 152.
16 A&P, 1922, p. 279.
17 McNeill, p. 153-154.
18 ibid., p. 154.
19 *The Missionary Messenger*, July/August 1922, p. 514.
20 ibid., July/August 1924, p. 201.
21 ibid., p. 200.
22 ibid., p. 201.
23 ibid., p. 204.

Chapter 9
The Flourishing, 1918-1925

1 *The Missionary Messenger*, September 1919, p. 230.
2 ibid., November 1919, p. 294.
3 ibid., p. 11.
4 ibid., July/August 1923, p. 200.
5 ibid., p. 199.
6 ibid., July/August 1924, p. 219.

7 ibid., January 1925, p. 3.
8 ibid., February 1925, p. 43.
9 MacGillivray, *The Planting of the Faith*, p. 256.
10 *The Missionary Messenger*, November 1923, p. 306.
11 ibid., May 1925, p. 144.
12 ibid., March 1923, p. 72.
13 ibid., January 1924, p. 10.
14 *The Missionary Messenger*, April 1921, p. 98.
15 ibid., September 1923, p. 269.
16 ibid., April 1925, p. 105.
17 ibid., May 1925, p. 156.
18 ibid., July 1920, p. 210.
19 ibid., April 1921, p. 99.
20 ibid., November 1921, p. 269.
21 ibid., December 1923, p. 350.
22 ibid., June 1920, p. 162.
23 ibid., October 1921, p. 234.
24 ibid., December 1923, p. 340.
25 ibid., April 1924, p. 102.
26 MacGillivray, p. 178.
27 ibid., p. 182.

Chapter 10 The Disruption, 1925

1 WMS Report 1914-1917; 1915, p. 123.
2 *The Missionary Messenger*, July/August 1919, p. 213.
3 ibid., December 1921, p. 289.
4 ibid., May 1923, p. 153.
5 ibid., June 1923, p. 188.
6 ibid., July/August 1924, p. 207.
7 *The Church Union Question, A Study of the Situation in Canada*, The Review Print, Paris, Canada, circa 1925. PCC Archives.
8 Priscilla Lee Reid, "The Role of Presbyterian Women in Canadian Development." *Enkindled by the Word, Essays on Presbyterianism in Canada*, editor Neil G. Smith. Compiled by the Centennial Committee of The Presbyterian Church in Canada, Presbyterian Publications, Toronto, 1966, p.117.
9 ibid.
10 N. Keith Clifford, *The Resistance to Church Union in Canada, 1904-1939*, University of British Columbia Press, Vancouver, 1985, p. 133.
11 ibid., p. 132.
12 ibid.
13 ibid., p. 133. Note: WMS traces its origins to 1864, not 1876.
14 ibid., p. 134.
15 ibid., p. 139.
16 ibid., p. 134.
17 Roberta Clare, "The Role of Women in the Preservation of the Presbyterian Church in Canada 1921-1928." *The Burning Bush and a few Acres of Snow: The Presbyterian Contribution to Canadian Life and Culture*, editor William Klempa. Ottawa, Canada. Carleton University Press, 1994, p.266-7.
18 ibid., p. 267.
19 R. G. MacBeth, *The Burning Bush and Canada*, John M. Poole, The Westminster Press, 401 Lumsden Building, Toronto, Canada, 1926, p. 267.
20 *The Presbyterian Record*, Vo. I, No. 6, June 1925, p. 171.
21 12th Annual Report of the Women's Missionary Society 1925, p. 15.
22 A&P, 1927, p. 37.
23 Roberta Clare, "The Role of Women in the Preservation of the Presbyterian Church in Canada 1921-1928." *The Burning Bush and a few Acres of Snow: The Presbyterian Contribution to Canadian Life and Culture*, editor William Klempa. Ottawa, Canada. Carleton University Press, 1994, p. 270.
24 ibid., p. 271.
25 *The Missionary Messenger*, July/August 1925, p. 210.
26 ibid., p. 220-222.
27 ibid., p. 226-227.
28 12th Annual Report of the Women's Missionary Society 1925, p. 7.
29 Minutes of the Provisional Women's Missionary Society of the Continuing Presbyterian Church in Canada, September 1924, p. 2.
30 ibid., p. 3.
31 ibid., p. 5.
32 Alice Inkster, *Retrospect 1874-1967* (Memoirs), p. 70-71.
33 Letters from Presbyterian Church Archives, 1925.
34 Letters from Presbyterian Church Archives, 1925.

35 Letters from Presbyterian Church Archives, 1925.
36 Letters from Presbyterian Church Archives, 1925.
37 Clifford, p. 190.
38 *Glad Tidings*, 1925-26-27, vol. 1,2,3, July/August 1925, p. 5.
39 12th Annual Report of the Women's Missionary Society W.D., Presbyterian Church in Canada, 1925, p. 10.

Chapter 11
A Time to Build, 1925-1931

1 *The Glad Tidings*, July/August 1925, p. 6.
2 ibid., The gavel bore the inscription, "Presbyterian WMS 1925 'Go', Matthew 28:19. 'Come', Acts 16:9. Amkhut Bhils pray: Acts 1:8." July/August 1925, p. 7.
3 ibid. p. 7-8.
4 *The Glad Tidings* name was selected by Olive Wagner from a number of suggestions…Miss Wagner was formerly matron of the 'Lucy M. Baker' School Home for Girls in Prince Albert, *The Lively Story*, p. 276.
5 ibid., p. 11.
6 A&P, 1928, Report of the General Board of Missions, p. 14.
7 *The Glad Tidings*, March 1926, p. 90.
8 *The Glad Tidings*, March 1931, p. 82.
9 ibid., July/August 1927, p. 258-9.
10 ibid., p. 265.
11 ibid., p. 266.
12 *Twelfth Annual Report of the Women's Missionary Society W.D.*, 1925, p. 47-48.
13 Archives, WMS file, 1927.
14 *The Glad Tidings*, May 1929, p. 168.
15 A&P, 1929, WMS Report, p. 80.
16 *The Glad Tidings*, December 1931, p. 409.
17 ibid., March 1926, p. 72.
18 ibid., July/August 1931, p. 252.
19 ibid., September 1931, p. 295.
20 ibid., May 1931, p. 179.
21 Robert K. Anderson, *Kimchi and Maple Leaves Under the Rising Sun*, p. 74.
22 ibid., p. 77.
23 ibid., p. 96-97.
24 *The Glad Tidings*, October 1931, p.329.
25 ibid., p. 330-1.

Chapter 12
The Depression Years, 1931-1939

1 *The Glad Tidings*, July/August 1931, p. 242.
2 ibid., March 1935, p. 97.
3 ibid., December 1937, p. 441.
4 ibid., September 1938, p. 324
5 ibid.
6 ibid., May 1935, p. 181.
7 ibid., November 1936, p. 387-8.
8 ibid., December 1936, p. 412.
9 ibid., June 1937, p. 239-40.
10 ibid., February 1938, p. 46.
11 ibid., p. 49.
12 ibid., June 1936, P. 202.
13 ibid., October 1937, p. 348-9.
14 ibid., March 1938, p. 99f.
15 ibid., March 1939, p. 106.
16 ibid., November 1939, p. 403.
17 ibid., p. 427.
18 ibid., March 1935, p. 93.
19 ibid., p. 103.
20 ibid., March 1945, p. 97.
21 ibid., March 1938, p. 109.
22 ibid., July/August 1938, p. 271-2.
23 ibid., April 1933, p. 151.

Chapter 13
Another War to End All Wars, 1940-1945

1 *The Glad Tidings*, January 1940, p. 1.
2 ibid., June 1943, p. 243-4.
3 ibid., July/August 1940, p. 269.
4 ibid., September 1940, p. 315.
5 ibid., January 1941, p. 3.
6 ibid., December 1940, p. 453.
7 ibid., September 1940, p. 328.
8 ibid., July/August 1942, p. 283.
9 ibid., July/August 1945, p. 266.
10 ibid., March 1943, p. 90.
11 ibid., April 1945, p. 156.
12 ibid., May 1943, p. 181
13 ibid., April 1944, p. 145.
14 ibid., September 1942, p. 330.
15 ibid., September 1945, p. 318.
16 ibid., April 1942, p. 150.

17 ibid., January 1943, p. 21.
18 ibid., February 1942, p. 50-1.
19 Robert K. Anderson, *Kimchi and Maple Leaves Under the Rising Sun*, see chapters 8 and 9, p. 121-170.
20 ibid., July/August 1941, p. 292-3.
21 ibid., March 1941, p. 99.
22 ibid., May 1941, p. 196-7.
23 ibid., January 1943, p. 17.
24 ibid., March 1943, p. 119-20.
25 ibid., November 1944, p. 399.
26 ibid., November 1945, p. 424.

Chapter 14 The Aftermath of War, 1946-1951

1 *The Glad Tidings*, March 1946, p. 90.
2 ibid., October 1948, p. 357.
3 ibid., September 1948, p. 324.
4 ibid., September 1950, p. 318-9.
5 ibid., July/August 1950, p. 278.
6 ibid., p. 280-1.
7 ibid., January 1946, p. 29.
8 ibid., July/August 1948, p. 268.
9 ibid., February 1950, p. 69-70.
10 ibid., November 1948, p. 430.
11 ibid.
12 ibid., February 1950, p. 69-70.
13 ibid., March 1949, p. 106.
14 ibid., February 1954, p. 66.
15 ibid., April 1951, p. 141.
16 ibid., May 1946, p. 186-7.
17 ibid., May 1948, p. 182.
18 ibid., March 1948, p. 116-8.
19 ibid., January 1951, p. 8-11.
20 ibid., January 1946, p. 159.
21 ibid., April 1951, p. 159.
22 ibid. March 1946, p. 101.
23 ibid., p. 102.
24 ibid., September 1946, p. 317.
25 ibid., November 1951, p. 436.
26 ibid., December 1951, p. 489.
27 ibid., April 1950, p. 139.
28 ibid., February 1946, p. 68.

Chapter 15 Changing Times, 1950-1972

1 *The Glad Tidings*, November 1952, p. 433-444.
2 ibid., February 1953, p. 54.
3 ibid., April 1953, p. 150.
4 ibid., July/August 1953, p. 308.
5 ibid., November 1953, p. 441.
6 ibid., August/September, 1971, p. 20.
7 ibid., July/August 1955, p. 295.
8 *Glad Tidings*, August/September 1970, p. 6. **Note:** December 1967 issue is titled *The Glad Tidings*, January 1968 issue is *Glad Tidings*.
9 *The Glad Tidings*, June 1956, p. 5.
10 ibid., May 1957. p. 17.
11 ibid., September 1964, p. 24.
12 ibid., July/August 1964, p. 1.
13 ibid., May 1964, p. 22.
14 ibid.
15 ibid., September 1964, p. 1-7.
16 *Glad Tidings*, October 1969, p. 15.
17 *The Glad Tidings*, December 1960, p. 23.
18 ibid., November 1956, p. 30.
19 ibid., September 1959, p. 22.
20 ibid., October 1952, p. 387.
21 ibid., June 1952, p. 261.
22 ibid., October 1952, p. 388.
23 ibid., February 1966, p. 4.
24 *Glad Tidings*, March 1971, p. 19.
25 After World War II, Formosa became known as Taiwan — the Chinese name for the Island. The end of the war brought the end of Japanese rule and a return to Chinese rule — now under Chiang Kai-shek.
26 *The Glad Tidings*, October 1955, p. 391.
27 ibid., October 1958, p. 37.
28 ibid., February 1959, p. 10.
29 ibid., May 1952, p. 198.
30 ibid., May 1953, p. 204.
31 In 1966, British Guiana received its independence from Britain and thereafter was known as Guyana.
32 WMS Annual Report, 1963, p. 74.
33 *The Glad Tidings*, September 1954, p. 352.
34 ibid., January 1958, p. 25.
35 ibid., September, 1959, p. 9.
36 Lois Klempa, "Part Five, Ordaining Women," *Turning Points, The Church Decides, Heritage Resources*, The Presbyterian Church in Canada, 1980, p. 57ff.
37 ibid., June 1953, p. 243-4.
38 ibid., p. 253.
39 ibid., October 1955, p. 394-5.

40 ibid., June 1957, p. 5-8.
41 ibid., July/August 1957, p. 1.
42 ibid., February 1958, p. 23.
43 ibid., April 1962, p. 15-16.
44 ibid., April 1967, p. 29.
45 *Call and Response*, p. 6.
46 *The Glad Tidings*, September 1960, p. 20.
47 ibid., May 1960, p. 21.
48 ibid., p. 22.
49 WMS Annual Report, 1964, p. 14-15.
50 *The Glad Tidings*, May 1967, p. 45-48.
51 ibid., April 1966, p. 18f.
52 WMS Annual Report 1966, p. 39.
53 ibid., p. 13.
54 *Glad Tidings*, August/September 1970, p. 11.
55 ibid., p. 9-10.
56 ibid., p. 10.
57 ibid., p. 14.
58 ibid., p. 10.
59 ibid., June/July 1971, p. 13.
60 Margaret E. McPherson, "Head, heart and Purse: The Presbyterian Women's Missionary Society in Canada, 1876-1925," *Prairie Spirit; Perspectives on the Heritage of the United Church of Canada in the West*, p. 149.

Chapter 16
New Ways, 1972-2001

1 Laura Burnett, "A New Year, A New Day, A New Challenge in Mission in the 70s," *Glad Tidings*, January, 1972, p. 4.
2 There is some confusion about the exact name of the new board. Some documents identify it as "The Board of World Mission." Others opt for "The Board of World Missions." For the purposes of this book, the former will be used except where direct quotations dictate otherwise.
3 Minutes of Joint GBM and WMS Committee, April 30th, 1968, p. 2.
4 While both missionary societies do currently include men in their membership, both groups continue to be better known as women's groups. The WMS (ED), however, in 1987 changed its name to the Atlantic Mission Society.
5 A&P, 1970, p. 47.
6 "A Responsibility for Change," *Glad Tidings*, May 1979 p. 3.
7 A&P, 1970, p. 47.
8 A&P, 1970, p. 262.
9 Mary Whale, Diary, PCC Archives, May 14, 1971.
10 WMS Council Executive minutes, October 24, 1972, p. 55.
11 Helen C. Young, "Working Together on the Total Mission Task," *Glad Tidings*, February 1972, p.10ff.
12 Laura Burnett, p. 4.
13 R. P. Carter, "Opting in to the Whole Mission Operation," *Glad Tidings*, January, 1972, p.10.
14 "Working Together on The Total Mission Task," *Glad Tidings*, February, 1972, pp. 11-12.
15 Giollo Kelly, Mary Whale and Louise Reith, "The Ongoing Responsibilities of the Women's Missionary Society," *Glad Tidings*, March, 1972, p. 22.
16 Louis de Groot, "A Look at The Board of World Mission," *Glad Tidings*, August-September, 1973, p. 3.
17 ibid, p. 3.
18 "Estimates," *Glad Tidings*, January, 1977, p. 9.
19 "General Assembly Establishes Board of Congregational Life," *Glad Tidings*, August/September 1972, p. 13
20 ibid., p. 13.
21 A&P, 1974, p. 243.
22 "Council '72," *Glad Tidings*, December 1972, p. 13.

Educating in Mission

1 Margaret Robertson, "Taking Mission to New Heights," *Glad Tidings*, January/February, 2000, p. 24.
2 Kelly, Whale and Reith, p. 25-27.
3 WMS 10th Annual Report, 1923, p. 77.
4 Kelly, Whale and Reith, p. 25.
5 "Questions People Ask," *Glad Tidings*, August/September, 1972, p. 17.
6 Jean Campbell, *A Lively Story*, p. 280
7 *Glad Tidings*, January, 1973, p. 36.
8 ibid., June/July 1992, p. 14.
9 ibid., November 1992, p. 29.
10 ibid., December 1992, p. 26.

11 Mollie Harback, "Decision over Teacups," *Glad Tidings*, January, 1984, p. 5.
12 "Voices from the Past," *Glad Tidings*, January/February, 1995, p. 4.
13 ibid.
14 WMS 85th Annual Report, 1999, p. 33.
15 Campbell, *A Lively Story*, p. 271.
16 In 1976 the General Assembly approved a revised aim and purpose for the WMS. It read: The Aim and Purpose of the society shall be to unite the women, youth and children of the Church in prayer, study and service for the advancement of the Kingdom of God at home and abroad. In 1986 the wording was changed in order to provide a broader focus and to be more inclusive. The new statement of purpose read: The Women's Missionary Society, Western Division, is a community of Christian women whose purpose, in response to the love of God in Jesus Christ, is to encourage one another and all the people of the church to be involved in local and world mission through prayer, study, service and fellowship. In 1997, the words "Christian women" were replaced by the word "Christians," in order to acknowledge those men who were members of the society. The reference to "Western Division" was also deleted from the purpose because there was no longer an "Eastern Division," the WMS(E.D.) having become the Atlantic Mission Society. The letters WD, however, remain as part of the legal name of the society.
17 Harback, p. 5.
18 ibid, p. 5.
19 "A Conversation with Louise Reith," *Glad Tidings*, November, 1974, p. 4. CGIT, or Canadian Girls in Training, is an ecumenical program for girls between the ages of 12 and 17, begun in 1915 and recognized by the Presbyterian Church in Canada in that year. Its purpose is to enable girls, *under the leadership of Jesus, to cherish health, seek truth, know God and serve others,* so as to become the girls God intends them to be. Explorers was an ecumenical program aimed at helping *juniors explore God's world for the purpose of locating and finding their place in it.* (The History of "Explorers," *Glad Tidings*, June/July 1975, p.7). The organization was recognized by the Canadian Presbyterians in 1940 as a suitable through- the-week channel for reaching nine-to-eleven year old boys and girls. COC, or Children of the Church, appeared on the scene sometime later and catered to younger children. Like Explorers, it was a weekday group, aiming to provide opportunities for education in the Christian faith.
20 In a personal letter from Helen Tetley to Rosemary Doran. Mabel Booth worked for the WMS from 1962 to 1976 and became National Secretary for Children's Work. She devoted much time and talent to the development of the Children of the Church and Explorer groups.
22 WMS 7th Annual Report, 1920, p. 69.
23 In 1994, General Assembly agreed to change the term deaconess to diaconal minister. Throughout its history, most WMS field staff have been women, though in the Residential Schools there were male principals. In October 1989, Rev. Blake Carter was the first male Area Educational Consultant appointed by the society.
24 "Profile," *Glad Tidings*, March 1978, p. 22.
25 *The Glad Tidings*, January, 1937, p.10.
26 *The Glad Tidings*, April, 1937, p. 142.
27 "A Conversation with Louise Reith," *Glad Tidings*, November 1974, pp 3-4.

Lean and Accountable

1 A&P, 1991, p. 473.
2 ibid, pp 472-3.
3 A&P, 1989, p. 27.
4 A&P, 1991, p. 399.
5 A&P, 1990, p. 520.
6 ibid, p. 543.
7 A&P, 1991, p. 398.

8 In 1995 the Service Agency was reconstituted as Support Services under the direction of a Chief Financial Officer.
9 A&P, 1990, p. 519.
10 A&P, 1991, p. 398.
11 A&P, 1994, p. 221.
12 ibid, p. 222
13 Joan Sampson, "A Challenge from the President," *Glad Tidings*, January, 1991, p. 15.
14 Joan Sampson, "From the President," *Glad Tidings*, January, 1992, p. 5.
15 A&P, 1990, p. 520.
16 WMS 79th Annual Report, 1993, p. xvii.
17 Irene Nesbitt, "Forward in Faith," *Glad Tidings*, July/August, 1996, p. 20.
18 A&P, 1990, p. 524.
19 "Reflections," *Glad Tidings*, July/August, 1998, p. 22.
20 Life and Mission Position Paper, presented to Council Executive, January 1997, p. 1.
21 Minutes of WMS Council Sub-Executive, January, 1996, p. 3.
22 WMS 73rd Annual Report, 1987, p. 14.
23 A&P, 1992, p. 37.
24 Minutes of Council Executive, February, 1994, p. 8.
25 ibid.
26 ibid, p. 10
27 A&P, 1994, p. 405.
28 ibid, p. 410.
29 ibid.
30 WMS 84th Annual Report, 1998, p. 15.
31 Triennium is an event for youth, organized every three years by the Presbyterian Church USA at Purdue University, Indiana. Several hundred young people from The Presbyterian Church in Canada attend and representatives from the denomination contribute to the planning and staffing of the event. For information on Youth in Mission (YIM), see the chapter Today's Missionaries.
32 Minutes of WMS Council Executive, October 1995, p. 6.

The Amount Available

1 "Statement of Giving," *Glad Tidings*, April, 1986, p. 4-5.
2 Although the WMS allocates money each year for the funding of regional staff positions, not all of the money may be required in any given year, depending on the number of positions filled. Money that is not used stays in the General Fund of the society.
3 A&P, 1970, p. 47.
4 Clara Hogg, "From the Treasurer," *Glad Tidings*, June-July 1979, p. 30.
5 "Forward in Faith," *Glad Tidings*, August/September, 1991, p. 12.
6 *Glad Tidings*, August/September, 1993, p. 10.
7 A&P, 1992, p. 465.
8 WMS 75th Annual Report, 1989, pp vii-viii.
9 WMS 77th Annual Report, 1991, p. vii.
10 ibid, p. ix.
11 In this instance the voice of the people was heard! A new fund was set up in 2001. $50,000 from undesignated legacies was allocated for *mission projects undertaken by WMS groups within their communities* ("Forward in Faith," *Glad Tidings*, January/February 2002, p. 30). This would enable local groups to pursue mission projects of their own choosing at the local level.
12 "The 86th Annual Council Meeting," *Glad Tidings*, July/August 2001, p. 26.

Landmarks

1 *Glad Tidings*, May, 1988, p. 30.
2 "Go and Tell," *Glad Tidings*, August/September 1989, p. 13.
3 L. June Stevenson, "Written in Love," *Glad Tidings*, May 1989, p. 3.
4 "News," *Glad Tidings*, August/September, 1982, p. 21.
5 Druse Bryan and Lois Klempa, "Biting the Apple, the Third Re-Imagining Community Gathering," *Glad Tidings*, May/June 1997, p. 29.
6 "Sophia" is the Greek name for the concept of "wisdom," as found in the Hebrew Scriptures. Feminist writings emphasize Sophia's important creative role in the divine scheme of things.

7 *Glad Tidings*, September/October 1997, p. 16.
8 World Council of Churches Message at the opening of the Decade, Easter, 1988, quoted by Anne Saunders in *Glad Tidings*, September/October, 1998, p. 4.
9 Margaret Robertson, "Journey to Africa," *Glad Tidings*, March/April 1999, p. 23.
10 Stories of individual women who made valuable contributions to the WMS and, through their experience in the society, to the Church and community at large can be found in *Gifts and Graces, Profiles of Canadian Presbyterian Women*, edited by John Moir, Committee on History, The Presbyterian Church in Canada.

Residential Schools

1 "News," *Glad Tidings*, August/ September, 1976, p. 22.
2 ibid.
3 L. June Stevenson, "The Gift," *Glad Tidings*, December 1991, p. 4. After the closing of the school as a residential school for Aboriginal children, it continued as an integrated school for children of the area. Steve Robinson was principal before, during and after integration.
4 Under the guidance of Elijah Harper, a spiritual leader of the Aboriginal Peoples, a Sacred Assembly was held in Hull, Quebec, in December, 1995. Representatives of the major denominations and other faith groups, along with government and Aboriginal leaders and their people, met to hear one another's stories. WMS members were among the official delegates. The goal of the assembly was to initiate dialogue and begin the journey to reconciliation.
5 Report on the response to a letter to Council from East Toronto Presbyterial about the article "No Clean Hands," *Presbyterian Record*, February, 1992, from Council Executive file for October, 1992.
6 Kay Blake, "Remembering Cecilia Jeffrey," *Glad Tidings*, June/July 1985, p. 10ff.
7 "Kay Blake's Story," *Presbyterian Record*, February, 1992, p.20.
8 Kay Rusaw, "Ioyan Mani — 'To Walk Beyond,'" *Glad Tidings*, May 1986, p. 10ff.
9 Gordon Williams, "Living our Faith," *Glad Tidings*, February, 1986, p. 5ff.
10 L. June Stevenson, "The Gift," pp. 5-6.
11 "To the Presbyterian Church in Canada from a former student of Cecilia Jeffrey Indian Residential School, Kenora, Ontario," *Glad Tidings*, October, 1994, p. 12.
12 A&P, 1994, p. 365ff.
13 ibid, p. 366.
14 Report on the response to a letter to Council re "No Clean Hands," October, 1992.
15 *Glad Tidings*, June/July, 1992, p. 16.
16 *Glad Tidings*, October, 1992, p. 15.
17 A&P, 1994, p. 376.
18 Sheina B. Smith, "White Man Go Home," *Glad Tidings*, May, 1973, p. 17.
19 "Sharing the Journey, Council 85," *Glad Tidings*, August/September, 1985, p. 5.
20 Marjorie Ross, "Mission is with...Native Canadians," *Glad Tidings*, October 1981, p. 7.
21 ibid., p. 8.
22 A&P, 1994, p. 376.
23 WMS 80th Annual Report WMS, 1994, p. 13.
24 "In the World," *Glad Tidings*, December 1994, p.21.
25 In late 2002, there were some 11,000 claims before the Government of Canada, of which about 1% related to The Presbyterian Church in Canada.
26 "No Clean Hands," *Presbyterian Record*, February 1992, p. 18.
27 A&P, 1999, p. 24-27.

Today's Missionaries

1 Wanda Thompson, "Lives Lived, From Murder Mysteries to Malawi," *Presbyterian Record*, February 2001, p. 51.

2 Cathy Victor, "The Women's Missionary Society, Past, Present and Future," p. 10, unpublished paper, 1998, used with permission.
3 L. de Groot, "The Future of Missions in India," *Glad Tidings*, June/July 1973, p. 8.
4 Jean Sonnenfeld, "If You Can't Say It ... Live It," *Glad Tidings*, October, 1973, p. 28.
5 "Dear Friends," *Glad Tidings*, October, 1990, p. 20.
6 *Presbyterian Record*, January 2001, p. 49.
7 John Congram, *This Presbyterian Church of Ours*, p. 31.
8 ibid., p. 31-32.
9 Agnew Johnston, "Why Christian Mission Today?" *Glad Tidings*, November 1973, p. 4.
10 May Nutt, "Pauline," *Glad Tidings*, May 1977, p. 4.
11 Clara Henderson, "Mission in the Context of Relationship," *Glad Tidings*, February 1989, p. 5.
12 "Partnership in Mission," *Glad Tidings*, May/June, 1998, p. 37.
13 Youth In Mission (YIM) pamphlet, The Presbyterian Church in Canada.

Who Are We?

1 Women's Missionary Society National Survey, 1993-94, p. 32.
2 "Council '80," *Glad Tidings*, August/September, 1980, p. 4. Another comment in the same context comes from ANN: The Newsletter of A New Network Within The Presbyterian Church in Canada which *identifies a New Year's Resolution — that all clergy be required to know at least as much about the work of the Church around the world as the average 75 year old WMS member!* — quoted in *Glad Tidings*, July/August 1999, p. 29.
3 Donald C. MacDonald, "A Message from the Moderator," *Glad Tidings*, December, 1983, p. 6.
4 John Congram, "A Message from the Moderator of the 123rd General Assembly," *Glad Tidings*, July/August, 1998 p. 5.
5 ibid.
6 ibid.
7 Richard Fee, *Still Moving*, 2000-2001, p. 4.
8 Victor, p. 12.
9 Joanne Watson, "A Ring of Lavender," *Glad Tidings*, January 1988, p. 30.
10 Jackie Phills, "What is the WMS?" *Glad Tidings*, August/September 1994, p. 30.
11 Margaret Greig, "Called to Make Justice: Religious Communities Working to End Sexual Misconduct and Domestic Violence," *Glad Tidings*, August/September 1993, p. 9.
12 Rosemary Doran, "Where are we going?" *Glad Tidings* May, 1974, p. 4.
13 Eileen Parish, "WMS Cameo," *Glad Tidings*, October, 1981, p. 12.
14 "The WMS Who Are They?" *From a Woman's Perspective*, May, 1989, Issue 17, p. 1. (used with permission)
15 ibid, p. 3.
16 In response to the article, Lois Klempa, Convener of the Anniversary Committee, wrote a letter which was not published by *From a Woman's Perspective*. In it she disputes the idea that the WMS is uncertain of its self-image. *I would have thought what we were trying to convey* [through the poster] *would be fairly obvious — a group of ordinary laywomen (no men, no clergy) stretching back into the past and forward into the future committed to prayer, study, service and fellowship (note the study book, bible and mite box), and if this does not 'convey a notion of discipleship', then I guess my 'notion of discipleship' is definitely way off the track.* ("The Convener Responds to FAWP," p. 2, reproduced with permission.)
17 Linda J. Bell, "New Partnerships in Mission," *Glad Tidings*, March 1993, p. 5.
18 "A Child's Lasting Impression," F*rom a Woman's Perspective*, May 1989, p. 9.
19 *Women's Missionary Society National Survey*, 1993-94, p. 19.
20 ibid, p. 27.
21 ibid, p. 29.
22 ibid, p. 29.

23 This was not the first such "plan." The WMS, faced with a challenge to the status quo, often responded in good Presbyterian fashion by forming a special committee or appointing a task force to examine the issue. For example, a Vision Committee was formed in 1988 to look at the goals and strategies of the society. In 1993 a Research Steering Committee came together to see how the WMS was perceived by people outside the society so that the organization might become more effective in the area of mission. It was this committee which proposed the survey that was carried out in 1993 and then in turn became a Research Task Force.
24 Alyson C. Huntly, *Naomi's Daughters*, United Church Publishing House, Toronto, 2000, p. 16, used with permission.
25 *Glad Tidings*, January/February, 1998, p. 36.
26 Huntly, p. 18-19.

Still Counting the Women

1 Quoted by John Congram, *Glad Tidings*, July/August 1998. p. 6.

Index

G

H

I

J

K

L

M

N

O

P

Q

R

S

W

Y

Z